THE MUSICALS NO ONE CAME TO SEE

GARLAND REFERENCE LIBRARY
OF THE HUMANITIES
(Vol. 563)

THE MUSICALS NO ONE CAME TO SEE
A Guidebook to
Four Decades of Musical-Comedy Casualties
on Broadway, Off-Broadway and in Out-of-Town Try-out,
1943–1983

Rick Simas

GARLAND PUBLISHING, INC. · NEW YORK & LONDON
1987

Library of Congress Cataloging-in-Publication Data

Simas, Rick, 1954–
The Musicals No One Came To See.

Includes indexes.
1. Musical revues, comedies, etc.—Bibliography.
2. Music trade—United States.   I. Title.
ML128.M78S5   1987   016.7821'0973   87-25095   ISBN 0-8240-8804-2

Cover design by Alison Lew

Printed on acid-free, 250-year-life paper
Manufactured in the United States of America

"In Peoria, Illinois, there's a small summer-stock theater that's been in existence for thirty-seven years. In that time, they've managed to produce 214 productions of *Brigadoon*, 810 productions of *My Fair Lady*, and 11,375 productions of *The Sound of Music*. Last year, the people of Peoria, Illinois, voted unanimously to never again allow Florence Henderson within the city limits. Tonight is dedicated to those very bored people of Peoria, Illinois. . . .

> The song was sweet, the song was funny,
> That song alone had backers puttin' up their money.
> It was a grand ole' Broadway tune
>   that had 'em dancin' in the aisles
> And the audience bustin' with excitement and smiles.
>
> But then the show closed up in Philly,
> Lots of money down the drain,
> And that poor song was never heard of again.
> Until tonight. That's why we're here. . . ."

"We Love a Broadway Song,"
lyric & music by Ed Linderman,
from the musical revue, *Broadway Jukebox*.

Contents

ACKNOWLEDGEMENTS

Alan Becker, BMI
David Cleaver, Theatrebooks
Mitch Douglas, ICM
Miles Kreuger, Institute for the American Musical
David E. LeVine, Dramatists Guild
David Morton, UCLA

Beyond these few individuals whose contributions were invaluable, there are many more without whose help, support and guidance this volume would not have been completed. Much thanks goes to all those who contributed in so many ways to the creation of this work. In particular, much homage is paid the authors, composers, lyricists and agents who contributed to the entries listed herein. Likewise, acknowledgement is due the unions, guilds, licensing agencies and theatrical producers who put me in direct contact with their members or clients.

Finally, much gratitude and admiration go to Jenny Redding—my editor, business partner and friend—without whose continual advice, encouragement and word–processing skill, this book would never have gone to press.

PREFACE

As far back as high school, I can recall a proverbially perplexed drama teacher asking me (as even then I had a rather avid interest in the musical theater), "Did you know there was a musical version of *Georgy Girl*? *Elmer Gantry*? *Lilies of the Field*? I wonder who owns the rights to those shows?" After checking all the available licensing catalogues (Samuel French, Tams–Witmark, Music Theatre International, *ad infinitum*), we found the shows were not listed. When we called Tams–Witmark and all the other licensing agencies for further information, they—of course—could offer none.

During my undergraduate days at San Francisco State University, my interest in musical theater grew with my involvement in such relatively obscure shows as *Dear World, She Loves Me, Shinbone Alley* and *Zorba*. Around that time, I tried to learn the status of Rick Besoyan's musical, *Mrs. 'Arris Goes to Paris* (he died before it was completed, and the rights reverted back to source author Paul Gallico), as well as the musical version of *How Green Was My Valley*, entitled *A Time for Singing* (available directly through authors Gerald Freedman and John Morris). While subsequent and rather lengthy research has turned up this information, I—of course—was unable to find out anything substantial at the time.

During my years as a high school teacher, I had an interest in producing *King of Hearts, F. Jasmine Addams, The Yearling* (before it was made available through Dramatic Publishing Company) and *Babes in the Wood* (which has since been made available through Broadway Play Publishing). By that time, I had learned how to contact authors through the Dramatists Guild, BMI or ASCAP, or by checking the copyright page of one of their published works—if, indeed, they had published anything. I found, however, that it took an inordinate amount of time to get any response, yet I was unable to find anyone with the expertise to advise me *how* to go about approaching authors or their agents. I soon realized that this was indeed unchartered territory—that there was a real need for a reference work listing the information I and so many others with whom I had been in contact, were seeking. I also began to notice around me a growing interest in "flop" musicals; record companies like Original Cast and DRG Records and American Entertainment Industries (AEI) were cropping up and releasing or re-releasing original cast albums of unsuccessful Broadway shows like *Ankles Aweigh, King of Hearts, Onward Victoria!* and *So Long, 174th Street*, and even shows which had closed out of town, like *The Baker's Wife, Nefertiti, Prettybelle* and *Snoopy!!!*. Blue Pear Records was then to come into existence, pressing "collector's albums" of previously unrecorded shows from bootleg tapes of live performances, and soon, albums of such obscure musical comedies as *Zenda, The Sap of Life, Drat! The Cat!* and *The Body Beautiful* were hitting the record stores.

When I arrived at U.C.L.A. in the fall of 1979, I was told how theater arts professor John Cauble had negotiated rights to productions of *Anyone Can Whistle* and *Dear World* before they were generally available through licensing agencies (Jerry Herman, Jerome Lawrence and Robert E. Lee were in residence for the latter), and how he had searched for the original orchestrations to the Kurt Weill musical *Johnny Johnson*, which had been lost. It was at this point, when faced with choosing a dissertation topic, that I decided to undertake what has grown into a rather enormous project. One of my advisors was music professor David Morton, curator of the university's popular music archive; he, along with musical-theater historian Miles Kreuger, founder of the Institute for the American Musical, encouraged my work, and I soon found myself spending several summers in New York City—the first, 1980, doing research at the New York Public Library's Billy Rose Theater Collection and the Dramatists Guild, and the second, 1983, talking with authors or their agents regarding unrepresented shows. Later, I was to travel to Washington, D.C., to examine the holdings of the Library of Congress. Since that time, I have been back to New York and heard from or met hundreds of authors, the vast majority of whom seem anxious to see their work produced in regional, summer stock, educational and community theaters across the country. I have met with representatives of AGAC, ASCAP, BMI, the Dramatists Guild, Broadway Play Publishing, the Dramatic Publishing Company, Music Theatre International, the Rodgers and Hammerstein Theatre Library, Samuel French, Inc. and the Tams-Witmark Music Library; all have been encouraging. Likewise, I have met with individuals from major theater book stores and out-of-print record shops, as well as theater producers, directors, agents and the like. They, too, have been enthusiastic about the work and adamant in their belief that such a catalogue is much needed by the theater community. After six years of travel, research and ongoing contact with authors or their representatives, *The Musicals No One Came to See: A Guidebook to Four Decades of Musical-Comedy Casualties on Broadway, Off-Broadway and in Out-of-Town Try-Out*, has emerged.

While every effort has been made to ensure the information listed herein is current and correct, it must go without saying that authors change agents, change addresses, disassociate themselves from guilds, and eventually pass on to join yet a greater fraternity. It is my intention to continually update the information—to make it as complete, current and useful to the theater-producing community as possible. To this end, I am most anxious to hear from individuals regarding particular shows, recordings, production materials, contacts and the like. Corrections and additions are most welcome and will certainly be added to future editions of this volume.

Rick Simas
c/o Garland Publishing, Inc.
136 Madison Avenue
New York, New York   10016

INTRODUCTION

For the past forty or more years, at least since the debut of Rodgers & Hammerstein's *Oklahoma!* in 1943, Broadway has annually produced a number of "modern" musical shows which, for whatever reasons, have been commercially unsuccessful. It is easy to dismiss these shows as ill–conceived, badly written or poorly produced, and therefore unworthy of revival; however, one cannot dismiss the fact that such milestones in the American musical theater as *Porgy and Bess, Pal Joey* and *Candide* were themselves commercial "flops" until successfully revived in later years. It is also worthwhile to note that such experimental shows as *Anyone Can Whistle, Celebration, Don't Play Us Cheap!* and *The Golden Apple*, which did not fare well at the box office, are today touted as forerunners to critically–acclaimed musical shows which soon followed in their trailblazing footsteps. It is also of note that most all great musical–theater writers have had their share of "unsuccessful" shows: Irving Berlin (*Miss Liberty, Mr. President*), Noel Coward (*The Girl Who Came to Supper, Sail Away*), Alan Jay Lerner (*Carmelina, Dance a Little Closer*) and Richard Rodgers (*Do I Hear a Waltz?, I Remember Mama*), to name but a few.

Some of Broadway's musical casualties—such as Mitch Leigh's *Cry for Us All* and Eddie Lawrence & Moose Charlap's *Kelly*—have gone on to become "cult favorites" with musical–theater enthusiasts. Others, such as Edward Albee & Bob Merrill's *Breakfast at Tiffany's* and Buster Davis' *Doctor Jazz*, were in such a state of flux throughout their out–of–town and New York previews that no one, except perhaps the original authors, knows what these shows might have become had they stabilized earlier in their try–out periods. Still other shows which, to a great extent, are flawed, nevertheless contain excellent material now rarely performed. Works such as Mel Brooks' *All American* and Jerry Herman's *Dear World* surely fall into this latter category.

1

Anyone with a serious interest in musical theater soon begins to wonder about these "other musicals"—the ones which may not have been hits but are certainly of interest and worthy of revival. Why does no one produce them? How does one acquire information about them? Who owns the rights, production materials and the like?

No one does these shows quite simply because the majority of them are not made available through any licensing agency; and those few that are made available are not performed often enough because the agencies handling them do not publicize and promote them in the same manner they do a popular show, like *Bye Bye Birdie, Hello, Dolly!* or *The Sound of Music*. To gain performance rights and production materials to an unrepresented show requires a great deal of research and concerted effort; that is, unless one knows exactly how to go about it.

According to the Dramatists Guild, following the close of a first–class production, all rights (unless otherwise specified) and materials (including scripts, scores and orchestrations) remain sole property of the authors; the original production company, however, participates in subsidiary rights and royalties from subsequent productions at a rate, and for a period of time, as specified in the production contract. The performance rights (excluding first–class production) and production materials of each property are bid upon by interested licensing agencies, the highest bidder granted jurisdiction to handle the performance rights within the United States; the property is then made available by the successful bidder for amateur, stock, educational and professional performance. This agency is responsible for the drawing–up of contracts, collecting and dispersing of royalties, and rental and/or sale of such production materials as scripts, scores, vocal parts and orchestrations.

Agencies that handle musical–theater properties exclusively or in large part include the Tams–Witmark Music Library, Music Theatre International, the Rodgers and Hammerstein Theatre Library, Samuel French, Inc. and the Dramatic Publishing Company. All are headquartered in New York City except for the Dramatic Publishing Company, which is in Illinois. Together, these licensing agencies make available to production companies and theater groups nationwide approximately 500 musical-theater properties that originated in New York.

But what happens to the musical shows these agencies do not consider commercial enough to purchase? How does the musical-theater producer, director or entrepreneur go about securing rights to an unrepresented show, and where would he find scripts and scores to such a property if they have never been published? While many of the 577 musical-theater properties compiled in this work are represented by licensing agencies and are generally available for theatrical production, over 400 shows included here, originating in New York between the 1943-44 and 1982-83 theater seasons, to date are not represented; thus, the rights and production materials to these shows are difficult if not impossible to locate and secure. The aim of this work is to make accessible to the theater-producing community these unrepresented works, as well as those musical-theater properties currently represented yet rarely produced.

Often, it seems, the producer, director or entrepreneur of musical theater at any level—be it professional, stock or educational theater—is unaware of the diversity of musical shows available to him. More often than not, his knowledge of musical theater is confined to touring companies of hit Broadway musicals that have played his town, long-run shows he's managed to take in during infrequent trips to New York, a number of original cast albums he's amassed over the years (the majority of which, again, are of hit Broadway shows or movies made from Broadway hits) or movie versions of Broadway originals he's seen at the local theater or on television. For these reasons, his knowledge of musical-theater properties from which he may select his theatrical organization's season is limited to a few "hit" Broadway musicals, the entire list of which does not represent even fifty percent of the musical theater produced in New York over the past four decades. Therefore, most musical-theater producers, directors or entrepreneurs settle for yet another rehash of such venerable war horses as *The Sound of Music, Bye Bye Birdie, Hello, Dolly!* or *My Fair Lady*, rather than seek out the relatively unknown musical-theater properties available (or that with careful "coercion" could be made available) to them.

Anyone with more than a passing interest in musical theater, then, has a stake in broadening his knowledge of these relatively obscure musical–theater properties; in this way, the production material from which he may select is all the more encompassing. For it must be understood that although a musical–theater property may have failed in the New York marketplace—be it on or off Broadway or in try–out—this is not necessarily an indication of the property's worth to other theatrical organizations. The "strike–it–rich or close–it–down" reality governing professional theater economics is often all too brutal to the shows that do not garner the rave reviews, captivate the finicky New York critics or immediately find their audience.

For example, New York theater critics and audiences in many ways tend toward the reactionary, resisting subject matter, concept or treatment that is experimental in nature. Such musicals as *Anyone Can Whistle, Prettybelle* and *La Strada*, may have fallen prey to this widely-acknowledged prejudice. New York critics also seem compelled to eschew sentimentality; generally, thumbs are down to any musical–theater production that does not treat its subject matter either seriously or nostalgically. Yet many musical–theater properties deemed "cute," "pretentious" or "sentimental" by the more jaded of New York critics and audiences may be exactly what a community–theater audience is looking for. *Henry, Sweet Henry* (based on *The World of Henry Orient*), *The Yearling* (based on the novel by Marjorie Kinnan Rawlings), *F. Jasmine Addams* (based on Carson McCullers' *The Member of the Wedding*) and *Look to the Lilies* (based on *Lilies of the Field*) are only a few properties that fall into this category. Other shows which may have problematic librettos, nevertheless contain excellent musical–comedy scores, reason enough for their successful revival (Jerry Herman's *Mack and Mabel*, Cole Porter's *Out of this World* and Stephen Schwartz's *The Baker's Wife*, for example). Others have script construction or development problems (e.g., *The Act, Darling of the Day* and *How Now, Dow Jones*) which, with the authors' permission, could perhaps be rectified through judicious cutting, editing or revision. It is even conceivable that the authors would welcome the opportunity to rework their own properties in hopes of reviving interest in a heretofore forgotten work.

It should also be realized that shows do fail in New York through little or no fault on the authors' part; while this is more often the exception than the rule, failure can be due in large part to casting errors, poor direction or choreography, design errors (in setting or scene shift, costume or lighting) or poor management. For example, the musical *Miss Moffat*, based on Emlyn Williams' play *The Corn is Green*, closed out of town when star Bette Davis, allegedly suffering from a spinal ailment, insisted on leaving the show. Both *Fade Out - Fade In*, the show marking Carol Burnett's return to the Broadway stage, and *Wildcat*, the show boasting Lucille Ball's musical-comedy debut, closed when the stars for whom these shows were written, bowed out early in the run. Author–composer–lyricist Bob Merrill believed his musical *The Prince of Grand Street* failed in try–out because star Robert Preston was miscast in the leading role. By the time replacement Herschel Bernardi was contacted, the show's producers had decided to fold out of town.

Seesaw, based on William Gibson's play *Two for the Seesaw*, had financial troubles when replacement director Michael Bennett (hired out of town to fix the show) insisted upon new sets and costumes. Star Lainie Kazan was then fired to be replaced by Michele Lee, but owing to a contract dispute, the show's producers were forced to pay both Kazan and Lee; already $400,000 over budget because of the new sets and costumes, the producers could not keep their heads above water and had to close the show prematurely.

Novelist–playwright William Goldman in his book *The Season* relates the following about the ill–fated musical *Mata Hari* which closed out of town:

> *Mata Hari* was the one genuinely ambitious musical of the [1967–68] year. With the spy–spoof fad at the flood, with Bonds and Flints and U.N.C.L.E. operatives all around us, the writers of *Mata Hari* had the really extraordinary notion of doing a musical play about the most famous female spy of them all. . . .
> When enough of the show was written to show to a producer, the three writers [Martin Charnin, Edward Thomas and Jerome Coopersmith] took it to David

Merrick. . . . Merrick agreed to produce the show, and at his suggestion, Vincente Minnelli was given the chance to direct it, and accepted.

This is probably always *the* step in the making of a musical: a director has got to get it up there. It's his baby, in a sense, and you have to go with him as long as you can, with his suggestions, his "feel"; if you don't, then you're involved in a mutinous situation, and it's hard enough getting a musical done without a mutiny going on. . . .

Rehearsals began. At first the show simply seemed undirected, misdirected. But by the time of the first–act run–through, Merrick was approached to do something about Minnelli. He refused. . . .

The first Washington preview . . . was a case of instant legend. Murphy's Law went into overdrive: wigs fell off, sets collapsed, dancers tripped over each other, and the audience wouldn't stop laughing in the wrong places. The culminating event occurred at the end when Mata Hari, shot dead by the firing squad and lying there breathing heavily in full view of the audience, raised her hand to her forehead. The next day, one Washington society column was headlined *MATA HARI HILARIOUS.*

The show opened there a few days later and got bombed. Again, and consistently, Merrick was requested to bring in a new director. Again, and consistently, Merrick refused. . . . The only prayer the show had was to get rid of Minnelli, but Merrick would have none of this. . . . Why? Merrick is as astute a showman as Broadway offers at the moment, and the best guess is that he was under heavy pressure at the time. He had three musicals dying on the road then [*The Happy Time* and *How Now, Dow Jones*, as well as *Mata Hari*], and he probably felt that the other two were more fixable. . . . *Mata Hari* was a musical with a concept, . . . you had to buy it from the start. Unified shows like *Mata Hari* are always hardest to fix out of town because they have a texture peculiarly their own. . . . Besides, *Mata Hari* didn't have much of an advance in New York compared with the other musicals that Merrick had in trouble. Perhaps if it had, he might have made a stab at saving it. But he didn't . . . and Merrick closed *Mata Hari* on the road.

Shows also fail due to what amounts to poor promotion, inopportune timing or what might be construed as bad reviewing. (Critics also have bad days, make bad judgments or dislike shows enjoyed by the majority of the audience.) States lyricist E.Y. Harburg in editor Otis Guernsey, Jr.'s *Playwrights, Lyricists, Composers on Theater:*

> Since the *New York Times* remains the one and only morning paper and most influential, the oligarchic power which it holds over a show is a monster that every author must be prepared to face. In the case of *Darling of the Day*, which was produced by top echelon authors and producers at a cost of $600,000, the drama department of the *Times* had the audacity to let its first–string critic review a ballet opening in preference to our show. The second– or third–string critic with strong psychic hostility toward what he called "Charm for the older generation," came to review us. To compound this injustice, we were given second billing on the drama page the next morning, and an off–Broadway revival of *House of Flowers* received the headline notice. . . . The young man's review was so obviously a subjective one and so venal that he misquoted lines of lyrics which later the *Times* had to correct.
>
> Mr. Walter Kerr, who had also seen the show on opening night, wrote a favorable Sunday review which is better evidence than anything I can say. But by the time this review appeared two weeks later in the Sunday *Times*, so much money had been lost on the show that the producers did not have the funds to counteract the damage done by the second stringer. In their desperation to rectify some of their injustice, the *Times* drama department finally sent Mr. Barnes to see the show. His review was short of excellent, but they failed to publish it. He managed during a Sunday piece to slip in one line saying "effortlessly the season's best musical."

A production staff not forced to deal in "Broadway terms" would not encounter these problems; therefore, in such cases, the script and score—depending upon the condition of these materials—need not be altered whatsoever.

It should be realized, however, that those shows which were never published or picked up by a licensing agency may now be in pieces; this is particularly true of those shows that closed in New York preview or out-of-town try-out. For example, the New York Public Library's Billy Rose Theater Collection at Lincoln Center is in possession of five different drafts of the libretto of *Breakfast at Tiffany's* (earlier entitled *Holly Golightly*) by one of the show's several librettists, Edward Albee. For over a decade, licensing agency Samuel French, Inc. has controlled the rights to Christopher Gore and Galt MacDermot's *Via Galactica*, as well as the Joel Grey vehicle, *Goodtime Charley*. Not until 1986 were they able to piece together script, score and orchestral parts to the latter; they are still at odds discussing the difficulties in reconstructing what's left of the former.

In 1980, under the title *I, Anastasia*, Music Theatre International added to its catalogue the musical *Anya* (adapted from the play *Anastasia*) some fifteen years after the show was produced on Broadway. However, MTI did not recover the orchestrations commissioned for the original 1965 production which, if not in the composers' possession, could be most anywhere: holed up in a stage manager's or conductor's trunk, donated to a library archive, or burned with the original production's sets, costumes and other miscellaneous holdings. Locating, securing rights to, and piecing together such a property is a painstaking job, demanding the drive, patience and tenacity only afforded a labor of love. But by re–discovering such a musical–theater property and bringing it back to life, the creative producer, director or entrepreneur has everything to gain; he may be bringing the work to the attention of local audiences and critics for the first time. And after all, a musical–theater producer or director stands to gain much more recognition for himself and his theatrical organization by creating a production of an "unknown" musical–theater work than by recreating yet another production of *Annie Get Your Gun, Oklahoma!* or *L'il Abner*, pretty much identical to those created by thousands of producers and directors before him.

Of course, the major concern of all producers and theatrical organizations is whether or not an endeavor is financially viable. This, a musical–theater producer, director or entrepreneur can only know once he understands the taste and sensibility of his theater's audience; however, it is also a theater's right, if not obligation, to guide its audience to a broader awareness and appreciation of artistic fare. This is especially true when a theater group is engaged in selling an entire season of theater rather than single theatrical events; for example, it would undoubtedly be much easier to sell the musical comedy *The Secret Life of Walter Mitty* on a five-show bill including, say, *Death of a Salesman, The Madwoman of Chaillot, The Good Doctor* and *Carousel*, rather than trying to sell it as a single evening of theater. Additionally, the way in which a "new" show is marketed is every bit as crucial to its success as the track record of an already-proven property. For example, there would certainly be interest in the theater community to see a musical comedy based on a popular work (e.g., John Steinbeck's *Of Mice and Men*, William Inge's *Picnic* or Vladimir Nabokov's *Lolita*), or composed by a successful musical-theater writer (Richard Rodgers' *Rex*, Alan Jay Lerner's *Love Life* or Leonard Bernstein's *1600 Pennsylvania Avenue*), or originally performed by famous actors (*Breakfast at Tiffany's*, which starred Mary Tyler Moore and Richard Chamberlain; *Soon*, which starred Richard Gere, Barry Bostwick and Nell Carter; or *We Take the Town*, which starred Robert Preston).

It is also true that a show's track record is not nearly as important to an audience as that of the producing organization itself; once a theater has built a reputation and has a solid audience base, it is more able to take risks on shows that are not "name draws." For example, the Megaw Theater, an Equity-waiver house in the Los Angeles area, in the summer of 1983 was able to successfully mount and sell a new musical adaptation of Oscar Wilde's *The Importance of Being Earnest* primarily because of the theater's outstanding track record. Likewise, there are high schools, colleges, little theaters and summer stock companies across the country that, because of their artistic reputation, enjoy a loyal following and can therefore afford to experiment with such shows. These are the companies (like Los Angeles' Odyssey Theater, cited below) that owe it to their audience, as well as the theatrical community at large, to revive shows which, for whatever reason, have failed to become part of the standard musical-theater repertoire.

It has been proven time and time again that when such shows are carefully chosen and creatively mounted, their success is all the more prominent, for it's truly as if the theater has brought a brand new work into the performance repertoire. Two cases in point are the Broadway revival of Leonard Bernstein's *Candide*, and the Los Angeles Equity–waiver production of Cliff Jones' *Rockabye Hamlet*, subsequently titled *Something's Rockin' in Denmark*.

The musical comedy *Candide*, directed by Tyrone Guthrie, opened on Broadway at the Martin Beck Theatre on December 1, 1956. The script, based on Voltaire's comic satire, was written by noted American playwright Lillian Hellman (her only foray into musical theater), with lyrics by famed Molière–translator Richard Wilbur in collaboration with John Latouche and Dorothy Parker, and music by noted American composer and conductor Leonard Bernstein. The production starred Barbara Cook, Robert Rounseville and Max Adrian. John Chapman, then drama critic for the *New York Daily News*, reviewed the show thusly:

> The opening at the Martin Beck of Leonard Bernstein's *Candide* Saturday evening was a truly notable event in the musical theatre. Sixty seconds after conductor Samuel Krachmalnick brought down his baton for the overture, one sensed that here was going to be an evening of uncommon quality.
>
> It developed into an artistic triumph—the best light opera, I think, since Richard Strauss wrote *Der Rosenkavalier* in 1911. It is a great contribution to the riches of the American musical–comedy stage. Many artists of many skills have had a hand in fashioning *Candide*, but it is Bernstein's profoundly sophisticated and witty score which puts it in a class by itself on Broadway. Now all I can hope is that Broadway, which is unpredictable and which does not always like to be jogged out of its routine, will cherish it as it should be cherished.

Chapman's foreboding was accurate, for despite a remarkable score, creditable performances and superlative musical virtuosity (the original cast album is still in print), the show folded after only seventy–three performances. Sixteen years later, Brooklyn's Chelsea Theatre group approached one of its advisory board, Broadway producer–director Harold Prince, with the idea of a revival. According to Prince in his book *Contradictions: Notes on Twenty–Six Years in the Theatre*:

> I had seen the original . . . and remembered it well. The
> score was exciting, but the performance confusing. I
> tend to think the production failed at the top from that
> confusion. . . . The book, music and physical production
> were inappropriate to one another.

Prince spent some time mulling over the project, and once his production of
A Little Night Music had opened on Broadway, he decided to collaborate on
the *Candide* revival. Reading Voltaire's original and comparing it to
Hellman's adaptation, he felt her structure was too rigid, her treatment too
serious:

> I had never read *Candide*. I was surprised by how light
> and irreverent and *unimportant* it is. Apparently he
> wrote it quickly and denied having written it, putting it
> down as a school–boy's prank. And that's the spirit of
> it. The three hundred and some odd years that separated
> Voltaire's writing it and the Guthrie version of it had
> served only to make a classic of it and spoil the fun.

Prince decided that while he would like to use Bernstein's score more or less
intact, he would have the script completely reworked with a new
environmental concept in mind. He suggested to Bob Kalfin, artistic
director of the Chelsea, that they "approach Lillian Hellman and ask her
whether she would be willing to write a new *Candide*,"

> I told her our scheme and she said that was what she
> had always wanted, but *Candide*? Never again! In that
> case, would she object to my asking someone else to
> work with me? Immediately she agreed. . . . I then
> called Hugh Wheeler. We met and listened to the
> album. Each of us took the Voltaire and underlined
> choice bits, going over what particularly delighted us.
> Hugh and I paid Bernstein a visit and told him our plan
> (he said it was what he had always wanted) and discussed
> new numbers. . . . Bernstein produced a file of melodies,
> themes, full songs in some instances, of discarded
> material from 1955–56. There was enough musical
> material to accommodate the new version, but who was

to write the new lyrics? Lenny had, in fact, written "I
Am Easily Assimilated" in its entirety, and the "Auto da
Fe" with John Latouche, which though discarded in 1956
became valuable to us. But he was scheduled for a series
of lectures at Harvard. Given the short time we had to
work, it seemed expeditious to ask Steve Sondheim to
help us out since I had never met Richard Wilbur.

Craig Zadan, in his book *Sondheim & Co.*, quotes Leonard Bernstein:

"This version of *Candide* was exactly what I wanted it to
be. . . . It's exciting, swift, pungent, funny and touching,
and it works just like sideshows at a fair. About half the
score went in the process, I am sorry to say. We lost
five songs that were on the original cast album"
(Goddard Lieberson's Broadway cast recording of the
original production was responsible for making the show
the most well-known and popular cult-musical the
theater has ever known, after its brief two-month
legitimate run) "although what's on the record is not the
full score by any means. . . . But there were other things
that had been written for the show and never used. They
found this music in old trunks and boxes and Steve wrote
new lyrics to them."

Continues Prince in *Contradictions*:

We opened over a ten-day period with critics at every
performance. We were sold out beforehand and the
Brooklyn run was extended two weeks. The reviews were
marvelous, many suggesting a move to Broadway [which
was accomplished with great success]. Earlier I have
said that each play seeds the next. Nowhere is it more
apparent than with the success of *Candide*.

Granted, Hal Prince had everything at his disposal in the re-making of
Candide: a brilliant composer, Leonard Bernstein, willing to rework his
original score and provide additional musical material with which to shape
new musical numbers; the most lauded musical-comedy lyricist of our time,

Stephen Sondheim, willing to augment existing lyrics and create new ones; a team of creative and industrious librettists, Hugh Wheeler and Hal Prince, conceiving a new structure for *Candide* and adapting it anew from the Voltaire classic; and the cooperation of the original authors or their estates, allowing Prince's team to reshape the material into a new, inventive production. While a community, stock or educational theater group certainly cannot command this kind of support, the work any theatrical producer, director or entrepreneur undertakes in pursuing such a project is basically the same and can by all means yield equivalent satisfaction and reward.

A case in point is the Los Angeles Odyssey Theater's production of Cliff Jones' *Something's Rockin' in Denmark* conceived by Bill Castellino. The musical *Rockabye Hamlet* (actually a rock opera) with book, music and lyrics by Cliff Jones, directed and choreographed by Gower Champion, opened on Broadway at the Minskoff Theatre, February 17, 1976. It closed a week later, having played only eight performances. Reported drama critic John Devere of the original production:

> Gower Champion's . . . brilliant directorial touches combine plot lines with rock technology, as in the counterpoint aria "Tis Pity, Tis True," when Claudius, Gertrude and Polonius simultaneously sing different and contrasting lyrics . . . while inadvertently (it seems) tangling their microphone ropes in a pattern almost as complex as the plot of *Hamlet* itself. . . . You may disagree with the concept, but the realization is glossy Broadway at its best. . . .
> *Rockabye Hamlet*, which delighted audiences, met with hatcheting hostility from critics; the fact that the musical dared tamper with a classic seemed to spur unusually vituperative venom. Not allowed the time to find its audience through successful word–of–mouth, *Rockabye Hamlet* will not be seen by the tens of thousands who would have appreciated its imaginative realization. When a show this exciting closes, unseen, something is rotten in the state of Broadway.

States author Cliff Jones in an interview with Abbie Bernstein in the December 17–23, 1981 issue of *Drama–Logue*:

It was *extemely* exciting in New York—we were playing the Minskoff Theatre, we previewed for three weeks and in the last week we were selling out every night; the audience would stop the show and get on their feet and cheer and scream. But the three major critics hated it and so overnight the show got killed. We ran another week and that was it. We knew that we had a real audience–pleaser simply because of the response we got during previews, but there was no money. I think what hurt more than anything was that it was a *good* show that went down the tubes.

And that was the last anyone heard of *Rockabye Hamlet* until five years later when Bill Castellino, a director for the Odyssey Theater—an Equity–waiver house in the Los Angeles area—took an interest in the property. Reports Gretchen Henkel in the November 12–18, 1981 issue of *Drama–Logue*:

Castellino himself was the catalyst for this project. He had never seen the Gower Champion version . . . when he lived in New York. But he had heard about it and what he heard, he liked. "The idea of the two forms mixing, the classical theme with the contemporary milieu," was what captivated him. . . .

In New York last Thanksgiving . . . Castellino tracked down the original producers of *Rockabye Hamlet*. He met with them and pitched himself as director and the Odyssey Theatre as a place to redo the play. Back in California, he got a form of the script and tape of the score and set about getting in touch with Cliff Jones. Jones was very interested in Castellino's approach to the piece and agreed to let him do it. There was a series of developmental meetings between Jones, Castellino and Ron Sossi (the Odyssey's artistic director); then Jones went home to rewrite the book. Included in this version of the piece (a composite of its three other productions, two in Canada and the New York one) is the new title song by Jerry Sternback [the musical director and arranger for the Odyssey production].

States Abbie Bernstein in her *Drama–Logue* article, "Many of the Los Angeles reviews of the current production have been extemely favorable and box office is robust." Critic Lee Melville's review of the Los Angeles production described it thusly:

Cliff Jones' pop opera, *Something's Rockin' in Denmark*, is "based on the legend of Hamlet," but doesn't try to be a new interpretation of the original; rather, Jones focuses more intently on the passions of the play. And in the hands of director–choreographer Bill Castellino . . . this opus is lively, dazzling, inventive and pure entertainment. . . .

Jones' work (he wrote the book, music and lyrics) was called *Rockabye Hamlet* and was directed by the estimable Gower Champion. It was one of Broadway's big disasters. Apparently Jones has done considerable rethinking and reworking, for this time he has come up with a winner. The music may not always be inspired (there are forty–nine numbers listed, including reprises) . . . but there are enough—at least a dozen—that hit you square in your rockin' bones to make you want to stand up and shout, "Hooray for being daring and taking chances." Castellino never stops generating energy on stage nor does he miss an opportunity for schtick, high drama, fun and outrageous antics; but, most importantly, he expertly combines it all into a cohesive unit.

And so once again is chronicled the success story of a director who, instead of turning out another carbon–copy production of the tried and true, had enough faith in his own ability to create something new and innovative for his theater's audience. Of course, not every musical production conceived by a theater group such as the Odyssey can be a new hit resurrected from obscurity. On the other hand, every musical–theater production need not be the revival of a show by Rodgers and Hammerstein, Lerner and Loewe, or Irving Berlin. Variety *is* the spice of life, and varying the fare with a show that requires more of a producer's and director's commitment, drive and artistry, can only help benefit their staff, their cast and their audience.

To further support the case for discovering obscure musical properties, any theater group producing musical shows over a period of years can corroborate that it is soon face to face with a dilemma not so quickly met by producers of straight dramatic fare. At present, only one or two of the several musical productions premiering each season on Broadway become hit shows; the list of proven musical–theater "draws" numbers less than some forty titles. Consistently choosing from this list greatly limits the scope and variety of musical–theater fare any group can present to its public; soon the group is repeating or "reviving" musical productions it has previously presented. And more importantly, the group thereby fails to expose its audience to the many musical-theater originals rarely, if ever, produced outside Manhattan.

Of course, it is much more difficult for the theatrical producer, director or entrepreneur to locate musical-theater librettos and scores—particularly those of unsuccessful shows—than to find at the local bookstore or library the script to most any straight dramatic play. This volume, then, serves as a reference guide to locating these lesser-known shows. It is compiled to introduce the musical-theater producer, director or enthusiast to these obscure musical-theater properties; to alert him to the whereabouts of existing scripts, scores and orchestrations; and to instruct him in how to go about contacting the authors, producers, agents or attorneys who control the rights to these properties. While producing a musical relegated to the ranks of obscurity is undoubtedly more difficult, it can also be all the more rewarding to the theater group that has painstakingly sought out the show best suited to its particular needs, and brought the material to life for what is sure to be the first time locally.

Indexed in this work are musical shows premiering in New York over a forty-year period—between the 1943-44 and 1982-83 theater seasons inclusive—which ran on or off Broadway for less than 300 performances or which closed in preview or pre-Broadway try-out. This seemingly arbitrary cut-off was chosen due to the fact that shows which ran for any longer a period (approximately nine months) were most often successful and thus became known to the theater-going public. However, shows such as *Coco* and *The Magic Show*—which did run longer than 300 performances—have been included in this work if, to date, no licensing agency has made them available for production.

This work does not include one-act musicals, musicals presented in a foreign language, musicals written to be performed by puppets, or revivals of musicals which premiered before the 1943-44 theater season *unless* the revival was substantially different from the original. Distinctions were more difficult to make in the cases of "musical revues," "plays with music" and "operas." The intention is to index only book–oriented musical–theater works which meet the requirements listed above; however, distinctions in many of these cases were difficult to make. For example, how does one decide whether a musical property is a "revue" or "comedy" when its scenes seem more like sketches, yet it is unified in concept, employs central recurring characters and has an integrated score (e.g., *La Grosse Valise, A History of the American Film, Runaways* and *Snoopy!!!*)? How does one decide what amount of music employed in what fashion separates a "play with music" from a bona fide musical–theater property (e.g., *Colette, Mrs. Patterson, The Pink Jungle* and *Tambourines to Glory*)? If a libretto is set entirely to music, yet the music is decidedly "musical–theater" in nature and the show is produced in a Broadway or off–Broadway house, how does one decide whether it is relegated to the ranks of musical theater or opera (e.g., *The Golden Apple, Kittiwake Island, Regina* and *The Umbrellas of Cherbourg*)? And how, then, does one classify "rock operas"—as musical–theater properties or operas (e.g., *The Lieutenant, Rockabye Hamlet, Sgt. Pepper's Lonely Heart's Club Band on the Road* and *The Survival of St. Joan*)?

For the purposes of this work, whenever the validity of a show as a musical–theater property was in doubt, *New York Times* reviews and *Best Plays* and *Theater World* entries were cross–checked; if any of these referred to or described the property as a musical (as was true in all of the cases cited above), it was included in this compilation. Conversely, none of the works of Gian–Carlo Menotti has been included here (though several were eligible according to opening date, length of run and theater of original production) as they were referred to in all sources consulted as operas. Only a selection of off–off–Broadway musical productions is included as documentation concerning the majority was so vague or unverifiable that most such shows could not be evaluated as musical–theater properties without actually locating and perusing their scripts and scores.

ORIGINAL CAST ALBUMS AND BOOTLEG TAPES

If certain shows described in this volume are unfamiliar, undoubtedly the best way of acquainting yourself with them is by listening to the original cast albums and reading the liner notes. However, because many of these shows did not run long enough to make an original cast album commercially viable, an authorized recording of the score is most likely not available. And even those shows that did release an album, because there is not a vast market for recordings of unsuccessful shows, it is more than likely these albums are now out of print. (Original cast albums which are no longer available are designated in the entries to follow as OP; those which have been reissued are marked RE.)

Because an album is no longer in print, however, does not mean a copy of it cannot be made available to you. For a price. Out-of-print recordings have become a multi-million-dollar industry in this country; within the last decade, several companies have appeared which deal almost exclusively in out-of-print show albums, one of the most accessible being:

> Original Cast Records   (203) 544-8288
> Box 496
> Georgetown, CT   06829

For a small fee, they will send you their catalogue listing which out-of-print records they make available at what prices. While it is wise to know these prices for comparison shopping, it is advisable to first check the used record shops, thrift stores, garage sales and flea markets in your own area before purchasing anything through the mail. While it may, in this manner, prove difficult to find a particular show album, over a period of time one can amass an admirable record collection for relatively little money. To locate a particular out-of-print recording, it is best to look through the local yellow pages under the heading, "Records." It is here you should find record shops advertising "used," "out-of-print" or "hard-to-find" records. Most all major cities have at least one such store. If you cannot locate the one in your particular area, ask at other record shops for advice regarding out-of-print items; they are bound to know the best local dealer. Having located the right store, check their price for a particular recording against the one listed by Original Cast Records; should it not compare favorably, try bargaining with the proprietor. If it is then advantageous to purchase the album from Original Cast Records, be sure to allow at least six weeks for delivery.

For those who wish further information regarding out-of-print cast albums, as well as virtually all other aspects of recorded show music, I recommend David Hummel's *The Collector's Guide to the American Musical Theatre* (Scarecrow Press, 1984). In turn, Mr. Hummel recommends as companion volumes to his book, Jack Raymond's *Show Music on Record* (Unger, 1982) and Brian Rust's *London Musical Shows on Record* (Gramophone, 1977). In Mr. Hummel's book, in addition to Original Cast Records, he lists the following sources for out-of-print records:

> A-1 Record Finders   (213) REC-ORDS
> P.O. Box #75071
> Los Angeles, CA   90075
>
> Music Masters   (212) 840-1958
> 25 W. 43rd Street
> New York, N.Y.   10036

If a cast album for a particular show was never recorded, this still does not mean an original cast recording of it can't be made available to you; it does mean, however, that the musical-comedy aficionado must then address the entire question of underground or bootleg recordings and whether or not he should patronize those parties who make a profit from an essentially stolen product.

It is generally acknowledged that illegal recordings of Broadway musicals have been made since the advent of recording equipment itself. I myself have listened to bootleg tapes of shows dating as far back as *Gentlemen Prefer Blondes*, which opened on Broadway, December 8, 1949; I therefore assume that "homemade recordings" exist for practically every show listed in this volume. Some of these are "sound–system quality," recorded through the theater's sound system once the closing notice had been posted and the stage manager realized that no authorized recording of the show would ever take place. Other bootleg recordings are far worse in quality, having been recorded from the auditorium by "a hundred little Sonys," either by collectors for their own private collections or exploiters who knew they could turn a fast buck on a recording of a show for which no cast album would ever by made. Obviously, these tapes are not available to the general public as they are illegal; they are made without clearance from the guilds and unions protecting the artists employed in the original productions, and no royalty earned from the sale of these cassettes goes to the people who created the shows they represent. However, if no cast album exists of a show, and there is no other way to reconstruct it, to resurrect it from obscurity, then obviously the tape serves a valuable purpose and must be employed to help return the musical–theater property to the performance repertoire. My advice to people in search of bootleg tapes is that they first learn the difference between the collector and the exploiter.

Be it known that in New York (and in a handful of other spots across the country, although primarily in New York), there exists a breed apart, made up of individuals who, quite frankly, *live* for the musical theater. They are playgoers, collectors, historians, devoted fans; they own most every original cast album (including those never released to the general public), the show posters, the reviews, the clippings, the photos, the Hirschfelds, the librettos, the bootleg cassettes and yes, even the videotapes. (There are also such videotapes available for viewing on the third floor of the New York Public Library at Lincoln Center; you must first, however, make an appointment to come in and view them.) These "musical–theater maniacs," for the most part, do not sell tapes for profit; generally, they trade with other collectors or will duplicate a tape for a "collector in need." These are the people with whom I recommend musical–theater directors, producers and entrepreneurs consult while working on resurrecting an obscure musical–theater property. I fell into league with one such person while in New York who then led me to a whole network of musical–theater experts; but it wasn't until I left New York that I truly came to realize how closely–knit and far–reaching this "musical–theater underground" is. . . . .

Some time after I'd been in communication with this network of individuals, I traveled to the Library of Congress in Washington, D.C., to pursue further research. While discussing with a librarian there the musical *Sherry!* (a musical–comedy version of the George S. Kaufman & Moss Hart play, *The Man Who Came to Dinner*), a young lawyer eavesdropping on our conversation approached me, introduced himself, and asked if I was the one working on the catalogue of unsuccessful Broadway musicals. Taken aback by my newfound fame, I replied affirmatively; he immediately offered to be of whatever assistance he could, and we subsequently had a rather lengthy discussion about the library's holdings (he was a resident and very familiar with the facility while I was only able to remain in town and work at the library for a week). He had heard by telephone of my work and was only too anxious to give me a hand, all thanks to this now infamous "New York underground."

While these are true "fanatics," hopelessly obsessed with the world of musical comedy, rest assured they are a gentle and loving species willing to do whatever they can, once they're convinced you're sincere in your quest. These are the people who keep obscure musical shows alive in their collections and memories, and whose help should be enlisted to bring such shows back to life on the stage. On the other hand, there are those who are only in business to make a fast buck, who charge as much as fifty dollars for a tape they illegally made one night in the theater, cassette recorder in hand. This is outrageous not only for the price (considering the quality of the product), but for the fact that no one involved with the original production receives any royalty from the sale. Unlike the collectors, these people do not support the professional theater, they exploit it. They make thousands of dollars peddling products they did not create, taking revenue away from the theater and giving nothing back in return. This is also true of such recording companies as Blue Pear Records which take these unauthorized live recordings, press a limited number of "collector's albums," and then peddle them in specialty record stores for anywhere between twenty and thirty dollars apiece.

The bottom line is that it's illegal to make bootleg tapes and certainly all the more so to sell them. The only function I believe such tapes fulfill is an historical one, in that they can serve to reconstruct a show should the original materials have disappeared. Therefore, if you are not relatively certain you want to produce a musical show for which no original cast album exists, I would advise avoiding the inherent difficulties in procuring a bootleg recording of it. Should a bootleg tape be essential to a musical-theater director, producer or entrepreneur in order to reconstruct a libretto, score or orchestration, the surest route is to visit any of the several book stores in New York City specializing in theater books, or record shops specializing in out-of-print records. Then, rather than asking point blank, "Where can I buy a bootleg tape of *Molly?*" it is far wiser to first explain your position and intention, i.e., "I'm a summer-stock director interested in producing the musical *Molly*. I'm looking for all the materials I can find on this show. Can you help me?" In this way, you should eventually come into contact with at least one or two people who can steer you to the collectors or historians in possession of the materials. If you cannot get to New York, my best advice is to then try the theater book stores and out-of-print record shops in your own area, using the same tactic. Needless to say, New York is the hub of professional musical theater, and you are likely to be more successful there in such endeavors than anywhere else in the world. That is not to say you can't achieve the same results in other cities such as Chicago, Boston or Los Angeles, but it is my experience that the search you undertake anywhere other than New York will be much longer and more indirect. Don't count on any luck in towns like Amarillo or Winnemucca; generally speaking, hardcore musical-comedy addicts do not gravitate to places where national touring companies don't play—i.e., bergs.

For those with a real interest in musical-theater recordings, David Hummel, in his *Collector's Guide to the American Musical Theatre*, highly recommends the publication *Show Music*, available from Max Preeo, 5800 Pebble Beach Blvd., Las Vegas, NV 89109:

This newsletter is published every other month and will keep the collector informed of all new releases on show music for stage, screen and television. . . . One thing that is very helpful to the collector is the "record sources" column. If a private album is issued, it will not only be reviewed, but you will be given the address where you will be able to obtain it—in many cases directly from the composer. . . . This publication is a MUST for anyone in the show music field.

And for the collector wishing to know the value of his or her records, there is *Osborne & Hamilton's Original Record Collectors Price Guide for Movie/TV Soundtracks & Original Cast Albums* (O'Sullivan, Woodside & Co., 1981) by Jerry Osborne and Bruce Hamilton. This book lists prices used in New York and Los Angeles and is based on sale prices of records in those areas, as well as collector's set mail order lists. . . . It is the first edition and will most likely be updated every few years to include new issues as well as an updating of prices.

SHEET MUSIC AND LIBRETTOS

Sheet music publishers are listed in this volume if individual song sheets, vocal selections or entire piano–vocal scores were printed for a particular show. However, because of the drastic changes that have taken place in the sheet–music industry over the past three decades and the virtual impossibility of verifying which songs were published and distributed for each show indexed, the specific song titles published are not listed. For those who wish more detailed information regarding sheet music, I recommend Steven Suskin's *Show Tunes 1905–1985: The Songs, Shows and Careers Of Broadway's Major Composers* (Dodd, Mead & Company, 1986). While many of the shows indexed herein were not written by "major" composers and therefore do not appear in Mr. Suskin's book, those shows he does include list all of the songs from the score which have been published. To locate sheet music still in print, one is advised to check the local music store, where it should be relatively easy to find what sheet music is available for a particular show. To locate sheet music no longer in print, the process is—of course—decidedly more complicated.

First, one should search out the music stores in the nearby area specializing in out–of–print sheet music; should there be no advertisement in the yellow pages under "Music–Sheet" specializing in "out–of–print" or "hard–to–find" music, one might then inquire at the local music stores where such a specialized dealer can be located. In his book *The Musical: Where to Find It* (Magnetic Indexes, 1984), Clyde Primm recommends:

Globe Music (213) 465–1777
5351 Santa Monica Blvd.
Los Angeles, CA 90029

Front Row Center (213) 852–0149
8127 W. Third Street
Los Angeles, CA 90048

Should this strategy not yield sufficient results, one might then attempt to contact the original music publisher himself. Virtually all major music publishers are located in New York City, and it is certainly easy enough to thumb through the Manhattan white pages at the local library in search of the publisher in question. One then need only write or call to find out what sheet music has been published and whether it is still possible to obtain copies of it. Of course, this is none too difficult *if* the publisher is listed; fortunately, most musical-theater sheet music printed over the past four decades has been published by one company—Chappell—and they do indeed maintain an office in New York (for the address, see below, under "How to Interpret the Entries"). However, one should be aware that music publishers today are no longer the giant corporations they once were. Many have gone out of business, sold off much of their holdings or merged with larger conglomerates. And those which have remained solvent have not done so by paying particularly close attention to their out-of-print stock; more often than not, these companies cannot locate the precious, hard-to-find material you seek, or else they simply don't find it lucrative enough to make a serious effort. Should you be unable to locate a particular publisher, or should he be unable to provide the answers or materials you seek, it is then my advice that you consult with one of the larger sheet music archives regarding their holdings. While I'm sure there exists a number of private collectors who could also be of help, my advice is that you first contact the Archive of Popular American Music/UCLA, the New York Public Library/Billy Rose Collection, or the Library of Congress/Copyright Office (for addresses, see below, under "How to Interpret the Entries"). Should these particular archives not be in possession of the material you're seeking, they are bound to know if the materials do exist and where to obtain them.

Regarding published librettos, the first step is to peruse the local libraries and book stores. Should this not yield results, one can always check with the library regarding their inter-library loan policy. (In this way, all of the published librettos listed herein should be available to library patrons; however, neither the New York Public Library nor the Library of Congress can loan their *unpublished* material.) It might also prove worthwhile to seek out the book store(s) nearest you which specialize in theater books, in much the same way as was described regarding out–of–print record and sheet music outlets. Again, Clyde Primm makes several recommendations in *The Musical: Where to Find It*, which include:

Theatrebooks, Inc.   (212) 757–2834
1576 Broadway
New York, N.Y.   10036

Drama Books   (415) 441–5343
511 Geary Street
San Francisco, CA   94102

Additionally, I recommend:

Larry Edmonds Bookshop, Inc.   (213) 463–3273
6658 Hollywood Boulevard
Hollywood, CA   90028

As a companion to this volume—particularly as regards published librettos, plot synopsis, and production requirements of musicals presently available for production—I highly recommend Tom Tumbusch's book from *The Theatre Student* series, *Guide to Broadway Musical Theatre* (Rosen Publishing, revised edition, 1983). Less informative but offering a comprehensive list of the musical shows made available by major licensing agencies and the published vocal selections or piano–vocal scores for each, is Richard Lynch's book, *Musicals! A Directory of Musical Properties Available for Production* (American Library Association, 1984).

For further information, particularly as regards musical–theater recordings and librettos, I recommend musical–theater historian Miles Kreuger at the Institute for the American Musical and, for recordings, David Hummel at the Archives of the American Musical Theatre (for addresses, see below, under "How to Interpret the Entries").

DISCREPANCIES

In researching, cross–checking and compiling such an enormous amount of data of such an obscure nature (documenting 577 shows over a forty–year period, a good number of which ran for less than a week, many written by authors and produced by groups never heard from again), discrepancies are bound to arise. Primarily five sources were used to locate, verify and document the entries in this work: *Theater World* yearbooks, *Best Plays* yearbooks, *Theater Information Bulletin*, *Variety* (as recorded in the theater statistics file of the New York Public Library's Billy Rose Collection, Lincoln Center) and *Notable Names in the American Theater*, revised edition, 1976. Generally, where discrepancies were found, the consensus is cited in the entry which appears in this work. For example, the musical *Rex* was recorded by *Best Plays* as having run forty–one performances, by *Theater World* as having run forty–eight performances, and by *Variety*/New York Public Library's statistics file and *Theater Information Bulletin* as having run forty–nine performances; it is too recent a show to appear in *Notable Names in the American Theater*. *Rex* is thus recorded in this work as having run forty–nine performances.

Certain discrepancies, however, were not as easy to reconcile. For example, occasionally no information whatsoever was available regarding a certain statistic; sometimes *all* available information conflicted; and other times the only information available, with regard to common sense, appeared to be incorrect. The following is a compilation of the discrepancies found throughout the research that could not be resolved in the fashion described above and the method by which each particular case was analyzed and recorded in this work.

TITLES OF SOURCE WORKS: Oftentimes, the source work of a musical–comedy adaptation was listed as "story" or "original work" by a particular author or authors with no source title given. Further research usually resulted in the discovery of the source's title; however, this was not always the case. Eleven sources of adaptations are listed in this work by author only as research did not reveal the source work's title. Seven of these musical–comedy adaptations—*Beg, Borrow, or Steal; The Girl from Nantucket; Morning Sun; Rhapsody; Spotlight; What a Killing* and *Wild and Wonderful*— were based on a "story" or "original work" by authors other than those who wrote the show's libretto. It is conceivable that the titles for the source works were not available as the works were never published and possibly never given titles. How is this possible? One explanation is that when setting about writing something as complicated as a musical–theater piece, oftentimes a "story" or "treatment" (whatever term given a basic plot outline and description of characters and song interpolations) is first created to sell the idea to a producer or theater company. Once terms guaranteeing production are reached, the writing of the actual libretto and score begins. In the case of *Spotlight*, librettist Richard Seff explained that his libretto was based on an earlier draft by Leonard Starr, who had since left the production team. For this reason, billing as regards source material had to be given as "based on a story by Leonard Starr."

One musical, *Lyle*, was based on a series of "children's books by Bernard Waber." No reference source consulted listed which books specifically were the sources for the musical adaptation; therefore, titles are not given. Two musicals were based on a series of short stories, *The Education of H*Y*M*A*N   K*A*P*L*A*N* on "stories by Leo Rosten" and *Hazel Flagg* on "stories by James Street." While there is a collection of stories by Rosten entitled *The Education of H*Y*M*A*N   K*A*P*L*A*N*, he also wrote other volumes of stories about Jewish immigrants which were used in the adaptation; none of the sources consulted, however, specifically listed which stories collected in which volumes were used. In the case of *Hazel Flagg*, author James Street has written a number of short stories; all of the reference sources consulted, however, failed to list which of these were used as source material for the musical adaptation. As for *Horseman, Pass By*, source material is listed as "poetry by William Butler Yeats"; however, nowhere was it listed exactly which poems served as the source for the musical adaptation.

Source materials originally written in a foreign language are listed by their standard English title followed in parentheses by the original foreign title. Source works which have not been translated into English or whose title is the same in English have been listed by foreign title only. The "Index to Sources of Adaptations" lists foreign titles as well as English translations of source works.

CLASSIFICATION OF SOURCE MATERIALS: Sources of adaptations for musical-theater properties were classified as one of the following: play, verse play, melodrama, commedia dell'arte scenario, *chante-fable*, folk tale, musical comedy, opera, operetta, radio/television serial, teleplay or screenplay; short story, biography, autobiography, novel, novella, scripture, poetry or epic poem; short stories (not published as a single work); collection (published as a single work containing any of the following: interviews, monologues, poetry, sermons, sketches or short stories); record album; or comic strip.

Several musical-theater properties were listed as being "suggested by . . .," "freely adapted from . . .," "sequel to . . .," or "suggested by characters from. . . ." In these cases, the source of adaptation is followed in parentheses by the phrase "suggested by," "freely adapted," "sequel" or "characters from."

COMPOSERS AND LYRICISTS: Six of the musical-theater properties cited in this work did not have scores written expressly for the property itself but rather interpolated musical numbers from existing sources: *Happy New Year* incorporated songs from Cole Porter's music and lyrics; *The Heebie Jeebies* centered around "the contemporary pop tunes the Boswell Sisters sang between 1930 and 1936"; *Hijinks!* interpolated music from a number of different sources; *The Last Minstrel Show* utilized music from the traditional minstrel repertoire; *The Madwoman of Central Park West* incorporated show music and pop tunes, as well as several original numbers written for the show; and *The 1940's Radio Hour* employed "hit tunes from the period." Three of these shows, *The Heebie Jeebies*, *The Last Minstrel Show* and *The 1940's Radio Hour*, did not cite any lyricists' or composers' names, nor was this information readily available in any of the references consulted. Instead, the musical numbers listed are so cited here.

THEATERS: Over a period of years, theater groups disband, regroup, change names; likewise, the theaters that they lease oftentimes change names. Among the theaters cited in this compilation, four operating under an off-Broadway contract have names that appear in different variations over a period of years. They are:

(Chelsea Theater Center's) Academy of Music
Chelsea Theater Center/Cheryl Crawford Theater
Chelsea Theater Center Upstairs Theater

Judson Hall
Judson Memorial Church
Judson Poet's Theater

Public Theater
Public Theater/Anspacher
Public/Cabaret Theater
Public/LuEsther Hall
Public/Martinson Hall
Public/Newman Theater
Public/Other Stage

Westside Arts Theater
Westside Theater
Westside Arts/Cheryl Crawford Theater
Westside Arts/Downstairs
Westside/Upstairs

No attempt has been made to reconcile the inconsistencies in the names of these theaters as it is conceivable that they indicate different theaters within the same structure (Westside Theater, Westside/Upstairs) or perhaps different structures owned or leased by the same producing organization (Public/Cabaret Theater, Public/ Martinson Hall).

CLASSIFICATION OF PRODUCTIONS: Whether a show is classified as a Broadway, off–Broadway or off–off–Broadway production involves more than the location within Manhattan of the theater where the production took place. (In fact, two of the theaters listed in the off–Broadway section of this volume are not even in Manhattan: the Academy of Music is in Brooklyn, and the Jones Beach Theater is on Long Island.) The classification of a production is determined by the actors' union, Actors' Equity Association, and recognized by the dramatists' organization, the Dramatists Guild, Inc. These organizations take into consideration a number of factors governing a production and then set regulations accordingly which govern the employment, rate of pay and working conditions of their members in the production.

The five reference sources used to locate, verify and document other statistics in this work were also consulted concerning the classification statistic of all production entries (which reported shows appearing at the Jones Beach Theater and the Academy of Music as off–Broadway productions). As stated above in reference to the run of *Rex*, where discrepancies were found, the consensus is cited in the entry which appears in this work.

Pre–Broadway shows were the most difficult to identify as most every musical production premiering anywhere in the United States other than New York City, New York, intends—eventually—to play on Broadway. Obviously, all of these "musical–theater hopefuls" could not be included in the pre–Broadway section of this work. Of the sixty–six entries catalogued, all but fourteen were listed in *Theater World* and/or *Best Plays* as being in pre–Broadway try–out or on pre–Broadway tour, suggesting the producer(s) had made arrangements for a Broadway theater and opening date. Six pre–Broadway entries closed in New York during Broadway previews. Four (*Peg*; *How Do You Do, I Love You*; *Hello, Sucker!* and *W.C.*) played the pre–Broadway Guber–Gross Music Fair circuit. And print material found in the clipping files of the New York Public Library's Billy Rose Collection indicated that the remaining four shows—*1491*, *Marianne*, *Sheba* and *A Song for Cyrano*—were of pre–Broadway calibre and were pursuing arrangements for a New York opening.

OPENING DATES: There were never more discrepancies found than in the case of opening date/length–of–run statistics. This is less true of Broadway than off– or off–off–Broadway shows, though there are cases, such as the Broadway musical *Savara*, which had no formal opening, for which the length of run is calculated from the first public performance. The reason opening date and length–of–run statistics for off– and off–off–Broadway shows are so erratic has to do with the concept of an "opening." A show will usually play in preview at reduced ticket prices a week to three weeks before its scheduled opening or press night. This gives the company a chance to settle into the theater, and the writers and directors a chance to rework their property in light of audience response. For off– and particularly off–off–Broadway shows, where production costs do not approach those of Broadway, oftentimes the opening—the date the press is invited to review the show and the ticket prices rise to scale—is postponed for weeks, sometimes months. For this reason, some of the references consulted (particularly *Best Plays*) tend to cite the date of first public performance as the opening date instead of the press date; they then calculate the run accordingly. Because the majority of literary sources consulted (as well as theater historians and librarians) are adamant in the belief that the opening date from which a length of run is calculated should be the date the production is opened to the critics, opening date and length–of–run statistics in this work refer to the press date from which time the length of run is calculated. Obviously, this does not include pre-Broadway shows, which never reach their New York opening; therefore, the date cited in pre-Broadway entries is indeed the date of first public performance. In these instances, no length–of–run statistic is given, for the show closed out of town (OT) before its New York debut.

ARRANGEMENT OF ENTRIES

The entries in this work are arranged alphabetically by title under the divisions "The Broadway Shows," "The Shows That Closed in Try–out or Preview," "The off–Broadway Shows and a Selection of off–off–Broadway Shows" and "The Shows That Ran Longer Than 300 Performances But Are Currently Unavailable for Production." As previously stated, the original Jones Beach shows are included in the off–Broadway section because of their classification in *Best Plays*. An appendix lists the works by opening date. Indices that appear at the back of the book arrange the entries according to title; source of adaptations; and source authors, librettists, composers and lyricists.

Each entry includes the following information:

(1) title
(2) source of adaptation (listed as original unless based on *specific* textual source(s), described by title, classification of text and source author, where available)
(3) author
(4) lyricist
(5) composer
(6) original producer
(7) original theater
(8) classification of production:
Broadway
off–Broadway
off–off–Broadway
pre–Broadway (closed out of town or in New York preview)
(9) opening date
(10) length of run (number of performances from opening night/press date; OT = closed out of town; Preview = closed in New York preview; NA = information not available)
(11) original stars (included only where they might aid in publicizing subsequent productions; NA = not applicable)
(12) *Theater World* reference annotation (indicates the entry in *Theater World*, which includes a full cast list, production photographs, credits, scene breakdown and listing of songs; NO ENTRY AVAIL = no listing appears in the *Theater World* annual)
(13) *Best Plays* reference annotation (indicates the entry in *Best Plays*, which includes all *Theater World* information except production photos, and a more complete scene breakdown and listing of songs; NO ENTRY AVAIL = no listing appears in the *Best Plays* annual)

(14) magazine criticism annotation(s) (magazine review annotations as listed in *The Reader's Guide to Periodical Literature*; il = illustrated; NO CRIT AVAIL = no magazine reviews available)

(15) *New York Times* criticism annotation(s) (NO CRIT AVAIL = no critical reviews available from the *New York Times*)

(16) *New York Theatre Critics Reviews* (NYTC) criticism annotation(s) (NO CRIT AVAIL = no critical reviews available from *New York Theatre Critics Reviews* annuals; in the case of pre–Broadway shows, which had no New York opening, critical review annotations are from William Torbert Leonard's *Broadway Bound*, cited below)

(17) publication data on published scripts (NA = no published script available)

(18) publication data on published sheet music (NA = no published sheet music available; NA followed by music company in parentheses = Library of Congress annotation indicating that while no music was published, this company holds the sheet music copyright and may be in possession of original music manuscript)

(19) publication data on original cast recordings (NA = not available; OP = out of print; RE = reissued)

(20) owners of rights; who to contact for royalty/copyright permission, listed in the order by which one should initiate contact (NO CONT AVAIL = no copyright owner could be located for this particular property; DG, Inc. = The Dramatists Guild, Inc.)

(21) where *unpublished* librettos exist (LC = Library of Congress; NYPL = New York Public Library/Billy Rose Collection; MCNY = Museum of the City of New York)

(22) where *unpublished* piano–conductor score exists (LC = Library of Congress; NYPL = New York Public Library/Billy Rose Collection; MCNY = Museum of the City of New York)

(23) where orchestrations exist (LC = Library of Congress; NYPL = New York Public Library/Billy Rose Collection; MCNY = Museum of the City of New York)

The material is compiled in the fashion calculated to be of most use to the theater–producing public. Utilizing the indices at the back of the book, one may locate a property by title; source author, librettist, composer, lyricist; or source of adaptation. If researching a show for which the title, author or source cannot be recalled, one might estimate when the show ran in New York and accordingly locate the property by opening date. The information listed in each entry gives a general profile of each show. *Best Plays* and *Theater World* yearbooks (generally available in any research library) will give further information concerning the original production. Magazine, *New York Times* and *New York Theatre Critics* reviews give the researcher specific information about the show's plot, casting requirements and artistic strengths and weaknesses.

The *New York Theatre Critics Reviews* annuals, which cite the reviews of all Broadway and some off-Broadway productions by all major New York newspapers, date from 1940 to the present and are available in most every research library. For pre-Broadway shows, which had no New York opening, critical review annotations are from William Torbert Leonard's reference work, *Broadway Bound: A Guide to Shows that Died Aborning* (Scarecrow, 1983). This volume, also available in most every research library, lists the show's credits, statistics, place and date of origin, as well as excerpts from all the available reviews. It is an invaluable tool for researching a show for which little information is available. Additionally, the New York Public Library's Billy Rose Theater Collection at Lincoln Center maintains clipping files on virtually every production that has played in New York or which closed prior to its scheduled New York opening. The research librarians there can be contacted concerning the photocopying and mailing of these materials (for address, see below, under "How to Interpret Entries").

HOW TO INTERPRET ENTRIES

The entries are organized according to the following format:

HERE'S WHERE I BELONG
(*Source*) *East of Eden* (novel) by John Steinbeck
(*Book*) Alex Gordon
(*Lyrics*) Alfred Uhry
(*Music*) Robert Waldman
(*Producer*) Mitch Miller
Billy Rose Theatre   Broadway
March 3, 1968   1 performance
(*Stars*) James Coco
Theatre World 67–68, p. 49
Best Plays 67–68, pp. 365–66
New Yorker 44:132 Mr 9 '68
New York Times 1968, Mr 4, 32:1
NYTC 1968:331
(*Published libretto*) NA
(*Published sheet music*) United Artists Music Co.
(*Original cast recording*) NA
(*Agent/contact*)   Alfred Uhry   Robert Waldman
                           c/o DG, Inc.   c/o DG, Inc.
(*Libretto*) NYPL NCOF+; same as (*Agent/Contact*)
(*Music, Orchestrations*) Same as (*Agent/contact*)

This entry is to be interpreted at follows:

The name of this musical, listed in alphabetical order according to title
        under the appropriate section, is *HERE'S WHERE I BELONG*.
It is based on (*Source*) John Steinbeck's novel, *East of Eden*.
The *Book*, or script without lyrics, is by Alex Gordon.
The *Lyrics* are by Alfred Uhry.
The *Music* is by Robert Waldman.
The *Producer* of the original production was Mitch Miller.
The original production played at the Billy Rose Theatre on Broadway.
Opening night—as well as closing night as the show ran for only one (1)
        performance—was March 3, 1968.
One of the *Stars* of the production was actor James Coco.
A full cast list, credits, scene breakdown, listing of songs and production
        photos, can be found in the *Theater World* yearbook, 1967–68
        volume, page 49.

36

Similar information (without photographs) can be found in the *Best Plays* yearbook, 1967–68 volume, pages 365–66.

A magazine review of this production can be found in volume 44 of *New Yorker* magazine on page 132, the issue of March 9, 1968.

A *New York Times* review of this production can be found either on microfilm of the *New York Times* or in bound volumes of the *New York Times Theater Reviews*, March 4, 1968 issue, page 32, column 1.

Reviews of this production from all major newspaper and television critics can be found in the *New York Theatre Critics Reviews* annual (NYTC), 1968 volume, page 331.

A *Published libretto* of this work is not available (NA).

The *Published sheet music* of this work is printed by United Artists Music Company.

An *Original cast recording* of this work is not available (NA).

For royalty quotation/copyright permission, *contact* Alfred Uhry or Robert Waldman c/o The Dramatists Guild, Inc. (DG, Inc.).

An unpublished *Libretto* of this work exists in the New York Public Library/Billy Rose Collection (NYPL) under the call number NCOF+, or can be located by contacting Mr. Uhry or Mr. Waldman c/o The Dramatists Guild, Inc. [Same as *(Agent/Contact)*].

To locate an unpublished piano–conductor score *(Music)* and *Orchestrations*, one should also contact Mr. Uhry or Mr. Waldman c/o The Dramatists Guild, Inc. [Same as *(Agent/contact)*].

Magazine review annotations are cited herein as described in *The Reader's Guide to Periodical Literature*. For example, il Life 36:67–8+ Mr 29 '54 is to be interpreted as an illustrated (il) review that appears in volume 36 of *Life* magazine, pages 67–68 and continuing on later pages (+) of the March 29, 1954 issue.

The following are standard abbreviations of magazines used in *The Reader's Guide to Periodical Literature* which are cited in the entries that follow:

America – *America*
Am Mercury – *American Mercury Magazine*
Bsns W – *Business Week*
CS Mon Mag – *Christian Science Monitor*, magazine section

Cath World – *Catholic World*
Chr Cent – *Christian Century* continuing *New Christian*
Chr Today – *Christianity Today*
Colliers – *Collier's*
Commentary – *Commentary*
Commonweal – *Commonweal*
Coronet – *Coronet*
Craft Horiz – *Craft Horizons*
Crawdaddy – *Crawdaddy*
Dance Mag – *Dance Magazine*
Down Beat – *Down Beat*
Ebony – *Ebony*
Encore – *Encore American and Worldwide News*
Esquire – *Esquire*
Forum – *Forum*
Harp Baz – *Harper's Bazaar*
Harper – *Harper's Magazine*
HiFi – *High Fidelity and Musical America*
Holiday – *Holiday*
Horizon – *Horizon*
Life – *Life*
Look – *Look*
Macleans – *Maclean's*
Mlle – *Mademoiselle*
Mod Mus – *Modern Music*
Mus Am – *Musical America*
NY – *New York*
NY Times Mag – *New York Times Magazine*
Nat R – *National Review*
Nation – *Nation*
New Leader – *New Leader*
New Repub – *New Republic*
New Yorker – *New Yorker*
Newsweek – *Newsweek*
Opera N – *Opera News*
People – *People*
Reporter – *The Reporter*
Roll Stone – *Rolling Stone*
Sat Eve Post – *Saturday Evening Post*
Sat R – *Saturday Review*
Sat R Lit – *Saturday Review of Literature*
Sch & Soc – *School and Society*
Seventeen – *Seventeen*
Sr Schol – *Senior Scholastic* (teacher edition)
Theatre Arts – *Theatre Arts Magazine*
Theatre Crafts – *Theatre Crafts*
Time – *Time*
Vogue – *Vogue*

New York Times review annotations (organized in bound volumes as the *New York Times Reviews* or on microfilm of the *New York Times*) are listed by year, month, day, section of newspaper (if applicable), pages and columns; for example, 1958, Ap 1, IX, 1:5 is to be interpreted as a review that appears in the April 1, 1958 edition of the *New York Times*, section IX, page one, column five. *New York Times* annotations for shows that closed in try–out or preview do not refer to reviews as these shows had no opening in New York. They are for the most part interviews, notices of cast or opening date changes, or other documented facts about a show during its try–out period. *New York Times* annotations for most of these pre–Broadway shows will only be found on microfilm and not in the bound volumes.

Magazine or *New York Times* annotations evidencing a date earlier than the opening date of a given New York production refer to pre–Broadway interviews/press releases, reviews of a previous production (London, off–Broadway or regional theater) or information regarding the same production during pre–Broadway tour. Magazine, *New York Times* or *New York Theatre Critics* reviews evidencing a date substantially later than the opening of a given production are either cast changes/closing notice/press releases or reviews of a revival production (London, Broadway or off–Broadway). These entries have been included so that the researcher has access to all available print material concerning a given show. Care should be taken in the analysis of these annotations so that the researcher does not waste time tracking down information not of use to his particular needs.

Following are the addresses and phone numbers of various guilds, associations, libraries and other arts organizations cited as contacts to authors or their works in the entries to follow.

AGAC/the Songwriters Guild   (212) 686–6820
276 Fifth Avenue
New York, N.Y. 10001

ASCAP   (213) 466–7681
6430 Sunset Boulevard
Los Angeles, CA 90028   [ASCAP also has a New York office; however, I've gotten better results with Los Angeles and therefore include that information here.]

*Archive of Popular American
    Music*   (213) 825-1665
Music Department
University of California
Los Angeles, CA   90024
ATTN: Victor T. Cardell

*Archives of the American Musical
    Theatre*   (616) 943-8260
P.O. Box 201
Grawn, MI   49637
ATTN: David Hummel

BMI   (212) 586-2000
320 W. 57th Street
New York, N.Y.   10019

Billy Rose Theater Collection   (212) 870-1639
New York Public Library
Lincoln Center
111 Amsterdam Avenue
New York, N.Y.   10023

Broadway Play Publishing, Inc.   (212) 627-1055
249 W. 29th Street
New York, N.Y.   10001

Chappell Music Company   (212) 399-6910
810 Seventh Avenue
New York, N.Y.   10019

The Dramatic Publishing Company   (815) 338-7170
P.O. Box 109
Woodstock, IL   60098

The Dramatists Guild, Inc.   (212) 398-9366
234 W. 44th Street
New York, N.Y.   10036

Dramatists Play Service, Inc.   (212) 683-8960
440 Park Avenue South
New York, N.Y.   10016

Institute for the American Musical   (213) 934-1221
121 N. Detroit Street
Los Angeles, CA   90036
ATTN: Miles Kreuger

Library of Congress   (202) 287-5000
Copyright Office
Reference and Bibliography Section
Washington, D.C.   20540

Library of Congress   (202) 287-5640
Photoduplication Service
Washington, D.C.   20540

Museum of the City of New York   (212) 534-1672
Theatre Collection
Fifth Avenue at 103rd Street
New York, N.Y.   10029

Music Theatre International   (212) 975-6841
810 Seventh Avenue
New York, N.Y.   10019

Performing Rights Society   01-580-5544
29-33 Berners Street
London WIP 4AA, England

Pioneer Drama Service   (303) 759-4297
2172 S. Colorado Blvd.
Box #22555
Denver, CO   80222

The Rodgers & Hammerstein   (212) 486-0643
   Theatre Library
598 Madison Avenue
New York, N.Y.   10022

Samuel French, Inc.   (212) 206-8125
45 W. 25th Street
New York, N.Y.   10036
ATTN: Musical Department

Samuel French, Ltd.   01-387-9373
52 Fitzroy Street
London, WIP 6JR, England
ATTN: John Bedding

Tams-Witmark Music Library, Inc.   (800) 221-7196
560 Lexington Avenue   [in New York, (800) 522-2181]
New York, N.Y.   10022

Theatre Maximus   (212) 765-5913
1650 Broadway
New York, N.Y.   10036

HOW TO CONTACT THE APPROPRIATE PARTIES
REGARDING COPYRIGHT, ROYALTY AND PRODUCTION MATERIALS

Once the theatrical organization has located what seems to be the ideal musical–theater property for its next season, or the musical–theater director has found the one property he most likely wants to undertake as his next project, the next step is to contact the people who control the rights to the work and have access to production materials. It is here that I give the most advice to theatrical groups or individuals interested in producing one of these shows, as well as to the authors, composers and lyricists of the shows indexed in this volume.

For theatrical groups and individuals interested in producing these works, the first thing to do is ascertain whether a particular property is made available for production by a licensing agency (e.g., Tams–Witmark Music Library, Music Theatre International, the Rodgers and Hammerstein Theatre Library, Samuel French, Inc., or the Dramatic Publishing Company). If so, it is most likely available to groups such as yours, unless it is listed herein "for future release," such as *Via Galactica, Rex, Colette*, etc. If the show is controlled by a licensing agency, you need not check its availability much more than three months prior to the time you intend to present it. Upon request, the licensing agency will then send you royalty and rental quotations as well as a perusal script and score (the latter for a small fee). In fact, because these shows are so rarely performed (with some exceptions, such as *Canterbury Tales* and *Working*, which are regularly produced in university theaters), it is my experience that the licensing agency will do whatever it can to give you speedy service and a fair quotation simply to get the show back into circulation. However, if you are interested in a property which is not available through a licensing organization, my advice, which is decidedly more complicated, is as follows:

42

First, while an author may be flattered that you're interested in presenting his work, keep in mind that the money he'll earn from this endeavor will hardly cover the time and effort he must devote to reconstruct the production materials (scripts, vocal scores, instrumental parts, etc.). Please bear in mind that you're dealing with an author's *livelihood*, that you cannot expect him or his representative to devote an inordinate amount of time sending out perusal scripts and scores, readying materials and drawing up contracts when his income for such work can never by commensurate with the time he must spend on it. For this reason, I recommend that whenever possible, you write to the author or his representative (listed in this volume as *Agent/contact) one full year* before you intend to produce such a property. (See the interview with composer Peter Link, below.) Relate to him your interest in his work, asking him how you might best be able to get more information about the property. If you do not hear back within six weeks, try a second letter. (It has been my experience that oftentimes authors are traveling or committed to other projects.) Should you receive a favorable reply, you might then make arrangements to receive a perusal script and score (or cassette recording of the music), and negotiate with the author as to possible terms (royalty and rental fees, stipulations regarding cuts, revision, billing, etc.) along with his involvement, if any, on the production. (It is often advantageous to seek the author's help in reworking the material or at least his permission in making changes should the material need revision.) This accomplished, the next step is to sign a written agreement accompanied with your organization's payment for performance clearance (royalty) and usage of production materials (rental fees), along with a refundable deposit for the materials (usually $250 if you are using orchestrations, $100 if you are not), should they not be returned in acceptable condition.

In addition to this *basic* advice, I offer the following four axioms:

1.   Do not pay royalty, rental and deposit fees until you have reached a *written* agreement with an author or his representative stating the copyright holders' permission allowing you to present (*a*) how many

performances of the work (*b*) on what dates (*c*) for what fee; rental of (*d*) specified production materials (*e*) for how long (*f*) for what fee; and a deposit on this material (*g*) for what amount (*h*) to be refunded in full when the material is returned in good condition (*i*) by what date.

2.   Be sure the person with whom you're negotiating represents *all* parties who have copyright claim to the material. In other words, if you enter into an agreement with Music Makers, Inc. (representatives for composer Mitch Leigh) to do a production of *Cry for Us All* (book by William Alfred, lyrics by William Alfred and Phyllis Robinson, music by Mitch Leigh), you had better be certain that Music Makers, Inc. has indeed been in touch with all the other copyright owners and that the terms Music Makers, Inc. has offered are equitable with them as well as Mr. Leigh. It is my advice that in the written agreement you obtain from the leasing agent (or *lessor*), something is stated to the effect that "in permitting the specified performances of this property, the lessor takes full responsibility for obtaining copyright permission from *all* copyright holders of the specified property. Should these performances constitute any infringement of copyright whatsoever, the *lessor* takes full responsibility for this infringement and is liable for any fees, penalties and damages thereby incurred." You should especially be aware of this need for *copyright consensus* when it is herein noted that a particular author is "not interested in soliciting further productions of this property." For example, in regards to the musical version of *Cafe Crown* (book by Hy Kraft, lyrics by Marty Brill, music by Albert Hague), while Messrs. Leonard M. & Sidney N. Herman, attorneys for the estate of Hy Kraft, were amenable to the possibility of future productions of Mr. Kraft's work, Albert Hague stated in a letter that he had no such interest. While it then makes more sense to first consult Mr. Kraft's estate in pursuing the rights to such a production, you must be certain that they have indeed secured permission from Mr. Hague before granting you production approval.

3.   When contacting an author through his guild, union, licensing agency, etc., address your letter c/o the organization and write *PLEASE FORWARD* on the envelope in bold letters. For example:

Mr. Alfred Uhry
c/o The Dramatists Guild, Inc.
234 West 44th Street
New York, N.Y.   10036

PLEASE FORWARD

Also, remember that these organizations are not in business to forward mail to their members. Allow adequate time for forwarding and send as few pieces of mail in this manner as possible. I guarantee that if you continually send mail to be forwarded, these organizations will eventually deny you forwarding privileges or request a fee for this service.

4.   Obviously, no author or agent is going to get rich from royalties to an obscure musical show; it is therefore assumed that authors or their representatives are willing to work with amateur, educational and stock groups because they want to see their work brought back to life and enjoyed by audiences. While your organization gives the author the chance to accomplish this, you must understand that in return he affords you the opportunity to produce an *original* musical–theater piece for your audience, as well as the advantage of his professional experience. Requesting perusal material from an author without any real intention of performing his work, or negligence in paying him fees or returning rented production materials in satisfactory condition, will most likely deter him from again entering into such an agreement. Others are thereby robbed of such a theatrical experience, and the goal of this work is nullified. I would hope that before any musical–theater group or individual enters into correspondence with an author or his representative that they have a genuine interest in his work, the prospective means to produce it, and the integrity to follow through with these plans should a written agreement be reached.

For authors, composers and lyricists of the shows that were never made available for further production, my advice is simply this:

While it's true you will probably never make an enormous amount of money from royalties to such a show, making it available to theatrical groups gives you the opportunity to rework or revise the show in order to see it enacted in the form in which you originally envisioned it; from this initial production there arises the possibility of either interesting a licensing agency in making it available to other groups or making it available yourself (as did composer Peter Link with his musical *King of Hearts*, cited below). You must also keep in mind that while any group may produce *Mame, Bye Bye Birdie* or *The Sound of Music* simply because it wants to do a musical comedy that will "pack the house," it takes a special theater individual to recognize the potential of an obscure musical–theater property, to be drawn to it because of its subject matter, source material, score or author(s). It's particularly frustrating to enjoy an original cast album over the years, only to find that when the opportunity finally arises to produce the show, the copyright owners and production materials are no where to be found. The following is just a sample of the more than fifty shows which released an original cast album yet are unavailable for production: *The Act, Ankles Aweigh, Bravo Giovanni, Christine, Coco, Darling of the Day, Flahooley, The Girl in Pink Tights, I Had a Ball, Jimmy, Juno, Kean, Kwamina, Nefertiti, The Nervous Set, Prettybelle, Saratoga, Seventh Heaven, A Time for Singing, Whoop–Up, Your Arms Too Short to Box with God.*

Should you receive a request regarding such a show, the best advice I can give is to first check with the other copyright holders to see if further productions of this work are feasible, and secondly, what materials (scripts, scores and orchestrations) are available and in what condition. Once you have the answers to these questions, you can respond appropriately to the inquiry. Be sure that when you do reply, that you speak for *all* copyright holders or advise the inquirer as to whom you represent. Also, bear in mind that many theater practitioners at the amateur or educational level can be intimidated by working professionals; therefore, it's best if your reply can be prompt and specific.

Should you be able to make the property available, the next logical step is to get estimates on having the materials duplicated (never give out originals of anything!) and decide on a reasonable royalty/rental/deposit quotation. In this regard, I recommend you peruse this volume for several shows with much the same track record as your own, but which are available for production. For example, if you're one of the copyright holders of *Darling of the Day* (a Broadway show which ran for thirty-two performances and is not available for production), that you find three similar shows that are available (e.g., *The Body Beautiful*, sixty performances on Broadway, Samuel French, Inc.; *Dear World*, 132 performances on Broadway, Tams-Witmark Music Library; and *A Family Affair*, sixty-five performances on Broadway, Music Theatre International), call these agencies for quotations based on the information the inquirer has given you for *Darling of the Day* (number of performances, seating capacity of the theater and ticket scale), and then devise a comparable quotation. Keep in mind that this initial production will probably only cover the costs of reconstructing, duplicating, binding and mailing production materials. However, this is a one-time cost (unless the show should become popular and you need to duplicate more copies); therefore, future productions will yield greater profit.

Rather than give further advice to authors on subsequent productions of their unrepresented works, I would instead like to cite composer Peter Link's experience with his musical *King of Hearts* which was not made available for release through a major licensing agency. Mr. Link is a recipient of the New York Drama Desk Award for his work on the musical *Salvation* and a two-time Tony Award nominee for his musical scores for Joseph Papp's production of *Much Ado About Nothing* and Neil Simon's *The Good Doctor*. He has also served as Composer-in-Residence for the New York Shakespeare Festival, where he wrote the scores for such shows as *Iphigenia, Comedy of Errors* and *Trelawney of the Wells*. His Broadway credits include *Ulysses in Nighttown* starring Zero Mostel and *Lysistrata* starring Melina Mercouri, as well as *King of Hearts*. The following interview was conducted on January 16, 1984:

* * * * *

Rick Simas: *King of Hearts* opened on Broadway October 22, 1978, and
ran for 48 performances. Do you want to say anything about the production,
any feelings you might have about it?

Peter Link: *King of Hearts* on Broadway was a perfect example of how a
production can become confused. I felt it was about a half to two–thirds
successful, and I would blame that on two things, really: a bad choice of
house in that *King of Hearts* is an intimate musical, and they put it into the
Minskoff; the reason they did that was because of money, because Jerry
Minskoff was going to come in with an extra $150,000 which they needed at
the time, and he wanted it in his house. In fact, when that decision was
made, no one would tell me for a week; everybody knew how I felt about
that.

R.S.:   Do you feel the show then moved away from the original concept,
from what you had originally intended it to be?

P.L.:   Definitely. *King of Hearts* is a small, intimate story about a crazy
group of loonies. It's *small*. It's not supposed to be in the biggest, most
blatant Broadway house in New York. The other major problem of the two
was that it had the wrong director. The director tried to fill that house and
made certain choices which completely missed; he never really connected
with the *heart* of the show. Consequently, the show was beautifully
mounted and well–cast, and basically the story was told, but it was not told
with the heart that it has. There were several critics who said it was wrong
to assume in the end Johnny would make the choice of going into the
asylum, that you don't just go live with crazy people. But the whole point of
the show was really—who's crazy, the people inside or the people outside?
The director missed on that, and he missed on many, many other things as
well.

R.S.:   One thing that always amazes me, once a production closes down,
is that the writer, composer and lyricist often don't collect the materials to

their show; they lose them, or they forget to recover them from the producer. Why does this happen? Why would a composer or writer not collect his materials once the show has closed?

P.L.: If the show has not been a runaway hit, and it closes, say, within two or three months, which was the case with *King of Hearts*, I think there's such a disenchantment that goes on with a composer or lyricist that rather than go in and clean everything up and pull your "flop" back together, you just move on. You move onto another project, or by the time it closes, for your own salvation, you're already onto another project. There's just no instinct to tidy it up because it's an enormous job, first of all, to get the books in order, do the erasures, find the lost pages and pull all that stuff together. And then the question becomes, where do you put it? We all live in New York City here, and there's just a modicum of space for storage. Luckily, Joe Kipness [the producer] with *King of Hearts* had taken all the scripts and music, put it in crates and stored it down in the basement of his restaurant, and it was sitting down there.

R.S.: How long did you work on *King of Hearts*, from concept to opening?

P.L.: About three years.

R.S.: That's what I usually hear, two to three years. That's why I can't believe, even though it must be difficult to go in and get the materials after a show closes, that when you spend three years of your life on something, you can just let it go by the wayside.

P.L.: Well, it's not a matter of *letting* it go by the wayside; it has *gone* by the wayside.

R.S.: But that's not the case with *King of Hearts* because it's still done now. I've heard of several productions myself.

P.L.: And that's because of the strange occurrence that happened afterwards. I mean, besides the hits I've been associated with, I've worked on another ten shows which were flops and didn't go on.

R.S.:   When *King of Hearts* closed on Broadway, was there any talk of releasing the rights through a licensing agency like Samuel French or Tams–Witmark?

P.L.:   If there was, I didn't hear about it. I was off in Milwaukee doing another show. I came back the day of the closing and saw the show, and I honestly felt—as disappointed and heartbroken as I was—I felt it was good that it closed. It just wasn't right.

R.S.:   How did the original cast album come about?

P.L.:   Bruce Yeko, who owns Original Cast Albums, had approached me a couple of times long before to do *King of Hearts*, and I had always said, "Well, you know, let's wait and see what happens on Broadway." And then we signed with Capitol, and of course when the show closed, Capitol then did not do the album. So Bruce, I guess, talked to me about it again, but I was off doing something else, and I'd had it up to my ears with *King of Hearts*. I just didn't want to deal with it; it was too emotional an experience. Six months later this young man from a Catholic high school down in New Jersey somewhere called me and said he would like to do *King of Hearts*, that he'd seen it a couple times on Broadway and would like to put it on. And I said, well, like you say, the show was in a shambles; I didn't like the final script; four or five of the best songs in the score were cut. I said, "I would not even let you do what was done on Broadway." He had seen the show in Westport as well and said, "I liked a lot of the stuff in Westport, and I wouldn't mind cutting it back together again." I said, "Well, it's just too much work for me." And he said, "I'll do the work; you just give me some direction." And I said, "Well, oh gosh, I don't care. If you want to meet me at Joe Kipness's, I'll go through the stuff." I had no idea what I was getting into. We went down to his basement one morning and stayed there 'til about four or five in the afternoon, going through crates and boxes of stuff. I must have ended up handing him about ten different drafts of scripts and literally six or seven crates of music that filled the back of his station wagon. He took that all home and came back with several drafts that he liked, and we sat for one other whole day from about nine a.m. to nine at night and just went over it; I told him what to use and what not to use and why—basically what scripts and that sort of thing. He went off, and I forgot about him for about nine months, and finally one day I got a script in the mail which was a pretty good rendition. He hadn't written a single line; it was just basically cuttings from scripts that had been written before, scripts with dialogue both by Steve Tesich, who was the original book writer, and Joe Stein, who was the Broadway book writer. At that point, I went down once to the high school to work with the cast, which was a delightful experience—to go into a rehearsal of *King of Hearts* and experience the joy that always should have been there but never was because the vibe of a director was so negative. About two weeks later, I went down and experienced what *King of Hearts* always should have been, which was a production that made people laugh and just completely fall apart emotionally at the end. It was a beautiful show. I then brought a couple of my friends down as well, and we saw it, and it was just. . . . It was like. . . . I said at the time that it was the final curtain on the show, that it was nice to end it that way. About two weeks later—for some reason now it was back in my life—Bruce Yeko called and offered me a questionable record deal to do *King of Hearts* for, I think, a budget of $6,000, which I said was impossible. But I worked it out, and I did it; I spent three or four months one summer doing it in my living room. I had a small recording studio in my living room and performed most of the instruments myself and used a little bit of money to hire in some musicians and buy some equipment which I needed, and most of the cast did it for nothing. I used people from the Westport and Broadway casts; people just trooped up to the apartment for a couple spare hours apiece over the course of about three months. Most albums, as you know, are made in one or two days. I came off with a piece which I was very proud of. I think the *King of Hearts* album is better made, quality-wise, than most Broadway albums you'll find. Even though it was made in my living room, it was really controlled, and basically the album was the way I heard the music.

R.S.:   You'd say it's a good representation of the show, then, of the score of the show?

P.L.:   Yes. I took out the things I never liked, that the director had asked me to write that I wrote begrudgingly, and put back in the songs that had been for God knows what reasons cut. At that point I felt, "Well, gee, this is kind of the final statement of this," and was ready to rest on that. Then the record started to sell like crazy, which was really surprising to me. I thought we'd sell twenty–six copies, and that would be it, but it became the largest–selling album of this record company which has done probably a hundred albums in the last few years. So I just felt that that was a really nice thing to have happen. Probably about another three months later, Leslie Laughton from the Royal Lyceum in Edinburgh,' Scotland, called me and had heard the album and seen the show on Broadway and wanted to do it at the Royal Lyceum. I jumped at the chance; somehow the flow had gotten going again, and I called Steve Tesich and Jake Brackman, the book writer and lyricist, back in, and we put together a final draft of the book which Steve rewrote, putting together all the right ideas for Edinburgh.   We spent maybe a week on that.

R.S.:   So this was a little different from the version done at the high school?

P.L.:   Oh yes. It was a lot different. In the one done at the high school, a lot of the book was by Joe Stein; it was a compilation of both.

R.S.:   The one you release now is which?

P.L.:   The one we release now is the Steve Tesich book. In fact, I've gone back to Joe and said, "Joe, no offense, but we're just using this." So Joe still gets a royalty but doesn't get credit on the book. We honestly went through all of Joe's material and just decided against it. Steve was the writer that I had hired originally and was the person that I always wanted to do *King of Hearts*. The reason Steve left was because he wouldn't write what the director wanted him to—but that's all watᵒr under the dam. I went to Edinburgh   and worked on the production with Leslie Laughton, and it was a terrific success, and again I came away from the experience thinking, "Well, great. That was really the final summation of *King of Hearts*." When I got home, the young man who had done it in Jersey called me and said that he was now teaching at another school and wanted to do it there. I did some massive xeroxing, and I had rearranged the score for a ten–piece orchestra in Edinburgh; I always felt it should be a small orchestra rather than twenty–six pieces. So I had those arrangements. I had a pretty good idea in Edinburgh that I would try to lease it out here or else try to get it to an agency like Tams–Witmark. Well, right away I started working with this guy, and various schools started to do it. Since then—without any effort on our part—there's probably between fifteen and thirty productions of it a year done around the United States. As the company builds and more and more is done, we're planning on putting together a brochure and doing a mailing. At one point, I decided to take it to . . . I can't remember . . . it was either Tams–Witmark or Music Theatre International. They were interested, and I sat down and looked at the numbers, and it honestly wasn't worth it to go with them. I felt we could make more money just doing it ourselves. And I've been right because they did a major production in New Zealand, a major production in Milwaukee just recently, and now they're talking about a kind of first–class revival at the Burt Reynolds Theatre down in Florida, putting together a cast that would possibly go to L.A. with it. Well, we'll see about that. . . .

R.S.:   How do you know what to charge for royalties? How did you work that out?

P.L.:   Well, basically I just "borrowed" everything from one of the larger companies. I made calls to them and pretended I was a high school teacher and asked, "What do you charge for this? And what do you charge for that?" and figured out, based on the figures that they gave me, what their basic royalties were. And I think we're compatible with what they do. We give people probably a little extra service in that sometimes when they call I can sit down and talk with the director and tell him the pitfalls to avoid and certain things about the set and how to build it, whereas Tams–Witmark can't offer that service. We charge about the same. In fact, I just took their contract, kind of changed the paragraphs around, and filled in the right blanks with our name, and that was about it. That way I knew I wouldn't be getting into any trouble.

R.S.:   If one of the authors of another show wanted to release his work in a similar way, it would help to know how you worked out the royalty agreement amongst the authors of *King of Hearts*. What I'm concerned about is that if a university or little theatre wants to produce a show and contacts an author or his representative, that the representative does indeed represent all the copyright holders; otherwise, the university or little theatre can get into legal difficulty for doing a show without all the copyright holders' permission.

P.L.:   Well, first of all, when you sign a contract originally, the subsidiary rights agreements are already established. It wasn't a matter of working out percentages or anything like that; those were numbers already established right from the very beginning. With the rest of the authors, getting permission was not hard. In fact, I just wrote them a letter and told them I was doing it. Because . . . how could they complain? They're going to make a little money, and it's going to be no trouble on their parts; besides, their good work would live on, so it was easy. The only little difficulty I had, and it wasn't even a difficulty, was telling Joe Stein that we were basically taking his name off the script. Joe's a good friend and a pro; they all are, every single guy involved. Everybody was delighted that at least *King of Hearts* was beginning to get its due.

R.S.:   Can you give me a ballpark figure of what you've made from this venture since the closing of the Broadway production?

P.L.:   That's difficult.

R.S.:   Enough to make it worthwhile?

P.L.:   Oh, definitely. I mean, I have personally profited besides the company. Basically, the company pays its expenses. We have paid probably three or four thousand dollars in royalties per year to the authors; not to each, but dividing it up. And unfortunately *King of Hearts* is really divided up; there are a lot of people involved. But, you know, around the first of the year, each guy gets a check, depending upon what his percentage was, for somewhere between. . . . I usually say you can take yourself out to lunch on it. The company has been able to pay for people to come in and do erasures and keep the scripts in good shape. I wouldn't say that it's a big money–maker for us, but it certainly is more than breaking even and enabling us to continue to put it out. We have three full sets of scripts and scores. We've been able to manage so far on that. To get a fourth would probably cost maybe five hundred dollars, the way we're doing it. Basically, we're not printing it at this point; we're xeroxing. So the xerox costs are expensive. But the big cost was my sitting down and cleaning up all the scores and getting all the notes exactly right and all the vocal scores. I spent probably a couple weeks solid on that; that was a lot of work, and that's what would be difficult to try and find someone to do. But it was my baby; *King of Hearts* was always my baby so I didn't mind doing it. Then I saw a profit on down the line, and I think it will continue to profit as the company grows and is able to promote it better. Because really the only way people have done it up to this point is by word of mouth.

R.S.:   That's why I'm writing this book. I'm listing some 575 shows of which over 400 were never made available through a licensing agency. I've worked with university and college theaters, in summer stock; people have heard of the shows, especially if an album was released, but they haven't an inkling how to go about finding the people who own the rights and have the materials.

P.L.:   That's true. We've called Tams–Witmark and Music Theatre International repeatedly, saying, "Couldn't you please tell people who call about *King of Hearts* that we exist?" They always say, "Oh yes, we'd be delighted to," but nobody ever does over there. Consequently, every time I hear from somebody, I always get the same remark at the beginning: "Boy, you don't know what it took to find you."

R.S.:   Well, that's what this book is all about.

P.L.:   That's why I'm completely behind it. It can only help us all.

R.S.:   Would you say it's worthwhile for other authors to do this same thing if they get a request to have produced one of their unreleased shows, or do you think that *King of Hearts* is an out–of–the–ordinary case? I mean, you have other shows that you haven't yet made available.

P.L.:   It completely depends on the show. First of all, *King of Hearts* is a hit show; it's a beautiful script, it's a wonderful show and it works. It got a bad production, and it had bad direction. A lot of shows that flop are flops, and they are flawed, heavily flawed. *King of Hearts* was flawed on Broadway, but I believe it was fixed to a great extent. I mean, there are certain elements of *King of Hearts* that may never work, if you know what I mean. I think there are certain elements of *Chorus Line* that may never work too, though. Every show is flawed to a certain extent.

R.S.:   So you'd say that if an author believes in his work, the personal satisfaction in seeing the show done the way it should be done (considering he'd already spent three years on it) is worthwhile in itself.

P.L.:   With a musical, quite honestly, I think if there were no album or tape, I wonder how difficult it would be to do for these high schools and that sort of thing.

R.S.:   Of course, you know a tape exists for almost every show.

P.L.:   Bootleg tapes, sure. But you can't sell those to high schools. You can get into deep trouble that way.

R.S.:   You, as an author, can use them to reconstruct, however. If you'd forgotten how the show was put together.

P.L.:   Yes. I'm just saying that in terms of a high school learning stuff, I mean, yes, it can be taught, but boy, it sure is a lot easier to have that album or something that the kids can actually hear and go, "Oh, that's what it's supposed to sound like."

R.S.:   Do you think that you'll ever make any of your other shows—*Iphigenia* or *Lysistrata* or *Earl of Ruston*—available?

P.L.:   Well, *Iphigenia* I'm still re-working for theatrical production in New York, so that is very possible. *Lysistrata*, I think, was maybe the worst musical ever invented, and I wouldn't touch it with a ten-foot pole. *Earl of Ruston* was also a failure as a piece of material so there's just no point in keeping something like that alive. Some of the music was real good from it, and there is an album on Capitol for those people who like to have those old show albums and that sort of stuff. But I don't think either one of those shows is really worth doing.

R.S.:   For the record, if a group wants to do *King of Hearts*, how do they get in touch with your licensing agency?

P.L.:   They can write: Peter Link
                                    c/o On Broadway Productions
                                    400 W. 43rd Street, #38D
                                    New York, N.Y.   10036

           Or call: (212) 239-0282.

R.S.:   And do you have any provisions for perusal scripts, scores and the like?

P.L.:   We offer a perusal script and score for no charge for one month. We also offer the *King of Hearts* album for a charge of $10.00.

R.S.:   The orchestrations that are available for the show are the ten-piece arrangements or the twenty-six or both?

P.L.:   No, just the ten-piece. People call and say, "Gee, I'd like to put the circus back in." I just . . . I don't change it, basically. People think they want to put the circus back in, but I know that the circus ruined the second act, so I won't let anybody change it. There's just one authorized script and one authorized score, and that's it.

R.S.:   Thanks for the information. I know it will help a lot of other authors who may also want to make their works available, as well as the theater–producing public who are looking for new and exciting musical–theater properties to tackle.

P.L.:   Thank you.

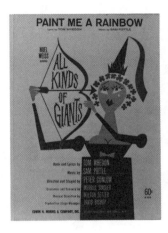

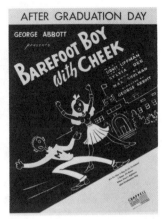

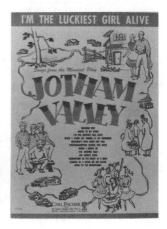

THE BROADWAY SHOWS

*THE ACT**

(*Source*) Original

(*Book*) George Furth

(*Lyrics*) Fred Ebb

(*Music*) John Kander

(*Producer*) Shubert Organization, Cy Feuer & Ernest H. Martin

Majestic Theater   Broadway

October 29, 1977   233 performances

(*Stars*) Liza Minnelli

Theatre World 77–78, p. 20

Best Plays 77–78, p. 356

America 137:423 D 10'77

       New Yorker 53:103 N 7 '77

       Newsweek il 90:49 S 5 '77

       Newsweek il 90:99 N 14 '77

       Sat R 5:44 O 1 '77

       Time 110:61 N 14 '77

New York Times 1977, O 31, 39:1

       New York Times 1977, N 6, II, 3:1

NYTC 1977:151

(*Published libretto*) Samuel French, Inc. (FOR FUTURE RELEASE)

(*Published sheet music*) UniChappell

(*Original cast recording*) DRG Records 6101

(*Agent/contact*) Samuel French, Inc. (FOR FUTURE RELEASE)

(*Libretto, Music, Orchestrations*) Same as (*Agent/contact*)

*Originally presented under title *SHINE IT ON*;

       subsequently presented under title *IN PERSON*

ALL AMERICAN

(*Source*) *Professor Fodorski* (novel) by Robert Lewis Taylor

(*Book*) Mel Brooks

(*Lyrics*) Lee Adams

(*Music*) Charles Strouse

(*Producer*) Edward Padula & L. Slade Brown

Winter Garden Theatre   Broadway

March 19, 1962   80 performances

(*Stars*) Ray Bolger

Theatre World 61–62, p. 84

Best Plays 61–62, pp. 292–94

America 107:278–9 My 19 '62

    New Yorker 38:104–6 Mr 31 '62

    Newsweek il 59:58 Ap 2 '62

    Theatre Arts 46:58 My '62

    Time 79:46 Mr 30 '62

New York Times 1962, Mr 20, 44:1

    New York Times 1962, Ap 8, II, 1:2

NYTC 1962:318

(*Published libretto*) Dramatic Publishing Company, 1972

    [adapted by June Walker Rogers; see (*Libretto*) for original

    manuscript]

(*Published sheet music*) Edwin H. Morris/Morley

(*Original cast recording*) OP Columbia KOL–5760/KOS–2160,

    RE Columbia Special Products AKOS–2160

(*Agent/contact*) Dramatic Publishing Company

(*Libretto*) NYPL RM7798/a, RM7798/b

(*Music, Orchestrations*) Same as (*Agent/contact*)

ALLAH BE PRAISED!

(*Source*) Original

(*Book*) George Marion, Jr.

(*Lyrics*) George Marion, Jr.

(*Music*) Don Walker & Baldwin Bergersen

(*Producer*) Alfred Bloomingdale

Adelphi Theatre   Broadway
April 20, 1944   20 performances
(*Stars*) Jack Albertson
NO ENTRY AVAIL
Best Plays 43–44, pp. 469–70
New Yorker 20:46 Ap 29 '44
New York Times 1944, Ap 21, 14:2
NYTC 1944: 207
(*Published libretto*) NA
(*Published sheet music*) Chappell
(*Original cast recording*) NA
(*Agent/contact*)

George Marion,	Don Walker	Baldwin Bergersen
Jr. Estate	c/o DG, Inc.	c/o DG, Inc.
c/o AGAC		

(*Libretto, Music, Orchestrations*) Same as (*Agent/contact*)

ALOHA
See *HEATHEN!*

*AMBASSADOR**
(*Source*) *The Ambassadors* (novel) by Henry James
(*Book*) Don Ettlinger & Anna Marie Barlow
(*Lyrics*) Hal Hackady
(*Music*) Don Gohman
(*Producer*) Gene Dingenary, Miranda d'Ancona & Nancy Levering
Lunt–Fontanne Theatre   Broadway
November 19, 1972   8 performances
(*Stars*) Howard Keel, Danielle Darrieux, Andrea Marcovicci
Theatre World 72–73, p. 29
Best Plays 72–73, pp. 342–43
New Yorker 48:123 D 2 '72
New York Times 1972, N 20, 46:1
NYTC 1972:177
(*Published libretto*) NA
(*Published sheet music*) Screen Gems–Columbia Publications

(*Original cast recording*) OP RCA(E) SER–5618 (Original London Cast)

(*Agent/contact*)   Don Ettlinger   Anna Marie Barlow   Hal Hackady
      c/o DG, Inc.   c/o DG, Inc.   c/o DG, Inc.

      Don Gohman Estate
      c/o ASCAP

(*Libretto*) LC Worthington Miner 11Aug61 DU53727 as *THE
   AMBASSADORS*; same as (*Agent/contact*)

(*Music, Orchestrations*) Same as (*Agent/contact*)

*Previously titled *THE AMBASSADORS*

THE AMBASSADORS

See *AMBASSADOR*

ANGEL

(*Source*) *Look Homeward, Angel* (novel) by Thomas Wolfe,
   (play) by Ketti Frings

(*Book*) Ketti Frings, Philip Rose & Peter Udell

(*Lyrics*) Peter Udell

(*Music*) Gary Geld

(*Producer*) Philip Rose & Ellen Madison

Minskoff Theatre   Broadway

May 10, 1978   5 performances

(*Stars*) Fred Gwynne

Theatre World 77–78, p. 46

Best Plays 77–78, pp. 373–75

New Yorker 54:91 My 22 '78

New York Times 1978, My 11, III, 17:1

NYTC 1978:284

(*Published libretto*) Samuel French, Inc., 1979

(*Published sheet music*) Udell Music–Geld Music

(*Original cast recording*) OP Geld–Udell–Abrams GUA–001

(*Agent/contact*) Samuel French, Inc.

(*Libretto, Music, Orchestrations*) Same as (*Agent/contact*)

ANKLES AWEIGH

(*Source*) Original

(*Book*) Guy Bolton & Eddie Davis

(*Lyrics*) Dan Shapiro

(*Music*) Sammy Fain

(*Producer*) Howard Hoyt, Reginald Hammerstein & Fred F. Finklehoff

Mark Hellinger Theatre   Broadway

April 18, 1955   176 performances

(*Stars*) Lew Parker, Betty & Jane Kean

Theatre World 54–55, p. 94

Best Plays 54–55, pp. 405–6

Cath World 181:228 Je '55

      Commonweal 62:330 Jl 1 '55

      New Yorker 31:71–2 Ap 30 '55

      Theatre Arts il 39:16, 88 Jl '55

      Time 65:78 My 2 '55

New York Times 1955, Ap 19, 27:1

      New York Times 1955, Ap 24, II, 1:1

NYTC 1955:329

(*Published libretto*) NA

(*Published sheet music*) Chappell

(*Original cast recording*) OP Decca DL–9025, RE AEI–1104

(*Agent/contact*)   Guy Bolton Estate   Dan Shapiro   Sammy Fain

               c/o Louis Aborn   c/o ASCAP   c/o DG, Inc.

               Tams–Witmark Music Library

(*Libretto*) LC Guy Bolton & Eddie David 14Oct42 DU82123; same as

      (*Agent/Contact*);

      Lee Davis

      Box 674/Pleasant Avenue

      Westhampton, N.Y.   11977

(*Music, Orchestrations*) Chappell Music Co.; same as (*Agent/contact*)

ANNE OF GREEN GABLES
(*Source*) *Anne of Green Gables* (novel) by L.M. Montgomery
(*Book*) Donald Harron
(*Lyrics*) Donald Harron & Norman Campbell
(*Music*) Norman Campbell
(*Producer*) City Center, Charlottetown Festival,
      Canadian National Music Theatre
City Center   Broadway
December 21, 1971   16 performances
(*Stars*) NA
Theatre World 71–72, p. 67
Best Plays 71–72, pp. 328–29
NO CRIT AVAIL
New York Times 1971, D 22, 30:1
      New York Times 1972, Ja 2, II, 1:1
NO CRIT AVAIL
(*Published libretto*) Samuel French, Inc., 1972
(*Published sheet music*) Chappell/Avonlea
(*Original cast recording*) OP CBS(E) 70053 (Original London Cast);
      Ready(C) LR–045 (Original Canadian Cast)
(*Agent/contact*) Samuel French, Inc.
(*Libretto, Music, Orchestrations*) Same as (*Agent/contact*)

*ANYA**
(*Source*) *Anastasia* (play) by Marcelle Maurette & Guy Bolton
(*Book*) George Abbott & Guy Bolton
(*Lyrics*) Robert Wright & George Forrest, based on themes by
      Sergei Rachmaninoff
(*Music*) Robert Wright & George Forrest
(*Producer*) Fred R. Fehlhaber
Ziegfeld Theatre   Broadway
November 29, 1965   16 performances
(*Stars*) Constance Towers, Lillian Gish
Theatre World 65–66, p. 37
Best Plays 65–66, pp. 387–89

Dance Mag 40:17 Ja '66

      New Yorker 41:142+ D 11 '65

      Time 86:78 D 10 '65

New York Times 1965, N 30, 48:1

NYTC 1965:243

(*Published libretto*) NA

(*Published sheet music*) Frank Music Corp.

(*Original cast recording*) OP United Artists UAL–4133/UAS–5133

(*Agent/contact*) Music Theatre International as *I, ANASTASIA*

      (adaptation of Broadway libretto)

(*Libretto*) NYPL RM402, RM473

(*Music, Orchestrations*) Same as (*Agent/contact*)

*Previously presented under title *A SONG FOR ANASTASIA*;

      subsequently titled *I, ANASTASIA*

ANYONE CAN WHISTLE

(*Source*) Original

(*Book*) Arthur Laurents

(*Lyrics*) Stephen Sondheim

(*Music*) Stephen Sondheim

(*Producer*) Kermit Bloomgarden & Diana Krasny

Majestic Theatre   Broadway

April 4, 1964   9 performances

(*Stars*) Angela Lansbury, Harry Guardino, Lee Remick

Theatre World 63–64, p. 100

Best Plays 63–64, pp. 330–32

NO CRIT AVAIL

New York Times 1964, Ap 6, 36:1

NYTC 1964:301

(*Published libretto*) Random House, 1965;

      Amiel Book Distrib. Corp., 1976

(*Published sheet music*) Burthen/Chappell

(*Original cast recording*) OP Columbia KOL–6080/KOS–2480, RE Columbia

      S–32608, Columbia Special Products AS–32608

(*Agent/contact*) Music Theatre International

(*Libretto*) NYPL RM7398; same as (*Agent/contact*)

(*Music, Orchestrations*) Same as (*Agent/contact*)

ARCHY & MEHITABEL

See *SHINBONE ALLEY*

ARE YOU WITH IT?

(*Source*) *Slightly Perfect* (novel) by George Malcolm–Smith

(*Book*) Sam Perrin & George Balzer

(*Lyrics*) Arnold B. Horwitt

(*Music*) Harry Revel

(*Producer*) Richard Kollmar & James W. Gardiner

Century Theatre/Shubert Theatre*   Broadway

November 10, 1945   264 performances

(*Stars*) Dolores Gray, Lew Parker, Joan Roberts

Theatre World 45–46, pp. 30–1

Best Plays 45–46, pp. 405–6

Cath World 162:359 Ja '46

      Colliers il 117:14–15 F 2 '46

      Commonweal 43:169 N 30 '45

      Life il 19:97–100 N 26 '45

      New Yorker 21:50+ N 24 '45

      Newsweek 26:69 N 26 '45

      Theatre Arts 30:14 Ja '46

New York Times 1945, N 12, 17:3

NYTC 1945:113

(*Published libretto*) NA

(*Published sheet music*) Chappell/Crawford Music Corp.

(*Original cast recording*) NA

(*Agent/contact*)   Arnold B. Horwitt Estate   Harry Revel Estate

                c/o ASCAP   c/o ASCAP

(*Libretto, Music, Orchestrations*) Same as (*Agent/contact*)

*Moved to Shubert Theatre 11/10/45

ARI

(*Source*) *Exodus* (novel) by Leon Uris
(*Book*) Leon Uris*
(*Lyrics*) Leon Uris*
(*Music*) Walt Smith
(*Producer*) Ken Gaston, Leonard Goldberg & Henry Stein
Mark Hellinger Theatre   Broadway
January 15, 1971   19 performances
(*Stars*) John Savage, David Cryer, Constance Towers
Theatre World 70–71, p. 29
Best Plays 70–71, pp. 304–5
New Yorker 46:66 Ja 23 '71
New York Times 1971, Ja 16, 16:1
NYTC 1971:386
(*Published libretto*) NA
(*Published sheet music*) NA
(*Original cast recording*) NA
(*Agent/contact*)   Leon Uris   Walt Smith
                         c/o DG, Inc.   c/o ASCAP
(*Libretto*) NYPL RM936; same as (*Agent/contact*)
(*Music, Orchestrations*) Same as (*Agent/contact*)

*At press time, Mr. Uris was not interested in soliciting further
        productions of this property

ARMS AND THE GIRL

(*Source*) *The Pursuit of Happiness* (play) by Lawrence Langner & Armina
        Marshall
(*Book*) Herbert & Dorothy Fields, Rouben Mamoulian
(*Lyrics*) Dorothy Fields
(*Music*) Morton Gould
(*Producer*) Theatre Guild & Anthony Brady Farrell
Forty–Sixth Street Theatre   Broadway
February 2, 1950   134 performances

(*Stars*) Pearl Bailey, Nanette Fabray
Theatre World 49–50, p. 81
Best Plays 49–50, p. 372
Cath World 171:67 Ap '50
     New Yorker 25:46–7 F 11 '50
     Newsweek il 35:80 F 13 '50
     Theatre Arts il 34:17 Ap '50
     Time il 55:53–4 F 13 '50
New York Times 1950, F 3, 28:2
NYTC 1950:235
(*Published libretto*) NA
(*Published sheet music*) Chappell/Crawford Music Corp.
(*Original cast recording*) OP Decca DL–5200; RE Columbia
     Special Products X–14879 (w/ *LOOK, MA, I'M DANCIN'!*)
(*Agent/contact*)

Chappell Music	Morton Gould	Rouben Mamoulian
ATTN: Irwin Robinson	c/o DG, Inc.	c/o DG, Inc.

(*Libretto*) NYPL NCOF+; same as (*Agent/contact*)
(*Music, Orchestrations*) Same as (*Agent/contact*)

AROUND THE WORLD
(*Source*) *Around the World in 80 Days* (novel) by Jules Verne
(*Book*) Orson Welles
(*Lyrics*) Cole Porter
(*Music*) Cole Porter
(*Producer*) Orson Welles
Adelphi Theatre   Broadway
May 31, 1946   75 performances
(*Stars*) Orson Welles
Theatre World 45–46, p. 105
Best Plays 45–46, pp. 448–49
Cath World 163:359–60 Jl '46
     Commonweal 44:238 Je 21 '46
     Life il 20:74–6 Je 17 '46
     New Yorker 22:48+ Je 8 '46

Newsweek 27:87 Je 10 '46

Theatre Arts il 30:473 Ag '46

Time 47:64 Je 3 '46

Time il 47:67 Je 10 '46

New York Times 1946, Je 1, 9:5

New York Times 1946, Je 9, II, 1:1

NYTC 1946:375

(*Published libretto*) NA

(*Published sheet music*) Chappell

(*Original cast recording*) NA

(*Agent/contact*)   Cole Porter Estate

c/o ASCAP

(*Libretto*) NYPL RM839, RM4203, RM4208; LC Mercury Enterprises,
        Inc. 13May46 DU3103; same as (*Agent/contact*)

(*Music, Orchestrations*) Same as (*Agent/contact*)

ASLEEP MY LOVE
See *PORTOFINO*

BAJOUR

(*Source*) *New Yorker* stories (short stories) by Joseph Mitchell

(*Book*) Ernest Kinoy

(*Lyrics*) Walter Marks

(*Music*) Walter Marks

(*Producer*) Edward Padula, Carroll & Harris Masterson, Norman Twain

Sam S. Shubert Theatre   Broadway

November 23, 1964   232 performances

(*Stars*) Herschel Bernardi, Nancy Dussault, Chita Rivera

Theatre World 64–65, p. 51

Best Plays 64–65, pp. 316–17

America 112:25 Ja 2 '65

Commonweal 81:422–3 D 18 '64

Dance Mag 39:19–20 Ja '65

New Yorker 40:88 D 5 '64

Newsweek 64:94 D 7 '64

Time 84:88 D 4 '64

New York Times 1964, N 24, 42:1

NYTC 1964:132

(*Published libretto*) Dramatic Publishing Company, 1976 [adapted
        by Marianne Brundage; see (*Libretto*) for original manuscript]

(*Published sheet music*) Mesquite Music Corp./Edwin H. Morris

(*Original cast recording*) OP Columbia KOL–6300/KOS–2700

(*Agent/contact*) Dramatic Publishing Company

(*Libretto*) NYPL RM391, NCOF+; LC (Performing Arts Reading Room)
        ML50/.M342B32

(*Music, Orchestrations*) Same as (*Agent/contact*)

BALLROOM

(*Source*) *Queen of the Stardust Ballroom* (teleplay) by Jerome Kass

(*Book*) Jerome Kass

(*Lyrics*) Alan & Marilyn Bergman

(*Music*) Billy Goldenberg

(*Producer*) Michael Bennett

Majestic Theatre   Broadway

December 14, 1978   116 performances

(*Stars*) Dorothy Loudon, Vincent Gardenia

Theatre World 78–79, p. 21

Best Plays 78–79, pp. 372–73

America 140:36 Ja 20 '79

        Dance Mag il 53:60–2 F '79

        Encore il 7:32–3 Ja 15 '79

        NY 12:64–5 Ja 8 '79

        New Leader 62:21 Ja 1 '79

        New Repub 180:25 Ja 27 '79

Newsweek il 93:56 Ja 1 '79

Sat R 6:52 F 17 '79

Time il 112:83 D 25 '78

New York Times 1978, D 15, III, 3:1

1978, D 24, II, 3:1

NYTC 1978:158

(*Published libretto*) Samuel French, Inc., 1981

(*Published sheet music*) G. Schirmer, Inc.

(*Original cast recording*) OP Columbia JS–35762

(*Agent/contact*) Samuel French, Inc.

(*Libretto*) NYPL NCOF+ 82–225

(*Music, Orchestrations*) Same as (*Agent/contact*)

BAREFOOT BOY WITH CHEEK

(*Source*) *Barefoot Boy With Cheek* (novel) by Max Shulman

(*Book*) Max Shulman

(*Lyrics*) Sylvia Dee

(*Music*) Sidney Lippman

(*Producer*) George Abbott

Martin Beck Theatre	Broadway
April 3, 1947	108 performances

(*Stars*) Nancy Walker, Red Buttons

Theatre World 46–47, pp. 100–1

Best Plays 46–47, pp. 474–75

Cath World 165:169 My '47

Commonweal 46:16 Ap 18 '47

New Repub 116:37 Ap 21 '47

New Yorker 23:46 Ap 12 '47

Newsweek 29:86 Ap 14 '47

Theatre Arts 31:41 Je '47

Time 49:70 Ap 14 '47

New York Times 1947, Ap 4, 20:2

NYTC 1947:402

(*Published libretto*) Dramatic Publishing Company, 1963

(*Published sheet music*) Chappell

(*Original cast recording*) NA

(*Agent/contact*)   Max Shulman   Sylvia Dee Estate   Sidney Lippman
                         c/o DG, Inc.   c/o ASCAP   c/o ASCAP

(*Libretto*) NYPL RM1082, NCOF+; same as (*Agent/contact*)

(*Music, Orchestrations*) LC Dramatic Pub. Co. 28Jan63 EP17589;
         same as (*Agent/contact*)

THE BARRIER*

(*Source*) *Mulatto* (play) by Langston Hughes

(*Book*) Langston Hughes

(*Lyrics*) Langston Hughes

(*Music*) Jan Meyerowitz

(*Producer*) Michael Myerberg & Joel Spector

Broadhurst Theatre   Broadway

November 2, 1950   4 performances

(*Stars*) NA

Theatre World 50–51, p. 38

Best Plays 50–51, pp. 323–24

CS Mon Mag p. 8 N 11'50

         Commonweal 53:172 N 24 '50

         Mus Am 70:244 F '50

         New Yorker 25:71 Ja 28 '50

         New Yorker 26:79–81 N 11 '50

         Newsweek 35:68 Ja 30 '50

         Sch & Soc 71:120 F 25 '50

         Theatre Arts por 35:12 Ja '51

         Time 55:68+ Ja 30 '50

New York Times 1950, N 3, 32:2

NYTC 1950:218

(*Published libretto*) NA

(*Published sheet music*) NA

(*Original cast recording*) NA

(*Agent/contact*)

Edwin B. Marks Music Corp.   Langston Hughes Estate
c/o Belwin–Mills Pub. Corp.   c/o Harold Ober
24 Deshon Drive   Associates Inc.
Melville, N.Y.   11747   40 E. 49th Street
                                         New York, N.Y.   10017
                                         ATTN: Wendy Schmalz

(*Libretto*) NYPL *MZ; same as (*Agent/contact*)
(*Music*) NYPL *MS; LC (Performing Arts Reading Room) M1503/
          .M624/B3/1950 as *THE MULATTO*; same as (*Agent/contact*)
(*Orchestrations*) Same as (*Agent/contact*)

*Previously titled *THE MULATTO*

THE BEAST IN ME
(*Source*) *Fables for Our Time* (collection) by James Thurber
(*Book*) James Costigan
(*Lyrics*) James Costigan
(*Music*) Don Elliott
(*Producer*) Bonard Productions
Plymouth Theatre   Broadway
May 16, 1963   4 performances
(*Stars*) Kaye Ballard, Bert Convy
Theatre World 62–63, p. 96
Best Plays 62–63, pp. 309–11
New Yorker 39:57 My 25 '63
          Newsweek il 61:93 My 27 '63
New York Times 1963, My 17, 29:1
NYTC 1963:324
(*Published libretto*) NA
(*Published sheet music*) NA (Sunbeam Music)
(*Original cast recording*) NA

(*Agent/contact*)   Don Elliott   James Costigan
                     c/o Don Elliott Productions   c/o I.C.M.
                     67 Park Avenue   8899 Beverly Blvd.
                     New York, N.Y.   10016   Los Angeles, CA
                                                             90048
                                                    ATTN: Ben Benjamin

(*Libretto*) NYPL RM532, RM533, RM2032; same as (*Agent/contact*)
(*Music, Orchestrations*) Same as (*Agent/contact*)

BEAUTIFUL MRS. FLYNN
See **MAGGIE FLYNN**

BEG, BORROW, OR STEAL*
(*Source*) Story (title unavailable) by Marvin Seiger & Bud Freeman
(*Book*) Bud Freeman
(*Lyrics*) Bud Freeman
(*Music*) Leon Pober
(*Producer*) Eddie Bracken, Carroll & Harris Masterson
Martin Beck Theatre   Broadway
February 10, 1960   5 performances
(*Stars*) Eddie Bracken, Betty Garrett, Estelle Parsons, Larry Parks
Theatre World 59–60, p. 62
Best Plays 59–60, pp. 317–18
New Yorker 36:101–2 F 20 '60
New York Times 1960, F 11, 39:4
NYTC 1960:370
(*Published libretto*) NA
(*Published sheet music*) NA (Vickers Music Co.)
(*Original cast recording*) OP Commentary CNT–02 (1959 Record Cast)
          as **CLARA**

(*Agent/contact*)

Bud Freeman
4311 Colfax Avenue
Studio City, CA 91604

Pober Productions
13900 Panay Way, #225M
Marina Del Ray, CA 90292

(*Libretto*) NYPL RM304; LC (Performing Arts Reading Room)

ML50/.P734B4; LC Vickers Music Co. 25Jan60 DU50346;

same as (*Agent/contact*)

(*Music, Orchestrations*) Same as (*Agent/contact*)

*Previously titled *CLARA*

BEGGAR'S HOLIDAY*

(*Source*) *The Beggar's Opera* (play) by John Gay

(*Book*) John Latouche

(*Lyrics*) John Latouche

(*Music*) Duke Ellington

(*Producer*) Perry Watkins, in association with John R. Sheppard, Jr.

Broadway Theatre
December 26, 1946

Broadway
108 performances

(*Stars*) Alfred Drake, Zero Mostel

Theatre World 46–47, pp. 64–5

Best Plays 46–47, pp. 451–52

Cath World 164:455–6 F '47

Commonweal 45:351–2 Ja 17 '47

Life il 22:75 F 24 '47

New Yorker 22:46–7 Ja 4 '47

Newsweek 29:64 Ja 6 '47

Sch & Soc 65:252 Ap 5 '47

Theatre Arts 31:16,27 Mr '47

Time 49:57 Ja 6 '47

New York Times 1946, D 27, 13:3

New York Times 1947, Ja 26, II, 1:1

NYTC 1946:204

(*Published libretto*) NA

(*Published sheet music*) Chappell/Mutual Music Society, Inc.

(*Original cast recording*) NA

(*Agent/contact*)   John Latouche Estate   Duke Ellington Estate
                         c/o ASCAP   c/o AGAC

(*Libretto*) NYPL RM2298, RM4554, *ZC–50; same as (*Agent/contact*)

(*Music, Orchestrations*) Same as (*Agent/contact*)

*Previously presented under title *TWILIGHT ALLEY*

BEN FRANKLIN IN PARIS

(*Source*) Original

(*Book*) Sidney Michaels

(*Lyrics*) Sidney Michaels*

(*Music*) Mark Sandrich, Jr.*

(*Producer*) George W. George & Frank Granat

Lunt–Fontanne Theatre   Broadway

October 27, 1964   215 performances

(*Stars*) Robert Preston, Susan Watson

Theatre World 64–65, p. 35

Best Plays 64–65, pp. 308–9

America 111:758 D 5 '64

       Commonweal 81:423 D 18 '64

       Dance Mag il 38:16 D '64

       Newsweek il 64:92 N 9 '64

       Sat R 47:53 N 14 '64

       Sr Schol il 86:21 Mr 4 '65

       Time il 84:52 N 6 '64

New York Times 1964, O 28, 52:1

NYTC 1964:181

(*Published libretto*) Random House, 1965

(*Published sheet music*) Edwin H. Morris

(*Original cast recording*) OP Capitol VAS/SVAS–2191

(*Agent/contact*) Samuel French, Inc.

(*Libretto*) LC (Performing Arts Reading Room) ML50/.S218B42;
     same as (*Agent/contact*)

(*Music, Orchestrations*) Same as (*Agent/contact*)

*Steven Suskin's *Show Tunes 1905–1985* credits two songs, "To Be Alone
    with You" and "Too Charming," by Jerry Herman

BIG TIME BUCK WHITE
See **BUCK WHITE**

BILLION DOLLAR BABY
(*Source*) Original
(*Book*) Betty Comden & Adolph Green
(*Lyrics*) Betty Comden & Adolph Green
(*Music*) Morton Gould
(*Producer*) Paul Feigay & Oliver Smith
Alvin Theatre   Broadway
December 21, 1945   220 performances
(*Stars*) Joan McCracken, William Tabbert
Theatre World 45–46, pp. 48–9
Best Plays 45–46, pp. 415–16
Cath World 162:458 F '46
          Life il 20:67+ Ja 21 '46
          Mod Mus 23 no2:145 [Ap] '46
          New Yorker 21:40 Ja 5 '46
          Newsweek il 26:78 D 31 '45
          Theatre Arts il 30:80–1 F '46
          Time il 46:64 D 31 '45
New York Times 1945, D 30, II, 1:1
NYTC 1945:61
(*Published libretto*) NA
(*Published sheet music*) Chappell
(*Original cast recording*) NA
(*Agent/contact*) Tams–Witmark Music Library

(*Libretto*) NYPL NCOF+; LC Betty Comden & Adolph Green
    23Aug46 DU4688; same as (*Agent/contact*)
(*Music, Orchestrations*) Same as (*Agent/contact*)

BILLY

(*Source*) *Billy Budd* (novel) by Herman Melville
(*Book*) Stephen Glassman*
(*Lyrics*) Ron Dante*
(*Music*) Ron Dante
(*Producer*) Bruce W. Stark & Joseph H. Shoctor
Billy Rose Theatre   Broadway
March 22, 1969   1 performance
(*Stars*) Laurence Naismith
Theatre World 68–69, p. 71
Best Plays 68–69, pp. 411–12
New Yorker 45:99 Mr 29 '69
New York Times 1969, Mr 24, 56:1
NYTC 1969:316
(*Published libretto*) NA
(*Published sheet music*) NA (Pamco Music, Inc.)
(*Original cast recording*) NA
(*Agent/contact*)   Seth Glassman   Ron Dante
                       484 W. 43rd Street, #19B c/o DG, Inc.
                       New York, N.Y.   10036
(*Libretto*) LC Robert Upton 9Aug68 DU72099; same as (*Agent/contact*)
(*Music, Orchestrations*) Same as (*Agent/contact*)

*In all publicity, Stephen Glassman is given sole authorship credit and Ron
    Dante sole lyricist/composer credit; however, LC copyright
    DU72099 gives Robert Upton sole authorship credit, Gene Allan sole
    lyricist credit and Ronald Dante sole composer credit

BILLY BISHOP GOES TO WAR
(*Source*) Original
(*Book*) John Gray & Eric Peterson
(*Lyrics*) John Gray & Eric Peterson
(*Music*) John Gray & Eric Peterson
(*Producer*) Mike Nichols & Lewis Allen
Morosco Theater*   Broadway*
May 29, 1980   12 performances*
(*Stars*) NA
Theatre World 79–80, p. 70
    Theatre World 80–81, p. 77
Best Plays 79–80, p. 399
    Best Plays 80–81, p. 387
Macleans il 91:70–1 D 4 '78
    New Yorker 56:112 Je 9 '80
    Newsweek il 95:106 Je 9 '80
    Time il 116:56 Ag 4 '80
New York Times 1980, Mr 13, III, 20:1
    New York Times 1980, My 30, III, 3:4
NYTC 1980:225
(*Published libretto*) Talonbooks, 1981
(*Published sheet music*) NA
(*Original cast recording*) Tapestry(C) GD–7372 (Original
    Canadian Cast)
(*Agent/contact*)   The Billy Bishop Company
               c/o Robert S. Fishko
               165 W. 46th Street
               New York, N.Y.   10036
(*Libretto*) NYPL RM869; same as (*Agent/contact*)
(*Music, Orchestrations*) Same as (*Agent/contact*)

*Subsequently moved off–Broadway to Theatre de Lys 6/17/80 where it ran
    for an additional 78 performances

BLIND DATE
See *JACKPOT*

THE BLOOD OF AN ENGLISHMAN
See *BLOOD RED ROSES*

BLOOD RED ROSES *
(*Source*) Original
(*Book*) John Lewin
(*Lyrics*) John Lewin
(*Music*) Michael Valenti
(*Producer*) Seymour Vall & Louis S. Goldman, in association
        with Rick Mandell & Bjorn I. Swanstrom
John Golden Theater   Broadway
March 22, 1970   1 performance
(*Stars*) NA
Theatre World 69–70, p. 46
Best Plays 69–70, pp. 319–20
New Yorker 46:82+ Mr 28 '70
New York Times 1970, Mr 23, 48:1
NYTC 1970:332
(*Published libretto*) NA
(*Published sheet music*) Remsen Music Corp./Frank Distrib. Corp.
(*Original cast recording*) NA
(*Agent/contact*)

Frank Music/	Michael Valenti	John Lewin
April–Blackwood	350 E. 67th Street	c/o DG, Inc.
1350 Sixth Avenue	New York, N.Y.	
New York, N.Y. 10022	10021	

(*Libretto*) NYPL RM4429 as *THE BLOOD OF AN ENGLISHMAN*; LC John
        Lewin 26Sept67 DU69720 as *THE BLOOD OF AN ENGLISHMAN*;
        same as (*Agent/contact*)

(*Music, Orchestrations*) Same as (*Agent/contact*)

*Previously titled *THE BLOOD OF AN ENGLISHMAN*

BLUES OPERA
See *ST. LOUIS WOMAN*

BOCCACCIO
(*Source*) *The Decameron* (collection) by Giovanni Boccaccio
(*Book*) Kenneth Cavander
(*Lyrics*) Kenneth Cavander
(*Music*) Richard Peaslee
(*Producer*) Rita Fredericks, Theatre Now, Inc. & Norman Kean
Edison Theatre   Broadway
November 24, 1975   7 performances
(*Stars*) Virginia Vestoff, D. Jamin Bartlett
Theatre World 75–76, p. 27
Best Plays 75–76, p. 334
New Yorker 51:119–20 D 8 '75
New York Times 1975, N 25, 42:1
NYTC 1975:145
(*Published libretto*) NA
(*Published sheet music*) NA
(*Original cast recording*) NA
(*Agent/contact*)

Joseph Taubman	Kenneth Cavander	Richard Peaslee
Tower 53, #14F	c/o WNET	90 Riverside Drive
159 W. 53rd Street	356 W. 58th Street	New York, N.Y. 10024
New York, N.Y.	New York, N.Y.	
10019	10019	

(*Libretto*) Bruce Savan; same as (*Agent/contact*)
(*Music, Orchestrations*) Richard Peaslee; same as (*Agent/contact*)

THE BODY BEAUTIFUL

(*Source*) Original

(*Book*) Joseph Stein & Will Glickman

(*Lyrics*) Sheldon Harnick

(*Music*) Jerry Bock

(*Producer*) Richard Kollmar & Albert Selden

Broadway Theatre   Broadway

January 23, 1958   60 performances

(*Stars*) Barbara McNair

Theatre World 57–58, p. 70

Best Plays 57–58, pp. 311–13

America 98:677 Mr 8 '58

       Cath World 187:70 Ap '58

       Dance Mag il 32:15 Mr '58

       New Yorker 33:54–6 F 1 '58

       Newsweek 51:55 F 3 '58

       Sat R 41:28 F 15 '58

       Theatre Arts il 42:17–8 Ap '58

       Time 71:78 F 3 '58

New York Times 1958, Ja 24, 15:2

NYTC 1958:386

(*Published libretto*) Samuel French, Inc., 1959

(*Published sheet music*) Sunbeam Music Corp./Valando Music

(*Original cast recording*) Blue Pear Records BP–1006 (Original

       Broadway Cast recorded live)

(*Agent/contact*) Samuel French, Inc.

(*Libretto*) NYPL NCOF+

(*Music, Orchestrations*) Same as (*Agent/contact*)

BRAVO GIOVANNI*

(*Source*) *The Crime of Giovanni Venturi* (novel) by Howard Shaw

(*Book*) A.J. Russell

(*Lyrics*) Ronny Graham

(*Music*) Milton Schafer

(*Producer*) Philip Rose

Broadhurst Theatre   Broadway
May 19, 1962   76 performances
(*Stars*) Michele Lee, Cesare Siepi, George S. Irving
Theatre World 61–62, p. 97
Best Plays 61–62, pp. 299–300
America 107:429–30 Je 23 '62
       Commonweal 76:304 Je 15 '62
       New Yorker 38:91–2 My 26 '62
       Newsweek il 59:65 Je 4 '62
       Sat R 45:24 Je 2 '62
       Theatre Arts il 46:67–9 Jl '62
       Time il 79:83 Je 1 '62
New York Times 1962, My 21, 41:2
       New York Times 1962, My 27, II, 1:1
NYTC 1962:276
(*Published libretto*) NA
(*Published sheet music*) Edwin H. Morris
(*Original cast recording*) OP Columbia KOL–5800/KOS–2200
(*Agent/contact*)   Ronny Graham   Milton Schafer   Philip Rose
                   c/o AGAC   c/o DG, Inc.   157 W. 57th Street
                                           New York, N.Y.
                                                10019
(*Libretto*) NYPL RM1958 as *THE CRIME OF GIOVANNI VENTURI*;
       same as (*Agent/contact*)
(*Music, Orchestrations*) Same as (*Agent/contact*)

*Previously titled *THE CRIME OF GIOVANNI VENTURI*

BRING BACK BIRDIE
(*Source*) *Bye Bye Birdie* (musical comedy) book by Michael
       Stewart, lyrics by Lee Adams, music by Charles Strouse (sequel)
(*Book*) Michael Stewart
(*Lyrics*) Lee Adams
(*Music*) Charles Strouse

(*Producer*) Lee Guber, Shelly Gross, Slade Brown & Jim Milford
Martin Beck Theater   Broadway
March 5, 1981   4 performances
(*Stars*) Donald O'Connor, Chita Rivera, Maria Karnilova
Theatre World 80–81, p. 43
Best Plays 80–81, pp. 368–70
NO CRIT AVAIL
New York Times 1981, Mr 6, III, 4:5
NYTC 1981:324
(*Published libretto*) NA
(*Published sheet music*) NA
(*Original cast recording*) Original Cast Records OC–8132
(*Agent/contact*) Tams–Witmark Music Library
(*Libretto, Orchestrations*) Same as (*Agent/contact*)
(*Music*) LC Charles Strouse & Lee Adams 5Mar81 PA–113–461;
        same as (*Agent/contact*)

A BROADWAY MUSCIAL
(*Source*) Original
(*Book*) William F. Brown
(*Lyrics*) Lee Adams
(*Music*) Charles Strouse
(*Producer*) Norman Kean, Garth H. Drabinsky
Lunt–Fontanne Theatre*   Broadway*
December 21, 1978   1 performance
(*Stars*) NA*
Theatre World 78–79, p. 23
Best Plays 78–79, pp. 373–74, 415–17
NO CRIT AVAIL
New York Times 1978, D 22, III, 3:1
NYTC 1978:150
(*Published libretto*) NA
(*Published sheet music*) NA
(*Original cast recording*) NA

(*Agent/contact*)

Charles Strouse	William F. Brown	Lee Adams
c/o Alvin Deutsch	164 Newtown Turnpike	c/o Alvin Deutsch
110 E. 59th Street	Westport, CT 06880	110 E. 59th Street
New York, N.Y. 10022		New York, N.Y. 10022

(*Libretto*) NYPL NCOF+ 81–1901; same as (*Agent/contact*)
(*Music, Orchestrations*) Same as (*Agent/contact*)

*Previously produced off–off–Broadway at Theatre of the Riverside
    Church, starring Helen Gallagher and Julius La Rosa

BUCK WHITE*
(*Source*) *Big Time Buck White* (play) by Joseph Dolan Tuotti
(*Book*) Oscar Brown, Jr.
(*Lyrics*) Oscar Brown, Jr.
(*Music*) Oscar Brown, Jr.
(*Producer*) Zev Bufman & High John Productions
George Abbott Theatre   Broadway
December 2, 1969   7 performances
(*Stars*) Muhammad Ali
Theatre World 69–70, p. 22
Best Plays 69–70, p. 307
NO CRIT AVAIL
New York Times 1969, D 3, 63:1
NYTC 1969:170
(*Published libretto*) NA
(*Published sheet music*) NA (Kama Sutra Music/High John Music, Inc.)
(*Original cast recording*) NA
(*Agent/contact*)
        Oscar Brown, Jr.
        855 Drexel Square,
        First Floor
        Chicago, IL 60615

(*Libretto*) LC Oscar C. Brown, Jr. 28Apr69 DU74249; same as
        (*Agent/contact*)
(*Music, Orchestrations*) Same as (*Agent/contact*)

*Previously titled *BIG TIME BUCK WHITE*

BUT NOT FOR MARRIAGE
See *PORTOFINO*

BUTTRIO SQUARE
(*Source*) *Buttrio Square* (play) by Hal Cranton
(*Book*) Billy Gilbert & Gen Genovese
(*Lyrics*) Gen Genovese
(*Music*) Arthur Jones & Fred Stamer
(*Producer*) Gen Genovese & Edward Woods
New Century Theatre   Broadway
October 14, 1952   7 performances
(*Stars*) Billy Gilbert
Theatre World 52–53, p. 21
Best Plays 52–53, p. 259
New Yorker 28:80 O 25 '52
        Time 60:76 O 27 '52
New York Times 1952, O 15, 40:2
NYTC 1952:238
(*Published libretto*) NA
(*Published sheet music*) Chappell
(*Original cast recording*) NA
(*Agent/contact*)   Gen Genovese   Arthur Jones (ASCAP '50)
                       c/o ASCAP   c/o ASCAP
(*Libretto, Music, Orchestrations*) Same as (*Agent/contact*)

BY THE BEAUTIFUL SEA
(*Source*) Original
(*Book*) Herbert & Dorothy Fields
(*Lyrics*) Dorothy Fields
(*Music*) Arthur Schwartz
(*Producer*) Robert Fryer & Lawrence Carr
Majestic Theatre   Broadway
April 8, 1954   270 performances
(*Stars*) Shirley Booth
Theatre World 53–54, pp. 92–4
Best Plays 53–54, pp. 349–50
America 91:171–2 My 8 '54
          Cath World 179:225 Je '54
          Commonweal 60:95–6 Ap 30 '54
          Life il 36:109–10+ My 17 '54
          Mlle il 38:125 Ap '54
          Nation 178:370 Ap 24 '54
          New Yorker 30:64–6 Ap 17 '54
          Newsweek il 43:66 Ap 19 '54
          Sat R 37:32 My 1 '54
          Theatre Arts il 38:18–9 Je '54
          Time il 63:85 Ap 19 '54
New York Times 1954, Ap 9, 20:1
          New York Times 1954, Ap 18, II, 1:1
NYTC 1954:335
(*Published libretto*) NA
(*Published sheet music*) Edwin H. Morris
(*Original cast recording*) OP Capitol S–531, RE Capitol T–11652
(*Agent/contact*) Music Theatre International
(*Libretto*) NYPL NCOF+, RM1475; same as (*Agent/contact*)
(*Music, Orchestrations*) Same as (*Agent/contact*)

CAFE CROWN
(*Source*) *Cafe Crown* (play) by Hy Kraft
(*Book*) Hy Kraft

(*Lyrics*) Marty Brill
(*Music*) Albert Hague*
(*Producer*) Philip Rose & Swanlee

Martin Beck Theatre	Broadway
April 17, 1964	3 performances

(*Stars*) Alan Alda, Sam Levene, Theodore Bikel
Theatre World 63–64, p. 108
Best Plays 63–64, pp. 334–35
Dance Mag il 38:26–7 My '64
      New Yorker 40:130 Ap 25 '64
New York Times 1964, Ap 18, 32:1
NYTC 1964:284
(*Published libretto*) NA
(*Published sheet music*) Harms
(*Original cast recording*) NA
(*Agent/contact*)

Philip Rose	Hy Kraft Estate	Marty Brill
157 W. 57th Street	c/o Leonard M. Herman	c/o DG, Inc.
New York, N.Y. 10019	2920 Commonwealth Avenue	
	Chicago, IL 60657	
Albert Hague		
c/o DG, Inc.		

(*Libretto*) NYPL NCOF+, RM2240; same as (*Agent/contact*)
(*Music, Orchestrations*) Same as (*Agent/contact*)

*At press time, Mr. Hague was not interested in soliciting further
    productions of this property

CANDIDE*

(*Source*) *Candide* (novel) by Voltaire
(*Book*) Lillian Hellman
(*Lyrics*) Richard Wilbur, John Latouche & Dorothy Parker
(*Music*) Leonard Bernstein
(*Producer*) Ethel Linder Reiner & Lester Osterman, Jr.

Martin Beck Theatre	Broadway

December 1, 1956   73 performances

(*Stars*) Barbara Cook, Max Adrian

Theatre World 56–57, pp. 56–7

       Theatre World 73–74, pp. 42–3, 104

Best Plays 56–57, pp. 340–2

       Best Plays 73–74, pp. 362–63, 382–83

America 130:262 Ap 6 '74

       Cath World 184:384–5 F '57

       Commentary 57:78 Je '74

       Commonweal 65:333–4 D 28 '56

       HiFi 24:MA31 Ap '74

       Mus Am il 76:26 D 15 '56

       Nat R 26:1049 S 13 '74

       Nation 183:527 D 15 '56

       Nation 218:30 Je 5 '74

       New Repub 135:30–1 D 17 '56

       New Repub 170:16+ Mr 30 '74

       New Yorker 32:52+ D 15 '56

       New Yorker 49:42–4 D 31 '73

       Newsweek 48:77 D 10'56

       Newsweek il 82:31 D 31 '73

       Opera N il 38:33 F 9 '74

       Reporter 16:35 Ja 24 '57

       Time 68:70 D 10 '56

       Time il 103:75 Mr 25 '74

New York Times 1956, D 3, 40:2

       New York Times 1956, D 9, II, 5:1

       New York Times 1973, D 21, 47:1

       New York Times 1973, D 30, II, 1:7

       New York Times 1974, F 24, II, 1:1

       New York Times 1974, Mr 12, 34:1

       New York Times 1974, Jl 10, 44:1

NYTC 1956:176

       NYTC 1974:337

(*Published libretto*) Random House, 1957; Avon YD14, 1970; in *The*
  Collected Plays of Lillian Hellman, Little, Brown & Company, 1971;
  Schirmer Books, 1976 (Broadway Revival libretto)
(*Published sheet music*) G. Schirmer, Inc.
(*Original cast recording*) Columbia OL–5180/OS–2350 (Original Broadway
  Cast); Columbia S2X–32923 (Broadway Revival Cast)**
(*Agent/contact*) Music Theatre International***
(*Libretto*) NYPL RM561 (Original Broadway libretto);
  NYPL NCOF+ 77–429, RM8231 (Broadway Revival libretto);
  same as (*Agent/contact*) (Broadway Revival libretto)
(*Music, Orchestrations*) Same as (*Agent/contact*)

*A revised version of **CANDIDE** was later produced, retaining majority of
  Wilbur–Latouche–Parker/Bernstein score, with additional lyrics by
  Stephen Sondheim and new book by Hugh Wheeler; that version (as
  well as others produced subsequent to Original Broadway) is
  substantially different from the original

**Videotaped performance of Broadway Revival Cast available at NYPL
  Billy Rose Collection, Lincoln Center, NCOV 47

***MTI makes available revised version by Hugh Wheeler, with additional
  lyrics by Stephen Sondheim; the Lillian Hellman version is no longer
  available for production

CANTERBURY TALES
(*Source*) *The Canterbury Tales* (collection) by Geoffrey
  Chaucer, as translated by Nevill Coghill
(*Book*) Martin Starkie & Nevill Coghill
(*Lyrics*) Nevill Coghill
(*Music*) Richard Hill & John Hawkins

(*Producer*) Management Three Productions, Frank Productions,
      Classic Presentations
Eugene O'Neill Theatre   Broadway
February 3, 1969   121 performances
(*Stars*) Hermione Baddeley, Sandy Duncan
Theatre World 68–69, p. 53
Best Plays 68–69, pp. 404–5
America 120:316 Mr 15 '69
      Dance Mag 43:26+ My '69
      Nat R 21:918 S 9 '69
      New Yorker 44:90 F 15 '69
      Newsweek il 73:113 F 17 '69
      Time il 91:68 Ap 12 '68
      Time il 93:62 F 14 '69
      Vogue 153:42 Mr 15 '69
New York Times 1969, F 4, 34:1
      New York Times 1969, F 16, II, 1:1
NYTC 1969:368
(*Published libretto*) NA
(*Published sheet music*) Frank Music Corp.
(*Original cast recording*) OP Capitol SW–229; OP Decca(E)
      SKL–4956, RE That's Entertainment(E) TER–1076 (Original London
      Cast)
(*Agent/contact*) Music Theatre International
(*Libretto*) NYPL RM4421; same as (*Agent/contact*)
(*Music, Orchestrations*) Same as (*Agent/contact*)

CAPTAIN'S PARADISE
See *OH CAPTAIN!*

*CARIB SONG**
(*Source*) Original
(*Book*) William Archibald
(*Lyrics*) William Archibald
(*Music*) Baldwin Bergersen
(*Producer*) George Stanton

Adelphi Theatre   Broadway
September 27, 1945   36 performances
(*Stars*) Eartha Kitt (chorus)
Theatre World 45–46, p. 18
Best Plays 45–46, pp. 386–87
Cath World 162:167 N '45
        Commonweal 43:17 O 19 '45
        New Yorker 21:50 O 6 '45
        Theatre Arts il (p. 626) 29:624+ N '45
        Time 46:78 O 8 '45
New York Times 1945, S 28, 17:2
NYTC 1945:157
(*Published libretto*) NA
(*Published sheet music*) Chappell
(*Original cast recording*) NA
(*Agent/contact*)   William Archibald Estate   Baldwin Bergersen
                          c/o Samuel French, Inc.   c/o DG, Inc.
(*Libretto*) LC William J. Archibald & B. Bergersen 3May45 DU93342
        as *PO' ME ONE*; same as (*Agent/contact*)
(*Music, Orchestrations*) Same as (*Agent/contact*)

*Previously titled *PO' ME ONE*

CARMELINA
(*Source*) *Buona Sera, Mrs. Campbell* (screenplay) by Melvin Frank,
        Denis Norden & Sheldon Keller
(*Book*) Alan Jay Lerner & Joseph Stein
(*Lyrics*) Alan Jay Lerner
(*Music*) Burton Lane
(*Producer*) Roger L. Stevens, J.W. Fisher, Joan Cullman,
        Jujamcyn Productions
St. James Theatre   Broadway
April 8, 1979   17 performances
(*Stars*) Cesare Siepi, Georgia Brown
Theatre World 78–79, p. 40

Best Plays 78–79, pp. 385–86
Esquire 91:88–9 Ap 24 '79
    NY 12:70–1 Ap 23 '79
    New Yorker 55:115 Ap 16 '79
    Time 113:50 Ap 23 '79
New York Times 1979, Ap 1, II, 7:1
    New York Times 1979, Ap 9, III, 13:1
    New York Times 1979, Ap 22, II, 7:1
NYTC 1979:292
(*Published libretto*) NA
(*Published sheet music*) Chappell & Co.
(*Original cast recording*) Original Cast Records OC–8019
(*Agent/contact*)

Alan Jay Lerner Estate	Burton Lane
c/o David Grossberg	c/o David Grossberg
30 N. La Salle Street	30 N. La Salle Street
New York, N.Y. 10027	New York, N.Y. 10027

Jujamcyn Productions
246 W. 44th Street
New York, N.Y. 10036
(*Libretto*) Same as (*Agent/contact*)
(*Music, Orchestrations*) Chappell & Co.; same as (*Agent/contact*)

CARNIVAL IN FLANDERS

(*Source*) *Carnival in Flanders* (*La Kermesse Heroique*) (screenplay) by
    Charles Spaak, Jacques Feyder & Bernard Zimmer
(*Book*) Preston Sturges
(*Lyrics*) Johnny Burke
(*Music*) James Van Heusen
(*Producer*) Paula Stone, Mike Sloane, Johnny Burke & James Van Heusen
New Century Theatre   Broadway
September 8, 1953   6 performances
(*Stars*) John Raitt, Pat Stanley, Dolores Gray

Theatre World 53–54, p. 9

Best Plays 53–54, pp. 301–2

America 89:629 S 26 '53

      Commonweal 58:634 O 2 '53

      New Yorker 29:74 S 19 '53

      Theatre Arts il 37:18 N '53

New York Times 1953, S 9, 38:2

NYTC 1953:286

(*Published libretto*) NA

(*Published sheet music*) Burke & Van Heusen, Inc.

(*Original cast recording*) NA

(*Agent/contact*)

      Van Heusen Music Corp.   Johnny Burke Estate

      301 E. 69th Street, #15B   c/o Samuel French, Inc.

      New York, N.Y. 10021

      ATTN: Miriam Stern

      Preston Sturges Estate

      c/o Samuel French, Inc.

(*Libretto, Music, Orchestrations*) Same as (*Agent/contact*)

CELEBRATION

(*Source*) Original

(*Book*) Tom Jones

(*Lyrics*) Tom Jones

(*Music*) Harvey Schmidt

(*Producer*) Cheryl Crawford & Richard Chandler

Ambassador Theatre   Broadway

January 22, 1969   110 performances

(*Stars*) Susan Watson

Theatre World 68–69, p. 48

Best Plays 68–69, p. 402

America 120:315 Mr 15 '69

      Dance Mag 43:71 Mr '69

      Life il 66:82–4+ Mr 14 '69

New Yorker 44:49 F 1 '69
Time il 93:72 Ja 31 '69
New York Times 1969, Ja 23, 55:2
New York Times 1969, F 2, II, 3:1
NYTC 1969:383
(*Published libretto*) In *The Fantasticks/Celebration:*
Two Musicals by Tom Jones and Harvey Schmidt,
Drama Book Specialists, 1973
(*Published sheet music*) Portfolio Music/Chappell & Co.
(*Original cast recording*) OP Capitol SW–198
(*Agent/contact*) Music Theatre International
(*Libretto*) NYPL NCOF+; same as (*Agent/contact*)
(*Music, Orchestrations*) Same as (*Agent/contact*)

CHARLIE AND ALGERNON*

(*Source*) *Flowers for Algernon* (novel) by Daniel Keyes
(*Book*) David Rogers
(*Lyrics*) David Rogers
(*Music*) Charles Strouse
(*Producer*) John F. Kennedy Center for the Performing Arts,
Isobel Robins Konecky, Fisher Theater Foundation
& Folger Theater Group

Helen Hayes Theater	Broadway
September 14, 1980	17 performances

(*Stars*) NA
Theatre World 80–81, p. 16
Best Plays 80–81, p. 347
NY il 13:44+ S 29 '80
New Yorker 56:76 S 22 '80
New York Times 1980, Mr 12, III, 23:1
New York Times 1980, S 15, III, 17:1
New York Times 1980, S 21, II, 3:1
NYTC 1980:168
(*Published libretto*) Dramatic Publishing Company, 1981
(*Published sheet music*) NA

(*Original cast recording*) Original Cast Records OC–8021 as
    FLOWERS FOR ALGERNON (Original London Cast)
(*Agent/contact*) Dramatic Publishing Company
(*Libretto*) NYPL NCOF+ 83–1024; NCOF+ 83–1023 as *FLOWERS FOR*
    ALGERNON
(*Music, Orchestrations*) Same as (*Agent/contact*)

*Previously presented under title *FLOWERS FOR ALGERNON*

CHRISTINE*
(*Source*) *My Indian Family* (novel) by Hilda Wernher
(*Book*) Pearl S. Buck & Charles K. Peck, Jr.
(*Lyrics*) Paul Francis Webster
(*Music*) Sammy Fain
(*Producer*) Oscar S. Lerman, Martin B. Cohen & Walter Cohen
Forty–Sixth Street Theatre   Broadway
April 28, 1960   12 performances
(*Stars*) Maureen O'Hara, Nancy Andrews
Theatre World 59–60, p. 94
Best Plays 59–60, pp. 339–40
America 103:267 My 14 '60
    New Yorker 36:114+ My 7 '60
    Sat R 43:28 My 14 '60
    Time il 75:56 My 9 '60
New York Times 1960, Ap 29, 27:1
NYTC 1960:272
(*Published libretto*) NA
(*Published sheet music*) Harms
(*Original cast recording*) OP Columbia OL–5520/OS–2026
(*Agent/contact*)   Sammy Fain   Paul Francis Webster
                   c/o DG, Inc.   c/o ASCAP

(*Libretto*) NYPL RM329; same as (*Agent/contact*)
(*Music, Orchestrations*) Same as (*Agent/contact*)

*Previously titled *MY INDIAN FAMILY*

CHRISTMAS IS COMIN' UPTOWN
See *COMIN' UPTOWN*

CINDERELLA '46
See *IF THE SHOE FITS*

CLARA
See *BEG, BORROW, OR STEAL*

CLEAVAGE
(*Source*) Original
(*Book*) Buddy & David Sheffield
(*Lyrics*) Buddy Sheffield
(*Music*) Buddy Sheffield
(*Producer*) Up Front Productions (Braxton Glasgow III, William J.
        O'Brien III, Morgan P. O'Brien & David E. Fite)
Playhouse Theatre   Broadway
June 23, 1982   1 performance
(*Stars*) NA
Theatre World 82–83, p. 8
Best Plays 82–83, p. 332
Nation 235:92–3 Jl 24–31 '82
NO CRIT AVAIL
NO CRIT AVAIL
(*Published libretto*) NA
(*Published sheet music*) NA
(*Original cast recording*) OP BI Records LP 36–24–36

(*Agent/contact*) NO CONT AVAIL

(*Libretto, Music*) LC Morris T. & David A. Sheffield 14Aug81
        PAu–339–080; same as (*Agent/contact*)

(*Orchestrations*) Same as (*Agent/contact*)

COME SUMMER

(*Source*) *Rainbow on the Road* (novel) by Esther Forbes

(*Book*) Will Holt

(*Lyrics*) Will Holt

(*Music*) David Baker

(*Producer*) Albert W. Selden & Hal James

Lunt-Fontanne Theatre   Broadway

March 18, 1969   7 performances

(*Stars*) Ray Bolger, Margaret Hamilton, Cathryn Damon

Theatre World 68–69, p. 70

Best Plays 68–69, pp. 411–12

New Yorker 45:99 Mr 29 '69

New York Times 1969, Mr 19, 43:1

NYTC 1969:319

(*Published libretto*) NA

(*Published sheet music*) Edwin H. Morris

(*Original cast recording*) NA

(*Agent/contact*)

    Will Holt   David Baker
    c/o Fifi Oscard Associates, Inc.   c/o William Morris Agency
    19 W. 44th Street   1350 Avenue of the Americas
    New York, N.Y.   10036   New York, N.Y.   10019
    ATTN: Charles Hunt   ATTN: Biff Liff

(*Libretto*) NYPL NCOF+, RM4460, RM5010, RM7794a,
        RM7794b; LC Will Holt 6Aug69 DU75953; same as (*Agent/contact*)

(*Music, Orchestrations*) Same as (*Agent/contact*)

*COMIN' UPTOWN**
(*Source*) *A Christmas Carol* (novel) by Charles Dickens
(*Book*) Philip Rose & Peter Udell
(*Lyrics*) Peter Udell
(*Music*) Garry Sherman
(*Producer*) Ridgely Bullock & Albert W. Selden, Columbia Pictures
Winter Garden Theatre   Broadway
December 20, 1979   45 performances
(*Stars*) Gregory Hines
Theatre World 79–80, p. 35
Best Plays 79–80, pp. 376–78
Encore il 9:38 Ja '80
       New Yorker 55:57 Ja 7 '80
New York Times 1979, D 21, III, 5:1
NYTC 1979:58
(*Published libretto*) Samuel French, Inc., 1981, as
       CHRISTMAS IS COMIN' UPTOWN
(*Published sheet music*) NA
(*Original cast recording*) NA
(*Agent/contact*) Samuel French, Inc.
(*Libretto, Music, Orchestrations*) Same as (*Agent/contact*)

*Subsequently titled *CHRISTMAS IS COMIN' UPTOWN*

THE CONQUERING HERO
(*Source*) *Hail, The Conquering Hero* (screenplay) by Preston Sturges
(*Book*) Larry Gelbart
(*Lyrics*) Norman Gimbel
(*Music*) Moose Charlap
(*Producer*) Robert Whitehead, Roger L. Stevens & Emka Ltd.
ANTA Theatre   Broadway
January 16, 1961   8 performances
(*Stars*) Tom Poston, John McMartin
Theatre World 60–61, p. 64

Best Plays 60–61, pp. 318–19
New Yorker 36:64 Ja 28 '61
New York Times 1961, Ja 17, 40:2
NYTC 1961:388
(*Published libretto*) NA
(*Published sheet music*) Douglas/Chappell
(*Original cast recording*) NA
(*Agent/contact*)

Larry Gelbart	Moose Charlap Estate	Norman Gimbel
807 N. Alpine Drive	c/o Sandra Charlap	c/o DG, Inc.
Beverly Hills, CA 90210	40 E. 62nd Street	
	New York, N.Y. 10021	

(*Libretto, Music, Orchestrations*) Same as (*Agent/contact*)

COPPER AND BRASS
(*Source*) Original
(*Book*) Ellen Violet & David Craig
(*Lyrics*) David Craig
(*Music*) David Baker
(*Producer*) Lyn Austin, Thomas Noyes & Anderson Lawler
Martin Beck Theatre   Broadway
October 17, 1957   36 performances
(*Stars*) Nancy Walker
Theatre World 57–58, p. 26
Best Plays 57–58, pp. 293–94
Dance Mag 31:13 D '57
        Nation 185:310 N 2 '57
        New Yorker 33:98–100 O 26 '57
        Theatre Arts il 41:26–7 D '57
        Time il 70:92 O 28 '57
New York Times 1957, O 18, 19:2
NYTC 1957:216
(*Published libretto*) NA
(*Published sheet music*) Chappell
(*Original cast recording*) NA

(*Agent/contact*)   David Baker   Ellen Violet
                     c/o Flora Roberts, Inc.   c/o DG, Inc.
                     157 W. 57th Street
                     New York, N.Y.   10019
(*Libretto*) NYPL NCOF+; LC David Baker, David Craig & Ellen Violet
      22May56 DU42577; same as (*Agent/contact*)
(*Music, Orchestrations*) Chappell Music Co.; same as (*Agent/contact*)

COPPERFIELD

(*Source*) *David Copperfield* (novel) by Charles Dickens
(*Book*) Al Kasha & Joel Hirschhorn
(*Lyrics*) Al Kasha & Joel Hirschhorn
(*Music*) Al Kasha & Joel Hirschhorn
(*Producer*) Don Gregory & Mike Merrick
ANTA Theater   Broadway
April 13, 1981   13 performances
(*Stars*) George S. Irving
Theatre World 80–81, p. 50
Best Plays 80–81, pp. 373–75
NY 14:60–1 Ap 27 '81
      New Yorker 57:143 Ap 27 '81
New York Times 1981, Ap 17, III, 3:1
      New York Times 1981, Ap 26, II, 3:2
NYTC 1981:286
(*Published libretto*) NA
(*Published sheet music*) NA (April Music/Blackwood Music, Inc.)
(*Original cast recording*) NA
(*Agent/contact*)   Joel Hirschhorn   Al Kasha
                     c/o DG, Inc.   c/o DG, Inc.
(*Libretto, Orchestrations*) Same as (*Agent/contact*)
(*Music*) LC April Music, Inc. & Blackwood Music, Inc.
      13Jan82 PAu–478–633; same as (*Agent/contact*)

COURTIN' TIME

(*Source*) *The Farmer's Wife* (play) by Eden Philpotts

(*Book*) William Roos

(*Lyrics*) Jack Lawrence & Don Walker

(*Music*) Jack Lawrence & Don Walker

(*Producer*) James Russo, Michael Ellis & Alexander H. Cohen

National Theatre/Royale Theatre*   Broadway

June 13, 1951   37 performances

(*Stars*) Joe E. Brown

Theatre World 51–52, p. 9

Best Plays 51–52, pp. 276–77

Cath World 173:386–7 Ag '51

       Commonweal 54:285 Je 29 '51

       Nation 172:594 Je 23 '51

       New Yorker 27:45 Je 23 '51

       Newsweek il 37:72 Je 25 '51

       Theatre Arts 35:6 S '51

       Time il 57:73 Je 25 '51

New York Times 1951, Je 14, 30:2

       New York Times 1951, Jl 1, II, 1:1

NYTC 1951:254

(*Published libretto*) NA

(*Published sheet music*) Harms

(*Original cast recording*) NA

(*Agent/contact*)

    Jack Lawrence   Don Walker   William E. Roos

    25 Sutton Place   c/o DG, Inc.   Box #1112

    New York, N.Y. 10022   Edgartown, MA 02539

    Alexander H. Cohen

    225 W. 44th Street

    New York, N.Y. 10036

(*Libretto*) NYPL NCOF+; LC Don Walker, Jack Lawrence 29Sep50 DU2557;
    same as (*Agent/contact*)
(*Music, Orchestrations*) Same as (*Agent/contact*)

*Transferred to the Royale Theatre 7/2/51

THE CRIME OF GIOVANNI VENTURI
See *BRAVO GIOVANNI*

CRY FOR US ALL*
(*Source*) *Hogan's Goat* (play) by William Alfred
(*Book*) William Alfred
(*Lyrics*) William Alfred & Phyllis Robinson
(*Music*) Mitch Leigh
(*Producer*) Mitch Leigh & C. Gerald Goldsmith
Broadhurst Theatre   Broadway
April 8, 1970   9 performances
(*Stars*) Robert Weede, Joan Diener, Helen Gallagher
Theatre World 69–70, p. 53
Best Plays 69–70, pp. 325–26
New Yorker 46:79–80 Ap 18 '70
        Time 95:51 Ap 20 '70
New York Times 1970, Ap 9, 48:2
NYTC 1970:304
(*Published libretto*) NA
(*Published sheet music*) Andrew Scott, Inc.
(*Original cast recording*) OP Project 3 TS–100SD
(*Agent/contact*)
    Mitch Leigh   William Alfred   Phyllis Robinson
    c/o Music Makers, Inc.   c/o DG, Inc.   c/o DG, Inc.
    200 Central Park South
    New York, N.Y.   10019
(*Libretto, Music, Orchestrations*) Same as (*Agent/contact*)

*Previously titled *WHO TO LOVE*

CYRANO

(*Source*) *Cyrano de Bergerac* (play) by Edmond Rostand, as
     translated by Anthony Burgess
(*Book*) Anthony Burgess
(*Lyrics*) Anthony Burgess
(*Music*) Michael J. Lewis
(*Producer*) Richard Gregson & APJAC International

Palace Theatre	Broadway
May 13, 1973	49 performances

(*Stars*) Christopher Plummer
Theatre World 72–73, p. 74
Best Plays 72–73, pp. 358–59
America 128:538 Je 9 '73
     Harp Baz 106:153 Mr '73
     Harp Baz 106:98+ Ap '73
     Nation 216:731 Je 4 '73
     New Yorker 49:54 My 26 '73
     Newsweek 81:83 My 28 '73
     Time 101:55 My 28 '73
New York Times 1973, My 14, 37:1
     New York Times 1973, My 20, II, 1:1
NYTC 1973:272
(*Published libretto*) NA
(*Published sheet music*) NA (Mediarts Music, Inc.)
(*Original cast recording*) OP A&M Records SP–3702

(*Agent/contact*)	Michael J. Lewis	Anthony Burgess
	c/o DG, Inc.	c/o McGraw–Hill, Inc.
		1221 Avenue of the Americas
		New York, N.Y. 10020
		ATTN: Lori Shapiro

(*Libretto*) NYPL RM7187, RM7435; same as (*Agent/contact*)
(*Music, Orchestrations*) Same as (*Agent/contact*)

DAARLIN' JUNO
See *JUNO*

DANCE A LITTLE CLOSER
(*Source*) *Idiot's Delight* (play) by Robert E. Sherwood
(*Book*) Alan Jay Lerner*
(*Lyrics*) Alan Jay Lerner*
(*Music*) Charles Strouse
(*Producer*) Frederick Brisson, Jerome Minskoff, James Nederlander,
        The Kennedy Center (Roger L. Stevens, Chairman)

Minskoff Theatre   Broadway
May 11, 1983   1 performance
(*Stars*) Len Cariou, George Rose
Theatre World 82–83, p. 57
Best Plays 82–83, pp. 363–65
Harp Baz il 116:38 My '83
        NY 16:94–5 My 23 '83
New York Times 1983, My 8, II, 1:1
        New York Times 1983, My 12, III, 18:5
        New York Times 1983, My 13, III, 10:5
        New York Times 1983, Je 12, II, 8:3
NYTC 1983:248
(*Published libretto*) NA
(*Published sheet music*) Valando/Columbia Pictures Corp.
(*Original cast recording*) CBS Special Products (FOR FUTURE RELEASE)
(*Agent/contact*)

Alan Jay Lerner Estate	Charles Strouse	Frederick Brisson
c/o David Grossberg	c/o DG, Inc.	Productions
30 N. La Salle Street		c/o Dwight D. Frye
New York, N.Y. 10027		35 W. 90th Street
		New York, N.Y. 10024

(*Libretto, Music, Orchestrations*) Same as (*Agent/contact*)

*At press time, the Alan Jay Lerner Estate was not interested in soliciting
    further productions of this property

*DARLING OF THE DAY**

(*Source*) *Buried Alive* (novel) by Arnold Bennett

(*Book*) Nunnally Johnson/Keith Waterhouse & Willis Hall**

(*Lyrics*) E.Y. Harburg

(*Music*) Jule Styne

(*Producer*) Theatre Guild, Joel Schenker

George Abbott Theatre   Broadway

January 27, 1968   32 performances

(*Stars*) Vincent Price, Patricia Routledge

Theatre World 67–68, p. 40

Best Plays 67–68, pp. 360–61

Dance Mag il 42:27–8 Ap '68

     New Yorker 43:77–8 F 3 '68

New York Times 1968, Ja 29, 26:2

     New York Times 1968, F 11, II, 3:1

NYTC 1968:370

(*Published libretto*) NA

(*Published sheet music*) Chappell–Styne, Inc./Chappell

(*Original cast recording*) OP RCA LOC/LSO–1149

(*Agent/contact*)

    Jule Styne   E.Y. Harburg Estate

    c/o DG, Inc.   c/o Ernie Harburg

                        2 Washington Square Village

                        New York, N.Y.   10012

(*Libretto*) NYPL RM4458, RM4459 as *THE GREAT ADVENTURE*; same as

     (*Agent/contact*)

(*Music, Orchestrations*) Same as (*Agent/contact*)

*Previously titled *THE GREAT ADVENTURE*;

    previously presented under title *MARRIED ALIVE!*

**Nunnally Johnson replaced by Keith Waterhouse & Willis Hall as

    book writer, all of whom refused authorship credit

THE DAY BEFORE SPRING
(*Source*) Original
(*Book*) Alan Jay Lerner*
(*Lyrics*) Alan Jay Lerner*
(*Music*) Frederick Loewe
(*Producer*) John C. Wilson

National Theatre	Broadway
November 22, 1945	165 performances

(*Stars*) Irene Manning
Theatre World 45–46, p. 38
Best Plays 45–46, p. 409
Cath World 162:360 Ja '46
      Commonweal 43:238 D 14 '45
      Life il 19:85–6+ D 17 '45
      New Yorker 21:52 D 1 '45
      Newsweek il 26:92 D 3 '45
      Theatre Arts 30:14 Ja '46
      Time 46:68 D 3 '45
New York Times 1945, N 23, 27:2
      New York Times 1945, D 2, II, 1:1
NYTC 1945:92
(*Published libretto*) NA
(*Published sheet music*) Feist/Lowal/Chappell
(*Original cast recording*) NA

(*Agent/contact*)	Alan Jay Lerner Estate	Frederick Loewe
	c/o David Grossberg	c/o ASCAP
	30 N. La Salle Street	
	New York, N.Y. 10027	

(*Libretto*) LC Alan Jay Lerner & Frederick Loewe 24Oct44 DU90988;
      same as (*Agent/contact*)
(*Music, Orchestrations*) Same as (*Agent/contact*)

*At press time, the Alan Jay Lerner Estate was not interested in soliciting
      further productions of this property

DEAR WORLD

(*Source*) *The Madwoman of Chaillot* (play) by Jean Giraudoux

(*Book*) Jerome Lawrence & Robert E. Lee

(*Lyrics*) Jerry Herman

(*Music*) Jerry Herman

(*Producer*) Alexander H. Cohen

Mark Hellinger Theatre   Broadway

February 6, 1969   132 performances

(*Stars*) Angela Lansbury

Theatre World 68–69, p. 56

Best Plays 68–69, pp. 405–6

America 120:512 Ap 26 '69

      Chr Cent 86:483–4 Ap 9 '69

      Dance Mag il 43:20+ Ap '69

      New Yorker 44:90 F 15 '69

      Newsweek il 73:113 F 17 '69

New York Times 1969, F 7, 33:1

      New York Times 1969, F 16, II, 1:1

NYTC 1969:363

(*Published libretto*) NA

(*Published sheet music*) Edwin H. Morris

(*Original cast recording*) OP Columbia BOS–3260, RE Columbia

      Special Products ABOS–3260

(*Agent/contact*) Tams–Witmark Music Library

(*Libretto*) NYPL RM4475; same as (*Agent/contact*)

(*Music, Orchestrations*) Same as (*Agent/contact*)

*DIFFERENT TIMES**

(*Source*) Original

(*Book*) Michael Brown

(*Lyrics*) Michael Brown

(*Music*) Michael Brown

(*Producer*) Bowman Productions, William L. Witt & William J. Gumprez

ANTA Theatre   Broadway
May 1, 1972   24 performances
(*Stars*) Mary Jo Catlett
Theatre World 71–72, p. 53
Best Plays 71–72, pp. 343–44
New Yorker 48:99 My 13 '72
New York Times 1972, My 2, 50:1
NYTC 1972:286
(*Published libretto*) NA
(*Published sheet music*) NA (Sunbury Music, Inc.)
(*Original cast recording*) NA
(*Agent/contact*)   Michael Brown
                       c/o ASCAP
(*Libretto*) NYPL RM7890, RM7891 as **MARVELOUS TIMES**, RM7892, RM7893,
        RM7894; LC Michael Brown 15Apr71 DU80243 as **MARVELOUS
        TIMES**; same as (*Agent/contact*)
(*Music, Orchestrations*) Same as (*Agent/contact*)

*Previously titled **MARVELOUS TIMES**

DO BLACK PATENT LEATHER SHOES REALLY REFLECT UP?
(*Source*) Do Black Patent Leather Shoes Really Reflect Up?
        (novel) by John R. Powers
(*Book*) John R. Powers
(*Lyrics*) James Quinn & Alaric Jans
(*Music*) James Quinn & Alaric Jans
(*Producer*) Mavin Prods., Inc., Libby Adler Mages &
        Daniel A. Goldman
Alvin Theater*   Broadway*
May 27, 1982   5 performances
(*Stars*) Russ Thacker
Theatre World 81–82, p. 32
Best Plays 81–82, pp. 339–40

NY il 15:62+ Je 7 '82
    New Yorker 58:112+ Je 7 '82
New York Times 1982, My 28, III, 3:5
NYTC 1982:257
(*Published libretto*) NA
(*Published sheet music*) NA
(*Original cast recording*) CBS Special Products DP–18852
(*Agent/contact*)   Mavin Productions
                         845 N. Michigan, Ste. 903E
                         Chicago, IL   60611
(*Libretto, Music, Orchestrations*) Same as (*Agent/contact*)

*Previously produced in Chicago, Detroit and Philadelphia

DO I HEAR A WALTZ?
(*Source*) *The Time of the Cuckoo* (play) by Arthur Laurents
(*Book*) Arthur Laurents
(*Lyrics*) Stephen Sondheim
(*Music*) Richard Rodgers
(*Producer*) Richard Rodgers
Forty–Sixth Street Theatre   Broadway
March 18, 1965   220 performances
(*Stars*) Sergio Franchi, Elizabeth Allen
Theatre World 64–65, p. 88
Best Plays 64–65, pp. 330–31
America 112:590–1 Ap 17 '65
    Commonweal 82:85–6 Ap 9 '65
    Dance Mag 39:28–9 My '65
    New Yorker 41:144 Mr 27 '65
    Newsweek 65:82 Mr 29 '65
    Sat R 48:36 Ap 3 '65
    Time 85:60 Mr 26 '65
New York Times 1965, Mr 19, 28:1
    New York Times 1965, Mr 28, II, 1:1

NYTC 1965:357

(*Published libretto*) Random House, 1966

(*Published sheet music*) Chappell

(*Original cast recording*) OP Columbia KOL–6370/KOS–2770, RE Columbia
    Special Products AKOS–2770

(*Agent/contact*) Rodgers & Hammerstein Theatre Library

(*Libretto*) NYPL RM4350; same as (*Agent/contact*)

(*Music, Orchestrations*) Same as (*Agent/contact*)

DOCTOR JAZZ

(*Source*) Original

(*Book*) Buster Davis*

(*Lyrics*) Buster Davis

(*Music*) Buster Davis

(*Producer*) Cyma Rubin

Winter Garden Theatre   Broadway

March 19, 1975   5 performances

(*Stars*) Bobby Van, Lola Falana

Theatre World 74–75, p. 49

Best Plays 74–75, pp. 345–46

NO CRIT AVAIL

New York Times 1975, Mr 20, 46:1

NYTC 1975:294

(*Published libretto*) NA

(*Published sheet music*) NA

(*Original cast recording*) NA

(*Agent/contact*)   Buster Davis**
                       c/o DG, Inc.

(*Libretto*) NYPL RM305, RM306; LC Buster Davis 11Mar74 DU89566;
    same as (*Agent/contact*)

(*Music, Orchestrations*) Same as (*Agent/contact*)

*In all publicity, Buster Davis is given full authorship credit; however,
the manuscript/promptscript filed with NYPL Billy Rose Collection
gives Paul Carter Harrison and Buster Davis authorship credit

**Mr. Davis' original libretto was altered for Broadway; at press time,
the author was not interested in soliciting further productions of
this Broadway version

*A DOLL'S LIFE**

(*Source*) *A Doll's House* (play) by Henrik Ibsen (sequel)
(*Book*) Betty Comden & Adolph Green
(*Lyrics*) Betty Comden & Adolph Green
(*Music*) Larry Grossman
(*Producer*) James M. Nederlander, Sidney Shlenker, Warner
Theatre Productions, Joseph Harris, Mary Lea Johnson,
Martin Richards, Robert Fryer, in association with Harold Prince
Mark Hellinger Theatre   Broadway
September 23, 1982   5 performances
(*Stars*) Betsy Joslyn, George Hearn, Peter Gallagher
Theatre World 82–83, p. 15
Best Plays 82–83, pp. 338–39
America 147:235 O 23 '82
        NY il 15:91–2 O 4 '82
        Nation 235:378–80 O 16 '82
        New Yorker 58:122 O 4 '82
        Theatre Crafts il 16:22–3+ N/D '82
New York Times 1982, F 23, III, 9:1
        New York Times 1982, Ap 8, III, 13:1
        New York Times 1982, illus, Jl 31, 9:1

New York Times 1982, S 19, II, 8:1

New York Times 1982, illus, S 27, III, 11:1

NYTC 1982:207

(*Published libretto*) Samuel French, Inc., 1983

(*Published sheet music*) Fiddleback/Bettdolph/Manor Lane/Valando

(*Original cast recording*) OP Original Cast Records OC–8241,

RE CBS Special Products P–18846

(*Agent/contact*) Samuel French, Inc.

(*Libretto*) NYPL NCOF+ 83–1500

(*Music, Orchestrations*) Same as (*Agent/contact*)

*Videotaped performance available at NYPL Billy Rose Collection, Lincoln
Center, NCOV 222

DONNYBROOK!

(*Source*) *The Quiet Man* (screenplay) by Frank Nugent, story
by Maurice Walsh

(*Book*) Robert E. McEnroe

(*Lyrics*) Johnny Burke

(*Music*) Johnny Burke

(*Producer*) Fred Hebert & David Kapp

Forty–Sixth Street Theatre   Broadway

May 18, 1961   68 performances

(*Stars*) Art Lund, Eddie Foy

Theatre World 60–61, p. 88

Best Plays 60–61, pp. 339–40

America 105:532 Jl 15 '61

Dance Mag il 35:20 Jl '61

New Yorker 37:72+ My 27 '61

Sat R 44:51 Je 17 '61

Theatre Arts il 45:9–10 Jl '61

Time il 77:79 My 26 '61

New York Times 1961, My 19, 23:1

New York Times 1961, My 28, II, 1:1

NYTC 1961:292

(*Published libretto*) NA

(*Published sheet music*) Harms

(*Original cast recording*) OP Kapp KDL/KDS–8500

(*Agent/contact*) Samuel French, Inc.

(*Libretto*) NYPL RM1267, NCOF+; LC (Performing Arts Reading Room)
ML50/.B9658D6; LC Robert E. McEnroe 5Sep61 DU53851; same as
(*Agent/contact*)

(*Music, Orchestrations*) Same as (*Agent/contact*)

DON'T PLAY US CHEAP!

(*Source*) Original

(*Book*) Melvin Van Peebles

(*Lyrics*) Melvin Van Peebles

(*Music*) Melvin Van Peebles

(*Producer*) Melvin Van Peebles

Ethel Barrymore Theater   Broadway

May 16, 1972   164 performances

(*Stars*) Esther Rolle, Mabel King

Theatre World 71–72, p. 55

Best Plays 71–72, p. 346

New Yorker 48:82 My 27 '72
      Newsweek 79:75 My 29 '72

New York Times 1972, My 17, 39:1
      New York Times 1972, My 28, II, 1:1

NYTC 1972:279

(*Published libretto*) *Don't Play Us Cheap: A Harlem Party*
(novelized version), Bantam, 1973

(*Published sheet music*) NA

(*Original cast recording*) OP Stax STS2–3006

(*Agent/contact*)   Melvin Van Peebles
                       353 W. 56th Street
                       New York, N.Y. 10019

(*Libretto*) LC Yeah, Inc. 8Sep72 DU84551; same as (*Agent/contact*)

(*Music, Orchestrations*) Same as (*Agent/contact*)

DRAT! THE CAT!
(*Source*) Original
(*Book*) Ira Levin
(*Lyrics*) Ira Levin
(*Music*) Milton Schafer
(*Producer*) Jerry Adler & Norman Rosemont
Martin Beck Theatre   Broadway
October 10, 1965   8 performances
(*Stars*) Elliott Gould, Leslie Ann Warren
Theatre World 65–66, p. 15
Best Plays 65–66, pp. 375–76
Dance Mag 39:138 D '65
        Sat R 48:74 O 30 '65
New York Times 1965, O 11, 54:2
NYTC 1965:319
(*Published libretto*) NA
(*Published sheet music*) Edwin H. Morris
(*Original cast recording*) Blue Pear Records BP–1005
        (Original Broadway Cast recorded live)
(*Agent/contact*) Samuel French, Inc.
(*Libretto*) NYPL RM4486; LC (Performing Arts Reading Room) ML50/
        .S295D72; LC Ira Levin 19Jul67 DU69201; same as (*Agent/contact*)
(*Music, Orchestrations*) Same as (*Agent/contact*)

DREAM WITH MUSIC
(*Source*) Original
(*Book*) Sidney Sheldon, Dorothy Kilgallen & Ben Roberts
(*Lyrics*) Edward Eager
(*Music*) Clay Warnick, based on classical themes
(*Producer*) Richard Kollmar
Majestic Theatre   Broadway
May 18, 1944   28 performances
(*Stars*) Vera Zorina
NO ENTRY AVAIL

Best Plays 43–44, pp. 477–78

Commonweal 40:156 Je 2 '44

      Nation 158:688 Je 10 '44

      New Yorker 20:40 My 27 '44

New York Times 1944, My 19, 15:2

NYTC 1944:188

(*Published libretto*) NA

(*Published sheet music*) Chappell

(*Original cast recording*) NA

(*Agent/contact*)

Edward Eager Estate	Clay Warnick	Sidney Sheldon
c/o ASCAP	c/o ASCAP	c/o William
		Morrow & Co.
		105 Madison Avenue
		New York, N.Y. 10016

(*Libretto, Music, Orchestrations*) Same as (*Agent/contact*)

THE DUCHESS MISBEHAVES

(*Source*) Original

(*Book*) Gladys Shelley, additional dialogue by Joe Bigelow

(*Lyrics*) Gladys Shelley

(*Music*) Dr. Frank Black

(*Producer*) A.P. Waxman

Adelphi Theatre	Broadway
February 13, 1946	5 performances

(*Stars*) NA

Theatre World 45–46, p. 72

Best Plays 45–46, pp. 427–28

New Yorker 22:44+ F 23 '46

New York Times 1946, F 14, 32:2

NYTC 1946:456

(*Published libretto*) NA

(*Published sheet music*) Chappell

(*Original cast recording*) NA

(*Agent/contact*)   Gladys Shelley
                         c/o DG, Inc.
(*Libretto, Music, Orchestrations*) Same as (*Agent/contact*)

DUDE
(*Source*) Original
(*Book*) Gerome Ragni
(*Lyrics*) Gerome Ragni
(*Music*) Galt MacDermot
(*Producer*) Adela & Peter Holzer
Broadway Theatre   Broadway
October 9, 1972   16 performances
(*Stars*) Ralph Carter, Delores Hall, Nell Carter
Theatre World 72–73, p. 15
Best Plays 72–73, pp. 330–31
Nation 215:410 O 30 '72
        New Yorker 48:30 S 23 '72
        New Yorker 48:76 O 21 '72
        Newsweek 80:111 O 30 '72
        Time 100:81 O 23 '72
        Vogue il 160:86–7 O 15 '72
New York Times 1972, O 10, 54:2
        New York Times 1972, O 22, II, 1:1
NYTC 1972:222
(*Published libretto*) NA
(*Published sheet music*) NA
(*Original cast recording*) OP Kilmarnock KIL–72007
(*Agent/contact*)   Gerome Ragni   Galt MacDermot
                       c/o Nat Shapiro   c/o DG, Inc.
                       157 W. 57th Street
                       New York, N.Y.   10019
(*Libretto*) LC Gerome Ragni 17May72 DU83530; same as (*Agent/contact*)

(Music, Orchestrations)   Arnold Arenstein;   same as *(Agent/contact)*
60 Sutton Place South
New York, N.Y.   10022

EARL OF RUSTON
(Source) Original
(Book) C.C. Courtney & Ragan Courtney
(Lyrics) C.C. Courtney & Ragan Courtney
(Music) Peter Link
(Producer) David Black
Billy Rose Theatre   Broadway
May 5, 1971   5 performances
(Stars) NA
Theatre World 70–71, p. 47
Best Plays 70–71, p. 315
New Yorker 47:102+ My 15 '71
New York Times 1971, My 6, 55:2
NYTC 1971:289
(Published libretto) NA
(Published sheet music) NA
(Original cast recording) OP Capitol ST–465
(Agent/contact)

Peter Link   C.C. Courtney   Ragan Courtney
c/o On Broadway Prods. c/o ASCAP   c/o ASCAP
400 W. 43rd Street, #38D
New York, N.Y.   10036
(Libretto, Music, Orchestrations) Same as *(Agent/contact)*

EAST OF EDEN
See *HERE'S WHERE I BELONG*

THE EDUCATION OF H*Y*M*A*N K*A*P*L*A*N
(Source) Stories (titles unavailable) by Leo Rosten
(Book) Benjamin Bernard Zavin
(Lyrics) Paul Nassau & Oscar Brand
(Music) Paul Nassau & Oscar Brand
(Producer) Andre Goulston, Jack Garren & Stephen Mellow
Alvin Theatre   Broadway
April 4, 1968   28 performances
(Stars) Tom Bosley, Hal Linden, Donna McKechnie
Theatre World 67–68, p. 54
Best Plays 67–68, pp. 369–70
Dance Mag 42:29 Je '68
        New Yorker 44:114 Ap 13 '68
        Time il 91:68 Ap 12 '68
New York Times 1968, Ap 5, 57:1
        New York Times 1968, Ap 14, II, 1:1
NYTC 1968:310
(Published libretto) Dramatic Publishing Company, 1968
(Published sheet music) Chantz/TRO
(Agent/contact) Dramatic Publishing Company
(Original cast recording) NA
(Libretto) NYPL RM3338, RM7484, RM7485, RM7486,
        RM7487, RM7488, RM7489, RM7490, RM7491
(Music, Orchestrations) Same as (Agent/contact)

FADE OUT – FADE IN*
(Source) Original
(Book) Betty Comden & Adolph Green
(Lyrics) Betty Comden & Adolph Green
(Music) Jule Styne
(Producer) Lester Osterman & Jule Styne
Mark Hellinger Theatre   Broadway
May 26, 1964**   271 performances**
(Stars) Carol Burnett, Jack Cassidy/Dick Shawn**

Theatre World 63–64, pp. 116–17

    Theatre World 64–65, pp. 74–5

Best Plays 63–64, pp. 339–40

    Best Plays 64–65, p. 294

America 111:114–15 Ag 1 '64

    Dance Mag il 38:17 Ag '64

    Life 57:30 S 25 '64

    Nation 198:611 Je 15 '64

    Newsweek il 63:69 Je 8 '64

    Sat R 47:28 Je 20 '64

    Time 83:75 Je 5 '64

New York Times 1964, My 27, 45:1

    New York Times 1964, Je 21, II, 1:1

    New York Times 1965, F 16, 40:2

NYTC 1964:248

(*Published libretto*) Random House, 1965

(*Published sheet music*) Stratford Music/Chappell & Co.

(*Original cast recording*) OP ABC Records SOC–3

(*Agent/contact*) Tams–Witmark Music Library

(*Libretto, Music, Orchestrations*) Same as (*Agent/contact*)

*Previously titled *A GIRL TO REMEMBER*

**Opened 5/26/64 and closed after 199 performances due to Miss Burnett's
    illness; reopened 2/15/65 for 72 additional performances, which made
    for a total run of 271 performances. The reopening included a slightly
    altered book and two new songs: "A Girl to Remember" (replacing "Lila
    Tremaine") and "Notice Me." Two other songs, "The Thirties" and "Go
    Home Train," were cut. There were also cast changes, notably Dick
    Shawn in the role originated by Jack Cassidy

A FAMILY AFFAIR
(*Source*) Original
(*Book*) James Goldman, John Kander & William Goldman
(*Lyrics*) James Goldman, John Kander & William Goldman
(*Music*) James Goldman, John Kander & William Goldman
(*Producer*) Andrew Siff
Billy Rose Theatre   Broadway
January 27, 1962   65 performances
(*Stars*) Larry Kert, Shelley Berman, Eileen Heckart, Morris Carnovsky
Theatre World 61–62, p. 72
Best Plays 61–62, pp. 282–83
America 106:737 Mr 3 '62
        Theatre Arts 46:58–9 Ap '62
        Time 79:61 F 9 '62
New York Times 1962, Ja 29, 17:1
NYTC 1962:374
(*Published libretto*) NA
(*Published sheet music*) Sunbeam Music/Valando Music
(*Original cast recording*) OP United Artists UAL–4099/UAS–5099
(*Agent/contact*) Music Theatre International
(*Libretto, Music, Orchestrations*) Same as (*Agent/contact*)

FEARLESS FRANK
(*Source*) Original
(*Book*) Andrew Davies
(*Lyrics*) Andrew Davies
(*Music*) Dave Brown
(*Producer*) Dave Black & Robert Fabian, in association
        with Oscar Lewenstein & Theodore P. Donahue, Jr.
Princess Theatre   Broadway
June 15, 1980   12 performances
(*Stars*) NA
Theatre World 80–81, p. 11
Best Plays 80–81, pp. 341–42

NY 13:49–50 Je 30 '80

    New Yorker 56:55 Je 30 '80

New York Times 1980, illus, Je 16, III, 13:1

NYTC 1980:212

(*Published libretto*) NA

(*Published sheet music*) NA

(*Original cast recording*) NA

(*Agent/contact*)   Andrew Davies   David Black

                  c/o Harvey Unna &   251 E. 51st Street

                     Stephen Durbridge, Ltd.   New York, N.Y.

                  14 Beaumont Mews   10022

                  Marylebone High Street

                  London WIN 4HE, England

(*Libretto, Music, Orchestrations*) Same as (*Agent/contact*)

THE FIG LEAVES ARE FALLING

(*Source*) Original

(*Book*) Allan Sherman

(*Lyrics*) Allan Sherman

(*Music*) Albert Hague

(*Producer*) Joseph Harris, Lawrence Carr & John Bowab

Broadhurst Theatre   Broadway

January 2, 1969   4 performances

(*Stars*) Barry Nelson, Dorothy Loudon, David Cassidy

Theatre World 68–69, p. 44

Best Plays 68–69, pp. 400–1

New Yorker 44:56 Ja 11 '69

        Newsweek 73:86 Ja 13 '69

New York Times 1969, Ja 3, 19:1

NYTC 1969:397

(*Published libretto*) NA

(*Published sheet music*) Playgoers Music/Sam Fox

(*Original cast recording*) NA

(*Agent/contact*)

Albert Hague	Allan Sherman Estate	Joseph P. Harris Assoc.
c/o DG, Inc.	c/o ASCAP	1500 Broadway
		New York, N.Y. 10036

(*Libretto*) NYPL RM4507; same as (*Agent/contact*)

(*Music, Orchestrations*) Same as (*Agent/contact*)

THE FIREBRAND OF FLORENCE*

(*Source*) *The Firebrand* (play) by Edwin Justus Mayer

(*Book*) Edwin Justus Mayer & Ira Gershwin

(*Lyrics*) Edwin Justus Mayer & Ira Gershwin

(*Music*) Kurt Weill

(*Producer*) Max Gordon

Alvin Theatre   Broadway

March 22, 1945   43 performances

(*Stars*) NA

Theatre World 44–45, p. 83

Best Plays 44–45, pp. 424–25

New Yorker 21:42 Mr 31 '45

        Time 45:60 Ap 2 '45

New York Times 1945, Mr 23, 13:4

NYTC 1945:241

(*Published libretto*) NA

(*Published sheet music*) Chappell

(*Original cast recording*) NA

(*Agent/contact*)   Kurt Weill Estate   Ira Gershwin Estate

                         c/o European American Music c/o ASCAP

                         11 West End Avenue

                         Totowa, NJ   07512

                         ATTN: Ronald Freed

(*Libretto*) NYPL RM178; RM179 as *MUCH ADO ABOUT LOVE*; LC Edwin
        Justus Mayer 14May45 DU93473; Kurt Weill Foundation

(Music, Orchestrations)   Kurt Weill Foundation
                                            Lincoln Towers
                                            142 West End Avenue, Ste 1R
                                            New York, N.Y.   10023

*Previously titled *MUCH ADO ABOUT LOVE*

THE FIRST
(Source) Original
(Book) Joe Siegel, with Martin Charnin
(Lyrics) Martin Charnin
(Music) Bob Brush
(Producer) Zev Bufman, Neil Bogart, Michael Harvey &
          Peter A. Bobley
Martin Beck Theater   Broadway
November 17, 1981   37 performances
(Stars) NA
Theatre World 81–82, p. 17
Best Plays 81–82, pp. 322–24
Dance Mag 56:98 F '82
          NY 14:88 N 30 '81
          New Yorker 57:110 D 7 '81
          Newsweek il 98:109 N 30 '81
New York Times 1981, illus, N 8, II, 1:2
          New York Times 1981, N 18, III, 25:1
NYTC 1981:110
(Published libretto) Samuel French, Inc., 1983
(Published sheet music) MPL Communications/Hal Leonard
(Original cast recording) NA
(Agent/contact) Samuel French, Inc.
(Libretto, Music, Orchestrations) Same as *(Agent/contact)*

FIRST IMPRESSIONS

(Source) Pride and Prejudice (novel) by Jane Austen, (play) by Helen
    Jerome

(Book) Abe Burrows

(Lyrics) Robert Goldman, Glenn Paxton & George Weiss

(Music) Robert Goldman, Glenn Paxton & George Weiss

(Producer) George Gilbert & Edward Specter Productions, Inc.

Alvin Theatre   Broadway

March 19, 1959   84 performances

(Stars) Hermione Gingold, Polly Bergen, Farley Granger

Theatre World 58–59, p. 106

Best Plays 58–59, pp. 331–32

Cath World 189:241–2 Je '59

        Commonweal 70:57–8 Ap 10 '59

        Dance Mag 33:16 Je '59

        New Yorker 35:89 Mr 28 '59

        Sat R 42:28 Ap 4 '59

        Theatre Arts il 43:23–4 My '59

        Time il 73:43 Mr 30 '59

New York Times 1959, Mr 20, 28:1

        New York Times 1959, Mr 29, II, 1:1

NYTC 1959:336

(Published libretto) Samuel French, Inc., 1962

(Published sheet music) Stratford Music/Chappell & Co.

(Original cast recording) OP Columbia OL–5400/OS–2014, RE Columbia
    Special Products AOS–2014

(Agent/contact) Samuel French, Inc.

(Libretto, Music, Orchestrations) Same as *(Agent/contact)*

FLAHOOLEY*

(Source) Original

(Book) E.Y. Harburg & Fred Saidy

(Lyrics) E.Y. Harburg

(*Music*) Sammy Fain

(*Producer*) Cheryl Crawford, E.Y. Harburg & Fred Saidy

Broadhurst Theatre   Broadway

May 14, 1951   40 performances

(*Stars*) Barbara Cook, Yma Sumac, Louis Nye

Theatre World 50–51, p. 116

Best Plays 50–51, pp. 370–71

Cath World 173:307 Jl '51

   Commonweal 54:189 Je 1 '51

   New Yorker 27:48+ My 26 '51

   Newsweek il 37:58 My 28 '51

   Theatre Arts 35:5 S '51

   Time 57:78 My 28 '51

New York Times 1951, My 15, 39:1

   New York Times 1951, My 20, II, 1:1

   New York Times 1952, Ag 13, 17:7

NYTC 1951:264

(*Published libretto*) NA

(*Published sheet music*) Chappell & Co.

(*Original cast recording*) OP Capitol S–284, RE Capitol T–11649

(*Agent/contact*)

  E.Y. Harburg Estate   Sammy Fain   Fred Saidy Estate

  c/o Ernie Harburg   c/o DG, Inc.   c/o Herman I. Meltzer

  2 Washington Square Village   551 Fifth Avenue

  New York, N.Y. 10012   New York, N.Y. 10017

(*Libretto*) NYPL NCOF+ 73–1869; LC Edgar Y. Harburg, Fred Saidy

   14Mar51 DU27037; same as (*Agent/contact*)

(*Music, Orchestrations*) Same as (*Agent/contact*)

*Subsequently presented under title *JOLLYANNA*

FLORA, THE RED MENACE

(*Source*) *Love Is Just Around the Corner* (novel) by Lester Atwell

(*Book*) George Abbott & Robert Russell
(*Lyrics*) Fred Ebb
(*Music*) John Kander
(*Producer*) Harold Prince

Alvin Theatre	Broadway
May 11, 1965	87 performances

(*Stars*) Liza Minnelli, Cathryn Damon, Bob Dishy
Theatre World 64–65, p. 103
Best Plays 64–65, pp. 336–38
America 113:121–2 Jl 31 '65
      Dance Mag il 39:23 Jl '65
      Nat R 17:561–2 Je 29 '65
      New Yorker 41:114 My 22 '65
      Newsweek 65:99 My 24 '65
      Sat R il 48:50 My 8 '65
      Time il 85:69 My 21 '65
      Vogue 146:38 Jl '65
New York Times 1965, My 12, 41:2
NYTC 1965:330
(*Published libretto*) NA
(*Published sheet music*) Sunbeam Music/Valando Music
(*Original cast recording*) OP RCA LOC/LSO–1111, RE RCA CBLI–2760
(*Agent/contact*)

John Kander	Fred Ebb	Harold Prince
c/o I.C.M.	c/o Morton Leavy	1270 Sixth Avenue
40 W. 57th Street	79 Madison Avenue	New York, N.Y. 10020
New York, N.Y. 10019	New York, N.Y. 10016	
ATTN: Bridget Aschenburg		

(*Libretto*) NYPL RM121, RM135, RM136, RM137; same as (*Agent/contact*)
(*Music, Orchestrations*) Same as (*Agent/contact*)

FLOWERS FOR ALGERNON
See **CHARLIE AND ALGERNON**

FOXY

(*Source*) *Volpone* (play) by Ben Jonson

(*Book*) Ian McLellan Hunter & Ring Lardner, Jr.

(*Lyrics*) Johnny Mercer

(*Music*) Robert Emmett Dolan

(*Producer*) David Merrick

Ziegfeld Theatre   Broadway

February 16, 1964   72 performances

(*Stars*) Bert Lahr, John Davidson, Larry Blyden, Cathryn Damon

Theatre World 63–64, p. 83

Best Plays 63–64, pp. 325–26

America 110:465 Mr 28 '64

      Commonweal 79:723 Mr 13 '64

      New Yorker 40:106 F 29 '64

      Newsweek 63:56 Mr 2 '64

      Sat R 47:23 Mr 7 '64

      Time il 83:61 F 28 '64

New York Times 1964, F 17, 26:1

      New York Times 1964, Mr 20, 30:1

NYTC 1964:349

(*Published libretto*) NA

(*Published sheet music*) Commander

(*Original cast recording*) OP SPM Records CO–4636

      (Original Broadway Cast recorded live)

(*Agent/contact*)

Robert Emmett	Johnny Mercer Foundation	Ian McLellan
Dolan Estate	32107 Lindero Canyon Rd.,	Hunter
c/o ASCAP	Ste 222	c/o ASCAP
	Westlake Village, CA	
	91361	

(*Libretto*) NYPL RM3120, RM6431, RM6960, RM6963, RM8219;

      LC (Performing Arts Reading Room) ML50/.D64F72; LC Ian

      McLellan Hunter & Ring Lardner, Jr. 2Dec63 DU59016; same as

      (*Agent/contact*)

(*Music, Orchestrations*) Same as (*Agent/contact*)

FRANK MERRIWELL, OR HONOR CHALLENGED
(*Source*) *Frank Merriwell's School Days* (novel) by Burt L.
        Standish (Gilbert Patten)
(*Book*) Skip Redwine, Larry Frank & Heywood Gould
(*Lyrics*) Skip Redwine & Larry Frank
(*Music*) Skip Redwine & Larry Frank
(*Producer*) Sandy Farber, Stanley Barnett & Nate Friedman
Longacre Theatre   Broadway
April 24, 1971   1 performance
(*Stars*) NA
Theatre World 70–71, p. 46
Best Plays 70–71, pp. 314–15
New Yorker 47:94 My 1 '71
New York Times 1971, Ap 26, 40:1
        New York Times 1971, My 9, II, 1:1
NYTC 1971:296
(*Published libretto*) Samuel French, Inc., 1971
(*Published sheet music*) NA
(*Original cast recording*) NA
(*Agent/contact*) Samuel French, Inc.
(*Libretto, Orchestrations*) Same as (*Agent/contact*)
(*Music*) NYPL JPB 78–33; same as (*Agent/contact*)

FREE AND EASY
See *ST. LOUIS WOMAN*

GANTRY
(*Source*) *Elmer Gantry* (novel) by Sinclair Lewis
(*Book*) Peter Bellwood
(*Lyrics*) Fred Tobias
(*Music*) Stanley Lebowsky
(*Producer*) Joseph Cates & Jerry Schlossberg
George Abbott Theatre   Broadway
February 14, 1970   1 performance

(*Stars*) Rita Moreno, Robert Shaw
Theatre World 69–70, p. 38
Best Plays 69–70, p. 315–16
New Yorker 46:62+ F 21 '70
        Sat R 53:61 F 28 '70
New York Times 1970, F 16, 44:1
        New York Times 1970, S 6, II, 1:1
NYTC 1970:370
(*Published libretto*) NA
(*Published sheet music*) NA
(*Original cast recording*) NA
(*Agent/contact*)

Tobias/Lebowsky, Ltd.	Jerry Schlossberg
162 W. 56th Street	1431 Cromwell Avenue
New York, N.Y. 10019	Bronx, N.Y. 10452

(*Libretto*) NYPL RM5027; same as (*Agent/contact*)
(*Music, Orchestrations*) Same as (*Agent/contact*)

THE GAY LIFE*

(*Source*) *Anatol* (play) by Arthur Schnitzler
(*Book*) Fay & Michael Kanin
(*Lyrics*) Howard Dietz & Arthur Schwartz
(*Music*) Howard Dietz & Arthur Schwartz
(*Producer*) Kermit Bloomgarden

Sam S. Shubert Theatre	Broadway
November 18, 1961	113 performances

(*Stars*) Barbara Cook, Elizabeth Allen
Theatre World 61–62, p. 48
Best Plays 61–62, pp. 270–72
America 106:737 Mr 3 '62
        Dance Mag 36:13–4 Ja '62
        Life il 52:49–51 Ja 19 '62
        New Yorker 37:118 D 2 '61
        Newsweek 58:79 D 4 '61

Theatre Arts il 46:11–2 F '62
Time 78:64 D 1 '61
New York Times 1961, N 20, 38:1
NYTC 1961:168
(*Published libretto*) Samuel French, Inc., 1986, as *THE HIGH LIFE*
(*Published sheet music*) Harms
(*Original cast recording*) OP Capitol WAO/SWAO–1560
(*Agent/contact*) Samuel French, Inc.
(*Libretto*) NYPL NCOF+ 83–1026
(*Music, Orchestrations*) Same as (*Agent/contact*)

*Subsequently titled *THE HIGH LIFE*

GEORGY
(*Source*) *Georgy Girl* (novel) by Margaret Forster,
          (screenplay) by Margaret Forster & Peter Nichols
(*Book*) Tom Mankiewicz
(*Lyrics*) Carole Bayer
(*Music*) George Fischoff
(*Producer*) Fred Coe, Joseph Harris & Ira Bernstein
Winter Garden Theatre   Broadway
February 26, 1970   4 performances
(*Stars*) Stephen Elliott
Theatre World 69–70, p. 42
Best Plays 69–70, pp. 317–18
New Yorker 46:83 Mr 7 '70
New York Times 1970, F 15, II, 1:1
          New York Times 1970, F 27, 26:1
NYTC 1970:354
(*Published libretto*) NA
(*Published sheet music*) Screen Gems–Columbia Music
(*Original cast recording*) NA

(*Agent/contact*)

George Fischoff Music Co.	Tom Mankiewicz	Carole Bayer
61–45 98th Street, #4E	c/o DG, Inc.	Sager
Rego Park, N.Y. 11374		c/o DG, Inc.

(*Libretto*) NYPL NCOF+; same as (*Agent/contact*)

(*Music, Orchestrations*) Same as (*Agent/contact*)

GIGI

(*Source*) *Gigi* (screenplay) by Alan Jay Lerner, music by Frederick
    Loewe, adapted from *Gigi* (novel) by Colette

(*Book*) Alan Jay Lerner

(*Lyrics*) Alan Jay Lerner

(*Music*) Frederic Loewe

(*Producer*) Arnold Saint–Subber, California Civic Light
    Opera Association

Uris Theatre   Broadway

November 13, 1973   103 performances

(*Stars*) Alfred Drake, Daniel Massey, Maria Karnilova, Agnes Moorehead

Theatre World 73–74, p. 20

Best Plays 73–74, pp. 351–52

Nation 217:603 D 3 '73

   New Yorker 49:80 N 26 '73

   Newsweek il 82:113 N 26 '73

   Time il 102:79 N 26 '73

New York Times 1973, N 14, 39:1

   New York Times 1973, N 25, II, 1:4

NYTC 1973:190

(*Published libretto*) NA

(*Published sheet music*) Chappell

(*Original cast recording*) RCA ABL–1–0404

(*Agent/contact*) Tams–Witmark Music Library

(*Libretto*) NYPL RM7960; same as (*Agent/contact*)

(*Music, Orchestrations*) Same as (*Agent/contact*)

THE GIRL FROM NANTUCKET
(*Source*) Story (title unavailable) by Fred Thompson & Berne Giler
(*Book*) Paul Stamford & Harold M. Sherman*
(*Lyrics*) Kay Twomey
(*Music*) Jacques Belasco
(*Producer*) Henry Adrian
Adelphi Theatre   Broadway
November 8, 1945   12 performances
(*Stars*) Jane Kean
Theatre World 45–46, p. 28
Best Plays 45–46, pp. 403–4
NO CRIT AVAIL
New York Times 1945, N 9, 17:2
NYTC 1945:121
(*Published libretto*) NA
(*Published sheet music*) Chappell
(*Original cast recording*) NA
(*Agent/contact*)   Harold M. Sherman
                       c/o DG, Inc.
(*Libretto*) NYPL NCOF+; same as (*Agent/contact*)
(*Music, Orchestrations*) Same as (*Agent/contact*)

*In all publicity, Paul Stamford & Harold M. Sherman are given authorship
        credit; however, the manuscript/promptscript filed with NYPL Billy
        Rose Collection gives Berne Giler sole authorship credit

THE GIRL IN PINK TIGHTS
(*Source*) Original
(*Book*) Jerome Chodorov & Joseph Fields
(*Lyrics*) Leo Robin
(*Music*) Sigmund Romberg
(*Producer*) Shepard Traube & Anthony B. Farrell
Mark Hellinger Theatre   Broadway
March 5, 1954   115 performances
(*Stars*) Zizi Jeanmaire

Theatre World 53–54, p. 84

Best Plays 53–54, pp. 343–46

America 91:79 Ap 17 '54

   Cath World 179:149 My '54

   Commonweal 60:95–6 Ap 30 '54

   Life il 36:67–8+ Mr 29 '54

   Mlle il 38:124 Ap '54

   Mus Am 74:7 Je '54

   Nation 178:246 Mr 20 '54

   New Yorker 30:71 Mr 13 '54

   Newsweek il 43:63 Mr 15 '54

   Theatre Arts il 38:24–5 Ap '54

   Theatre Arts il 38:16–7 My '54

   Time 63:87 Mr 15 '54

New York Times 1954, Mr 6, 13:2

NYTC 1954:354

(*Published libretto*) NA

(*Published sheet music*) Chappell/Edwin H. Morris

(*Original cast recording*) OP Columbia ML/OL–4890, RE Columbia Special
   Products AOL–4890

(*Agent/contact*)

Shepard Traube	Sigmund Romberg Estate	Jerome Chodorov
168 W. 86th Street	c/o Mirose Agency, Inc.	c/o I.C.M.
New York, N.Y.	301 E. 69th St., #15B	40 W. 57th St.
10024	New York, N.Y. 10021	New York, N.Y.
	ATTN: Miriam Stern	10019
		ATTN: Mitch Douglas

Leo Robin	Joseph Fields Estate
c/o DG, Inc.	c/o Dramatists Play Service

(*Libretto, Music, Orchestrations*) Tams–Witmark Music Library;
   same as (*Agent/contact*)

A GIRL TO REMEMBER
See **FADE OUT–FADE IN**

THE GIRL WHO CAME TO SUPPER

(*Source*) *The Sleeping Prince* (play) by Terence Rattigan

(*Book*) Harry Kurnitz

(*Lyrics*) Noel Coward

(*Music*) Noel Coward

(*Producer*) Herman Levin

Broadway Theatre Broadway

December 8, 1963 112 performances

(*Stars*) Jose Ferrer, Florence Henderson, Tessie O'Shea

Theatre World 63–64, p. 58

Best Plays 63–64, pp. 315–16

America 110:26 Ja 4 '64

New Yorker 39:62 D 21 '63

Sat R 47:52 Ja 11 '64

Time 82:81 D 20 '63

Vogue 143:62 F 1 '64

New York Times 1963, D 9, 49:1

NYTC 1963:178

(*Published libretto*) NA

(*Published sheet music*) Chappell

(*Original cast recording*) OP Columbia KOL–6020/KOS–2420

(*Agent/contact*)

Noel Coward Estate Harry Kurnitz Estate

c/o Michael Imison c/o Charles Goldring

Playwrights, Ltd. 9044 Melrose Ave.,

150 W. 47th Street, #5F Ste #101

New York, N.Y. 10017 Los Angeles, CA 90069

(*Libretto, Music, Orchestrations*) Same as (*Agent/contact*)

THE GOLDEN APPLE

(*Source*) Original

(*Book*) John Latouche

(*Lyrics*) John Latouche

(*Music*) Jerome Moross

(*Producer*) Alfred De Liagre, Jr., Roger L. Stevens, T. Edward
        Hambleton & Norris Houghton
Alvin Theatre*   Broadway
April 20, 1954*   125 performances
(*Stars*) Kaye Ballard, Stephen Douglass, Portia Nelson
Theatre World 53–54, p. 96
Best Plays 53–54, pp. 346–47
America 91:24–5+ Ap 3 '54
        Cath World 179:148 My '54
        Commonweal 60:95 Ap 30 '54
        Commonweal 76:210 My 18 '62
        Harper 208:91–2 My '54
        Life il 36:163–4+ Ap 12 '54
        Mus Am il 74:7 Je '54
        Nation 178:265–6 Mr 27 '54
        New Yorker 30:60+ Mr 20 '54
        Sat R 37:23 Mr 27 '54
        Theatre Arts il 38:80 My '54
        Theatre Arts il 38:23 Je '54
        Theatre Arts il 38:22–5 Ag '54
        Theatre Arts il 46:59–61 Ap '62
        Time il 63:96+ Mr 22 '54
New York Times 1954, Mr 12, 15:2
        New York Times 1954, Mr 21, II, 1:1
        New York Times 1962, F 13, 38:2
NYTC 1954:346
(*Published libretto*) Random House, 1954; in *Theatre* (annual), 1954
(*Published sheet music*) Chappell
(*Original cast recording*) OP RCA LOC–1014, RE Elektra EKL–5000
(*Agent/contact*) Tams–Witmark Music Library
(*Libretto, Music, Orchestrations*) Same as (*Agent/contact*)

*Originally opened off–Broadway at the Phoenix Theatre 3/11/54
        before transferring on Broadway to the Alvin Theatre

GOLDILOCKS
(*Source*) Original
(*Book*) Walter & Jean Kerr
(*Lyrics*) Joan Ford, Walter & Jean Kerr
(*Music*) Leroy Anderson
(*Producer*) The Producers Theatre & Robert Whitehead
Lunt–Fontanne Theatre   Broadway
October 11, 1958   161 performances
(*Stars*) Elaine Stritch, Don Ameche
Theatre World 58–59, p. 16
Best Plays 58–59, pp. 294–95
America 100:255 N 22 '58
        Cath World 188:333 Ja '59
        Chr Cent 75:1338 N 19 '58
        Dance Mag il 32:16–7 N '58
        New Repub 139:22 O 27 '58
        New Yorker 34:55 O 18 '58
        Reporter 19:37–8 N 13 '58
        Theatre Arts il (p. 11) 42:12 D '58
        Time il 72:100 O 20 '58
        Vogue il 132:104 N 15 '58
New York Times 1958, O 13, 33:1
        New York Times 1958, O 19, II, 1:1
NYTC 1958:273
(*Published libretto*) Samuel French, Inc., 1958; Doubleday & Co.,
        Inc., 1959; in *Mary, Mary & Other Plays*, Crest Books, 1964
(*Published sheet music*) Ankerford Music/Mills Music
(*Original cast recording*) OP Columbia OL-5340/OS-2007, RE Columbia
        Special Products COS-2007
(*Agent/contact*) Samuel French, Inc.
(*Libretto*) NYPL NCOF+, RM2026, RM8362; same as (*Agent/contact*)
(*Music, Orchestrations*) Same as (*Agent/contact*)

*GOOD NEWS (revival)**

(*Source*) Original

(*Book*) Lawrence Schwab, Buddy de Sylva & Frank Mandel,
        adapted by Garry Marshall

(*Lyrics*) Buddy de Sylva, Lew Brown & Ray Henderson

(*Music*) Buddy de Sylva, Lew Brown & Ray Henderson

(*Producer*) Harry Rigby & Terry Allen Kramer

St. James Theatre   Broadway

December 23, 1974   16 performances

(*Stars*) Alice Faye, Stubby Kaye, John Payne/Gene Nelson**

Theatre World 74–75, p. 32

Best Plays 74–75, pp. 333–34

Nat R 26:819 Jl 19 '74

        New Yorker 50:50 Ja 6 '75

        Newsweek 85:64 Ja 6 '75

        Time 105:94 Ja 6 '75

New York Times 1974, D 24, 8:1

NYTC 1974:110

(*Published libretto*) Samuel French, Inc. [Original Broadway
        libretto; for Broadway Revival libretto, see (*Libretto*) below]

(*Published sheet music*) Chappell/Anne–Rachel

(*Original cast recording*) OP Unnamed label SA–101/4 (Broadway
        Revival Cast recorded live)

(*Agent/contact*) Samuel French, Inc./Tams–Witmark Music Library***

(*Libretto*) LC (Performing Arts Reading Room) ML50/.H5G7; Tams–Witmark
        Music Library

(*Music, Orchestrations*) Same as (*Agent/contact*)

*This revival included as it was substantially different from its
        original New York production

**Gene Nelson replaced John Payne in the leading role for Broadway opening

***Samuel French, Inc. makes available to all groups Original Broadway
        libretto, score and orchestrations; Tams–Witmark makes available
        to professional and semi–professional groups Broadway Revival
        libretto, score and orchestrations

GOODTIME CHARLEY

(*Source*) Original
(*Book*) Sidney Michaels
(*Lyrics*) Hal Hackady
(*Music*) Larry Grossman
(*Producer*) Max Brown & Byron Goldman, Robert Victor & Stone Widney

Palace Theatre   Broadway
March 3, 1975   104 performances

(*Stars*) Joel Grey, Ann Reinking
Theatre World 74–75, p. 42
Best Plays 74–75, pp. 341–42
America 132:246 Mr 29 '75
      Dance Mag 49:28+ My '75
      New Yorker 51:92 Mr 17 '75
      Time il 105:73 Mr 17 '75
New York Times 1975, Mr 4, 40:1
NYTC 1975:324
(*Published libretto*) Samuel French, Inc., 1986
(*Published sheet music*) Dramatis Music/Screen Gems–Columbia
(*Original cast recording*) OP RCA ARL-1-1001
(*Agent/contact*) Samuel French, Inc.
(*Libretto, Music, Orchestrations*) Same as (*Agent/contact*)

GOT TU GO DISCO

(*Source*) "Cinderella" (folk tale)
(*Book*) John Zodrow
(*Lyrics*) Kenny Lehman, Wayne Morrison, John Davis, Ray Chew,
      Nat Adderley, Jr., Thomas Jones, Steve Boston & Eugene Narmore
(*Music*) Betty Rowland & Jerry Powell
(*Producer*) Jerry Brandt, in association with Roy Rifkind,
      Julie Rifkind, Bill Spitalsky & WKTU–Radio 92

Minskoff Theatre   Broadway
June 25, 1979   8 performances

(*Stars*) Irene Cara
Theatre World 79–80, p. 12
Best Plays 79–80, pp. 356–57
NY 12:54–8 Je 25 '79
New York Times 1979, Je 26, III, 7:5
NYTC 1979:192
(*Published libretto*) NA
(*Published sheet music*) NA
(*Original cast recording*) NA
(*Agent/contact*)

John Zodrow	Ken Lehman
1297 Calle Las Trancas	950 E. 14th St., #3D
Thousand Oaks, CA 91360	Brooklyn, N.Y. 11230

(*Libretto*) LC John Zodrow 6Apr79 PAu–96–741; same as (*Agent/contact*)
(*Music, Orchestrations*) Same as (*Agent/contact*)

THE GRAND TOUR

(*Source*) *Jacobowsky and the Colonel (Jacobowsky und der Oberst)*
     (play) by Franz Werfel, as adapted by S.N. Behrman
(*Book*) Michael Stewart & Mark Bramble
(*Lyrics*) Jerry Herman
(*Music*) Jerry Herman
(*Producer*) James N. Nederlander, Diana Shumlin, Jack Schlissel,
     in association with Carole J. Shorenstein & Stewart F. Lane
Palace Theatre   Broadway
January 11, 1979   61 performances
(*Stars*) Joel Gray, Ron Holgate
Theatre World 78–79, p. 26
Best Plays 78–79, pp. 375–77
NY 12:119 Ja 29 '79
     Nation 228:156 F 10 '79
     New Leader 62:21–2 Ja 29 '79
     New Yorker 54:88 Ja 22 '79

Newsweek il 93:86 Ja 22 '79
Time il 113:84 Ja 22 '79
New York Times 1979, Ja 12, III, 3:1
New York Times 1979, Ja 21, II, 3:1
NYTC 1979:390
(Published libretto) Samuel French, Inc., 1980
(Published sheet music) MacMillan Performing Arts/G. Schirmer
(Original cast recording) OP Columbia JS–35761
(Agent/contact) Samuel French, Inc.
(Libretto, Music, Orchestrations) Same as (Agent/contact)

THE GRASS HARP*

(Source) The Grass Harp (novel and play) by Truman Capote
(Book) Kenward Elmslie
(Lyrics) Kenward Elmslie
(Music) Claibe Richardson
(Producer) Richard Barr, Charles Woodward & Michael Harvey

Martin Beck Theatre	Broadway
November 2, 1971	7 performances

(Stars) Barbara Cook, Karen Morrow
Theatre World 71–72, p. 19
Best Plays 71–72, pp. 320–21
America 125:427 N 20 '71
New Yorker 47:66 N 13 '71
New York Times 1971, N 3, 41:2
NYTC 1971:196
(Published libretto) Samuel French, Inc., 1973
(Published sheet music) Thackery Falls Music
(Original cast recording) Painted Smiles PS–1354
(Agent/contact) Samuel French, Inc.
(Libretto) NYPL RM4502, RM5028 as YELLOW DRUM, NCOF+ 82–774
(Music, Orchestrations) Same as (Agent/contact)

*Previously titled YELLOW DRUM

THE GREAT ADVENTURE
See *DARLING OF THE DAY*

GREAT TO BE ALIVE!
(*Source*) Original
(*Book*) Walter Bullock & Sylvia Regan
(*Lyrics*) Walter Bullock
(*Music*) Abraham Ellstein
(*Producer*) Vinton Freedley, Anderson Lawler & Russell Markert
Winter Garden Theatre   Broadway
March 23, 1950   52 performances
(*Stars*) Vivienne Segal
Theatre World 49–50, p. 94
Best Plays 49–50, p. 376
Cath World 171:149 My '50
        New Yorker 26:46+ Ap 1 '50
        Newsweek il 35:73 Ap 3 '50
        Theatre Arts il 34:18 My '50
        Time 55:51 Ap 3 '50
New York Times 1950, Mr 24, 28:2
NYTC 1950:324
(*Published libretto*) NA
(*Published sheet music*) Chappell
(*Original cast recording*) NA
(*Agent/contact*)
   Sylvia Regan Ellstein   Walter Bullock Estate
   55 E. 9th Street   c/o ASCAP
   New York, N.Y.   10003
(*Libretto*) NYPL NCOF+; LC Walter Bullock & Sylvia Regan Dunp. 2545;
        same as (*Agent/contact*)
(*Music, Orchestrations*) Same as (*Agent/contact*)

GREENWILLOW

(Source) *Greenwillow* (novel) by B.J. Chute

(Book) Lesser Samuels & Frank Loesser*

(Lyrics) Frank Loesser*

(Music) Frank Loesser*

(Producer) Robert A. Willey & Frank Productions, Inc.

Alvin Theatre   Broadway

March 8, 1960   97 performances

(Stars) Anthony Perkins, Pert Kelton

Theatre World 59–60, p. 76

Best Plays 59–60, pp. 327–28

Commonweal 72:16 Ap 1 '60

    New Yorker 36:117 Mr 19 '60

    Newsweek il 55:116 Mr 21 '60

    Time 75:74 Mr 21 '60

New York Times 1960, Mr 9, 38:1

    New York Times 1960, Mr 20, II, 1:1

    New York Times 1970, D 8, 60:1

NYTC 1960:325

(Published libretto) NA

(Published sheet music) Frank Music

(Original cast recording) OP RCA LOC/LSO–2001, RE Columbia

    Special Products P–13974

(Agent/contact)   Frank Loesser Estate

                  c/o Music Theatre International

(Libretto) NYPL RM1977A; same as (Agent/contact)

(Music, Orchestrations) Same as (Agent/contact)

*At press time, the Frank Loesser Estate was not interested in

    soliciting further productions of this property

HALLELUJAH, BABY!

(Source) Original

(Book) Arthur Laurents

(Lyrics) Betty Comden & Adolph Green

(Music) Jule Styne
(Producer) Albert W. Selden & Hal James, James C. Nusbaum &
        Harry Rigby
Martin Beck Theatre   Broadway
April 26, 1967   293 performances
(Stars) Leslie Uggams
Theatre World 66–67, pp. 60–1
Best Plays 66–67, pp. 391–92
America 116:879 Je 24 '67
        Chr Cent 84:1106 Ag 30 '67
        Commonweal 86:342–5 Je 9 '67
        Dance Mag 41:78–9 Je '67
        Nat R 19:976–7 S 5 '67
        New Yorker 43:150 My 6 '67
        Newsweek il 69:116 My 8 '67
        Sat R 50:66 My 13 '67
        Time il 89:58 My 5 '67
New York Times 1967, Ap 27, 51:1
        New York Times 1967, My 7, II, 1:1
NYTC 1967:312
(Published libretto) NA
(Published sheet music) Stratford/Chappell
(Original cast recording) OP Columbia KOL–6690/KOS–3090
(Agent/contact) Music Theatre International
(Libretto) NYPL RM2247, RM4479; same as *(Agent/contact)*
(Music, Orchestrations) Same as *(Agent/contact)*

HAMLET, A CONTEMPORARY MUSICAL
See *ROCKABYE HAMLET*

THE HAPPIEST GIRL IN THE WORLD
(Source) *Lysistrata* (play) by Aristophanes
(Book) Fred Saidy & Henry Myers
(Lyrics) E.Y. Harburg

(*Music*) Jacques Offenbach
(*Producer*) Lee Guber
Martin Beck Theatre   Broadway
April 3, 1961   96 performances
(*Stars*) Cyril Ritchard, Janice Rule
Theatre World 60–61, p. 80
Best Plays 60–61, pp. 332–33
America 105:410 Je 3 '61
      Dance Mag il 35:13–14 My '61
      Nation 192:358 Ap 22 '61
      Newsweek 57:69 Ap 17 '61
      New Yorker 37:76 Ap 15 '61
      Theatre Arts il (p. 30) 45:32 Je '61
      Time il 77:106+ Ap 14 '61
New York Times 1961, Ap 4, 42:1
NYTC 1961:314
(*Published libretto*) NA
(*Published sheet music*) Edlee Music Corp./Chappell
(*Original cast recording*) OP Columbia KOL–5650/KOS–2050
(*Agent/contact*) Tams–Witmark Music Library
(*Libretto*) NYPL RM5542, NCOF+; same as (*Agent/contact*)
(*Music, Orchestrations*) Same as (*Agent/contact*)

HAPPY AS LARRY

(*Source*) *Happy as Larry* (verse play) by Donagh MacDonagh
(*Book*) Donagh MacDonagh
(*Lyrics*) Donagh MacDonagh
(*Music*) Mischa & Wesley Portnoff
(*Producer*) Leonard Sillman
Coronet Theatre   Broadway
January 6, 1950   3 performances
(*Stars*) Burgess Meredith
Theatre World 49–50, p. 62
Best Plays 49–50, pp. 366–67
New Yorker 25:48 Ja 14 '50

Newsweek 35:74 Ja 16 '50

Theatre Arts il 34:14 Mr '50

Time 55:45 Ja 16 '50

NTY 1950, Ja 7, 11:2

New York Times 1961, Ap 26, 36:1

NYTC 1950:394

(*Published libretto*) NA

(*Published sheet music*) NA

(*Original cast recording*) NA

(*Agent/contact*)   Mischa Portnoff Estate

c/o ASCAP

(*Libretto, Music, Orchestrations*) Same as (*Agent/contact*)

HAPPY END

(*Source*) Original*

(*Book*) Elisabeth Hauptmann, adapted by Michael Feingold

(*Lyrics*) Bertolt Brecht, adapted by Michael Feingold

(*Music*) Kurt Weill

(*Producer*) Michael Harvey & The Chelsea Theater Center

Martin Beck Theatre**   Broadway**

May 7, 1977   75 performances

(*Stars*) Meryl Streep

Theatre World 76–77, p. 73

Best Plays 76–77, pp. 310–11

Nation 224:603 My 14 '77

New Yorker 53:59 My 9 '77

Newsweek 79:50 Ap 24 '72

Sat R 4:49 Je 11 '77

Time il 409:89 Je 13 '77

Time 105:58 Mr 10 '75

New York Times 1977, Ap 27, III, 17:3

New York Times 1977, Jl 1, III, 3:1

NYTC 1977:239

(*Published libretto*) Samuel French, Inc., 1982; Methuen, Inc., 1982

(*Published sheet music*) European–American Music Corp.

(*Original cast recording*) OP Columbia OL–5630/OS–2032 (Original Record
         Cast, in German)

(*Agent/contact*) Samuel French, Inc.

(*Libretto*) NYPL RM1102, RM1103, RM1104; LC (Performing Arts Reading
         Room) ML50/.W42H42 (Leo Kerz/Eric Bentley translation)

(*Music, Orchestrations*)   European–American Music Corp.

                                   11 West End Avenue

                                   Totowa, NJ   07512

*While *HAPPY END* was billed as an adaptation "from a short story
         by Dorothy Lane, " it is believed to be an original work by Bertolt
         Brecht & Elisabeth Hauptmann

**First produced in Berlin, 1929

HAPPY NEW YEAR

(*Source*) *Holiday* (play) by Philip Barry

(*Book*) Burt Shevelove

(*Lyrics*) Cole Porter, edited by Buster Davis*

(*Music*) Cole Porter, edited by Buster Davis*

(*Producer*) Leonard Soloway, Allan Francis, Hale Matthews &
         Marble Arch Productions

Morosco Theatre   Broadway

April 27, 1980   25 performances

(*Stars*) John McMartin

Theatre World 79–80, p. 58

Best Plays 79–80, pp. 391–92

Dance Mag 54:94 Jl '80

         NY 13:59–61 My 12 '80

         Time 115:83 My 12 '80

New York Times 1980, Ap 27, II, 1:4
        New York Times 1980, Ap 28, III, 3:1
NYTC 1980:272
(*Published libretto*) Samuel French, Inc., 1982
(*Published sheet music*) In *Music & Lyrics by Cole Porter*, 2 vols.,
        Chappell
(*Original cast recording*) NA
(*Agent/contact*) Samuel French, Inc.
(*Libretto*) NYPL RM6915
(*Music*) LC Burt Shevelove & The Cole Porter Musical and Literary Property
        Trusts 10Feb82 PA–134–791; same as (*Agent/contact*)
(*Orchestrations*) Same as (*Agent/contact*)

*Musical numbers interpolated by Buster Davis from existing
        Cole Porter material

THE HAPPY TIME
(*Source*) *The Happy Time* (collection) by Robert L. Fontaine (characters from)
(*Book*) N. Richard Nash
(*Lyrics*) Fred Ebb
(*Music*) John Kander
(*Producer*) David Merrick
Broadway Theatre   Broadway
January 18, 1968   286 performances
(*Stars*) Robert Goulet, David Wayne
Theatre World 67–68, p. 38
Best Plays 67–68, pp. 358–59
America 118:356 Mr 16 '68
        Dance Mag 42:27 Ap '68
        Nation 206:186+ F 5 '68
        New Yorker 43:84+ Ja 27 '68

Newsweek 71:76 Ja 29 '68
Sat R 51:45 F 3 '68
New York Times 1968, Ja 19, 32:2
New York Times 1968, Ja 28, II, 3:1
NYTC 1968:378
(*Published libretto*) Dramatic Publishing Company, 1969
(*Published sheet music*) Sunbeam/Valando
(*Original cast recording*) OP RCA LOC/LSO–1144
(*Agent/contact*) Dramatic Publishing Company
(*Libretto*) NYPL RM4424
(*Music, Orchestrations*) Same as (*Agent/contact*)

HAPPY TOWN

(*Source*) Original
(*Book*) Max Hampton*
(*Lyrics*) Harry M. Haldane*
(*Music*) Gordon Duffy & Paul Nassau*
(*Producer*) B & M Productions

Fifty–Fourth Street Theatre	Broadway
October 7, 1959	5 performances

(*Stars*) NA
Theatre World 59–60, p. 16
Best Plays 59–60, pp. 293–94
New Yorker 35:134 O 17 '59
New York Times 1959, O 8, 49:2
NYTC 1959:279
(*Published libretto*) NA
(*Published sheet music*) NA
(*Original cast recording*) NA

(*Agent/contact*)	Allan A. Buckhantz	Harry M. Haldane
	c/o Directors Guild	4714 Commons Drive, #2
	of America, Inc.	Annandale, VA 22003
	7950 W. Sunset Blvd.	
	Hollywood, CA 90046	

Gordon Duffy
P.O. Box #52
Pebble Beach, CA 93953
(*Libretto*) NYPL RM6861; LC (Performing Arts Reading Room)
ML50/.D8398H3; LC Allan A. Buckhantz & Harry M. Haldane
16Jun58 DU47438, 17Aug59 DU49553; same as (*Agent/contact*)
(*Music, Orchestrations*)
Gordon Duffy
P.O. Box #52
Pebble Beach, CA 93953

*In all publicity, Max Hampton is given sole authorship credit, Harry M.
Haldane sole lyricist credit and Gordon Duffy & Paul Nassau
composer credit; however, the manuscript/promptscript filed with
LC Performing Arts Reading Room gives Allan A. Buckhantz &
Harry Haldane authorship credit and Allan A. Buckhantz, Harry
Haldane & Gordon Duffy lyricist and composer credit

HARRY IV, PARTS 1 THRU 37
See *HURRY, HARRY*

HAZEL FLAGG
(*Source*) Stories (titles unavailable) by James Street; *Nothing Sacred*
(screenplay) by Ben Hecht
(*Book*) Ben Hecht
(*Lyrics*) Bob Hilliard
(*Music*) Jule Styne
(*Producer*) Jule Styne & Anthony B. Farrell
Mark Hellinger Theatre   Broadway
February 11, 1953   190 performances
(*Stars*) Helen Gallagher

Theatre World 52–53, p. 95
Best Plays 52–53, pp. 286–88
America 88:661 Mr 14 '53
      Cath World 177:70 Ap '53
      Commonweal 57:552 Mr 6 '53
      Dance Mag il 27:12–15+ Mr '53
      Life il 34:102–4+ Mr 9 '53
      Look il 17:20 Mr 24:53
      Nation 176:193 F 28 '53
      New Yorker 29:58 F 21 '53
      Newsweek il 41:62 F 23 '53
      Sat R 36:38 F 28 '53
      Theatre Arts 37:14–15 F '53
      Theatre Arts 37:15 My '53
      Time il 61:86 F 23 '53
New York Times 1953, F 12, 22:2
NYTC 1953:362
(*Published libretto*) NA
(*Published sheet music*) Chappell
(*Original cast recording*) OP RCA LOC–1010, RE RCA CBM1–2207
(*Agent/contact*) Tams-Witmark Music Library
(*Libretto*) NYPL NCOF+; LC (Performing Arts Reading Room)
      ML50/.S955H4; same as (*Agent/contact*)
(*Music, Orchestrations*) Same as (*Agent/contact*)

HEATHEN!*
(*Source*) Original
(*Book*) Robert Helpmann & Eaton Magoon, Jr.
(*Lyrics*) Eaton Magoon, Jr.
(*Music*) Eaton Magoon, Jr.
(*Producer*) Leonard J. Goldberg, Ken Gaston & R. Paul Woodville
Billy Rose Theatre   Broadway
May 21, 1972   1 performance
(*Stars*) Russ Thacker

Theatre World 71–72, p. 56

Best Plays 71–72, pp. 346–47

New Yorker 48:84 My 27 '72

New York Times 1972, My 22, 43:1

NYTC 1972:276

(*Published libretto*) NA

(*Published sheet music*) NA

(*Original cast recording*) OP Hawaiian Recording and Publishing HOS–101
    as *ALOHA* (1981 New Zealand Cast)

(*Agent/contact*)   Eaton Magoon, Jr.   Robert Helpmann

                    P.O. Box #2061   c/o DG, Inc.

                    Honolulu, HI 96805

(*Libretto*) LC Eaton Magoon, Jr. 25Jan65 DU62113 as *THANK HEAVEN
    FOR THE HEATHEN*, Eaton Magoon, Jr. 24Apr72 DU83499; same
    as (*Agent/contact*)

(*Music, Orchestrations*) Same as (*Agent/contact*)

*Previously titled *THANK HEAVEN FOR THE HEATHEN*;
    subsequently presented under the title *ALOHA*

HEAVEN ON EARTH

(*Source*) Original

(*Book*) Barry Trivers

(*Lyrics*) Barry Trivers

(*Music*) Jay Gorney

(*Producer*) Monte Proser, in association with Ned C. Litwack

New Century Theatre   Broadway

September 16, 1948   12 performances

(*Stars*) David Burns

Theatre World 48–49, p. 14

Best Plays 48–49, pp. 380–81

New Yorker 24:53 S 25 '48

    Newsweek 32:79 S 27 '48

New York Times 1948, S 17, 29:2
New York Times 1948, S 26, II, 1:1
NYTC 1948:240
(*Published libretto*) NA
(*Published sheet music*) Chappell
(*Original cast recording*) NA
(*Agent/contact*)   Jay Gorney   Barry Trivers Estate
                      270 West End Avenue   c/o ASCAP
                      New York, N.Y.   10023
(*Libretto*) LC Barry Trivers 1c 15Jan48 DU12394; same as (*Agent/contact*)
(*Music, Orchestrations*) Same as (*Agent/contact*)

HENRY, SWEET HENRY

(*Source*) *The World of Henry Orient* (novel) by Nora Johnson, (screenplay)
by Nora & Nunnally Johnson
(*Book*) Nunnally Johnson
(*Lyrics*) Bob Merrill
(*Music*) Bob Merrill
(*Producer*) Edward Specter & Norman Twain
Palace Theatre   Broadway
October 23, 1967   80 performances
(*Stars*) Don Ameche, Louise Lasser, Alice Playten
Theatre World 67–68, p. 23
Best Plays 67–68, pp. 347–48
America 117:624 N 18 '67
Newsweek 70:89A N 6 '67
Sat R 50:26 N 11 '67
New York Times 1967, O 24, 51:2
New York Times 1967, N 5, II, 3:1
New York Times 1967, D 22, 38:1
NYTC 1967:241
(*Published libretto*) Samuel French, Inc., 1969
(*Published sheet music*) Merrill Music Corp./Ampco

(*Original cast recording*) OP ABC Records SOC–4
(*Agent/contact*) Samuel French, Inc.
(*Libretto*) NYPL NCOF+
(*Music, Orchestrations*) Same as (*Agent/contact*)

HER FIRST ROMAN

(*Source*) *Caesar and Cleopatra* (play) by George Bernard Shaw
(*Book*) Ervin Drake
(*Lyrics*) Ervin Drake*
(*Music*) Ervin Drake*
(*Producer*) Joseph Cates, Harry Fownes, Warner Bros.–Seven Arts
Lunt–Fontanne Theatre   Broadway
October 20, 1968   17 performances
(*Stars*) Richard Kiley, Leslie Uggams
Theatre World 68–69, p. 24
Best Plays 68–69, pp. 386–87
New Yorker 44:139–40 O 26 '68
        Newsweek 72:118 N 4 '68
New York Times 1968, O 21, 53:3
        New York Times 1968, N 3, II, 1:1
NYTC 1968:200
(*Published libretto*) NA
(*Published sheet music*) W–7 Music Corp./Lindabet Music Corp.
(*Original cast recording*) OP SPM Records CO–7751 (Original Broadway Cast
        recorded live)
(*Agent/contact*)   Ervin Drake
                       c/o DG, Inc.
(*Libretto, Music, Orchestrations*) Same as (*Agent/contact*)

*Steven Suskin's *Show Tunes 1905–1985* credits three songs, "Caesar
        Is Wrong," "Old Gentleman" and "Ptolemy," lyrics by Sheldon
        Harnick, music by Jerry Bock

*HERE'S WHERE I BELONG**
(*Source*) *East of Eden* (novel) by John Steinbeck
(*Book*) Alex Gordon****
(*Lyrics*) Alfred Uhry
(*Music*) Robert Waldman
(*Producer*) Mitch Miller

Billy Rose Theatre	Broadway
March 3, 1968	1 performance

(*Stars*) James Coco
Theatre World 67–68, p. 49
Best Plays 67–68, pp. 365–66
New Yorker 44:132 Mr 9 '68
New York Times 1968, Mr 4, 32:1
NYTC 1968:331
(*Published libretto*) NA
(*Published sheet music*) United Artists Music Company
(*Original cast recording*) NA

(*Agent/contact*)	Alfred Uhry	Robert Waldman
	c/o DG, Inc.	c/o DG, Inc.

(*Libretto*) NYPL NCOF+; same as (*Agent/contact*)
(*Music, Orchestrations*) Same as (*Agent/contact*)

*Previously titled *EAST OF EDEN*

**In all publicity, Alex Gordon is given sole authorship credit; however,
        the manuscript/promptscript filed with NYPL Billy Rose
        Collection gives Terrence McNally sole authorship credit

THE HIGH LIFE
See *THE GAY LIFE*

A HISTORY OF THE AMERICAN FILM
(*Source*) Original
(*Book*) Christopher Durang
(*Lyrics*) Christopher Durang
(*Music*) Mel Marvin*
(*Producer*) Judith Gordon & Richard S. Bright
ANTA Theater   Broadway
March 30, 1978   21 performances
(*Stars*) NA
Theatre World 77–78, p. 41
Best Plays 77–78, pp. 368–70
Horizon il 21:25–31 Mr '78
          NY 11:100 Ap 17 '78
          Nation 226:443 Ap 15 '78
          New Repub 178:25 Ap 22 '78
          New Yorker 54:91–2 Ap 10 '78
          Newsweek 91:63 Ap 10 '78
          Sat R 5:42 My 27 '78
New York Times 1977, Mr 21, 41:1
          New York Times 1977, Mr 27, II, 4:4
          New York Times 1977, My 23, 22:1
          New York Times 1977, Je 5, II, 3:1
          New York Times 1978, Mr 31, III, 3:4
NYTC 1978:310
(*Published libretto*) Samuel French, Inc., 1978; Avon Books, 1978
(*Published sheet music*) NA
(*Original cast recording*) NA
(*Agent/contact*) Samuel French, Inc.
(*Libretto*) LC Christopher Durang & Mel Marvin 21Jun78 PAu–38–586
(*Music, Orchestrations*) Same as (*Agent/contact*)

*Music to Mr. Durang's lyrics has been written by other composers and
          performed in subsequent productions of the play

HIT THE TRAIL *
(*Source*) Original
(*Book*) Frank O'Neill
(*Lyrics*) Elizabeth Miele
(*Music*) Frederico Valerio
(*Producer*) Elizabeth Miele

Mark Hellinger Theatre	Broadway
December 2, 1954	4 performances

(*Stars*) Irra Petina, Robert Wright
Theatre World 54–55, p. 44
Best Plays 54–55, pp. 380–81
New Yorker 30:98 D 11 '54
        Theatre Arts il 39:16, 92 F '55
New York Times 1954, D 3 31:2
NYTC 1954:228
(*Published libretto*) NA
(*Published sheet music*) Chappell & Co. as *ON WITH THE SHOW!*
(*Original cast recording*) NA
(*Agent/contact*) NO CONT AVAIL
(*Libretto*) LC Elizabeth Miele, Frank O'Neill 6Aug54 DU37650 as
        ON WITH THE SHOW!; same as (*Agent/contact*)
(*Music, Orchestrations*) Same as (*Agent/contact*)

*Previously titled *ON WITH THE SHOW!*

HOLD IT!
(*Source*) Original
(*Book*) Matt Brooks & Art Arthur
(*Lyrics*) Sam Lerner
(*Music*) Gerald Marks
(*Producer*) Sammy Lambert

National Theatre	Broadway
May 5, 1948	46 performances

(*Stars*) Red Buttons

Theatre World 47–48, p. 110

Best Plays 47–48, pp. 402–3

New Yorker 24:48 My 15, '48

      Newsweek 31:89 My 17 '48

      Theatre Arts 32:14+ Je '48

New York Times 1948, My 6, 31:5

NYTC 1948:274

(*Published libretto*) NA

(*Published sheet music*) Sam Fox Pub. Comp.

(*Original cast recording*) NA

(*Agent/contact*) NO CONT AVAIL

(*Libretto, Music, Orchestrations*) Same as (*Agent/contact*)

HOLLYWOOD PINAFORE (OR THE LAD WHO LOVED A SALARY)

(*Source*) H.M.S. Pinafore (operetta) by W.S. Gilbert & Sir Arthur Sullivan

(*Book*) W.S. Gilbert, revised by George S. Kaufman

(*Lyrics*) W.S. Gilbert, revised by George S. Kaufman

(*Music*) Sir Arthur Sullivan

(*Producer*) Max Gordon, in association with Meyer Davis

Alvin Theatre   Broadway

May 31, 1945   52 performances

(*Stars*) Victor Moore, William Gaxton, Shirley Booth

Theatre World 44–45, pp. 96–7

Best Plays 44–45, pp. 434–35

Cath World 161:351 Jl '45

      Commonweal 42:213 Je 15 '45

      Nation 160:705 Je 23 '45

      New Yorker 21:38 Je 9 '45

      Newsweek il 25:93 Je 11 '45

      Sat R Lit il 28:24–5 Je 16 '45

      Theatre Arts 29:389 Jl '45

      Time il 45:58 Je 11 '45

New York Times 1945, Je 1, 20:1

New York Times 1945, Je 10, II, 1:1

New York Times 1945, Je 17, II, 4:5

NYTC 1945:203

(*Published libretto*) Condensed version in *By George*, St. Martin's
     Press, 1979

(*Published sheet music*) NA

(*Original cast recording*) NA

(*Agent/contact*)   George S. Kaufman Estate
                        c/o Samuel French, Inc.

(*Libretto, Music, Orchestrations*) Same as (*Agent/contact*)

HOME, SWEET HOMER*

(*Source*) *The Odyssey* (epic poem) by Homer

(*Book*) Roland Kibbee & Albert Marre

(*Lyrics*) Charles Burr

(*Music*) Mitch Leigh

(*Producer*) John F. Kennedy Center for the Performing Arts

Palace Theatre   Broadway

January 4, 1976   1 performance

(*Stars*) Yul Brynner, Joan Diener

Theatre World 75–76, p. 37

Best Plays 75–76, pp. 338–39

Time 104:54 D 30 '74

        New Yorker 51:55 Ja 12 '76

New York Times 1976, Ja 5, 36:1

NYTC 1976:398

(*Published libretto*) NA

(*Published sheet music*) NA (Andrew Scott, Inc. & Renleigh Music, Inc.)

(*Original cast recording*) NA

(*Agent/contact*)

Mitch Leigh   Albert Marre   Charles Burr Estate

c/o Music Makers, Inc.   c/o DG, Inc.   c/o BMI

200 Central Park South

New York, N.Y.   10019

(*Libretto, Music, Orchestrations*) Same as (*Agent/contact*)

*Previously presented under title **ODYSSEY**

HOT SPOT
(*Source*) Original
(*Book*) Jack Weinstock & Willie Gilbert
(*Lyrics*) Martin Charnin
(*Music*) Mary Rodgers
(*Producer*) Robert Fryer, Lawrence Carr & John Herman
Majestic Theatre   Broadway
April 19, 1963   43 performances
(*Stars*) Judy Holliday, Joseph Campanella, Conrad Bain
Theatre World 62–63, p. 92
Best Plays 62–63, pp. 306–7
Commonweal 78:225 My 17 '63
        New Yorker 39:82 Ap 27 '63
        Newsweek il 61:54 Ap 29 '63
        Theatre Arts il (p. 12) 47:66 Je '63
        Time il 81:58 Ap 26 '63
New York Times 1963, Ap 20, 17:2
NYTC 1963:336
(*Published libretto*) NA
(*Published sheet music*) Melrose Music Corp./Edwin H. Morris/
        Williamson Music
(*Original cast recording*) NA
(*Agent/contact*)

Robert Fryer	Martin Charnin	Mary Rodgers
Los Angeles Music Ctr	c/o DG, Inc.	c/o DG, Inc.
135 N. Grand Avenue		
Los Angeles, CA 90012		

Jack Weinstock Estate   William Gilbert Estate (ASCAP '71)
c/o Dorothy Griffith   c/o ASCAP
473 S.W. 28th Avenue
Delray Beach, FL 33445

(*Libretto, Orchestrations*) Same as (*Agent/contact*)

(*Music*) Institute for the American Musical; same as (*Agent/contact*)

HOUSE OF FLOWERS

(*Source*) Original

(*Book*) Truman Capote

(*Lyrics*) Truman Capote & Harold Arlen

(*Music*) Harold Arlen

(*Producer*) Arnold Saint–Subber

Alvin Theater   Broadway

December 30, 1954   165 performances

(*Stars*) Pearl Bailey, Diahann Carroll, Geoffrey Holder, Ray Walston,
       Alvin Ailey

Theatre World 54–55, p. 65

Best Plays 54–55, pp. 389–90

Cath World 180:469 Mr '55

       Commonweal 61:454-5 Ja 28 '55
       Dance Mag 42:28+ Ap '68
       Mlle 40:142 N '54
       Nation 180:106 Ja 29 '55
       New Yorker 30:62 Ja 8 '55
       Newsweek 45:62 Ja 10 '55
       Sat R 38:31 Ja 15 '55
       Theatre Arts il 39:30-1+ Ja '55
       Theatre Arts il 39:20-1, 90-1 Mr '55
       Time il 65:34 Ja 10 '55
       Time 91:75 F 9 '68
       Vogue 125:125 Ja '55

New York Times 1954, D 31, 11:2

New York Times 1968, Ja 29, 26:2

NYTC 1954:189

(*Published libretto*) Random House, 1968 (Off–Broadway Revival)*

(*Published sheet music*) Harwin Music Corp./Edwin H. Morris

(*Original cast recording*) OP Columbia ML/OL–4969, RE Columbia Special
Products COS–2320; OP United Artists UAS–5180 (Off–Broadway
Revival)

(*Agent/contact*)   Harold Arlen
c/o DG, Inc.

(*Libretto*) NYPL NCOF+; same as (*Agent/contact*)

(*Music, Orchestrations*) Same as (*Agent/contact*)

*HOUSE OF FLOWERS was revised and rewritten for 1968 off–Broadway
revival

HOW NOW, DOW JONES

(*Source*) Original

(*Book*) Max Shulman

(*Lyrics*) Carolyn Leigh

(*Music*) Elmer Bernstein

(*Producer*) David Merrick, Edwin H. Morris & Co.

Lunt–Fontanne Theatre   Broadway

December 7, 1967   221 performances

(*Stars*) Anthony Roberts, Brenda Vaccaro, Tommy Tune

Theatre World 67–68, p. 32

Best Plays 67–68, pp. 355–56

America 118:330 Mr 9 '68

Chr Cent 85:269 F 28 '68

Dance Mag 42:29+ F '68

Nation 206:28 Ja 1 '68

New Yorker 43:97 D 16 '67

Newsweek 70:94+ D 18 '67

New York Times 1967, D 8, 53:1
     New York Times 1967, D 22, 38:1
     New York Times 1967, D 24, II, 3:2
NYTC 1967:190
(*Published libretto*) Samuel French, Inc., 1968
(*Published sheet music*) Carwin Music/Edwin H. Morris
(*Original cast recording*) OP RCA LOC/LSO–1142
(*Agent/contact*) Samuel French, Inc.
(*Libretto, Music, Orchestrations*) Same as (*Agent/contact*)

HURRY, HARRY *
(*Source*) Original
(*Book*) Jeremiah Morris, Lee Kalcheim & Susan Perkis
(*Lyrics*) David Finkle
(*Music*) Bill Weeden
(*Producer*) Peter Grad
Ritz Theatre   Broadway
October 12, 1972   2 performances
(*Stars*) NA
Theatre World 72–73, p. 16
Best Plays 72–73, pp. 331–32
NO CRIT AVAIL
New York Times 1972, O 13, 33:1
NYTC 1972:220
(*Published libretto*) NA
(*Published sheet music*) NA (Cherry River Music Comp.)
(*Original cast recording*) NA
(*Agent/contact*)

Bill Weeden	David Finkle	Lee Kalcheim
312 W. 102nd Street	112 W. 78th Street	c/o DG, Inc.
New York, N.Y. 10025	New York, N.Y. 10024	

Susan Perkis
c/o DG, Inc.

(*Libretto, Music, Orchestrations*) Same as (*Agent/contact*)

*Previously presented off–off–Broadway under title *HARRY IV,
     PARTS 1 THRU 37*

I, ANASTASIA
See *ANYA*

I CAN GET IT FOR YOU WHOLESALE
(*Source*) *I Can Get It For You Wholesale* (novel) by Jerome Weidman
(*Book*) Jerome Weidman
(*Lyrics*) Harold Rome
(*Music*) Harold Rome
(*Producer*) David Merrick
Sam S. Shubert Theater   Broadway
March 22, 1962   300 performances
(*Stars*) Barbra Streisand, Elliott Gould
Theatre World 1961–62, pp. 86–7
Best Plays 61–62, pp. 294–95
Dance Mag il 36:18 My '62
          Life il 52:103–4+ My 18 '62
          Nation 194:338 Ap 14 '62
          Newsweek 59:58 Ap 2 '62
          Sat R 45:28 Ap 14 '62
          Theatre Arts 46:58+ My '62
          Time il 79:46 Mr 30 '62
New York Times 1962, Mr 23, 29:1
          New York Times 1962, Ap 8, II, 1:2
NYTC 1962:314
(*Published libretto*) Random House, 1962
(*Published sheet music*) Florence Music Co./Chappell

(*Original cast recording*) OP Columbia KOL–5780/KOS–2180, RE Columbia
      Special Products AKOS–2180
(*Agent/contact*) Tams–Witmark Music Library
(*Libretto*) NYPL NCOF+; same as (*Agent/contact*)
(*Music, Orchestrations*) Same as (*Agent/contact*)

I HAD A BALL
(*Source*) Original
(*Book*) Jerome Chodorov
(*Lyrics*) Jack Lawrence & Stan Freeman
(*Music*) Jack Lawrence & Stan Freeman
(*Producer*) Joseph Kipness

Martin Beck Theatre	Broadway
December 15, 1964	199 performances

(*Stars*) Buddy Hackett, Richard Kiley, Karen Morrow
Theatre World 64–65, p. 61
Best Plays 64–65, pp. 319–20
America 112:335 Mr 6 '65
      New Yorker 40:50 D 26 '64
      Newsweek il 64:57 D 28 '64
      Sat R 48:32 Ja 2 '65
      Time 84:62 D 25 '64
New York Times 1964, D 16, 50:1
NYTC 1964:107
(*Published libretto*) NA
(*Published sheet music*) Mesquite Music Corp./Edwin H. Morris
(*Original cast recording*) OP Mercury OCM–2210/OCS–6210
(*Agent/contact*)

Jack Lawrence	Stan Freeman	Jerome Chodorov
25 Sutton Place	c/o ASCAP	c/o I.C.M.
New York, N.Y. 10022		40 W. 57th Street
		New York, N.Y. 10019
		ATTN: Mitch Douglas

(*Libretto*) NYPL RM2068; LC (Performing Arts Reading Room)
    M150/.F852I22; same as (*Agent/contact*)
(*Music, Orchestrations*) Same as (*Agent/contact*)

I REMEMBER MAMA

(*Source*) *I Remember Mama* (play) by John Van Druten, based on *Mama's
    Bank Account* (collection) by Kathryn Forbes
(*Book*) Thomas Meehan
(*Lyrics*) Martin Charnin & Raymond Jessel
(*Music*) Richard Rodgers
(*Producer*) Alexander H. Cohen & Hildy Parks
Majestic Theatre   Broadway
May 31, 1979   108 performances
(*Stars*) Liv Ullmann, George Hearn
Theatre World 78–79, p. 52
Best Plays 78–79, pp. 392–94
NY 12:74 Je 18 '79
    New Leader 62:23–4 Je 18 '79
    New Yorker 55:79 Je 11 '79
    Newsweek il 93:75 Je 11 '79
    Time il 113:62 Je 11 '79
New York Times 1979, Je 1, III, 3:1
    New York Times 1979, Je 10, II, 5:1
NYTC 1979:227
(*Published libretto*) NA
(*Published sheet music*) Rememba Enterprises, Inc./MCA
(*Original cast recording*) Polydor 827337–1 (Original Record Cast)
(*Agent/contact*) Rodgers & Hammerstein Theatre Library
(*Libretto, Music, Orchestrations*) Same as (*Agent/contact*)

IF THE SHOE FITS*

(*Source*) "Cinderella" (folk tale)
(*Book*) June Carroll & Robert Duke

(*Lyrics*) June Carroll
(*Music*) David Raksin
(*Producer*) Leonard Sillman
Century Theatre   Broadway
December 5, 1946   21 performances
(*Stars*) NA
Theatre World 46–47, p. 56
Best Plays 46–47, pp. 446–47
New Yorker 22:64 D 14 '46
New York Times 1946, D 6, 29:4
NYTC 1946:226
(*Published libretto*) NA
(*Published sheet music*) Chappell
(*Original cast recording*) NA
(*Agent/contact*)   June Carroll   David Raksin
                       c/o DG, Inc.   c/o ASCAP
(*Libretto*) LC Leonard Sillman 19Oct45 DU96210 as **CINDERELLA '46**; same
        as (*Agent/contact*)
(*Music, Orchestrations*) Same as (*Agent/contact*)

*Previously titled **CINDERELLA '46**

*I'M SOLOMON***
(*Source*) *King Solomon and the Cobbler* (play) by Sammy Gronemann
(*Book*) Anne Croswell & Dan Almagor**
(*Lyrics*) Anne Croswell**
(*Music*) Ernest Gold
(*Producer*) Zvi Kolitz, Solomon Sagall & Abe Margolies
Mark Hellinger Theatre   Broadway
April 23, 1968   7 performances
(*Stars*) Dick Shawn, Karen Morrow
Theatre World 67–68, p. 57
Best Plays 67–68, pp. 372–73
New Yorker 44:129 My 4 '68

New York Times 1968, Ap 24, 51:1
NYTC 1968:297
(*Published libretto*) NA
(*Published sheet music*) NA (Edwin H. Morris)
(*Original cast recording*) NA
(*Agent/contact*)   Anne Croswell
                         c/o DG, Inc.
(*Libretto*) LC Erich Segal 2Oct67 DU69750; same as (*Agent/contact*)
(*Music, Orchestrations*)
                         Edwin H. Morris & Co.;   same as (*Agent/contact*)
                         c/o MPL Communications
                         39 W. 54th Street
                         New York, N.Y.   10019

*Previously titled *IN SOMEONE ELSE'S SANDALS*

**In all publicity, Anne Croswell & Dan Almagor are given authorship credit
    and Anne Croswell lyricist credit; however, LC copyright DU69750
    gives authorship and lyricist credit to Erich Segal & Sammy
    Gronemann

IN PERSON
See *THE ACT*

IN SOMEONE ELSE'S SANDALS
See *I'M SOLOMON*

*INNER CITY**
(*Source*) *The Inner City Mother Goose* (novel) by Eve Merriam
(*Book*) Eve Merriam & Tom O'Horgan
(*Lyrics*) Eve Merriam

(*Music*) Helen Miller
(*Producer*) Joseph Kipness, Lawrence Kasha, Tom O'Horgan & RCA Records
Ethel Barrymore Theatre   Broadway
December 19, 1971   97 performances
(*Stars*) Linda Hopkins
Theatre World 71–72, p. 27
Best Plays 71–72, p. 327
Nation 214:61 Ja 10 '72
New York Times 1971, D 20, 48:1
     New York Times 1971, D 26, II, 1:5
NYTC 1971:147
(*Published libretto*) NA
(*Published sheet music*) NA (Sunbeam Music, Inc.)
(*Original cast recording*) OP RCA LSO–1171
(*Agent/contact*) Samuel French, Inc. as *STREET DREAMS: THE INNER*
     CITY MUSICAL
(*Libretto, Music, Orchestrations*) Same as (*Agent/contact*)

*Subsequently titled *STREET DREAMS: THE INNER CITY MUSICAL*

IS THERE LIFE AFTER HIGH SCHOOL

(*Source*) *Is There Life After High School?* (novel) by Ralph Keyes
(*Book*) Jeffrey Kindley
(*Lyrics*) Craig Carnelia
(*Music*) Craig Carnelia
(*Producer*) Clive Davis, Francois de Menil, Harris Maslansky & Twentieth
     Century-Fox Theater Prods., Inc.
Ethel Barrymore Theater   Broadway
May 7, 1982   12 performances
(*Stars*) NA
Theatre World 81–82, p. 30
Best Plays 81–82, pp. 337–38

New Yorker 58:114–15 My 17 '82

New York Times 1981, Ap 26, XXIII, 24:4

New York Times 1982, illus, My 8, 17:1

NYTC 1982:295

(*Published libretto*) Samuel French, Inc., 1983

(*Published sheet music*) NA

(*Original cast recording*) Original Cast Records OC–8240

(*Agent/contact*) Samuel French, Inc.

(*Libretto, Orchestrations*) Same as (*Agent/contact*)

(*Music*) LC Craig Carnelia 10Feb83 PA–164–341; same as (*Agent/contact*)

IT'S A BIRD . . . IT'S A PLANE . . . IT'S SUPERMAN

(*Source*) "Superman" (comic strip) by Jerome Siegel & Joseph Shuster

(*Book*) David Newman & Robert Benton

(*Lyrics*) Lee Adams

(*Music*) Charles Strouse

(*Producer*) Harold Prince, in association with Ruth Mitchell

Alvin Theatre   Broadway

March 29, 1966   129 performances

(*Stars*) Bob Holiday, Jack Cassidy, Linda Lavin

Theatre World 65–66, p. 72

Best Plays 65–66, pp. 405–6

America 114:704 My 14 '66

Commonweal 84:156 Ap 22 '66

Dance Mag 40:25 My '66

Life il 60:25 Mr 11 '66

New Yorker 42:81 Ap 9 '66

Newsweek 67:94 Ap 11 '66

Sat R 49:62 Ap 16 '66

Time il 78:81 Ap 8 '66

New York Times 1966, Mr 30, 34:1

NYTC 1966:310

(*Published libretto*) Condensed version in *Best Plays of 1965–66*, Dodd,
      Mead, 1966

(*Published sheet music*) Morley Music Co./Edwin H. Morris

(*Original cast recording*) OP Columbia KOL–6570/KOS–2970, RE Columbia
      Special Products AKOS–2970

(*Agent/contact*) Tams–Witmark Music Library

(*Libretto*) NYPL NCOF+, RM4384; LC (Performing Arts Reading Room)
      ML50/S9355I82; same as (*Agent/contact*)

(*Music, Orchestrations*) Same as (*Agent/contact*)

IT'S SO NICE TO BE CIVILIZED

(*Source*) Original

(*Book*) Micki Grant

(*Lyrics*) Micki Grant

(*Music*) Micki Grant

(*Producer*) Jay Julien, Arnon Milchan & Larry Kalish

Martin Beck Theatre   Broadway

June 3, 1980   8 performances

(*Stars*) Mabel King, Vivian Reed

Theatre World 80–81, p. 9

Best Plays 80–81, p. 340

NO CRIT AVAIL

New York Times 1980, Je 4, III, 22:1

NYTC 1980:220

(*Published libretto*) Samuel French, Inc., 1982

(*Published sheet music*) NA

(*Original cast recording*) NA

(*Agent/contact*) Samuel French, Inc.

(*Libretto*) LC Micki Grant 3Oct79 PAu–142–856

(*Music*) LC Micki Grant 2Nov82 PA–161–862; same as (*Agent/contact*)

(*Orchestrations*) Same as (*Agent/contact*)

IZZY AND MOE
See *NOWHERE TO GO BUT UP*

*JACKPOT**
(*Source*) Original
(*Book*) Guy Bolton, Sidney Sheldon & Ben Roberts
(*Lyrics*) Howard Dietz & Vernon Duke
(*Music*) Howard Dietz & Vernon Duke
(*Producer*) Vinton Freedley
Alvin Theatre   Broadway
January 13, 1944   67 performances
(*Stars*) Nanette Fabray
NO ENTRY AVAIL
Best Plays 43–44, pp. 448–49
New Yorker 19:34+ Ja 22 '44
          Theatre Arts 28:142 Mr '44
New York Times 1944, Ja 14, 15:2
NYTC 1944:284
(*Published libretto*) NA
(*Published sheet music*) T.B. Harms
(*Original cast recording*) NA
(*Agent/contact*)

Guy Bolton Estate	Sidney Sheldon	Howard Dietz Estate
c/o Louis Aborn	c/o William Morrow & Co.	c/o ASCAP
Tams–Witmark	105 Madison Avenue	
Music Library	New York, N.Y. 10016	

Vernon Duke Estate
c/o Kay McCracken Duke
407 Vance Street
Pacific Palisades, CA   90272
(*Libretto*) NYPL RM4827; MCNY; same as (*Agent/contact*)
          Lee Davis
          Box #674/Pleasant Avenue
          Westhampton, N.Y.   11977

(*Music, Orchestrations*) Same as (*Agent/contact*)

*Previously titled *BLIND DATE*

JENNIE

(*Source*) *Laurette* (biography) by Marguerite Courtney
(*Book*) Arnold Schulman
(*Lyrics*) Howard Dietz & Arthur Schwartz
(*Music*) Howard Dietz & Arthur Schwartz
(*Producer*) Cheryl Crawford & Richard Halliday
Majestic Theatre   Broadway
October 17, 1963   82 performances
(*Stars*) Mary Martin
Theatre World 63–64, p. 35
Best Plays 63–64, pp. 308–10
America 109:644 N 16 '63
        New Yorker 39:113 O 26 '63
        Newsweek 62:91 O 28 '63
        Sat R 46:18 N 2 '63
        Theatre Arts il 48:67 Ja '64
        Time il 82:75 O 25 '63
New York Times 1963, O 18, 35:2
NYTC 1963:234
(*Published libretto*) NA
(*Published sheet music*) Harms, Inc.
(*Original cast recording*) OP RCA LOC/LSO–1083
(*Agent/contact*)

Arnold Schulman	Howard Dietz Estate	Arthur Schwartz Estate
c/o DG, Inc.	c/o ASCAP	c/o Samuel French, Inc.

(*Libretto, Music, Orchestrations*) MCNY; same as (*Agent/contact*)

JIMMY

(*Source*) *Beau James* (biography) by Gene Fowler, (screenplay) by
    Jack Rose & Melville Shavelson
(*Book*) Melville Shavelson
(*Lyrics*) Bill & Patti Jacob
(*Music*) Bill & Patti Jacob
(*Producer*) Jack L. Warner & Don Saxon
Winter Garden Theatre   Broadway
October 23, 1969   84 performances
(*Stars*) Frank Gorshin, Anita Gillette
Theatre World 69–70, p. 18
Best Plays 69–70, pp. 302–3
America 121:544–5 N 29 '69
        Commonweal 91:382–3 D 26 '69
        New Yorker 45:128 N '69
        Newsweek il 74:94 N 3 '64
New York Times 1969, O 24, 38:1
        New York Times 1969, N 9, II, 1:1
NYTC 1969:218
(*Published libretto*) NA
(*Published sheet music*) Riverside Drive Music/TRO
(*Original cast recording*) OP RCA LSO–1162
(*Agent/contact*)
    Shannon Shor   Melville Shavelson
    55 Central Park West   11947 Sunshine Terrace
    New York, N.Y. 10023   Studio City, CA 91604
(*Libretto*) NYPL RM4430; same as (*Agent/contact*)
(*Music, Orchestrations*) Same as (*Agent/contact*)

JOLLYANNA
See *FLAHOOLEY*

JOTHAM VALLEY
(*Source*) Original
(*Book*) Cecil Broadhurst
(*Lyrics*) Cecil Broadhurst
(*Music*) Cecil Broadhurst, Frances Hadden & Will Reed
(*Producer*) Moral Re–Armament (Howard Reynolds & Lena Ashwell)
Forty–Eighth Street Theatre/Coronet Theatre*   Broadway
February 6, 1951   31 performances
(*Stars*) NA
Theatre World 50–51, p. 81
NO ENTRY AVAIL
Cath World 173:70 Ap '51
New York Times 1951, F 7, 37:2
NO CRIT AVAIL
(*Published libretto*) NA
(*Published sheet music*) Moral Re–Armament, Inc.
(*Original cast recording*) NA
(*Agent/contact*)   Cecil Broadhurst
                         c/o ASCAP
(*Libretto*) LC Cecil Broadhurst, Moral Re–Armament, Inc. 22Jan51 DU26536;
        same as (*Agent/contact*)
(*Music, Orchestrations*) Same as (*Agent/contact*)

*Transferred to Coronet Theatre 2/19/51

A JOYFUL NOISE
(*Source*) *The Insolent Breed* (novel) by Borden Deal
(*Book*) Edward Padula
(*Lyrics*) Oscar Brand & Paul Nassau
(*Music*) Oscar Brand & Paul Nassau
(*Producer*) Edward Padula, Slade Brown & Sid Bernstein
Mark Hellinger Theatre   Broadway

December 15, 1966   12 performances

(*Stars*) John Raitt, Susan Watson, Karen Morrow, Tommy Tune (chorus)

Theatre World 66–67, p. 38

Best Plays 66–67, pp. 376–77

New Yorker 42:45 D 24 '66

     Newsweek 68:45 D 26 '66

     Dance Mag 41:23 F '67

New York Times 1966, D 16, 57:1

NYTC 1966:202

(*Published libretto*) NA

(*Published sheet music*) Churchill Music/TRO

(*Original cast recording*) NA

(*Agent/contact*)   Edward Padula   Oscar Brand

                  159 W. 53rd Street   c/o DG, Inc.

                  New York, N.Y.   10019

(*Libretto*) NYPL NCOF+, RM4414, RM4487; same as (*Agent/contact*)

(*Music, Orchestrations*) Same as (*Agent/contact*)

*JUNO**

(*Source*) *Juno and the Paycock* (play) by Sean O'Casey

(*Book*) Joseph Stein

(*Lyrics*) Marc Blitzstein

(*Music*) Marc Blitzstein

(*Producer*) The Playwright's Company, Oliver Smith & Oliver Rea

Winter Garden Theatre   Broadway

March 9, 1959   16 performances

(*Stars*) Shirley Booth, Melvyn Douglas

Theatre World 58–59, p. 98

Best Plays 58–59, pp. 326–27

Dance Mag 33:22 Ap '59

     New Repub 140:20 Mr 30 '59

     New Yorker 35:97 Mr 21 '59

     Newsweek 53:76 Mr 23 '59

     Theatre Arts 43:65–6 My '59

Time 73:60 Mr 23 '59

New York Times 1959, Mr 10, 41:1

New York Times 1959, Mr 15, II, 1:1

NYTC 1959:351

(*Published libretto*) NA

(*Published sheet music*) Chappell

(*Original cast recording*) OP Columbia OL–5380/OS–2013, RE Columbia
Special Products COS–2013

(*Agent/contact*) Joseph Stein Marc Blitzstein Estate
  c/o DG, Inc. c/o ASCAP

(*Libretto*) NYPL RM269, NCOF+; NCOF+ 77–426 as *DAARLIN' JUNO*;
Samuel French, Inc.; same as (*Agent/contact*)

(*Music, Orchestrations*) Samuel French, Inc.; same as (*Agent/contact*)

*Previously titled *DAARLIN' JUNO*

KEAN

(*Source*) *Kean* (play) by Jean–Paul Sartre, based on *Kean, ou Désordre
et Génie* (play) by Alexandre Dumas, père

(*Book*) Peter Stone

(*Lyrics*) Robert Wright & George Forrest

(*Music*) Robert Wright & George Forrest

(*Producer*) Robert Lantz

Broadway Theatre Broadway

November 2, 1961 92 performances

(*Stars*) Alfred Drake

Theatre World 61–62, p. 45

Best Plays 61–62, pp. 268–70

Commonweal 75:389 Ja 5 '62

Dance Mag il 35:23 D '61

Nation 193:438 N 25 '61

New Yorker 37:117 N 11 '61

Newsweek 58:94 N 13 '61

Theatre Arts il 45:17–24 D '61

Theatre Arts il 46:11–12 Ja '62

Time 78:66 N 10 '61

New York Times 1961, N 3, 28:2

New York Times 1961, N 12, II, 1:1

NYTC 1961:180

(*Published libretto*) NA

(*Published sheet music*) Express Music/Frank Distrib. Corp.

(*Original cast recording*) OP Columbia KOL–5720/KOS–2120

(*Agent/contact*)

Peter Stone	Robert Wright & George Forrest
c/o DG, Inc.	c/o DG, Inc.

(*Libretto*) NYPL NCOF+; same as (*Agent/contact*)

(*Music, Orchestrations*) Same as (*Agent/contact*)

*KELLY**

(*Source*) Original

(*Book*) Eddie Lawrence

(*Lyrics*) Eddie Lawrence

(*Music*) Moose Charlap

(*Producer*) David Susskind, David Melnick & Joseph E. Levine

Broadhurst Theatre Broadway

February 6, 1965   1 performance

(*Stars*) Don Francks, Anita Gillette, Jessie White

Theatre World 64–65, p. 72

Best Plays 64–65, pp. 325–26

New Yorker 40:76 F 13 '65

Sat Eve Post il 238:32–4+ Ap 24 '65

Time 85:64 F 19 '65

New York Times 1965, F 8, 28:2

NYTC 1965:382

(*Published libretto*) NA

(*Published sheet music*) Chappell/Thomason Music
(*Original cast recording*) Original Cast Records OC–8025 (Original Demo
        Recording)
(*Agent/contact*)   Eddie Lawrence   Moose Charlap Estate
                          435 E. 57th Street   c/o Sandra Charlap
                          New York, N.Y.   10022   40 E. 62nd Street
                                                      New York, N.Y.   10021
(*Libretto*) NYPL NCOF+, RM502z; same as (*Agent/contact*)
(*Music, Orchestrations*) Same as (*Agent/contact*)

*Previously titled *NEVER GO THERE ANYMORE*

KING OF HEARTS
(*Source*) *King of Hearts* (*Le Roi de Coeur*) (screenplay) by Philippe
        de Broca, Maurice Bressy & Daniel Boulanger
(*Book*) Steve Tesich/Joseph Stein*
(*Lyrics*) Jacob Brackman
(*Music*) Peter Link
(*Producer*) Joseph Kipness, Patty Grubman & Jerome Minskoff
Minskoff Theatre   Broadway
October 22, 1978   48 performances
(*Stars*) Millicent Martin
Theatre World 78–79, p. 16
Best Plays 78–79, pp. 368–69
NY 11:134 N 6 '78
        New Yorker 54:131 O 30 '78
        Newsweek il 92:92 N 6 '78
New York Times 1978, Ag 8, III, 3:1
        New York Times 1978, O 24, p. 58
        New York Times 1978, N 6, 54:3
        New York Times 1978, N 21, III, 9:1
NYTC 1978:200
(*Published libretto*) NA

(*Published sheet music*) NA (Colgems–EMI Music, Inc.)

(*Original cast recording*) Original Cast Records OC–8028

(*Agent/contact*)   Peter Link

                         c/o On Broadway Productions

                         400 W. 43rd Street, #38D

                         New York, N.Y.   10036

(*Libretto, Orchestrations*) Same as (*Agent/contact*)

(*Music*) LC Colgems–EMI Music, Inc. 16Nov78 PAu–69–676; same as (*Agent/
     contact*)

*Steve Tesich was replaced by Joseph Stein as book writer

KING OF SCHNORRERS*

(*Source*) *The King of Schnorrers* (novella) by Israel Zangwill

(*Book*) Judd Woldin**

(*Lyrics*) Judd Woldin**

(*Music*) Judd Woldin**

(*Producer*) Eric Krebs & Sam Landis

Playhouse Theatre***   Broadway

November 28, 1979***   63 performances

(*Stars*) NA

Theatre World 79–80, p. 92

Best Plays 79–80, pp. 373–75

NO CRIT AVAIL

New York Times 1979, O 12, III, 5:5

     New York Times 1979, N 29, III, 17:5

NYTC 1979:80

(*Published libretto*) Samuel French, Inc., 1982, as **PETTICOAT LANE**

(*Published sheet music*) Alaiyo Music

(*Original cast recording*) NA

(*Agent/contact*) Samuel French, Inc.

(*Libretto*) NYPL RM6837; LC Judd Wolden 19Dec77 DU106832, 18Oct78
     PAu–79–248.

(*Music, Orchestrations*) Same as (*Agent/contact*)

*Previously presented under title *PETTYCOAT LANE*; subsequently
     titled *PETTICOAT LANE*; subsequently presented off–Broadway
     under title *TATTERDEMALION*

**In all publicity, Judd Woldin is given sole authorship credit; however,
     the manuscript/promptscript filed with NYPL Billy Rose Collection
     gives Paul Avila Mayer sole authorship credit, Shimon Wincelberg &
     Diana Lampert lyricist credit and Bernard Herrman sole composer
     credit

***Originally opened off–Broadway at the Harold Clurman Theater 10/9/79
     before transferring on Broadway to the Playhouse Theatre

KRONBORG
See *ROCKABYE HAMLET*

KWAMINA
(*Source*) Original
(*Book*) Robert Alan Aurthur
(*Lyrics*) Richard Adler
(*Music*) Richard Adler
(*Producer*) Alfred de Liagre, Jr.
Fifty–Fourth Street Theatre   Broadway
October 23, 1961   32 performances
(*Stars*) Sally Ann Howes, Brock Peters, Robert Guillaume
Theatre World 61–62, p. 36
Best Plays 61–62, pp. 264–66
America 106:257 N 18 '61
       Dance Mag 35:23 D '61

New Repub 145:23 N 6 '61

New Yorker 37:126 N 4 '61

Newsweek 58:69 N 6 '61

Sat R 44:39 N 18 '61

Theatre Arts 46:13–14 Ja '62

Time 78:44 N 3 '61

New York Times 1961, O 24, 42:1

New York Times 1961, N 12, II, 1:1

NYTC 1961:206

(*Published libretto*) NA

(*Published sheet music*) Sahara Music/Chappell

(*Original cast recording*) OP Capitol WAO/SWAO–1645

(*Agent/contact*)   Richard Adler

c/o DG, Inc.

(*Libretto, Music, Orchestrations*) Same as (*Agent/contact*)

*LA GROSSE VALISE**

(*Source*) Original

(*Book*) Robert Dhery

(*Lyrics*) Harold Rome

(*Music*) Gerard Calvi

(*Producer*) Joseph Kipness & Arthur Lesser

Fifty–Fourth Street Threatre   Broadway

December 14, 1965   7 performances

(*Stars*) NA

Theatre World 65–66, p. 45

Best Plays 65–66, pp. 391–92

Dance Mag 40:14–5+ F '66

New Yorker 41:50 D 25 '65

New York Times 1965, D 15, 52:1

NYTC 1965:218

(*Published libretto*) NA

(*Published sheet music*) Chappell

(*Original cast recording*) OP Vogue(F) LD–593–30 (Original French

Cast) as *LA GROSSE VALSE*

(*Agent/contact*)   Harold Rome
                         c/o DG, Inc.
(*Libretto*) LC Joseph Fields 29Dec65 DU64643, 29Dec65 DU64645;
        same as (*Agent/contact*)
(*Music, Orchestrations*) Same as (*Agent/contact*)

*Previously presented under title *LA GROSSE VALSE*

LA GROSSE VALSE
See *LA GROSSE VALISE*

LA STRADA
(*Source*) *La Strada* (screenplay) by Federico Fellini, Ennio Flaiano &
        Tullio Pinelli
(*Book*) Charles K. Peck, Jr.
(*Lyrics*) Lionel Bart/additional material by Martin Charnin & Elliott
        Lawrence*
(*Music*) Lionel Bart/additional material by Martin Charnin & Elliott
        Lawrence*
(*Producer*) Charles K. Peck, Jr. & Canyon Productions, Inc.
Lunt–Fontanne Theatre   Broadway
December 14, 1969   1 performance
(*Stars*) Bernadette Peters, Larry Kert
Theatre World 69–70, p. 25
Best Plays 69–70, pp. 308–9
New Yorker 45:57 D 20 '69
New York Times 1969, D 15, 63:1
NYTC 1969:158
(*Published libretto*) NA
(*Published sheet music*) NA (United Artists Music, Ltd.)
(*Original cast recording*) NA

(*Agent/contact*)   Lionel Bart**   Martin Charnin
                      c/o MacNaughton Lowe   c/o DG, Inc.
                         Representation, Ltd.
                      194 Old Brompton Road
                      London SW5 OAS, England

(*Libretto, Orchestrations*) Same as (*Agent/contact*)

(*Music*) LC United Artists Music, Ltd. 16Oct68 EU79532; same as
        (*Agent/contact*)

*Program note issued opening night, "At this performance, additional
    music and lyrics by Martin Charnin & Elliott Lawrence"

**At press time, Mr. Bart was not interested in soliciting further
    productions of this property

A LADY SAYS YES

(*Source*) Original

(*Book*) Clayton Ashley (Maxwell Maltz)

(*Lyrics*) Stanley Adams

(*Music*) Fred Spielman & Arthur Gershwin

(*Producer*) J.J. Shubert, in association with Clayton Ashley

Broadhurst Theatre Broadway

January 10, 1945   87 performances

(*Stars*) Jack Albertson

Theatre World 44–45, p. 66

Best Plays 44–45, pp. 409–10

NO CRIT AVAIL

New York Times 1945, Ja 11, 18:5

NYTC 1945:294

(*Published libretto*) NA

(*Published sheet music*) Grand Music Corp.

(*Original cast recording*) NA

(*Agent/contact*)

| Stanley Adams | Fred Spielman | Arthur Gershwin Estate |
| c/o ASCAP | c/o ASCAP | c/o ASCAP |

The Shubert Organization
234 W. 44th Street
New York, N.Y.   10036
(*Libretto, Music, Orchestrations*) Same as (*Agent/contact*)

LET IT RIDE!

(*Source*) *Three Men on a Horse** (play) by John Cecil Holm & George Abbott
(*Book*) Abram S. Ginnes, with additional material by Ronny Graham
(*Lyrics*) Jay Livingston & Ray Evans
(*Music*) Jay Livingston & Ray Evans
(*Producer*) Joel Spector

Eugene O'Neill Theatre   Broadway
October 12, 1961   68 performances

(*Stars*) George Gobel
Theatre World 61–62, p. 24
Best Plays 61–62, pp. 260–61
Commonweal 75:154 N 3 '61
        Dance Mag 35:22 D '61
        New Yorker 37:129 O 21 '61
        Theatre Arts 45:13 D '61
        Time 78:64 O 20 '61
New York Times 1961, O 13, 27:4
NYTC 1961:230
(*Published libretto*) NA
(*Published sheet music*) G. Schirmer, Inc.
(*Original cast recording*) OP RCA LOC/LSO–1064
(*Agent/contact*)   Jay Livingston & Ray Evans
                      c/o Edward Traubner
                      1849 Sawtelle Blvd.
                      Los Angeles, CA   90025

(*Libretto, Music, Orchestrations*)

Jay Livingston	Ray Evans
c/o DG, Inc.	c/o DG, Inc.

Three Men on a Horse had previously been musicalized on Broadway in 1941 as *BANJO EYES* by Joe Quillan & Izzy Elinson, lyrics by John Latouche & Harold Adamson, music by Vernon Duke, and starring Eddie Cantor

THE LIAR

(*Source*) "The Liar" (commedia dell'arte scenario) by Carlo Goldoni
(*Book*) Edward Eager & Alfred Drake
(*Lyrics*) Edward Eager
(*Music*) John Mundy
(*Producer*) Dorothy Willard & Thomas Hammond

Broadhurst Theatre	Broadway
May 18, 1950	12 performances

(*Stars*) Martin Balsam, Walter Matthau (chorus roles)
Theatre World 49–50, p. 108
Best Plays 49–50, p. 380
CS Mon Mag p. 6 My 27 '50
      New Yorker 26:49 My 27 '50
      Newsweek il 35:69 My 29 '50
      Theatre Arts il 34:17 Jl '50
New York Times 1950, My 19, 30:2
NYTC 1950:296
(*Published libretto*) NA
(*Published sheet music*) Chappell
(*Original cast recording*) NA
(*Agent/contact*)

Alfred Drake	Edward Eager Estate	John Mundy Estate
c/o DG, Inc.	c/o AGAC	c/o ASCAP

(*Libretto*) NYPL NCOF+; same as (*Agent/contact*)
(*Music*) NYPL MNZ–Amer/MsB; same as (*Agent/contact*)
(*Orchestrations*) Same as (*Agent/contact*)

THE LIEUTENANT
(*Source*) Original
(*Book*) Gene Curty, Nitra Scharfman & Chuck Strand
(*Lyrics*) Gene Curty, Nitra Scharfman & Chuck Strand
(*Music*) Gene Curty, Nitra Scharfman & Chuck Strand
(*Producer*) Joseph S. Kutrzeba & Spofford J. Beadle
Lyceum Theatre   Broadway
March 9, 1975   9 performances
(*Stars*) NA
Theatre World 74–75, p. 44
Best Plays 74–75, pp. 342–43
America 132:247 Mr 29 '75
New York Times 1975, Mr 10, 42:1
NYTC 1975:314
(*Published libretto*) NA
(*Published sheet music*) NA
(*Original cast recording*) OP Unnamed label, unnumbered
(*Agent/contact*)

Chuck Strand	Nitra Schafrman	Gene Curty
22 Suydam Drive	c/o DG, Inc.	c/o ASCAP
Melville, N.Y. 11747		

(*Libretto*) LC Charles G. Strand, Eugene P. Curty & Nitra Scharfman
        1Nov74 DU92210; same as (*Agent/contact*)
(*Music, Orchestrations*) Same as (*Agent/contact*)

LITTLE JOHNNY JONES (revival)*
(*Source*) Original
(*Book*) George M. Cohan, adapted by Alfred Uhry
(*Lyrics*) George M. Cohan
(*Music*) George M. Cohan
(*Producer*) James M. Nederlander, Steven Leber, David Krebs & John F.
        Kennedy Center

Alvin Theatre   Broadway
March 21, 1982   1 performance
(*Stars*) Donny Osmond
Theatre World 81–82, p. 26
Best Plays 81–82, pp. 334–35
People 17:95–7 F 1 '82
New York Times 1982, Mr 22, III, 12:3
NYTC 1982:330
(*Published libretto*) NA
(*Published sheet music*) Vogel/Cohan Pub. Comp. (Original Broadway
          production)
(*Original cast recording*) NA
(*Agent/contact*) Tams–Witmark Music Library
(*Libretto*) NYPL NCOF+ 83–1503; same as (*Agent/contact*)
(*Music, Orchestrations*) Same as (*Agent/contact*)

*This revival included as it was substantially different from its original
     New York production

*LITTLE ME**
(*Source*) *Little Me* (novel) by Patrick Dennis
(*Book*) Neil Simon
(*Lyrics*) Carolyn Leigh
(*Music*) Cy Coleman
(*Producer*) Cy Feuer & Ernest H. Martin
Lunt–Fontanne Theatre   Broadway
November 17, 1962   257 performances
(*Stars*) Sid Caesar
Theatre World 62–63, p. 34–5
Best Plays 62–63, pp. 287–88
America 107:1258 D 15 '62
          Commonweal 77:280 D 7 '62
          Dance Mag il 37:24+ Ja '63

Life il 53:113–15 N 30 '62

Nation 195:411 D 8 '62

NY 15:57 F 1 '81

NY Times Mag il p. 75–6 N 4 '62

New Leader 65:22 F 8 '82

New Yorker 38:118+ D 1 '62

New Yorker 57:114 F 1 '82

Newsweek il 60:51–4 N 26 '62

Newsweek il 99:77 F 1 '82

Reporter 27:43–4 D 20 '62

Sat R 45:51 D 8 '62

Theatre Arts il 46:17–19+ N '62

Theatre Arts il 47:12 Ja '63

Time il 80:53 N 30 '62

Time 119:65 F 1 '82

New York Times 1962, O 10, 58:2

New York Times 1962, N 19, 41:3

New York Times 1962, D 2, II, 1:1

New York Times 1982, illus, Ja 22, III, 3:1

New York Times 1982, Ja 31, II, 5:1

NYTC 1962:196

NYTC 1982:393

(*Published libretto*) In *The Collected Plays of Neil Simon, Volume II*, Random House, 1979

(*Published sheet music*) Edwin H. Morris

(*Original cast recording*) OP RCA LOC/LSO-1078; OP Pye(E) NPL-18107/ NPS-83023 (Original London Cast)

(*Agent/contact*) Tams–Witmark Music Library

(*Libretto*) NYPL RM4266; same as (*Agent/contact*)

(*Music, Orchestrations*) Same as (*Agent/contact*)

*LITTLE ME was revised for 1982 Broadway revival, starring   James Coco

LOOK, MA, I'M DANCIN'!
(*Source*) Original
(*Book*) Jerome Lawrence & Robert E. Lee
(*Lyrics*) Hugh Martin
(*Music*) Hugh Martin
(*Producer*) George Abbott

Adelphi Theatre	Broadway
January 29, 1948	188 performances

(*Stars*) Nancy Walker, Harold Lang
Theatre World 47–48, pp. 76–7
Best Plays 47–48, pp. 379–80
Cath World 166:553 Mr '48
      Commonweal 47:447 F 13 '48
      Forum 109:155 Mr '48
      New Repub 118:32 F 16 '48
      New Yorker 23:40 F 7 '48
      Newsweek il 31:70 F 9 '48
      Sat R Lit 31:26–7 F 21 '48
      Time il 51:55 F 9 '48
New York Times 1948, Ja 30, 20:2
      New York Times 1948, F 8, II, 1:1
      New York Times 1948, F 8, II, 2:1
NYTC 1948:364
(*Published libretto*) NA
(*Published sheet music*) Chappell
(*Original cast recording*) OP Decca DL–5231; RE Columbia Special Products
      X–14878 (w/*ARMS AND THE GIRL*)
(*Agent/contact*)

Jerome Lawrence	Robert E. Lee	Hugh Martin
c/o DG, Inc.	c/o DG, Inc.	1800 W. Hillcrest Dr., #329
		Newbury Park, CA 91320

(*Libretto*) LC Jerome Lawrence & Robert E. Lee 19Nov46 DU6011;
      same as (*Agent/contact*)
(*Music, Orchestrations*) Same as (*Agent/contact*)

*LOOK TO THE LILIES**

(*Source*) *Lilies of the Field* (novel) by William E. Barrett, (screenplay)
     by James Poe
(*Book*) Leonard Spigelgass
(*Lyrics*) Sammy Cahn
(*Music*) Jule Styne
(*Producer*) Edgar Lansbury, Max J. Brown, Richard Lewine & Ralph Nelson
Lunt–Fontanne Theatre   Broadway
March 29, 1970   25 performances
(*Stars*) Shirley Booth, Al Freeman, Jr.
Theatre World 69–70, p. 48
Best Plays 69–70, pp. 320–21
New Yorker 46:61–2 Ap 4 '70
     Time 95:98 Ap 13 '70
New York Times 1970, Mr 30, 59:1
     New York Times 1970, Ap 12, II, 3:7
NYTC 1970:322
(*Published libretto*) NA
(*Published sheet music*) Chappell–Styne, Inc./Laursteed
(*Original cast recording*) NA
(*Agent/contact*)

Jule Styne	Edgar Lansbury	Sammy Cahn
c/o DG, Inc.	1650 Broadway	c/o Edward Traubner
	New York, N.Y. 10019	1849 Sawtelle Blvd.
Leonard Spigelgass		Los Angeles, CA 90025
c/o DG, Inc.		

(*Libretto*) NYPL RM6885; RM5006 as *SOME KIND OF MAN*; same as
     (*Agent/contact*)
(*Music, Orchestrations*) Same as (*Agent/contact*)

*Previously titled *SOME KIND OF MAN*

LOST IN THE STARS
(*Source*) *Cry the Beloved Country* (novel) by Alan Paton
(*Book*) Maxwell Anderson
(*Lyrics*) Maxwell Anderson
(*Music*) Kurt Weill
(*Producer*) Playwrights' Company
Music Box Theater   Broadway
October 30, 1949   281 performances
(*Stars*) Todd Duncan
Theatre World 49–50, pp. 30–1
          Theatre World 71–72, p. 48
Best Plays 49–50, pp. 358–59
          Best Plays 71–72, pp. 340–41
America 126:515 My 13 '72
          Am Mercury 70:170–2 F '50
          Cath World 170:226 D '49
          Commonweal 51:212 N 25 '49
          Forum 112:340 D '49
          Life il 27:143–6+ N 14 '49
          Mus Am il 69:9 N 15 '49
          Nation 169:478 N 12 '49
          Nation 214:603–4 My 8 '72
          New Repub 121:19 N 21 '49
          New Yorker 25:64 N 5 '49
          New Yorker 25:58 N 12 '49
          New Yorker 48:103 Ap 29 '72
          Newsweek il 34:80 N 7 '49
          Sat R il 55:64 My 6 '72
          Sat R Lit il 32:31–2 N 26 '49
          Sat R Lit 32:43 D 31 '49
          Theatre Arts il 34:11 Ja '50
          Time 54:80 N 7 '49
New York Times 1949, O 31, 21:2
          New York Times 1949, N 6, II, 1:1
          New York Times 1972, Ap 19, 382:2
          New York Times 1972, Ap 30, II, 3:1

NYTC 1949:241

    NYTC 1972:308

(*Published libretto*) Williams Sloane Assoc., 1949; in *Theatre Arts*, December
    1950; in *Famous American Plays of the 1940's*, Dell, 1960; in *Great
    Musicals of The American Theatre*, vol. 2, Chilton, 1976

(*Published sheet music*) Chappell

(*Original cast recording*) OP Decca DL–8028, RE Decca DL–9120/79120

(*Agent/contact*) Rodgers & Hammerstein Theatre Library

(*Libretto*) NYPL RM75, RM7788, NCOF+; same as (*Agent/contact*)

(*Music, Orchestrations*) Same as (*Agent/contact*)

LOUISIANA LADY

(*Source*) *Creoles* (novel) by Samuel Shipman & Kenneth Perkins

(*Book*) Isaac Green, Jr. & Eugene Berton

(*Lyrics*) Monte Carlo & Alma Sanders

(*Music*) Monte Carlo & Alma Sanders

(*Producer*) Hal Shelton

Century Theatre   Broadway

June 2, 1947   4 performances

(*Stars*) NA

Theatre World 47–48, p. 6

Best Plays 47–48, pp. 339–40

NO CRIT AVAIL

New York Times 1947, Je 3, 35:2

NYTC 1947:362

(*Published libretto*) NA

(*Published sheet music*) Chappell

(*Original cast recording*) NA

(*Agent/contact*)   Eugene Berton
                 c/o DG, Inc.

(*Libretto, Music, Orchestrations*) Same as (*Agent/contact*)

LOVE LIFE
(*Source*) Original
(*Book*) Alan Jay Lerner*
(*Lyrics*) Alan Jay Lerner*
(*Music*) Kurt Weill
(*Producer*) Cheryl Crawford
Forty–Sixth Street Theatre   Broadway
October 7, 1948   252 performances
(*Stars*) Nanette Fabray, Ray Middleton
Theatre World 48–49, p. 28–30
Best Plays 48–49, pp. 386–88
Cath World 168:161 N '48
         Commonweal 49:94 N 5 '48
         Forum 111:32–3 Ja '49
         Harper 198:110 Ja '49
         New Repub 119:28 N 1 '48
         New Yorker 24:52 O 16 '48
         Newsweek il 32:89 O 18 '48
         Sch & Soc 68:385–6 D 4 '48
         Theatre Arts il (p. 13) 33:18 Ja '49
         Time 52:82 O 18 '48
New York Times 1948, O 8, 31:2
NYTC 1948:201
(*Published libretto*) NA
(*Published sheet music*) Chappell
(*Original cast recording*) NA
(*Agent/contact*)
         Kurt Weill Estate   Alan Jay Lerner Estate
         c/o European American Music   c/o David Grossberg
         11 West End Avenue   30 N. La Salle Street
         Totowa, NJ   07512   New York, N.Y.   10027
         ATTN: Ronald Freed
(*Libretto*) NYPL RM8302, NCOF+; Kurt Weill Foundation

(*Music, Orchestrations*)   Kurt Weill Foundation
                                 Lincoln Towers
                                 142 West End Avenue, Ste 1R
                                 New York, N.Y.   10023

*At press time, the Alan Jay Lerner Estate was not interested in
    soliciting further productions of this property

LOVELY LADIES, KIND GENTLEMEN
(*Source*) *Teahouse of the August Moon* (novel) by Vern J. Sneider,
        (play) by John Patrick
(*Book*) John Patrick
(*Lyrics*) Stan Freeman & Franklin Underwood
(*Music*) Stan Freeman & Franklin Underwood
(*Producer*) Herman Levin
Majestic Theatre   Broadway
December 28, 1970   19 performances
(*Stars*) Kenneth Nelson, David Burns, Ron Husmann
Theatre World 70–71, p. 28
Best Plays 70–71, pp. 302–3
Dance Mag 45:82 Mr '71
        New Yorker 46:51 Ja 9 '71
New York Times 1970, D 29, 38:1
NYTC 1970:114
(*Published libretto*) Samuel French, Inc., 1971
(*Published sheet music*) Ruxton Music/Eastgate/TRO
(*Original cast recording*) NA
(*Agent/contact*) Samuel French, Inc.
(*Libretto, Music, Orchestrations*) Same as (*Agent/contact*)

LUTE SONG
(*Source*) *The Lute (Pi–Pa–Ki)* (play) by Ming Kao
(*Book*) Sidney Howard & Will Irwin

(*Lyrics*) Bernard Hanighan

(*Music*) Raymond Scott

(*Producer*) Michael Myerberg

Plymouth Theatre   Broadway

February 6, 1946   142 performances

(*Stars*) Mary Martin, Yul Brynner, Mildred Dunnock

Theatre World 45–46, pp. 70–1

        Theatre World 58–59, p. 127

Best Plays 45–46, pp. 426–27

        Best Plays 58–59, pp. 329–30

Am Mercury 62:587–90 My '46

        Cath World 162:553 Mr '46

        Cath World 189:159 My '59

        Commonweal 43:479 F 22 '46

        Dance Mag 33:23 Ap '59

        Life il 20:53–6 Mr 4 '46

        Mod Mus 23 no2:145 [Ap] '46

        Nation 162:240 F 23 '46

        New Repub 114:254 F 18 '46

        New Yorker 22:48+ F 16 '46

        Sat R Lit il 29:28–9 Mr 2 '46

        Theatre Arts il (p207–8) 30:199–200 Ap '46

        Theatre Arts 43:67–8 My '59

        Time il 47:49 F 18 '46

New York Times 1946, F 7, 29:2

        New York Times 1946, F 17, II, 1:1

        New York Times 1948, O 12, 32:3

        New York Times 1959, Mr 13, 24:1

NYTC 1946:459

(*Published libretto*) Dramatic Publishing Company, 1955

(*Published sheet music*) Capitol Songs/Goldsen, Inc./Criterion Music Corp.

(*Original cast recording*) OP Decca DL–8030 (w/**ON THE TOWN**)

(*Agent/contact*) Dramatic Publishing Company

(*Libretto*) NYPL RM254, RM5493, NCOF+

(*Music, Orchestrations*) Same as (*Agent/contact*)

LYSISTRATA
(*Source*) *Lysistrata* (play) by Aristophanes
(*Book*) Michael Cacoyannis
(*Lyrics*) Peter Link*
(*Music*) Peter Link*
(*Producer*) David Black & David Seltzer
Brooks Atkinson Theatre   Broadway
November 13, 1972   8 performances
(*Stars*) Melina Mercouri, Priscilla Lopez
Theatre World 72–73, p. 28
Best Plays 72–73, pp. 338–39
NO CRIT AVAIL
New York Times 1972, N 14, 54:1
NYTC 1972:190
(*Published libretto*) NA
(*Published sheet music*) NA
(*Original cast recording*) NA
(*Agent/contact*)   Peter Link
                       c/o On–Broadway Productions
                       400 W. 43rd Street, #38D
                       New York, N.Y.   10036
(*Libretto, Music, Orchestrations*) Same as (*Agent/contact*)

*At press time, Mr. Link was not interested in soliciting further
    productions of this property

MACK AND MABEL
(*Source*) Original
(*Book*) Michael Stewart
(*Lyrics*) Jerry Herman
(*Music*) Jerry Herman
(*Producer*) David Merrick

Majestic Theatre   Broadway
October 6, 1974   65 performances
(*Stars*) Bernadette Peters, Robert Preston
Theatre World 74–75, p. 10
Best Plays 74–75, pp. 320–21
America 131:284+ N 9 '74
            Nation 219:414 O 26 '74
            New Repub 171:41+ N 2 '74
            New Yorker 50:141 O 14 '74
            Newsweek il 84:56 O 21 '74
            Time 104:93 O 21 '74
New York Times 1974, O 7, 54:1
            New York Times 1974, O 13, II, 1:16
NYTC 1974:234
(*Published libretto*) Samuel French, Inc., 1976
(*Published sheet music*) Jerryco/Edwin H. Morris/Charles Hansen
(*Original cast recording*) OP ABC Records ABCH–830, RE MCA Records
            MCL–1728
(*Agent/contact*) Samuel French, Inc.
(*Libretto*) NYPL NCOF+ 83–1027
(*Music, Orchestrations*) Same as (*Agent/contact*)

*THE MADWOMAN OF CENTRAL PARK WEST**
(*Source*) Original
(*Book*) Phyllis Newman & Arthur Laurents
(*Lyrics*) Various lyricists**
(*Music*) Various composers**
(*Producer*) Gladys Rackmil, Fritz Holt & Barry M. Brown
22 Steps Theatre   Broadway
June 13, 1979   85 performances
(*Stars*) Phyllis Newman
Theatre World 79–80, p. 10
Best Plays 79–80, p. 354
NY 12:95 J1 9 '79
            New Yorker 55:57+ Je 25 '79

New York Times 1979, My 16, III, 20:3
    New York Times 1979, Je 14, III, 15:1
NYTC 1979:212
(*Published libretto*) NA
(*Published sheet music*) NA (Fiddleback Music Pub. Comp., Inc.)
(*Original cast recording*) NA
(*Agent/contact*)

Phyllis Newman	Arthur Laurents	Gladys Rackmil
c/o DG, Inc.	c/o DG, Inc.	1650 Broadway
		New York, N.Y. 10019

(*Libretto, Music, Orchestrations*) Same as (*Agent/contact*)

*Subsequently produced on television for Mobil Showcase Network's
    Summershow, available at NYPL Billy Rose Collection, Lincoln
    Center, NCOX 97

**Peter Allen, Leonard Bernstein, Jerry Bock, Martin Charnin, John
    Clifton, Betty Comden, Fred Ebb, Jack Feldman, Adolph Green,
    Sheldon Harnick, John Kander, Edward Kleban, Barry Manilow,
    Phyllis Newman, Joseph Raposo, Mary Rodgers, Carole Bayer Sager,
    Stephen Sondheim, Bruce Sussman

MAGDALENA
(*Source*) Original
(*Book*) Frederick Hazlitt Brennan & Homer Curran
(*Lyrics*) Robert Wright & George Forrest
(*Music*) Heitor Villa-Lobos
(*Producer*) Homer Curran

Ziegfeld Theatre	Broadway
September 20, 1948	88 performances

(*Stars*) John Raitt
Theatre World 48–49, p. 15
Best Plays 48–49, pp. 381–82
Cath World 168:158–9 N '48

Colliers il 122:24–5 N 20 '48

Commonweal 48:618 O 8 '48

New Repub 119:29 O 11 '48

New Yorker 24:50 O 2 '48

Sch & Soc 68:301–2 O 30 '48

Theatre Arts il (pp. 16–17) 33:18 Ja '49

Time il 52:59 O 4 '48

New York Times 1948, Jl 28, 27:2

New York Times 1948, S 21, 31:2

New York Times 1948, S 26, II, 1:1

New York Times 1948, S 26, II, 7:1

New York Times 1948, N 7, II, 6:5

NYTC 1948:235

(*Published libretto*) NA

(*Published sheet music*) Villa–Lobos Music Corp./J.J. Robbins & Sons

(*Original cast recording*) NA

(*Agent/contact*)   Robert Wright & George Forrest
                               c/o DG, Inc.

(*Libretto, Orchestrations*) Same as (*Agent/contact*)

(*Music*) NYPL *MS; same as (*Agent/contact*)

MAGGIE

(*Source*) *What Every Woman Knows* (play) by Sir James M. Barrie

(*Book*) Hugh Thomas

(*Lyrics*) William Roy

(*Music*) William Roy

(*Producer*) Franklin Gilbert & John Fearnley

National Theatre   Broadway

February 18, 1953   5 performances

(*Stars*) Keith Andes

Theatre World 52–53, p. 98

Best Plays 52–53, p. 289

Commonweal 57:577 Mr 13 '53

New Yorker 29:65 F 28 '53

Newsweek 41:84 Mr 2 '53

Sat R 36:35 Mr 7 '53

Theatre Arts 37:14 Ja '53

Theatre Arts 37:15 My '53

Time 61:77 Mr 2 '53

New York Times 1953, F 19, 20:2

NYTC 1953:351

(*Published libretto*) NA

(*Published sheet music*) Chappell

(*Original cast recording*) NA

(*Agent/contact*)   William Roy

c/o ASCAP

(*Libretto*) NYPL NCOF+; Samuel French, Inc.;

same as (*Agent/contact*)

(*Music, Orchestrations*) Samuel French, Inc.;

same as (*Agent/contact*)

*MAGGIE FLYNN**

(*Source*) Original

(*Book*) Hugo Peretti, Luigi Creatore, George David Weiss &

Morton Da Costa**

(*Lyrics*) Hugo Peretti, Luigi Creatore & George David Weiss

(*Music*) Hugo Peretti, Luigi Creatore & George David Weiss

(*Producer*) John Bowab

ANTA Theatre   Broadway

October 23, 1968   82 performances

(*Stars*) Shirley Jones, Jack Cassidy

Theatre World 68–69, p. 27

Best Plays 68–69, pp. 387–89

America 119:530 N 23 '68

Dance Mag 42:106 D '68

New Yorker 44:125 N 2 '68

Newsweek 72:118 N 4 '68

New York Times 1968, O 24, 52:1

New York Times 1968, N 3, II, 1:1

NYTC 1968:196

(*Published libretto*) Samuel French, Inc., 1968

(*Published sheet music*) Valando Music/HLG Music Corp.

(*Original cast recording*) OP RCA LSOD–2009

(*Agent/contact*) Samuel French, Inc.

(*Libretto*) NYPL NCOF+, RM4426, RM4499; LC (Performing Arts Reading
        Room) ML50/.W443M32 as *BEAUTIFUL MRS. FLYNN*

(*Music, Orchestrations*) Same as (*Agent/contact*)

*Previously titled *BEAUTIFUL MRS. FLYNN*

**In all publicity, Hugo Peretti, Luigi Creatore, George David Weiss
        & Morton Da Costa are given authorship credit; however, the
        manuscript filed with LC Performing Arts Reading Room gives John
        Flaxman sole authorship credit

MAKE A WISH

(*Source*) *The Good Fairy (A Jo Tündér)* (play) by Ferenc Molnar

(*Book*) Preston Sturges

(*Lyrics*) Hugh Martin

(*Music*) Hugh Martin

(*Producer*) Harry Rigby, Jule Styne & Alexander H. Cohen

Winter Garden Theatre   Broadway

April 18, 1951   102 performances

(*Stars*) Nanette Fabray, Harold Lang, Helen Gallagher, Stephen Douglass

Theatre World 50–51, p. 107

Best Plays 50–51, pp. 362–63

Cath World 173:228 Je '51

        Commonweal 54:88 My 4 '51

        Life il 30:137–8 My 14 '51

        Mus Am 71:7+ Jl '51

        Nation 172:403 Ap 28 '51

New Yorker 27:58 Ap 28 '51

Newsweek il 37:53 Ap 30 '51

Theatre Arts il 35:14 Je '51

Time 57:89 Ap 30 '51

New York Times 1951, Ap 19, 38:1

New York Times 1951, My 20, II, 1:1

NYTC 1951:294

(*Published libretto*) NA

(*Published sheet music*) Edwin H. Morris & Co.

(*Original cast recording*) OP RCA LOC–1002, RE RCA CBM1–2033

(*Agent/contact*)

Hugh Martin	Preston Sturges Estate	Harry Rigby
1800 W. Hillcrest Dr.,	c/o Samuel French, Inc.	1600 Broadway
#329		New York, N.Y. 10019
Newbury Park, CA 91320		

Jule Styne	Alexander H. Cohen
c/o DG, Inc.	225 W. 44th Street
	New York, N.Y. 10036

(*Libretto, Music, Orchestrations*) Same as (*Agent/contact*)

*MARINKA**

(*Source*) Original

(*Book*) George Marion, Jr. & Karl Farkas

(*Lyrics*) George Marion, Jr.

(*Music*) Emmerick Kalman

(*Producer*) Jules J. Leventhal & Harry Howard

Winter Garden Theatre/Barrymore Theatre**   Broadway

July 18, 1945   165 performances

(*Stars*) Joan Roberts

Theatre World 45–46, p. 9

Best Plays 45–46, pp. 380–81

Cath World 161:509–10 S '45

Commonweal 42:381 Ag 3 '45

New Yorker 21:40 Jl 28 '45

Newsweek il 26:65 Jl 30 '45

Sat R Lit il 28:22–3 S 29 '45

Time il 46:72 Jl 30 '45

New York Times 1945, Jl 19, 19:2

NYTC 1945:186

(*Published libretto*) NA

(*Published sheet music*) Remick

(*Original cast recording*) NA

(*Agent/contact*)

George Marion, Jr. Estate   Emmerick Kalman Estate

c/o AGAC   c/o ASCAP

(*Libretto*) NYPL NCOF+; MCNY; same as (*Agent/contact*)

(*Music, Orchestrations*) Same as (*Agent/contact*)

*Previously titled *SONG OF VIENNA*

**Moved to Barrymore Theatre 10/01/45

MARLOWE

(*Source*) Original

(*Book*) Leo Rost

(*Lyrics*) Leo Rost & Jimmy Horowitz

(*Music*) Jimmy Horowitz

(*Producer*) Tony Conforti, in association with

         Robert R. Blume, Billy Gaff, Howard P. Effron

Rialto Theatre   Broadway

October 12, 1981   48 performances

(*Stars*) NA

Theatre World 81–82, p. 10

Best Plays 81–82, pp. 315–16

NO CRIT AVAIL

New York Times 1981, O 13, III, 7:4

         New York Times 1981, D 1, 30:2

NYTC 1981:151
(*Published libretto*) NA
(*Published sheet music*) NA
(*Original cast recording*) NA
(*Agent/contact*)   Leo Rost
                     c/o DG, Inc.
(*Libretto, Music, Orchestrations*) Same as (*Agent/contact*)

MARRIED ALIVE!
See *DARLING OF THE DAY*

MARVELOUS TIMES
See *DIFFERENT TIMES*

MEMPHIS BOUND*
(*Source*) *H.M.S. Pinafore* (operetta) by W.S. Gilbert & Sir Arthur
           Sullivan
(*Book*) Albert Barker & Sally Benson
(*Lyrics*) Don Walker & Clay Warnick
(*Music*) Don Walker & Clay Warnick
(*Producer*) John Wildberg
Broadway Theatre   Broadway
May 24, 1945   36 performances
(*Stars*) Bill Robinson
Theatre World 44–45, p. 95
Best Plays 44–45, pp. 432–43
Cath World 161:350 Jl '45
          Commonweal 42:191 Je 8 '45
          Life il 18:57–8+ Je 25 '45
          Nation 160:705 Je 23 '45
          New Yorker 21:36+ Je 2 '45
          Theatre Arts 29:389 Jl '45
          Time il 45:85 Je 4 '45

New York Times 1945, My 25, 23:2

New York Times 1945, Je 10, II, 1:1

NYTC 1945:207

(Published libretto) NA

(Published sheet music) Crawford Music Corp.

(Original cast recording) NA

(Agent/contact)   Don Walker   Clay Warnick

c/o DG, Inc.   c/o ASCAP

(Libretto) LC Don Walker & Henry Clay Warnick 13May44 DU89046 as *U.S.S. PINAFORE; OR, NOT TONIGHT, JOSEPHINE!*; same as *(Agent/contact)*

(Music, Orchestrations) Same as *(Agent/contact)*

*Previously titled *U.S.S. PINAFORE; OR, NOT TONIGHT, JOSEPHINE!*

MERLIN

(Source) Original

(Book) Richard Levinson & William Link

(Lyrics) Don Black

(Music) Elmer Bernstein

(Producer) Ivan Reitman, Columbia Pictures Stage Productions, Marvin A. Krauss, Manes M. Nederlander

Mark Hellinger Theatre   Broadway

February 13, 1983   199 performances

(Stars) Chita Rivera, Doug Henning

Theatre World 82–83, p. 36

Best Plays 82–83, pp. 349–51

Dance Mag il 57:92–3+ Ap '83

Harp Baz il por 116:204–5+ D '82

NY il 16:77–8 F 28 '83

New Leader 66:20 Mr 7 '83

New Yorker 59:82 F 28 '83

Time il 121:63 F 7 '83

New York Times 1983, illus, Ja 31, III, 22:5
        New York Times 1983, F 13, II, 1:1
        New York Times 1983, F 20, II, 3:1
NYTC 1983:370
(*Published libretto*) NA
(*Published sheet music*) Hal Leonard/Dick James, Inc./Dejamus, Inc.
(*Original cast recording*) NA
(*Agent/contact*)

Elmer Bernstein	Don Black	Richard Levinson
c/o ASCAP	c/o DG, Inc.	c/o DG, Inc.

        William Link
        c/o DG, Inc.
(*Libretto, Music, Orchestrations*) Same as (*Agent/contact*)

MERRILY WE ROLL ALONG*

(*Source*) *Merrily We Roll Along* (play) by George S. Kaufman & Moss Hart
(*Book*) George Furth
(*Lyrics*) Stephen Sondheim
(*Music*) Stephen Sondheim
(*Producer*) Lord Grade, Martin Starger, Robert Fryer & Harold Prince
Alvin Theater   Broadway
November 16, 1981   16 performances
(*Stars*) Lonny Price
Theatre World 81–82, p. 16
Best Plays 81–82, pp. 321–22
NY 14:87–8 N 30 '81
        New Yorker 57:110 D 7 '81
        Newsweek 98:109 N 30 '81
        Time il 118:90 N 30 '81
New York Times 1981, illus, N 17, III, 9:1
NYTC 1981:104

(*Published libretto*) NA
(*Published sheet music*) Revelation/Rilting/Valando
(*Original cast recording*) RCA CBL1–4197
(*Agent/contact*) Music Theatre International
(*Libretto, Music, Orchestrations*) Same as (*Agent/contact*)

*Subsequently revised by George Furth & Stephen Sondheim and presented
        by La Jolla Playhouse, CA

MINNIE'S BOYS
(*Source*) Original
(*Book*) Arthur Marx
(*Lyrics*) Hal Hackady
(*Music*) Larry Grossman
(*Producer*) Arthur Whitelaw, Max J. Brown & Byron Goldman
Imperial Theatre   Broadway
March 26, 1970   76 performances
(*Stars*) Shelly Winters
Theatre World 69–60, p. 47
Best Plays 69–70, pp. 320–21
Commonweal 92:222 My 15 '70
        Dance Mag 44:84 Je '70
        New Yorker 46:61 Ap 4 '70
        Newsweek il 75:98–9 Ap 6 '70
        Sat R 53:20 Ap 11 '70
        Time 95:98+ Ap 13 '70
New York Times 1970, F 15, II, 1:1
        New York Times 1970, Mr 27, 27:1
        New York Times 1970, Ap 5, II, 3:1
NYTC 1970:325
(*Published libretto*) NA
(*Published sheet music*) New York Times Music Corp. (Sunbeam)/Charles
        Hansen

(*Original cast recording*) Project 3 TS–6200–SD
(*Agent/contact*) Samuel French, Inc.
(*Libretto*) NYPL RM5049; LC (Performing Arts Reading Room)
        ML50/.G8855M5; same as (*Agent/contact*)
(*Music, Orchestrations*) Same as (*Agent/contact*)

MR. PRESIDENT
(*Source*) Original
(*Book*) Howard Lindsay & Russell Crouse
(*Lyrics*) Irving Berlin
(*Music*) Irving Berlin
(*Producer*) Leland Hayward
St. James Theatre   Broadway
October 20, 1962   265 performances
(*Stars*) Nanette Fabray, Robert Ryan
Theatre World 62–63, p. 19–21
Best Plays 62–63, pp. 280–82
America 107:1230 D 8 '62
        Bsns W il p. 31 S 29 '62
        Commonweal 77:279 D 7 '62
        Dance Mag il 36:98 D '62
        Nat R 14:78–9 Ja 29 '63
        New Yorker 38:147 O 27 '62
        Newsweek 60:74 N 5 '62
        Reporter 27:43 D 20 '62
        Sat R 45:40 N 3 '62
        Theatre Arts il 46:14–16 N '62
        Theatre Arts il (p. 13) 46:14 D '62
        Time il 80:62 S 7 '62
        Time il 80:82 N 2 '62
        Vogue il 140:144–7+ N 1 '62
New York Times 1962, Ag 29, 18:4
        New York Times 1962, S 26, 36:1
        New York Times 1962, O 14, II, 1:7
        New York Times 1962, O 22, 34:2

NYTC 1962:238

(*Published libretto*) NA

(*Published sheet music*) Irving Berlin Music Corp.

(*Original cast recording*) OP Columbia KOL–5870/KOS–2270, RE Columbia
        Special Products AKOS–2270

(*Agent/contact*) Music Theatre International

(*Libretto*) NYPL RM1543, RM4263, RM5873, RM5874; LC (Performing Arts
        Reading Room) ML50/.B512M6; same as (*Agent/contact*)

(*Music, Orchestrations*) Same as (*Agent/contact*)

MR. RUMPLE

See *RUMPLE*

MR. STRAUSS GOES TO BOSTON

(*Source*) Original

(*Book*) Leonard L. Levinson

(*Lyrics*) Robert B. Sour

(*Music*) Robert Stolz

(*Producer*) Felix Brentano

Century Theatre   Broadway

September 6, 1945   12 performances

(*Stars*) Arlene Dahl, Harold Lang (chorus)

Theatre World 45–46, p. 10

Best Plays 45–46, pp. 381–82

NO CRIT AVAIL

New York Times 1945, S 7, 20:2

NYTC 1945:180

(*Published libretto*) NA

(*Published sheet music*) Broadcast Music, Inc.

(*Original cast recording*) NA

(*Agent/contact*) NO CONT AVAIL

(*Libretto*) LC Felix Brentano 18May44 DU88989; same as (*Agent/contact*)

(*Music, Orchestrations*) Same as (*Agent/contact*)

MRS. PATTERSON

(*Source*) Original

(*Book*) Charles Sebree & Greer Johnson

(*Lyrics*) Charles Sebree & Greer Johnson

(*Music*) James Shelton

(*Producer*) Leonard Sillman

National Theater   Broadway

December 1, 1954   101 performances

(*Stars*) Eartha Kitt

Theatre World 54–55, p. 43

Best Plays 54–55, pp. 379–80

America 92:345 D 25 '54

      Commonweal 61:406 Ja 14 '55

      Nation 179:538 D 18 '54

      New Yorker 30:97 D 11 '54

      Newsweek 44:60 N 1 '54

      Sat R 38:62 Ja 1 '55

      Theatre Arts il 39:15, 21+ F '55

      Time il D 13 '54

New York Times 1954, D 2, 37:1

      New York Times 1957, F 6, 20:2

NYTC 1954:231

(*Published libretto*) NA

(*Published sheet music*) Garland Music/Keys Music

(*Original cast recording*) OP RCA LOC–1017

(*Agent/contact*)   James H. Shelton Estate
                     c/o ASCAP

(*Libretto*) NYPL RM1440; LC Greer Johnson 8Oct51 DU28912;

      same as (*Agent/contact*)

(*Music, Orchestrations*) Same as (*Agent/contact*)

MOLLY

(*Source*) "The Goldbergs" (radio and television serial) by Gertrude

      Berg (characters from)

(*Book*) Louis Garfinkle & Leonard Adelson

(*Lyrics*) Leonard Adelson & Mack David

(*Music*) Jerry Livingston

(*Producer*) Don Saxon, Don Kaufman, George Daly & Complex IV

Alvin Theatre   Broadway

November 1, 1973   68 performances

(*Stars*) Kaye Ballard

Theatre World 73–74, p. 18

Best Plays 73–74, pp. 348–49

New Yorker 49:114 N 12 '73

      Newsweek il 82:81 N 12 '73

      Time 102:97 N 19 '73

New York Times 1973, N 2, 46:1

      New York Times 1973, N 11, II, 1:1

NYTC 1973:206

(*Published libretto*) NA

(*Published sheet music*) Hallmark Music Co./Theatrical Music Co./Sam Fox
      Pubs. Co.

(*Original cast recording*) NA

(*Agent/contact*)

Louis Garfinkle	Leonard Adelson	Mack David
c/o DG, Inc.	c/o Scott Adelson	c/o ASCAP
	1617 Manning Avenue	
Jerry Livingston	Los Angeles, CA 90024	
c/o DG, Inc.		

(*Libretto, Music, Orchestrations*) Same as (*Agent/contact*)

MUCH ADO ABOUT LOVE
See *THE FIREBRAND OF FLORENCE*

THE MULATTO
See *THE BARRIER*

*MUSIC IN MY HEART**
(*Source*) Original
(*Book*) Patsy Ruth Miller
(*Lyrics*) Forman Brown
(*Music*) Piotr Ilich Tchaikovsky, adapted by Franz Steininger
(*Producer*) Henry Duffy
Adelphi Theatre   Broadway
October 2, 1947   124 performances
(*Stars*) Robert Carroll, Vivienne Segal
Theatre World 47–48, p. 19
Best Plays 47–48, pp. 355–56
Cath World 166:171 N '47
            New Yorker 23:54 O 11 '47
            Newsweek 30:81 O 13 '47
            Sch & Soc 66:508–9 D 27 '47
            Theatre Arts 31:16 N '47
New York Times 1947, O 3, 30:2
NTYC 1947:324
(*Published libretto*) NA
(*Published sheet music*) Robbins
(*Original cast recording*) NA
(*Agent/contact*)   Franz K.W. Steininger Estate   Forman Brown
                     c/o ASCAP   c/o ASCAP
(*Libretto*) LC Patsy Ruth Miller 29May47 DU9800;
       same as (*Agent/contact*)
(*Music, Orchestrations*) Same as (*Agent/contact*)

*Originally presented under title *SONG WITHOUT WORDS*

MUSIC IS
(*Source*) *Twelfth Night* (play) by William Shakespeare
(*Book*) George Abbott
(*Lyrics*) Will Holt
(*Music*) Richard Adler
(*Producer*) Richard Adler, Roger Berlind & Edward R. Downe, Jr.

St. James Theatre   Broadway
December 20, 1976   8 performances
(*Stars*) Christopher Hewett
Theatre World 76–77, p. 45
Best Plays 76–77, pp. 298–99
NO CRIT AVAIL
New York Times 1976, D 21, 44:1
NYTC 1976:58
(*Published libretto*) NA
(*Published sheet music*) Music of the Times Pub. Corp.
(*Original cast recording*) NA
(*Agent/contact*)   Richard Adler
                      8 E. 83rd Street
                      New York, N.Y.   10028
(*Libretto, Music, Orchestrations*) Same as (*Agent/contact*)

MY DARLIN' AIDA
(*Source*) *Aida* (opera) by Giuseppe Verdi
(*Book*) Charles Friedman
(*Lyrics*) Charles Friedman
(*Music*) Verdi, as adapted by Charles Friedman
(*Producer*) Robert L. Joseph
Winter Garden Theatre   Broadway
October 27, 1952   89 performances
(*Stars*) Dorothy Sarnoff
Theatre World 52–53, p. 30
Best Plays 52–53, pp. 264–66
Cath World 176:228 D '52
          Commonweal 57:164 N 21 '52
          Mus Am 72:9 D 15 '52
          New Yorker 28:86+ N 8 '52
          Newsweek 40:94–5 N 10 '52
          Theatre Arts il 37:24–5 Ja '53
          Time il 60:72 N 10 '52

New York Times 1952, O 28, 36:4

NYTC 1952:218

(*Published libretto*) In *Theatre Arts*, June 1953

(*Published sheet music*) Chappell

(*Original cast recording*) NA

(*Agent/contact*)   Charles Friedman

                c/o DG, Inc.

(*Libretto*) NYPL NCOF+; LC Charles Friedman 25Oct47 DU11516;
     same as (*Agent/contact*)

(*Music, Orchestrations*) Same as (*Agent/contact*)

MY INDIAN FAMILY
See *CHRISTINE*

MY OLD FRIENDS
(*Source*) Original

(*Book*) Mel Mandel & Norman Sachs

(*Lyrics*) Mel Mandel & Norman Sachs

(*Music*) Mel Mandel & Norman Sachs

(*Producer*) Larry Abrams & Belwin/Mills Publishing Corp.

22 Steps Theatre*   Broadway*

April 12, 1979*   53 performances

(*Stars*) NA

Theatre World 78–79, p. 84

Best Plays 78–79, pp. 386–87; 433–34

Time il 113:142 F 5 '79

New York Times 1979, F 13, II, 13:1

NO CRIT AVAIL

(*Published libretto*) Samuel French, Inc., 1980

(*Published sheet music*) NA (Multimood Music, Inc.)

(*Original cast recording*) NA

(*Agent/contact*) Samuel French, Inc.

(*Libretto, Orchestrations*) Same as (*Agent/contact*)

(*Music*) Multimood Music, Inc. 17Jul79 PAu–127–542, 9Oct79 PAu–154–164;
    same as (*Agent/contact*)

*Previously produced off–off–Broadway at La Mama; opened off–Broadway
    at the Orpheum Theatre 1/12/79 before transferring on Broadway to
    the 22 Steps Theatre

MY ROMANCE
(*Source*) *Romance* (play) by Edward Sheldon
(*Book*) Rowland Leigh
(*Lyrics*) Rowland Leigh
(*Music*) Sigmund Romberg*
(*Producer*) The Shuberts
Sam S. Shubert Theatre*   Broadway*
October 19, 1948*   95 performances
(*Stars*) Anne Jeffreys
Theatre World 48–49, pp. 36–7
Best Plays 48–49, pp. 390–91
NO CRIT AVAIL
New York Times 1948, O 20, 38:5
NYTC 1948:186
(*Published libretto*) NA
(*Published sheet music*) T.B. Harms
(*Original cast recording*) NA
(*Agent/contact*)

Sigmund Romberg Estate	Rowland Leigh Estate	Shubert Organization
c/o Mirose Agency, Inc.	c/o ASCAP	234 W. 44th Street
301 E. 69th Street, #15B		New York, N.Y. 10036
New York, N.Y. 10021		
ATTN: Miriam Stern		

(*Libretto, Music, Orchestrations*) Same as (*Agent/contact*)

*Previously produced out of town at Shubert Theatre, New Haven, 2/12/48,
     with music by Denes Agay, additional music by Philip Redowski

NELLIE BLY
(*Source*) Original
(*Book*) Joseph Quillan*
(*Lyrics*) Johnny Burke
(*Music*) James Van Heusen
(*Producer*) Nat Karson & Eddie Cantor
Adelphi Theatre   Broadway
January 21, 1946   16 performances
(*Stars*) Victor Moore, William Gaxton
Theatre World 45–46, p. 61
Best Plays 45–46, pp. 422–23
Newsweek 27:80 F 4 '46
        Theatre Arts 30:137 Mr '46
        Time 47:63 F 4 '46
New York Times 1946, Ja 22, 32:2
        New York Times 1946, Ja 27, II, 1:1
NYTC 1946:481
(*Published libretto*) NA
(*Published sheet music*) Burke & Van Heusen/Bourne
(*Original cast recording*) NA
(*Agent/contact*)   Johnny Burke Estate   James Van Heusen
                         c/o Samuel French, Inc.   c/o DG, Inc.
(*Libretto*) NYPL NCOF+; LC Morrie Ryskind & Siegfried Herzig 14Nov45
        DU96111; same as (*Agent/contact*)

(Music, Orchestrations) Same as *(Agent/contact)*

*In all publicity, Joseph Quillan is given sole authorship credit;
   however, the manuscript/promptscript filed with NYPL Billy Rose
   Collection gives Morrie Ryskind & Sig Herzig authorship credit

THE NERVOUS SET

(Source) The Nervous Set (novel) by Jay Landesman
(Book) Jay Landesman & Theodore J. Flicker
(Lyrics) Fran Landesman
(Music) Tommy Wolf
(Producer) Robert Lantz

Henry Miller's Theatre   Broadway
May 12, 1959   23 performances

(Stars) Larry Hagman
Theatre World 58–59, p. 115
Best Plays 58–59, pp. 336–37
Nation 188:483 My 23 '59
      New Yorker 35:72+ My 23 '59
      Reporter 20:35–6 Je 11 '59
      Sat R 42:26 My 30 '59
      Theatre Arts il 43:10–11 Jl '59
      Time 73:50 My 25 '59
New York Times 1959, My 13, 43:1
NYTC 1959:306
(Published libretto) NA
(Published sheet music) Empress Music/Frank Distrib. Corp.
(Original cast recording) OP Columbia OL–5430/OS–2018
(Agent/contact)

Jay Landesman	Mary Wolf	Hope Wurdack
8 Duncan Terrace	7949 Belton Drive	The Theater Factory
London N1 8BZ, England	Los Angeles, CA	364 Jefferson Road
	90045	St. Louis, MO 63119

(*Libretto*) LC Jay Irving Landesman & Theodore J. Flicker 31Mar59
        DU48732; same as (*Agent/contact*)
(*Music, Orchestrations*)
        Frank Music Corporation;   same as (*Agent/contact*)
        39 W. 54th Street
        New York, N.Y. 10019

NEVER GO THERE ANYMORE
See *KELLY*

THE 1940's RADIO HOUR
(*Source*) Original
(*Book*) Walton Jones
(*Lyrics*) Various lyricists*
(*Music*) Various composers*
(*Producer*) Jujamcyn Productions, Joseph P. Harris, Ira Bernstein
        & Roger Berlind
St. James Theater   Broadway
October 7, 1979   105 performances
(*Stars*) NA
Theatre World 79–80, p. 19
Best Plays 79–80, pp. 362–63
America 141:237 O 27 '79
        Horizon il 22:4+ D '79
        NY 12:97 O 22 '79
        New Yorker 55:147–8 O 15 '79
        Newsweek il 94:130 O 22 '79
New York Times 1979, O 8, III, 13:1
        New York Times 1979, O 26, III, 6:1
        New York Times 1979, N 4, II, 27:1
NYTC 1979:138
(*Published libretto*) Samuel French, Inc., 1981
(*Published sheet music*) NA
(*Original cast recording*) NA

(*Agent/contact*) Samuel French, Inc.

(*Libretto*) LC 29Jun77 DU104299, 5Oct78 PAu–52–596, 6Apr79 PAu–96–811, 7Aug79 PAu–127–967

(*Music, Orchestrations*) Same as (*Agent/contact*)

*No listing given. *New York Times* cites the following musical numbers: "Ain't She Sweet," "Chattanooga Choo Choo," "Hey, Daddy," "How's About You," "I'll Never Smile Again," "Rose of the Rio Grande," "Strike Up the Band," "You, You're Driving Me Crazy"

NOWHERE TO GO BUT UP*

(*Source*) Original

(*Book*) James Lipton

(*Lyrics*) James Lipton

(*Music*) Sol Berkowitz

(*Producer*) Kermit Bloomgarden, Herbert Greene & Steven H. Scheuer

Winter Garden Theatre   Broadway

November 10, 1962   9 performances

(*Stars*) Tom Bosley, Dorothy Loudon, Martin Balsam, Bert Convy

Theatre World 62–63, p. 32

Best Plays 62–63, pp. 284–85

Dance Mag 37:24 Ja '63

    Dance Mag 37:28–9 F '63

    New Yorker 38:147 N 17 '62

    Theatre Arts 46:15 D '62

New York Times 1962, O 9, 46:6

    New York Times 1962, N 12, 36:2

NYTC 1962:209

(*Published libretto*) NA

(*Published sheet music*) Chappell

(*Original cast recording*) NA

(*Agent/contact*)   James Lipton   Sol Berkowitz
                c/o DG, Inc.   46–36 Hamford Street
                                       Douglaston, N.Y. 11362

(*Libretto*) James Lipton
(*Music, Orchestrations*) Sol Berkowitz

*Previously titled *IZZY AND MOE*

ODYSSEY
See *HOME, SWEET HOMER*

OH, BROTHER!
(*Source*) *The Menaechmi* (play) by Plautus, *The Comedy of Errors*
      (play) by William Shakespeare (freely adapted)
(*Book*) Donald Driver
(*Lyrics*) Donald Driver
(*Music*) Michael Valenti
(*Producer*) Zev Bufman, The Kennedy Center, Fisher Theater Foundation,
      Joan Cullman, Sidney Shlenker
ANTA Theater   Broadway
November 10, 1981   3 performances
(*Stars*) Judy Kaye
Theatre World 81–82, p. 14
Best Plays 81–82, pp. 319–20
NY 14:86–7 N 23 '81
New York Times 1981, N 11, III, 23:4
NYTC 1981:124
(*Published libretto*) Samuel French, Inc., 1982
(*Published sheet music*) MacMusic/MacMillan Perf. Arts, Inc.
(*Original cast recording*) Original Cast Records OC–8342
(*Agent/contact*) Samuel French, Inc.
(*Libretto*) LC Donald Driver & Dion Driver 25Sep80 PAu–276–104
(*Music*) LC MacMusic Company 22Sep82 PA–150–595; same as
      (*Agent/contact*)
(*Orchestrations*) Same as (*Agent/contact*)

OH CAPTAIN!*

(*Source*) *The Captain's Paradise* (screenplay) by Alec
        Coppel & Nicholas Phipps
(*Book*) Al Morgan & Jose Ferrer
(*Lyrics*) Jay Livingston & Ray Evans
(*Music*) Jay Livingston & Ray Evans
(*Producer*) Howard Merrill & Theatre Corp. of America
Alvin Theatre   Broadway
February 4, 1958   192 performances
(*Stars*) Tony Randall, Abbe Lane
Theatre World 57–58, p. 78
Best Plays 57–58, pp. 315–16
America 99:26 Ap 5 '58
        Cath World 187:70 Ap '58
        Dance Mag il 32:15 Mr '58
        New Repub 138:22–3 Mr 3 '58
        New Yorker 33:55 F 15 '58
        Newsweek 51:66 F 17 '58
        Theatre Arts il 42:20–1 Ap '58
        Time il 71:84 F 17 '58
New York Times 1958, F 5, 21:2
NYTC 1958:370
(*Published libretto*) NA
(*Published sheet music*) Chappell
(*Original cast recording*) OP Columbia OL/OS–5280, RE Columbia Special
        Products AOS–2002
(*Agent/contact*) Tams–Witmark Music Library
(*Libretto*) NYPL RM6683; RM7744 as *CAPTAIN'S PARADISE*;
        same as (*Agent/contact*)
(*Music, Orchestrations*) Same as (*Agent/contact*)

*Originally titled *CAPTAIN'S PARADISE*

ON A CLEAR DAY YOU CAN SEE FOREVER
(*Source*) Original
(*Book*) Alan Jay Lerner
(*Lyrics*) Alan Jay Lerner
(*Music*) Burton Lane
(*Producer*) Alan Jay Lerner & Rogo Productions
Mark Hellinger Theater   Broadway
October 17, 1965   280 performances
(*Stars*) Barbara Harris, John Cullum
Theatre World 65–66, p. 20–1
Best Plays 65–66, pp. 377–78
Dance Mag il 39:138–9 D '65
            Holiday 39:118+ Ja '66
            Nation 201:398 N 22 '65
            New Yorker 41:108 O 30 '65
            Newsweek il 66:84+ N 1 '65
            Sat R 48:41–2 N 6 '65
            Time 86:84 O 29 '65
New York Times 1965, O 18, 44:1
NYTC 1965:308
(*Published libretto*) Random House, 1966
(*Published sheet music*) Chappell & Co./Levlane Corp.
(*Original cast recording*) RCA LOCD/LSOD–2006
(*Agent/contact*) Tams–Witmark Music Library
(*Libretto*) NYPL RM141, RM4598, NCOF+; same as (*Agent/contact*)
(*Music, Orchestrations*) Same as (*Agent/contact*)

ON WITH THE SHOW!
See *HIT THE TRAIL*

ONWARD, VICTORIA!
(*Source*) Original
(*Book*) Charlotte Anker & Irene Rosenberg
(*Lyrics*) Charlotte Anker & Irene Rosenberg

(*Music*) Keith Herrmann
(*Producer*) John N. Hart, Jr., in association with Hugh J.
       Hubbard & Robert M. Browne
Martin Beck Theater*   Broadway*
December 14, 1980   1 performance
(*Stars*) Jill Eikenberry
Theatre World 78–79, p. 120
       Theatre World 80–81, p. 31
Best Plays 78–79, p. 451
       Best Plays 80–81, pp. 358–59
New Yorker 56:55 D 22 '80
New York Times 1980, D 15, III, 15:3
       New York Times 1980, D 26, III, 3:1
NYTC 1980:71
(*Published libretto*) NA
(*Published sheet music*) NA
(*Original cast recording*) Original Cast Records OC–8135
(*Agent/contact*)

Charlotte Anker	Irene Rosenberg	Keith Herrmann
11049 Seven Hill Lane	4203 Bradley Lane	c/o DG, Inc.
Potomac, MD 20854	Chevy Chase, MD	
	20815	

(*Libretto*) NYPL NCOF+ 83–1028; LC Charlotte Anker & Irene Rosenberg
       29May81 PAu–300–441; same as (*Agent/contact*)
(*Music, Orchestrations*) Keith Hermann

*Previously produced off–off–Broadway at the Manhattan Theater Club and
       the Joseph Jefferson Theater

OUT OF THIS WORLD
(*Source*) *Amphitryon 38* (play) by Jean Giraudoux, as translated
       by S.N. Behrman (suggested by)
(*Book*) Dwight Taylor & Reginald Lawrence

(*Lyrics*) Cole Porter
(*Music*) Cole Porter
(*Producer*) Arnold Saint–Subber & Lemuel Ayers
New Century Theatre   Broadway
December 21, 1950   157 performances
(*Stars*) Charlotte Greenwood
Theatre World 51–51, p. 59
Best Plays 50–51, p. 336
CS Mon Mag il p. 9 D 30 '50
        Cath World 173:69 Ap '51
        Commonweal 53:349 Ja 12 '51
        New Yorker 26:44 D 30 '50
        New Yorker 49:94 Mr 17 '73
        Newsweek 37:35 Ja 1 '51
        Theatre Arts il 35:19 F '51
        Time il 57:42 Ja 1 '51
New York Times 1950, D 22, 17:3
        New York Times 1951, My 20, II, 1:1
        New York Times 1955, S 21, 20:3
NYTC 1950:166
(*Published libretto*) NA
(*Published sheet music*) Melrose
(*Original cast recording*) OP Columbia ML–54390, ML/OL–4390, RE
        Columbia Special Products CML–4390
(*Agent/contact*) Tams–Witmark Music Library
(*Libretto*) NYPL RM268A, RM6867, RM7795, RM8079, NCOF+;
        same as (*Agent/contact*)
(*Music, Orchestrations*) Same as (*Agent/contact*)

*PACIFIC OVERTURES**
(*Source*) Original
(*Book*) John Weidman
(*Lyrics*) Stephen Sondheim
(*Music*) Stephen Sondheim

(*Producer*) Harold Prince, in association with Ruth Mitchell

Winter Garden Theatre   Broadway

January 11, 1976   193 performances

(*Stars*) Mako

Theatre World 75–76, p. 39

Best Plays 75–76, pp. 339–40

America 134:128 F 14 '76

   Nation 222:124 Ja 31 '76

   New Repub 174:20 F 7 '76

   New Yorker 51:44 Ja 19 '76

   Newsweek il 87:59 Ja 26 '76

   Opera N 40:45–6 F 28 '76

   Sat R 3:43–4 Ap 3 '76

   Time il 107:46–8 Ja 26 '76

New York Times 1976, Ja 12, 39:1

   New York Times 1976, Ja 18, II, 1:7

NYTC 1976:388

(*Published libretto*) Dodd Mead & Co., 1977

(*Published sheet music*) Revelation Music Publishing Corp./
   Rilting Music, Inc.

(*Original cast recording*) RCA ARL–1–1367

(*Agent/contact*) Music Theatre International

(*Libretto, Music, Orchestrations*) Same as (*Agent/contact*)

*Videotaped performance available at NYPL Billy Rose Collection, Lincoln
   Center, NCOV 65

PAINT YOUR WAGON

(*Source*) Original

(*Book*) Alan Jay Lerner

(*Lyrics*) Alan Jay Lerner

(*Music*) Frederick Loewe

(*Producer*) Cheryl Crawford

Sam S. Shubert Theatre   Broadway

November 12, 1951   289 performances
(Stars) Kay Medford
Theatre World 51–52, pp. 50–1
Best Plays 51–52, pp. 292–93
Cath World 174:308 Ja '52
          Commonweal 55:199 N 30 '51
          Nation 173:484–5 D 1 '51
          New Repub 126:22 Ja 7 '52
          New Yorker 27:67 N 24 '51
          Newsweek il 38:84 N 26 '51
          Sat R il 35:27 Jl 5 '52
          Sch & Soc 75:246 Ap 19 '52
          Theatre Arts 36:72 F '52
          Theatre Arts il 36:33–5 D '52
          Time il 58:87 N 26 '51
New York Times 1951, N 13, 32:2
          New York Times 1951, N 18, II, 1:1
NYTC 1951:172
(Published libretto) Coward–McCann, Inc., 1952; Chappell & Co., Ltd.
          (London), 1952; in *Theatre Arts*, December 1952 (revised libretto)
(Published sheet music) Chappell
(Original cast recording) OP RCA LOC–1006, RE RCA LSO–1006(e)
(Agent/contact) Tams–Witmark Music Library
(Libretto, Music, Orchestrations) Same as *(Agent/contact)*

PARK
(Source) Original
(Book) Paul Cherry
(Lyrics) Paul Cherry
(Music) Lance Mulcahy
(Producer) Edwin Pakula & Eddie Bracken Ventures
John Golden Theatre   Broadway
April 22, 1970   5 performances

(*Stars*) Joan Hackett
Theatre World 69–70, p. 56
Best Plays 69–70, p. 327
NO CRIT AVAIL
New York Times 1970, Ap 23, 47:1
NYTC 1970:270
(*Published libretto*) Samuel French, Inc., 1970
(*Published sheet music*) NA (Sunbeam Music, Inc./Valando Music,
        Inc.)
(*Original cast recording*) NA
(*Agent/contact*) Samuel French, Inc.
(*Libretto, Music, Orchestrations*) Same as (*Agent/contact*)

PARK AVENUE
(*Source*) Original
(*Book*) Nunnally Johnson & George S. Kaufman
(*Lyrics*) Ira Gershwin
(*Music*) Arthur Schwartz
(*Producer*) Max Gordon
Shubert Theatre   Broadway
November 4, 1946   72 performances
(*Stars*) David Wayne, Mary Wickes
Theatre World 46–47, p. 36
Best Plays 46–47, pp. 434–35
Cath World 164:361 Ja '46
        Nation 163:629 N 30 '46
        New Yorker 22:59 N 16 '46
        Newsweek 28:98 N 18 '46
        Time 48:64+ N 18 '46
New York Times 1946, N 5, 31:2
NYTC 1946:275
(*Published libretto*) NA
(*Published sheet music*) Putnam/T.B. Harms
(*Original cast recording*) NA

(*Agent/contact*)

Arthur Schwartz	Ira Gershwin Estate	Nunnally Johnson Estate
Estate	c/o ASCAP	c/o Samuel French, Inc.
c/o Samuel French, Inc.		

George S. Kaufman Estate
c/o Samuel French, Inc.

(*Libretto*) NYPL RM7225; same as (*Agent/contact*)

(*Music, Orchestrations*) Same as (*Agent/contact*)

PETTICOAT (PETTYCOAT) LANE
See *KING OF SCHNORRERS*

PICKWICK

(*Source*) *The Pickwick Papers* (novel) by Charles Dickens

(*Book*) Wolf Mankowitz

(*Lyrics*) Leslie Bricusse

(*Music*) Cyril Ornadel

(*Producer*) David Merrick & Bernard Delfont

Forty–Sixth Street Theatre	Broadway
October 4, 1965	56 performances

(*Stars*) Harry Secombe, Charlotte Rae

Theatre World 65–66, p. 11

Best Plays 65–66, pp. 372–74

America 113:509 O 30 '65

  Dance Mag 39:24 N '65

  New Yorker 41:195 O 16 '65

  Newsweek 66:114 O 18 '65

  Sat R 48:74 O 23 '65

  Time 86:75 O 15 '65

  Vogue 146:71 N 15 '65

New York Times 1965, O 6, 5:3

NYTC 1965:265

(*Published libretto*) NA

(*Published sheet music*) Chappell/Delfont Music, Ltd.
(*Original cast recording*) OP Philips(E) SAL–3431,
          RE Philips(E) 6382–070 (Original London Cast)
(*Agent/contact*) Samuel French, Ltd. (London)
(*Libretto*) LC (Performing Arts Reading Room) ML50/.073P52; LC
          Wolf Mankowitz Presentations, Ltd., Cheina Enterprises,
          Ltd. & Cyril Ornadel Enterprises, Ltd. 13May65 DU62928;
          same as (*Agent/contact*)
(*Music, Orchestrations*) Same as (*Agent/contact*)

PIPE DREAM
(*Source*) *Sweet Thursday* (novel) by John Steinbeck
(*Book*) Oscar Hammerstein, II
(*Lyrics*) Oscar Hammerstein, II
(*Music*) Richard Rodgers
(*Producer*) Rodgers & Hammerstein
Sam S. Shubert Theatre   Broadway
November 30, 1955   246 performances
(*Stars*) William Johnson, Helen Traubel
Theatre World 55–56, pp. 69–71
Best Plays 55–56, pp. 364–5
America 94:417–18 Ja 7 '56
          Cath World 182:388 F '56
          Commonweal 63:331 D 30 '55
          Nation 181:544 D 17 '55
          New Yorker 31:104+ D 10 '55
          Newsweek il 46:110 D 12 '55
          Sat R 38:24 D 17 '55
          Sat R 39:13 S 15 '56
          Theatre Arts il 40:12–13 F '56
          Time il 66:67 D 12 '55
New York Times 1955, D 1, 44:1
          New York Times 1955, D 11, II, 5:1
NYTC 1955:198
(*Published libretto*) Viking Press, 1956

(*Published sheet music*) Williamson Music
(*Original cast recording*) OP RCA LOC–1023, RE RCA LOC/LSO–1097(e)
(*Agent/contact*) Rodgers & Hammerstein Music Library
(*Libretto*) NYPL NCOF+; same as (*Agent/contact*)
(*Music, Orchestrations*) Same as (*Agent/contact*)

*PLATINUM**
(*Source*) Original
(*Book*) Will Holt & Bruce Vilanch
(*Lyrics*) Will Holt
(*Music*) Gary William Friedman
(*Producer*) Gladys Rackmil, Fritz Holt & Barry M. Brown
Mark Hellinger Theatre   Broadway
November 12, 1978   33 performances
(*Stars*) Alexis Smith
Theatre World 78–79, p. 18
Best Plays 78–79, p. 370
Encore il 7:30–1 D 18 '78
        New Yorker 54:117 N 20 '78
        Newsweek 92:70 N 27 '78
        Roll Stone p. 29 F 8 '79
New York Times 1978, N 13, III, 15:2
        New York Times 1978, N 19, II, 3:1
NYTC 1978:191
(*Published libretto*) NA
(*Published sheet music*) NA (WB Music Corp.)
(*Original cast recording*) OP Unnamed label CX–335 (Original Broadway Cast
        recorded live); CBS Special Products (FOR FUTURE RELEASE) as
        SUNSET (off–Broadway Revival cast)
(*Agent/contact*)
    Will Holt   Gary William Friedman   Gladys Rackmil
    45 E. 66th Street   c/o DG, Inc.   1650 Broadway
    New York, N.Y. 10021   New York, N.Y. 10019

(*Libretto, Music, Orchestrations*) Same as (*Agent/contact*)

*Previously presented under the title *SUNSET*; subsequently revised
    and presented under the title *SUNSET*

PLAY ME A COUNTRY SONG
(*Source*) Original
(*Book*) Jay Broad
(*Lyrics*) John R. Briggs & Harry Manfredini
(*Music*) John R. Briggs & Harry Manfredini
(*Producer*) Frederick R. Selch
Virginia Theatre   Broadway
June 27, 1982   1 performance
(*Stars*) Mary Jo Catlett
Theatre World 82–83, p. 9
Best Plays 82–83, pp. 332–33
New Yorker 58:90 Jl 5 '82
New York Times 1982, Mr 12, III, 2:2
        New York Times 1982, Je 28, III, 14:3
NYTC 1982:250
(*Published libretto*) NA
(*Published sheet music*) NA (Live Music Pub. Corp.)
(*Original cast recording*) NA
(*Agent/contact*)   Jay Broad
                       c/o DG, Inc.
(*Libretto, Music, Orchestrations*) Same as (*Agent/contact*)

PO' ME ONE
See *CARIB SONG*

POLONAISE
(*Source*) Original
(*Book*) Gottfried Reinhardt & Anthony Veiller
(*Lyrics*) John Latouche
(*Music*) Frederic Chopin, adapted by Bronislaw Kaper
(*Producer*) W. Horace Schmidlapp, in association with Harry
      Bloomfield

Alvin Theatre/Adelphi Theatre*	Broadway
October 6, 1945	113 performances

(*Stars*) NA
Theatre World 45–46, p. 20
Best Plays 45–46, pp. 396–97
NO CRIT AVAIL
New York Times 1945, O 8, 20:2
      New York Times 1945, O 14, II, 1:1
NYTC 1945:149
(*Published libretto*) NA
(*Published sheet music*) Chappell/Robbins
(*Original cast recording*) OP RCA Camden CAL–210 (w/*EILEEN*)
(*Agent/contact*)

John Latouche Estate	Bronislaw Kaper	Gottfried Reinhardt
c/o ASCAP	c/o ASCAP	c/o DG, Inc.

(*Libretto*) LC Gottfried Reinhardt & Anthony Veiller 19Apr45 DU93135;
      same as (*Agent/contact*)
(*Music, Orchestrations*) Same as (*Agent/contact*)

*Moved to Adelphi Theatre 12/03/45

*PORTOFINO**
(*Source*) Original
(*Book*) Richard Ney
(*Lyrics*) Richard Ney & Sheldon Harnick
(*Music*) Louis Bellson & Will Irwin
(*Producer*) Richard Ney

Adelphi Theatre   Broadway
February 21, 1958   3 performances
(*Stars*) Helen Gallagher
Theatre World 57–58, p. 87
Best Plays 57–58, pp. 320–21
New Yorker 34:58+ Mr 1 '58
New York Times 1958, F 22, 8:3
NYTC 1958:346
(*Published libretto*) NA
(*Published sheet music*) NA (Sunbeam Music Corp.)
(*Original cast recording*) NA
(*Agent/contact*)   Louis Bellson
                         P.O. Box #1560
                         Lake Havasu City, AZ 86403
(*Libretto*) NYPL RM7713 as *ASLEEP MY LOVE*; LC Richard Ney 28Jun57
        DU45193 as *BUT NOT FOR MARRIAGE*; same as (*Agent/contact*)
(*Music, Orchestrations*) Same as (*Agent/contact*)

*Previously titled *ASLEEP MY LOVE*;
        subsequently titled *BUT NOT FOR MARRIAGE*

POUSSE–CAFE
(*Source*) *The Blue Angel (Der Blaue Engel)* (screenplay) by Robert
        Liebmann, Karl Zuckmayer & Karl Vollmoeller
(*Book*) Jerome Weidman
(*Lyrics*) Marshall Barer & Fred Tobias
(*Music*) Duke Ellington
(*Producer*) Guy De La Passardiere
Forty–Sixth Street Theatre   Broadway
March 18, 1966   3 performances
(*Stars*) Theodore Bikel, Lilo

Theatre World 65–66, p. 69
Best Plays 65–66, pp. 403–4
Dance Mag 40:24 My '66
      New Yorker 42:120 Mr 26 '66
      Newsweek 67:88 Mr 28 '66
New York Times 1966, Mr 19, 19:2
NYTC 1966:326
(*Published libretto*) NA
(*Published sheet music*) Tempo Music, Inc.
(*Original cast recording*) NA
(*Agent/contact*)

Jerome Weidman	Marshall Barer	Fred Tobias
c/o DG, Inc.	1718 Main Street	c/o DG, Inc.
	Venice, CA 90291	
Duke Ellington Estate		
c/o AGAC		

(*Libretto, Music, Orchestrations*) Same as (*Agent/contact*)

RAINBOW JONES
(*Source*) Original
(*Book*) Jill Williams
(*Lyrics*) Jill Williams
(*Music*) Jill Williams
(*Producer*) Rubykate, Inc., Phil Gillin & Gene Bambic

Music Box Theatre	Broadway
February 13, 1974	1 performance

(*Stars*) NA
Theatre World 73–74, p. 39
Best Plays 73–74, pp. 359–60
NO CRIT AVAIL
New York Times 1974, F 14, 57:1
NYTC 1974:390
(*Published libretto*) Pioneer Drama Service, 1979
(*Published sheet music*) Wren Music/Edwin H. Morris & Co.
(*Original cast recording*) NA

(*Agent/contact*) Pioneer Drama Service
(*Libretto, Music, Orchestrations*) Same as (*Agent/contact*)

RED, WHITE, AND MADDOX

(*Source*) Original
(*Book*) Don Tucker & Jay Broad
(*Lyrics*) Don Tucker
(*Music*) Don Tucker
(*Producer*) Edward Padula

Cort Theatre	Broadway
January 26, 1969	41 performances

(*Stars*) NA
Theatre World 68–69, p. 50
Best Plays 68–69, p. 403
America 120:232 F 22 '69
  Nation 208:221 F 17 '69
  New Repub 160:29–30 F 22 '69
  New Yorker 44:49 F 1 '69
  Sat R 51:32 O 26 '68
  Sat R 52:33 F 15 '69
  Time 92:73 N 29 '68
  Vogue 153:42 Mr 15 '69
New York Times 1968, O 5, 71:4
  New York Times 1968 N 3, 87:1
  New York Times 1969, Ja 27, 27:1
  New York Times 1969, F 2, II, 3:1
NYTC 1969:379
(*Published libretto*) NA
(*Published sheet music*) Sunbeam Music/Valando Music
(*Original cast recording*) NA
(*Agent/contact*)

Edward Padula	Don Tucker	Jay Broad
159 W. 53rd Street	c/o BMI	c/o DG, Inc.
New York, N.Y. 10019		

(*Libretto*) NYPL RM4409, same as (*Agent/contact*)

(*Music, Orchestrations*) Same as (*Agent/contact*)

REGGAE

(*Source*) Original

(*Book*) Melvin Van Peebles, Kendrew Lascelles & Stafford Harrison

(*Lyrics*) Ras Karbi, Michael Kamen, Kendrew Lascelles, Max Romeo,
  Randy Bishop, Jackie Mittoo & Stafford Harrison

(*Music*) Ras Karbi, Michael Kamen, Kendrew Lascelles, Max Romeo, Randy
  Bishop, Jackie Mittoo & Stafford Harrison

(*Producer*) Michael Butler & Eric Nezhad, with David Cogan

Biltmore Theater   Broadway

March 27, 1980   21 performances

(*Stars*) NA

Theatre World 79–80, p. 51

Best Plays 79–80, pp. 388–89

Newsweek il 95:93+ Ap 7 '80

New York Times 1980, Mr 16, II, 6:1

  New York Times 1980, Mr 28, III, 3:1

NYTC 1980:307

(*Published libretto*) NA

(*Published sheet music*) NA

(*Original cast recording*) NA

(*Agent/contact*)

Michael Butler	Kendrew Lascelles	Melvin Van Peebles
1000 Oak Brook Road	c/o DG, Inc.	353 W. 56th Street
Oak Brook, IL 60521		New York, N.Y. 10019

(*Libretto, Music, Orchestrations*) Same as (*Agent/contact*)

REGINA

(*Source*) *The Little Foxes* (play) by Lillian Hellman

(*Book*) Marc Blitzstein

(*Lyrics*) Marc Blitzstein

(*Music*) Marc Blitzstein

(*Producer*) Cheryl Crawford & Clinton Wilder

Forty–Sixth Street Theatre   Broadway

October 31, 1949   56 performances

(*Stars*) Jane Pickens, Brenda Lewis, Priscilla Gillette

Theatre World 49–50, p. 32

Best Plays 49–50, p. 359

Am Mercury 70:172–3 F '50

       Cath World 170:228–9 D '49

       Commonweal 51:228–9 D '49

       Mus Am 69:9 D 1 '49

       Nation 169:478 N 12 '49

       New Repub 121:22 D 5 '49

       New Yorker 25:56–8 N 12 '49

       New Yorker 28:103–5 Je 14 '52

       Newsweek 34:84–5 N 14 '49

       Sat R Lit 32:54–5 N 19 '49

       Sch & Soc 71:24–5 Ja 14 '50

       Theatre Arts por 34:12 Ja '50

       Time 54:46 N 14 '49

New York Times 1949, N 1, 32:2

       New York Times 1949, N 13, II, 1:1

       New York Times 1952, Je 2, 25:4

       New York Times 1978, N 18, 11:5

NYTC 1949:237

(*Published libretto*) Chappell, 1953

(*Published sheet music*) Chappell

(*Original cast recording*) OP Columbia O3L–260, RE Odyssey Y3–35236

(*Agent/contact*) Tams–Witmark Music Library

(*Libretto, Music, Orchestrations*) Same as (*Agent/contact*)

REX

(*Source*) Original

(*Book*) Sherman Yellen

(*Lyrics*) Sheldon Harnick

(*Music*) Richard Rodgers

(*Producer*) Richard Adler, Roger Berlind & Edward R. Downe, Jr.

Lunt–Fontanne Theatre   Broadway

April 25, 1976   49 performances

(*Stars*) Nicol Williamson, Penny Fuller

Theatre World 75–76, p. 51

Best Plays 75–76, pp. 347–49

New Yorker 52:75 My 3 '76

       Newsweek 87:76 My 10 '76

       Sat R 3:44 Ap 3 '76

       Time 107:87 My 10 '76

New York Times 1976, Ap 26, 38:1

       New York Times 1976, My 9, II, 5:1

NYTC 1976:286

(*Published libretto*) NA

(*Published sheet music*) Williamson Music

(*Original cast recording*) OP RCA ABL1–1683

(*Agent/contact*) Rodgers & Hammerstein Music Library (FOR FUTURE
       RELEASE)

(*Libretto*) NYPL RM7830; same as (*Agent/contact*)

(*Music, Orchestrations*) Same as (*Agent/contact*)

RHAPSODY

(*Source*) Story (title unavailable) by A.N. Nagler

(*Book*) Leonard L. Levinson & Arnold Sundgaard

(*Lyrics*) John Latouche, additional lyrics by Russell
       Bennett & Blevins Davis

(*Music*) Fritz Kreisler, adapted by Russell Bennett

(*Producer*) Blevins Davis, in association with Lorraine Mannville
       Dresselhuys

Century Theatre   Broadway
November 22, 1944   13 performances
(*Stars*) NA
Theatre World 44–45, p. 45
Best Plays 44–45, pp. 399–400
NO CRIT AVAIL
New York Times 1944, N 23, 37:2
NYTC 1944:75
(*Published libretto*) NA
(*Published sheet music*) NA
(*Original cast recording*) NA
(*Agent/contact*)

    Arnold Sundgaard   John Latouche Estate   Fritz Kreisler Estate
    c/o DG, Inc.   c/o ASCAP   c/o ASCAP

(*Libretto*) NYPL NCOF+, same as (*Agent/contact*)
(*Music, Orchestrations*) Same as (*Agent/contact*)

THE ROAR OF THE GREASE PAINT – THE SMELL OF THE CROWD

(*Source*) Original
(*Book*) Leslie Bricusse & Anthony Newley
(*Lyrics*) Leslie Bricusse & Anthony Newley
(*Music*) Leslie Bricusse & Anthony Newley
(*Producer*) David Merrick, in association with Bernard Delfont
Sam S. Shubert Theatre   Broadway
May 16, 1965   232 performances
(*Stars*) Anthony Newley, Cyril Ritchard
Theatre World 64–65, pp. 104–6
Best Plays 64–65, p. 338
America 112:867–8 Je 12 '65
        Cath World il 201:151–2 My '65
        Dance Mag il 39:22–3 Jl '65
        New Yorker 41:56 My 29 '65
        Newsweek 65:76 My 31 '65
        Reporter 32:45–6 Ap 8 '65
        Sat R il 48:38 Je 5 '65

Time il 85:83 My 28 '65
New York Times 1965, My 17, 46:2
NYTC 1965:326
(*Published libretto*) NA
(*Published sheet music*) Concord Music/Musical Comedy Prod., Inc./TRO
(*Original cast recording*) OP RCA LOC/LSO–1109
(*Agent/contact*) Tams–Witmark Music Library
(*Libretto, Music, Orchestrations*) Same as (*Agent/contact*)

THE ROBBER BRIDEGROOM*

(*Source*) *The Robber Bridegroom* (novella) by Eudora Welty
(*Book*) Alfred Uhry
(*Lyrics*) Alfred Uhry
(*Music*) Robert Waldman
(*Producer*) John Houseman, Margot Harley & Michael B. Kapon
Biltmore Theatre**			Broadway**
October 9, 1976			145 performances
(*Stars*) Barry Bostwick
Theatre World 75–76, p. 91
		Theatre World 76–77, p. 31
Best Plays 75–76, pp. 322–23
		Best Plays 76–77, pp. 293–94
America 133:inside back cover N 15 '75
		New Yorker 51:102 O 20 '75
		New Yorker 52:61 O 25 '76
		Time 108:87 O 25 '76
New York Times 1975, O 8, 27:1
		New York Times 1975, O 19, II, 1:1
		New York Times 1976, O 11, 35:1
NYTC 1975:206
		NYTC 1976:156
(*Published libretto*) Drama Book Specialists, 1978
(*Published sheet music*) Macmillan Perf. Arts Music/G. Schirmer
(*Original cast recording*) Columbia Special Products P–14589

(*Agent/contact*) Music Theatre International
(*Libretto, Music, Orchestrations*) Same as (*Agent/contact*)

*Subsequently produced on television for *Broadway on Showtime*,
    available at NYPL Billy Rose Collection, Lincoln Center, NCOX 367

**Previously produced off–Broadway at the Harkness Theatre

*ROCKABYE HAMLET**
(*Source*) *Hamlet* (play) by William Shakespeare
(*Book*) Cliff Jones
(*Lyrics*) Cliff Jones
(*Music*) Cliff Jones
(*Producer*) Lester Osterman Productions, Joseph Kipness, Martin Richards,
    Victor D'Arc & Marilyn Strauss

Minskoff Theatre	Broadway
February 17, 1976	8 performances

(*Stars*) Beverly D'Angelo
Theatre World 75–75, p. 41
Best Plays 75–76, pp. 342–43
New Yorker 52:76 Mr 1 '76
New York Times 1976, F 18, 23:1
NYTC 1976:368
(*Published libretto*) NA
(*Published sheet music*) NA (Elsinore Music/Champlain Productions, Ltd.)
(*Original cast recording*) OP Rising(C) RILP–103 (Original Canadian Cast)
(*Agent/contact*)   Cliff Jones
                51 Forest Heights Blvd.
                Willowdale, Ontario, Canada M2L 2K7
(*Libretto*) NYPL RM8052; LC Cliff E.B. Jones 4Mar74 DU89573 as
    HAMLET, A CONTEMPORARY ROCK MUSICAL; same as
    (*Agent/contact*)

(*Music*) LC Cliff E.B. Jones 4Mar74 DU89573 as *HAMLET, A*
       CONTEMPORARY ROCK MUSICAL; same as (*Agent/contact*)
(*Orchestrations*) Same as (*Agent/contact*)

*Previously titled *HAMLET, A CONTEMPORARY MUSICAL*;
       previously presented under title *KRONBORG*; subsequently
       presented under title *SOMETHING'S ROCKIN' IN DENMARK*

THE ROCKY HORROR SHOW

(*Source*) Original
(*Book*) Richard O'Brien
(*Lyrics*) Richard O'Brien
(*Music*) Richard O'Brien
(*Producer*) Lou Adler & Michael White
Belasco Theatre   Broadway
March 10, 1975   32 performances
(*Stars*) Tim Curry, Meat Loaf
Theatre World 74–75, p. 45
Best Plays 74–75, pp. 343–44
Dance Mag 49:28+ My '75
       Time il 105:85 Mr 24 '75
New York Times 1975, Mr 11, 26:1
NYTC 1975:311
(*Published libretto*) Samuel French, Inc., 1983
(*Published sheet music*) Druidcrest Music/Hollenbeck Music
(*Original cast recording*) OP Ode Records SP–77026, RE Ode Records
       ODE–9009 (Original Los Angeles Cast); UK Records(E) UKAL–1006
       (Original London Cast)
(*Agent/contact*) Samuel French, Inc.
(*Libretto*) LC Richard O'Brien 21Nov74 DU92365
(*Music, Orchestrations*) Same as (*Agent/contact*)

*RUMPLE**

(*Source*) Original
(*Book*) Irving Phillips
(*Lyrics*) Frank Reardon
(*Music*) Ernest G. Schweikert
(*Producer*) Paula Stone & Mike Sloan

| Alvin Theatre | Broadway |
| November 6, 1957 | 45 performances |

(*Stars*) Stephen Douglass, Eddie Foy, Gretchen Wyler
Theatre World 57–58, p. 40
Best Plays 57–58, pp. 299–300
New Yorker 33:104+ N 16 '57
     Newsweek 50:90 N 18 '57
     Theatre Arts il 42:22 Ja '58
     Time il 70:78 N 18 '57
New York Times 1957, N 7, 42:2
NYTC 1957:188
(*Published libretto*) NA
(*Published sheet music*) Chappell
(*Original cast recording*) NA
(*Agent/contact*)

Irving Phillips	Frank C. Reardon	Ernest G.
2807 E. Sylvia Street	c/o ASCAP	Schweikert Estate
Phoenix, AZ 85032		c/o ASCAP

(*Libretto*) LC Irving Walter Philips 14Aug57 DU45257 as **MR.**
    RUMPLE; same as (*Agent/contact*)
(*Music, Orchestrations*) Same as (*Agent/contact*)

*Previously titled **MR. RUMPLE**

*RUNAWAYS**

(*Source*) Original
(*Book*) Elizabeth Swados
(*Lyrics*) Elizabeth Swados
(*Music*) Elizabeth Swados

(*Producer*) Joseph Papp
Plymouth Theatre**   Broadway**
May 13, 1978**   267 performances
(*Stars*) NA
Theatre World 77–78, p. 47
Best Plays 77–78, pp. 375–76
America 138:349 Ap 29 '78
     Commonweal 105:498 Ag 4 '78
     Crawdaddy p. 20 Jl '78
     Encore il 7:30 My 22 '78
     NY 11:70–1 Mr 27 '78
     NY 11:77 My 29 '78
     Nation 226:379–80 Ap 1 '78
     New Repub 178:24 Ap 22 '78
     New Yorker 54:88 Mr 20 '78
     Newsweek il 91:74–5 Mr 27 '78
     Roll Stone p. 54–6 Je 15 '78
     Sat R 5:24 My 13 '78
     Sat R 5:24 Jl 8 '78
     Time 111:84 Mr 20 '78
New York Times 1978, Mr 10, III, 3:4
     New York Times 1978, Mr 22, III, 17:1
     New York Times 1978, My 2, II, 5:1
     New York Times 1978, My 15, III, 15:1
NYTC 1978:278
(*Published libretto*) Bantam Books, 1979; Samuel French, Inc., 1980
(*Published sheet music*) NA
(*Original cast recording*) Columbia JS–35410
(*Agent/contact*) Samuel French, Inc.
(*Libretto*) NYPL NCOF+ 79–971
(*Music, Orchestrations*) Same as (*Agent/contact*)

*Videotaped performance available at NYPL Billy Rose Collection,
    Lincoln Center, NCOV 77
*Originally produced off–Broadway at the Public/Theater Cabaret
    3/9/78 before transferring on Broadway to the Plymouth Theatre

SADIE THOMPSON

(*Source*) *Rain* (short story) by Somerset Maugham, (play) by John Colton
      & Clemence Randolph

(*Book*) Howard Dietz & Rouben Mamoulian

(*Lyrics*) Howard Dietz

(*Music*) Vernon Duke

(*Producer*) A.P. Waxman

Alvin Theatre   Broadway

November 16, 1944   60 performances

(*Stars*) June Havoc

Theatre World 44–45, p. 42

Best Plays 44–45, pp. 397–98

Cath World 160:357 Ja '45

      Colliers il 115:12–13 Ja 6 '45

      Commonweal 41:174–5 D 1 '44

      Life il 17:43–6+ D 11 '44

      Nation 159:698 D 2 '44

      New Yorker 20:46 N 25 '44

      Newsweek il 24:100 N 27 '44

      Theatre Arts il (p. 8) 29:12+ Ja '45

      Time il 44:48 N 27 '44

New York Times 1944, N 17, 25:2

      New York Times 1944, N 26, II, 1:1

NYTC 1944:84

(*Published libretto*) NA

(*Published sheet music*) Paramount

(*Original cast recording*) NA

(*Agent/contact*)

Howard Dietz Estate	Vernon Duke Estate	Rouben Mamoulian
c/o ASCAP	c/o Kay McCracken Duke	c/o DG, Inc.
	407 Vance Street	
	Pacific Palisades, CA 90272	

(*Libretto*) NYPL NCOF+; MCNY; same as (*Agent/contact*)
(*Music*) MCNY; same as (*Agent/contact*)
(*Orchestrations*) Same as (*Agent/contact*)

SAIL AWAY
(*Source*) Original
(*Book*) Noel Coward
(*Lyrics*) Noel Coward
(*Music*) Noel Coward
(*Producer*) Bonard Productions & Charles Russell
Broadhurst Theatre   Broadway
October 3, 1961   167 performances
(*Stars*) Elaine Stritch
Theatre World 61–62, p. 14
Best Plays 61–62, pp. 257–58
Commonweal 75:154 N 3 '61
         Dance Mag il 35:28 N '61
         Nation 193:361 N 4 '61
         New Repub 145:22 N 6 '61
         New Yorker 37:162+ O 14 '61
         Newsweek 58:101 O 16 '61
         Reporter 25:53 O 26 '61
         Sat R 44:34 O 21 '61
         Theatre Arts il 45:10–11 D '61
         Time il 78:58 O 13 '61
New York Times 1961, Ag 10, 17:7
         New York Times 1961, O 4, 48:5
         New York Times 1962, Je 23, 14:3
NYTC 1961:251
(*Published libretto*) NA
(*Published sheet music*) Chappell
(*Original cast recording*) OP Capitol WAO/SWAO–1643; Stanyan(E)
         SR–10027 (Original London Cast)

(Agent/contact)   Noel Coward Estate

c/o Michael Imison Playwrights Ltd.

150 W. 47th Street, #5F

New York, N.Y. 10036

(Libretto) NYPL RM518, RM2040, NCOF+; same as *(Agent/contact)*

(Music, Orchestrations) Same as *(Agent/contact)*

ST. LOUIS WOMAN*

(Source) God Sends Sunday (novel) by Arna Bontemps

(Book) Arna Bontemps & Countee Cullen

(Lyrics) Johnny Mercer

(Music) Harold Arlen

(Producer) Edward Gross

Martin Beck Theatre   Broadway

March 30, 1946   113 performances

(Stars) Pearl Bailey

Theatre World 45–46, p. 85

Best Plays 45–46, p. 436

Cath World 163:170 My '46

    Commonweal 44:14 Ap 19 '46

    Forum 105:937–8 Je '46

    Life 20:63–4 Ap 29 '46

    Mod Mus 23 no2:146 [Ap] '46

    New Yorker 22:46+ Ap 6 '46

    Newsweek il 27:84 Ap 15 '46

    Sat R Lit il 29:24 Ap 27 '46

    Time il 47:47 Ap 8 '46

New York Times 1946, Ap 1, 22:2

NYTC 1946:415

(Published libretto) In *Black Theater*, Dodd, Mead & Comp., 1971

(Published sheet music) A–M Music/Crawford/DeSylva, Brown & Henderson, Inc.

(Original cast recording) OP Capitol L–355, RE Capitol H–355/ DW–2742

(*Agent/contact*)
> Johnny Mercer Foundation   Harold Arlen
> 32107 Lindero Canyon Rd., Ste 222   c/o DG, Inc.
> Westlake Village, CA   91361

(*Libretto*) LC Countee Cullen & Arna Bontemps 13Dec44 DU91614;
> same as (*Agent/contact*)

(*Music, Orchestrations*) Same as (*Agent/contact*)

*Subsequently revised and presented under titles *FREE AND*
> *EASY* and *BLUES OPERA*

SARATOGA

(*Source*) *Saratoga Trunk* (novel) by Edna Ferber
(*Book*) Morton DaCosta
(*Lyrics*) Johnny Mercer
(*Music*) Harold Arlen
(*Producer*) Robert Fryer

Winter Garden Theatre   Broadway
December 7, 1959   80 performances

(*Stars*) Howard Keel, Carol Lawrence
Theatre World 59–60, p. 50
Best Plays 59–60, pp. 309–10
America 102:594+ F 13 '60
> New Yorker 35:81 D 19 '59
> Newsweek 54:83 D 21 '59
> Sat R 42:25 D 26 '59
> Theatre Arts il 44:17–21 Ja '60
> Time 74:34 D 21 '59
> Vogue il 135:114–15 F 1 '60

New York Times 1959, D 8, 59:4
NYTC 1959:195
(*Published libretto*) NA
(*Published sheet music*) Harwin Music Corp./Edwin H. Morris & Co.
(*Original cast recording*) OP RCA LOC/LSO–1051

(*Agent/contact*)

Morton DaCosta	Robert Fryer	Johnny Mercer
R.F.D. 3, Dorothy Road	Los Angeles	Foundation
West Redding, CT 06896	Music Center	32107 Lindero
	135 N. Grand Avenue	Canyon Rd., Ste. 222
Harold Arlen	Los Angeles, CA 90012	Westlake Village, CA
c/o DG, Inc.		91361

(*Libretto*) NYPL NCOF+; LC (Performing Arts Reading Room)
    ML50/.A7S4; LC Morton DaCosta 29Dec59 DU50179;
    same as (*Agent/contact*)

(*Music, Orchestrations*) Same as (*Agent/contact*)

SARAVA

(*Source*) *Dona Flor and Her Two Husbands (Dona Flor e Seus Dois
    Maridos)* (novel) by Jorge Amado, (screenplay) by Bruno Barreto

(*Book*) N. Richard Nash

(*Lyrics*) N. Richard Nash

(*Music*) Mitch Leigh

(*Producer*) Eugene V. Wolsk & Mitch Leigh

Mark Hellinger Theatre   Broadway

January 11, 1979*   140 performances*

(*Stars*) Tovah Feldshuh

Theatre World 78–79, p. 30

Best Plays 78–79, pp. 377–78

New Leader 62:21–2 Mr 12 '79

    New Yorker 55:92 Mr 5 '79

New York Times 1979, F 12, III, 12:1

    New York Times 1979, Mr 4, II, 5:2

NYTC 1979:364

(*Published libretto*) NA

(*Published sheet music*) Andrew Scott, Inc.

(*Original cast recording*) NA
(*Agent/contact*)

Mitch Leigh	Eugene V. Wolsk	N. Richard Nash
c/o Music Makers, Inc.	165 W. 46th Street	c/o DG, Inc.
200 Central Park South	New York, N.Y. 10036	
New York, N.Y. 10019		

(*Libretto, Music, Orchestrations*) Same as (*Agent/contact*)

SARAVA had no official opening; however, previews began
          1/11/79 and number of performances is calculated from that date

SEESAW

(*Source*) *Two for the Seesaw* (play) by William Gibson
(*Book*) Michael Stewart/Michael Bennett*
(*Lyrics*) Dorothy Fields
(*Music*) Cy Coleman
(*Producer*) Joseph Kipness, Lawrence Kasha, James Nederlander,
          George M. Steinbrenner III & Lorin E. Price
Uris Theatre   Broadway
March 18, 1973   296 performances
(*Stars*) Michele Lee, Ken Howard, Tommy Tune
Theatre World 72–73, p. 64–5
Best Plays 72–73, pp. 354–55
America 128:336 Ap 14 '73
          Dance Mag il 47:58A–58C Je '73
          Harp Baz 106:153 Mr '73
          Nation 216:508 Ap 16 '73
          New Yorker 49:74 Mr 24 '73
          Newsweek il 81:83 Ap 2 '73
          Time il 101:71 Ap 2 '73
New York Times 1973, Mr 19, 46:1
          New York Times 1973, Mr 25, II, 1:1
NYTC 1973:324

(*Published libretto*) Samuel French, Inc., 1975
(*Published sheet music*) Notable Music Co./Aldi Music Co.
(*Original cast recording*) OP Buddah 95006–1, RE Columbia Special
        Products X–15563
(*Agent/contact*) Samuel French, Inc.
(*Libretto*) NYPL RM8336
(*Music, Orchestrations*) Same as (*Agent/contact*)

*Michael Stewart, who quit the show out of town and refused authorship
        credit, was replaced by director Michael Bennett as book writer

THE SELLING OF THE PRESIDENT
(*Source*) *The Selling of the President* (novel) by Joe McGinniss
(*Book*) Jack O'Brien* & Stuart Hample
(*Lyrics*) Jack O'Brien*
(*Music*) Bob James
(*Producer*) John Flaxman, Harold Hastings & Franklin Roberts
Shubert Theatre   Broadway
March 22, 1972   5 performances
(*Stars*) Pat Hingle, Barbara Barrie, Karen Morrow
Theatre World 71–72, p. 40
Best Plays 71–72, pp. 335–36
Look il 35:52–3 S 7 '71
        Newsweek 77:121 Ap 12 '71
New York Times 1972, Mr 23, 50:1
NYTC 1972:351
(*Published libretto*) NA
(*Published sheet music*) Edwin H. Morris/Charles Hansen Music
(*Original cast recording*) NA
(*Agent/contact*)   Jack O'Brien   Stuart Hample
                 c/o Old Globe Theatre   c/o DG, Inc.
                 Balboa Park
                 San Diego, CA   92112

(*Libretto*) NYPL RM5163; same as (*Agent/contact*)
(*Music, Orchestrations*) Same as (*Agent/contact*)

*At press time, Mr. O'Brien was not interested in soliciting
    further productions of this property

SEVEN BRIDES FOR SEVEN BROTHERS

(*Source*) *Seven Brides for Seven Brothers* (screenplay) by Frances
    Goodrich, Albert Hackett & Dorothy Kingsley, songs by Johnny
    Mercer & Gene de Paul, adapted from "The Sobbin' Women"
    (short story) by Stephen Vincent Benét
(*Book*) Lawrence Kasha & David Landay
(*Lyrics*) Johnny Mercer; new songs by Al Kasha & Joel Hirschhorn
(*Music*) Gene de Paul; new songs by Al Kasha & Joel Hirschhorn
(*Producer*) Kaslan Productions
Alvin Theatre   Broadway
July 8, 1982   5 performances
(*Stars*) Debby Boone
Theatre World 82–83, p. 11
Best Plays 82–83, pp. 333–34
NY il 15:60–1 Jl 19 '82
        New Yorker 58:69 Jl 19 '82
New York Times 1982, Je 3, III, 14:4
        New York Times 1982, Jl 9, III, 3:1
        New York Times 1982, Jl 10, 10:6
        New York Times 1982, Jl 13, II, 3:5
NYTC 1982:247
(*Published libretto*) NA
(*Published sheet music*) NA (Morning Picture Music, Inc./Fire and
    Water Songs); Robbins Music Corp. (Original Motion Picture)
(*Original cast recording*) First Night Records(E) Cast 2 (Original
    London Cast)

(*Agent/contact*) Tams–Witmark Music Library

(*Libretto*) NYPL NCOF+ 82–778; LC Lawrence Kasha, David Landay, Al
          Kasha & Joel Hirschhorn 12Nov82 PAu–478–722; same as
          (*Agent/contact*)

(*Music, Orchestrations*) Same as (*Agent/contact*)

SEVENTEEN

(*Source*) *Seventeen* (novel) by Booth Tarkington

(*Book*) Sally Benson

(*Lyrics*) Kim Gannon

(*Music*) Walter Kent

(*Producer*) Milton Berle, Sammy Lambert & Bernie Foyer

Broadhurst Theatre   Broadway

June 21, 1951   180 performances

(*Stars*) Frank Albertson, Kenneth Nelson

Theatre World 51–52, p. 10

Best Plays 51–52, pp. 277–78

Cath World 173:386 Ag '51

          Commonweal 54:309 Jl 6 '51

          Life il 31:57–8 Jl 23 '51

          Mus Am 71:34 Jl '51

          New Yorker 27:39 Je 30 '51

          Newsweek il 38:74 Jl 2 '51

          Theatre Arts il 35:6–7 S '51

          Time il 58:55 Jl 2 '51

New York Times 1951, Je 22, 16:6

          New York Times 1951, Jl 1, II, 9:5

NYTC 1951:250

(*Published libretto*) Samuel French, Inc., 1954

(*Published sheet music*) Leeds Music Corp.

(*Original cast recording*) OP RCA LOC–1003, RE RCA CBM1–2034

(*Agent/contact*) Samuel French, Inc./Tams–Witmark Music Library*

(*Libretto*) NYPL RM4868; Tams–Witmark Music Library
(*Music, Orchestrations*) Same as (*Agent/contact*)

*Samuel French, Inc. makes this property available to amateur and
      educational groups; Tams–Witmark licenses professional and
      semi–professional productions

SEVENTH HEAVEN
(*Source*) *Seventh Heaven* (play) by Austin Strong
(*Book*) Victor Wolfson & Stella Unger
(*Lyrics*) Stella Unger
(*Music*) Victor Young
(*Producer*) Gant Gaither & William Bacher
ANTA Theatre'   Broadway
May 26, 1955   44 performances
(*Stars*) Chita Rivera, Bea Arthur, Ricardo Montalban, Robert Clary,
      Gloria De Haven
Theatre World 54–55, p. 104
Best Plays 54–55, pp. 416–17
America 93:298 Je 11 '55
      Cath World 181:307–8 Jl '55
      Commonweal 62:329 Jl 1 '55
      NY Times Mag il p. 19 My 15 '55
      Nation 180:510 Je 11 '55
      Sat R 38:25 Je 11 '55
      Theatre Arts il 39:18–19 Ag '55
      Time il 65:57 Je 6 '55
New York Times 1955, My 27, 16:2
NYTC 1955:302
(*Published libretto*) NA
(*Published sheet music*) Chappell
(*Original cast recording*) OP Decca DL–9001

(*Agent/contact*)

Stella Unger Estate	Victor Wolfson	Victor Young Estate
c/o Robert L. Unger	c/o DG, Inc.	c/o Gold, Herscher,
25 W. 81st Street, #17A		Marks & Pepper
New York, N.Y. 10024		8500 Wilshire Blvd., #614
		Beverly Hills, CA 90211
		ATTN: Daniel Herscher

(*Libretto, Music, Orchestrations*) Same as (*Agent/contact*)

70, GIRLS, 70

(*Source*) *Breath of Spring* (play) by Peter Coke, *Make Mine*
        Mink (screenplay) by Michael Pertwee
(*Book*) Joe Masteroff*
(*Lyrics*) Fred Ebb
(*Music*) John Kander
(*Producer*) Arthur Whitelaw & Seth Harrison
Broadhurst Theartre   Broadway
April 15, 1971   36 performances
(*Stars*) Hans Conried, Mildred Natwick
Theatre World 70–71, p. 45
Best Plays 70–71, pp. 313–14
America 124:615–6 Je 12 '71
        Dance Mag 45:81–2 Je '71
        Nation 212:570–1 My 3 '71
        New Yorker 47:93–4 Ap 24 '71
New York Times 1971, Ap 16, 29:2
NYTC 1971:302
(*Published libretto*) NA
(*Published sheet music*) Sunbeam/Music Valando Music
(*Original cast recording*) OP Columbia S–30589
(*Agent/contact*) Samuel French, Inc.
(*Libretto*) NYPL NCOF+ 73–1864, RM7779, RM7780, RM7781;
        same as (*Agent/contact*)

(*Music, Orchestrations*) Same as (*Agent/contact*)

*In all publicity, Joe Masteroff is given sole authorship credit; however,
        the manuscript/promptscript filed with NYPL Billy Rose Collection
        gives Fred Ebb & Norman Martin authorship credit

SHANGRI–LA

(*Source*) *Lost Horizon* (novel) by James Hilton
(*Book*) James Hilton, Jerome Lawrence & Robert E. Lee
(*Lyrics*) James Hilton, Jerome Lawrence & Robert E. Lee
(*Music*) Harry Warren
(*Producer*) Robert Fryer & Lawrence Carr
Winter Garden Theatre   Broadway
June 31, 1956   21 performances
(*Stars*) Jack Cassidy, Carol Lawrence, Harold Lang, Alice Ghostley
Theatre World 55–56, p. 114
Best Plays 56–57, pp. 313–14
America 95:330 Je 30 '56
        Cath World 183:388 Ag '56
        Sat R 39:22 Je 30 '56
        Theatre Arts il 40:16 Ag '56
        Time 67:86+ Je 25 '56
New York Times 1956, Je 14, 40:1
NYTC 1956:293
(*Published libretto*) NA
(*Published sheet music*) Horizon Music Co./Edwin H. Morris
(*Original cast recording*) OP The Sound of Broadway 300/1
        (1960 Television Cast w/*SHINBONE ALLEY*)
(*Agent/contact*)
        Jerome Lawrence   Robert E. Lee
        c/o DG, Inc.   c/o DG, Inc.

        Harry Warren Estate
        c/o ASCAP

(*Libretto*) NYPL NCOF+; same as (*Agent/contact*)
(*Music, Orchestrations*) Same as (*Agent/contact*)

SHELTER

(*Source*) Original
(*Book*) Gretchen Cryer
(*Lyrics*) Gretchen Cryer
(*Music*) Nancy Ford
(*Producer*) Richard Fields & Peter Flood
John Golden Theatre   Broadway
February 6, 1973   31 performances
(*Stars*) Marcia Rodd
Theatre World 72–73, p. 54
Best Plays 72–73, pp. 348–49
New Yorker 48:79 F 17 '73
New York Times 1973, F 7, 31:1
         New York Times 1973, F 18, II, 1:4
NYTC 1973:370
(*Published libretto*) Samuel French, Inc., 1973
(*Published sheet music*) NA (Multimood Music, Inc./Marylebone
         Music, Inc.)
(*Original cast recording*) NA
(*Agent/contact*) Samuel French, Inc.
(*Libretto, Music, Orchestrations*) Same as (*Agent/contact*)

SHERRY!

(*Source*) *The Man Who Came to Dinner* (play) by George S. Kaufman &
         Moss Hart
(*Book*) James Lipton
(*Lyrics*) James Lipton
(*Music*) Laurence Rosenthal
(*Producer*) Lee Guber, Frank Ford & Shelly Gross

Alvin Theatre   Broadway
March 28, 1967   72 performances
(*Stars*) Clive Revill, Elizabeth Allen, Dolores Gray
Theatre World 66–67, p. 56
Best Plays 66–67, pp. 385–86
America 116:736–7 My 13 '67
      Chr Cent 84:870–1 Jl 5 '67
      Commonweal 86:208–10 My 5 '67
      Dance Mag 41:27–8 My '67
      New Yorker 43:138 Ap 8 '67
      Newsweek 69:109 Ap 10 '67
      Vogue 149:142 My '67
New York Times 1967, Mr 29, 39:1
      New York Times 1967, Ap 9, II, 1:1
NYTC 1967:332
(*Published libretto*) NA
(*Published sheet music*) Chappell
(*Original cast recording*) NA
(*Agent/contact*)
    James Lipton   Laurence Rosenthal   Guber/Gross Inc.
    c/o DG, Inc.   c/o DG, Inc.   32 E. 57th Street
                                       New York, N.Y. 10022
(*Libretto*) Institute for the American Musical; same as (*Agent/contact*)
(*Music, Orchestrations*) Same as (*Agent/contact*)

SHINBONE ALLEY *
(*Source*) *Archy and Mehitabel* (collection) by Don Marquis
(*Book*) Joe Darion & Mel Brooks
(*Lyrics*) Joe Darion
(*Music*) George Kleinsinger
(*Producer*) Peter Lawrence
Broadway Theater   Broadway
April 13, 1957   49 performances

(*Stars*) Eartha Kitt, Eddie Bracken

Theatre World 56–57, p. 110

Best Plays 56–57, pp. 367–68

America 97:216 My 11 '57

       Cath World 185:228–9 Je '57

       Chr Cent 74:762 Je 19 '57

       Commonweal 66:204 My 24 '57

       New Yorker 33:82+ Ap 20 '57

       Newsweek 49:69–70 Ap 22 '57

       Theatre Arts il 41:15–16 Je '57

       Time 69:90 Ap 22 '57

New York Times 1957, Ap 15, 23:2

       New York Times 1957, Ap 28, II, 1:1

NYTC 1957:292

(*Published libretto*) Chappell & Co., 1957, as *ARCHY & MEHITABEL*;

       in *The Best Short Plays of 1957–1958*, Beacon Press, 1958, as

       ARCHY & MEHITABEL

(*Published sheet music*) Helena Music Corp./Chappell

(*Original cast recording*) OP Columbia ML/OL–4963, RE Columbia

       Special Products AOL–4963 as *ARCHY & MEHITABEL*

       (Original Record Cast); OP Mastertone 1251 (Original

       Broadway Cast recorded live); OP Sound of Broadway 300/1

       (Original Television Cast w/*SHANGRI–LA*)

(*Agent/contact*) Music Theatre International

(*Libretto*) NYPL NCOF+; same as (*Agent/contact*)

(*Music, Orchestrations*) Same as (*Agent/contact*)

*Previously titled *ARCHY & MEHITABEL*

SHINE IT ON

See *THE ACT*

SIMPLY HEAVENLY

(*Source*) *Simple Takes a Wife* (novel) by Langston Hughes

(*Book*) Langston Hughes

(*Lyrics*) Langston Hughes

(*Music*) David Martin

(*Producer*) Stella Holt

The Playhouse*   Broadway*

August 20, 1957*   62 performances

(*Stars*) Claudia McNeil

Theatre World 56–57, p. 159

Best Plays 57–58, pp. 283–84

Cath World 185:388–9 Ag '57

   Nation 185:230 O 5 '57

   Sat R 40:24 S 7 '57

New York Times 1957, My 22, 28:2

   New York Times 1957, Je 2, II, 1:1

NYTC 1957:264

(*Published libretto*) Dramatists Play Service, Inc., 1959;

   in *Five Plays by Langston Hughes*, Indiana Univ. Press, 1968;

   in *Black Theater*, Dodd, Mead & Comp., 1971

(*Published sheet music*) Bourne, Inc.

(*Original cast recording*) OP Columbia OL–5240

(*Agent/contact*) Dramatists Play Service, Inc.

(*Libretto*) NYPL RM575, NCOF+

(*Music, Orchestrations*) Same as (*Agent/contact*)

*Originally opened off–Broadway at the 85th Street Playhouse 5/21/57

   before transferring on Broadway to The Playhouse

1600 PENNSYLVANIA AVENUE

(*Source*) Original

(*Book*) Alan Jay Lerner*

(*Lyrics*) Alan Jay Lerner*

(*Music*) Leonard Bernstein*
(*Producer*) Roger L. Stevens & Robert Whitehead
Mark Hellinger Theatre   Broadway
May 4, 1976   7 performances
(*Stars*) Ken Howard, Patricia Routledge
Theatre World 75–76, p. 55
Best Plays 75–76, pp. 350–51
New Yorker 52:124 My 17 '76
        Newsweek 87:96 My 17 '76
        Sat R 3:44–5 Ap 3 '76
        Time 107:69–70 My 31 '76
New York Times 1976, My 5, 48:1
NYTC 1976:244
(*Published libretto*) NA
(*Published sheet music*) Music of the Times Pub. Corp.
(*Original cast recording*) NA
(*Agent/contact*)   Alan Jay Lerner Estate   Leonard Bernstein
                        c/o David Grossberg   c/o DG, Inc.
                        30 N. La Salle Street
                        New York, N.Y.   10027
(*Libretto, Music, Orchestrations*) Same as (*Agent/contact*)

*At press time, neither the Alan Jay Lerner Estate nor Mr. Bernstein
        was interested in soliciting further productions of this property

SKYSCRAPER
(*Source*) *Dream Girl* (play) by Elmer Rice
(*Book*) Peter Stone
(*Lyrics*) Sammy Cahn
(*Music*) James Van Heusen
(*Producer*) Cy Feuer & Ernest H. Martin
Lunt–Fontanne Theatre   Broadway
November 13, 1965   241 performances

(*Stars*) Julie Harris, Peter Marshall, Charles Nelson Reilly
Theatre World 65–66, p. 32
Best Plays 65–66, pp. 384–85
America 114:180 Ja 29 '66
      Commonweal 83:316 D 10 '65
      Dance Mag 40:16 Ja '66
      Holiday 39:118+ Ja '66
      Life il 60:90–2 F 4 '66
      New Yorker 41:149 N 20 '65
      Newsweek il 66:91 N 29 '65
      Sat R 48:76 D 4 '65
      Time 86:67 N 26 '65
New York Times 1965, N 15, 48:1
NYTC 1965:274
(*Published libretto*) Samuel French, Inc., 1967
(*Published sheet music*) Harms
(*Original cast recording*) OP Capitol VAS/SVAS–2422
(*Agent/contact*) Samuel French, Inc.
(*Libretto*) NYPL RM405, RM2246, NCOF+
(*Music, Orchestrations*) Same as (*Agent/contact*)

SLEEPY HOLLOW
(*Source*) "The Legend of Sleepy Hollow" (short story) by Washington Irving
(*Book*) Russell Maloney & Miriam Battista
(*Lyrics*) Russell Maloney & Miriam Battista
(*Music*) George Lessner
(*Producer*) Lorraine Lester
St. James Theatre   Broadway
June 3, 1948   12 performances
(*Stars*) Jo Sullivan, Mary McCarty
Theatre World 48–49, p. 6
Best Plays 48–49, pp. 375–76
New Yorker 24:44 Je 12 '48

Newsweek il 31:86 Je 14 '48

Time 51:64 Je 14 '48

New York Times 1948, Je 4, 26:3

NYTC 1948:258

(*Published libretto*) NA

(*Published sheet music*) Chappell

(*Original cast recording*) NA

(*Agent/contact*)   George Lessner

58 Van Etten Blvd.

New Rochelle, N.Y.   10804

(*Libretto, Music, Orchestrations*) Same as (*Agent/contact*)

SO LONG, 174TH STREET

(*Source*) *Enter Laughing* (play) by Joseph Stein, (novel) by Carl Reiner

(*Book*) Joseph Stein

(*Lyrics*) Stan Daniels

(*Music*) Stan Daniels

(*Producer*) Frederick Brisson, The Harkness Organization & Wyatt
      Dickerson

Harkness Theatre   Broadway

April 27, 1976   16 performances

(*Stars*) Robert Morse, George S. Irving

Theatre World 75–76, p. 52

Best Plays 75–76, pp. 349–50

New Yorker 52:104 My 10 '76

Newsweek 87:76 My 10 '76

New York Times 1976, Ap 28, 34:1

New York Times 1976, My 9, II, 5:1

NYTC 1976:282

(*Published libretto*) NA

(*Published sheet music*) NA (Frank Music Corp.)

(*Original cast recording*) Original Cast Records OC-8131

(*Agent/contact*)

Stan Daniels	Joseph Stein	Frederick Brisson Prods.
4754 Alonzo Avenue	c/o DG, Inc.	c/o Dwight D. Frye
Encino, CA 91316		35 W. 90th Street
		New York, N.Y. 10024

(*Libretto, Music, Orchestrations*) Same as (*Agent/contact*)

SOME KIND OF MAN
See *LOOK TO THE LILIES*

SOMETHING MORE!
(*Source*) *Portofino P.T.A.* (novel) by Gerald Green
(*Book*) Nate Monaster
(*Lyrics*) Marilyn & Alan Bergman
(*Music*) Sammy Fain
(*Producer*) Lester Osterman
Eugene O'Neill Theatre   Broadway
November 10, 1964   15 performances
(*Stars*) Barbara Cook, Arthur Hill, Hal Linden
Theatre World 64–65, p. 40
Best Plays 64–65, pp. 311–12
Dance Mag 39:18–19 Ja '65
        Time 84:81 N 20 '64
New York Times 1964, N 11, 36:1
NYTC 1964:159
(*Published libretto*) NA
(*Published sheet music*) Chappell–Styne, Inc.
(*Original cast recording*) NA
(*Agent/contact*)

Marilyn & Alan Bergman	Sammy Fain	Nate Monaster
c/o The Lantz Office, Inc.	c/o DG, Inc.	c/o DG, Inc.
888 Seventh Avenue		
New York, N.Y. 10019		

(*Libretto, Music, Orchestrations*) Same as (*Agent/contact*)

SOMETHING'S AFOOT*

(*Source*) Original

(*Book*) James McDonald, David Vos & Robert Gerlach

(*Lyrics*) James McDonald, David Vos & Robert Gerlach

(*Music*) James McDonald, David Vos & Robert Gerlach;
    additional music by Ed Linderman

(*Producer*) Emanuel Azenburg, Dasha Epstein & John Mason Kirby

Lyceum Theatre   Broadway

May 27, 1976   61 performances

(*Stars*) Tessie O'Shea

Theatre World 75–76, p. 59

Best Plays 75–76, p. 353

New Yorker 52:79 Je 7 '76
    Time 107:74 Je 7 '76

New York Times 1976, My 28, III, 14:4
    New York Times 1976, Je 6, II, 5:1

NYTC 1976:234

(*Published libretto*) Samuel French, Inc., 1976

(*Published sheet music*) New York Times Music Corp./Music of the
    Times Pub. Corp.

(*Original cast recording*) NA

(*Agent/contact*) Samuel French, Inc.

(*Libretto, Music, Orchestrations*) Same as (*Agent/contact*)

*Subsequently produced on television for *Broadway on Showtime*,
    available at NYPL Billy Rose Collection, Lincoln Center, NCOX 375

SOMETHING'S ROCKIN' IN DENMARK
See **ROCKABYE HAMLET**

A SONG FOR ANASTASIA
See **ANYA**

SONG OF VIENNA
See *MARINKA*

SONG WITHOUT WORDS
See *MUSIC IN MY HEART*

SOPHIE
(*Source*) Original
(*Book*) Philip Pruneau
(*Lyrics*) Steve Allen
(*Music*) Steve Allen
(*Producer*) Len Bedsow, Hal Grossman, Michael Pollock
      & Max Fialkov

| Winter Garden Theatre | Broadway |
| April 15, 1963 | 8 performances |

(*Stars*) Art Lund
Theatre World 62–63, p. 89
Best Plays 62–63, pp. 305–6
Newsweek 61:54 Ap 29 '63
      Theatre Arts 47:66 Je '63
New York Times 1963, Ap 16, 32:1
NYTC 1963:344
(*Published libretto*) NA
(*Published sheet music*) Rosemeadow Pub. Corp.
(*Original cast recording*) AEI Records AEI–1130 (Original Demo Recording)
(*Agent/contact*)   Steve Allen
                15201 Burbank Blvd., Ste #B
                Van Nuys, CA 91411
(*Libretto*) LC (Performing Arts Reading Room) ML50/.Z99S672; LC
      Philip Pruneau 30Apr62 DU55374; same as (*Agent/contact*)
(*Music, Orchestrations*) Same as (*Agent/contact*)

STREET DREAMS: THE INNER CITY MUSICAL
See *INNER CITY*

STREET SCENE
(*Source*) *Street Scene* (play) by Elmer Rice
(*Book*) Elmer Rice
(*Lyrics*) Langston Hughes
(*Music*) Kurt Weill
(*Producer*) Dwight Deere Wiman & The Playwrights' Company
Adelphi Theatre   Broadway
January 9, 1947   148 performances
(*Stars*) Anne Jeffreys
Theatre World 46–47, p. 70
Best Plays 46–47, pp. 454–55
Cath World 164:453 F '47
        Commonweal 45:397 Ja 31 '47
        Life 22:78 F 24 '47
        New Repub 116:40 F 10 '47
        New Yorker 22:44+ Ja 18 '47
        Newsweek 29:84 Ja 20 '47
        Sat R Lit 30:24–6 F 1 '47
        Theatre Arts 31:12–13+, 26–7 Mr '47
        Time 49:69 Ja 20 '47
New York Times 1947, Ja 10, 17:2
        New York Times 1947, Ja 19, II, 1:1
NYTC 1947:490
(*Published libretto*) Chappell & Co., 1948
(*Published sheet music*) Chappell
(*Original cast recording*) OP Columbia ML/OL–4139,
        RE Columbia Special Products COL–4139
(*Agent/contact*) Rodgers & Hammerstein Theatre Library
(*Libretto*) NYPL RM47; LC Elmer Rice & Langston Hughes 22Nov46
        DU6104; same as (*Agent/contact*)
(*Music, Orchestrations*) Same as (*Agent/contact*)

STRIDER: THE STORY OF HORSE

(*Source*) "Kholstomer: The Story of a Horse" (short story) by Leo
       Tolstoy, translated by Tamara Bering Sunguroff
(*Book*) Bob Kalfin & Steve Brown
(*Lyrics*) Uri Riashetsev, translated by Steve Brown
(*Music*) Mark Rozovsky & S. Vetkin, adapted with additional music
       by Norman L. Berman
(*Producer*) Chelsea Theater Center/Robert Kalfin
Helen Hayes Theatre*   Broadway*
November 14, 1979*   214 performances*
(*Stars*) Roger DeKoven
Theatre World 78–79, p. 97
       Theatre World 79–80, p. 27
Best Plays 78–79, pp. 439–40
       Best Plays 79–80, pp. 372–73
NY 12:74 Je 18 '79
       New Repub 181:26–8 D 8 '79
       Newsweek il 94:141 D 3 '79
       Time il 114:60 Ag 27 '79
New York Times 1979, Je 1, III, 7:1
       New York Times 1979, N 23, III, 6:5
NYTC 1979:188
(*Published libretto*) Samuel French, Inc., 1981
(*Published sheet music*) Carbert Music, Inc./
       Bienstock Pub. Comp./MacMusic Company
(*Original cast recording*) NA
(*Agent/contact*) Samuel French, Inc.
(*Libretto*) NYPL NCOF+ 84–1039, RM634
(*Music, Orchestrations*) Same as (*Agent/contact*)

*Originally opened off–Broadway at the Chelsea Westside Theater
       5/31/79 before transferring on Broadway to the Helen Hayes Theatre

THE STUDENT GYPSY, OR THE PRINCE OF LIEDERKRANZ
(*Source*) Original
(*Book*) Rick Besoyan
(*Lyrics*) Rick Besoyan
(*Music*) Rick Besoyan
(*Producer*) Sandy Farber

Fifty–Fourth Street Theatre	Broadway
September 30, 1963	16 performances

(*Stars*) Eileen Brennan, Dom DeLuise
Theatre World 63–64, p. 20
Best Plays 63–64, pp. 304–5
Newsweek 62:77 O 14 '63
      Theatre Arts 47:13 D '63
New York Times 1963, O 1, 34:1
NYTC 1963:266
(*Published libretto*) NA
(*Published sheet music*) Sunbeam Music/Valando Music
(*Original cast recording*) NA
(*Agent/contact*) Samuel French, Inc.
(*Libretto*) NYPL RM2055, RM6137, RM6138; LC (Performing Arts
      Reading Room) ML50/.B5647S82; same as (*Agent/contact*)
(*Music*) NYPL *MS–Amer.; same as (*Agent/contact*)
(*Orchestrations*) Same as (*Agent/contact*)

SUBWAYS ARE FOR SLEEPING
(*Source*) *Subways Are for Sleeping* (novel) by Edmund G. Love
(*Book*) Betty Comden & Adolph Green
(*Lyrics*) Betty Comden & Adolph Green
(*Music*) Jule Styne
(*Producer*) David Merrick

St. James Theatre	Broadway
December 27, 1961	205 performances

(*Stars*) Sydney Chaplin, Carol Lawrence, Orson Bean, Phyllis Newman

Theatre World 61–62, p. 62

Best Plays 61–62, pp. 276–78

America 106:737 Mr 3 '62

       Dance Mag 36:13 Mr '62

       New Yorker 37:56 Ja 6 '62

       Newsweek 59:44 Ja 8 '62

       Theatre Arts il (p. 61) 46:60 Mr '62

       Time il 79:52 Ja 5 '62

New York Times 1961, D 28, 22:1

NYTC 1961:135

(*Published libretto*) NA

(*Published sheet music*) Stratford Music Corp./Chappell

(*Original cast recording*) OP Columbia KOL–5730/KOS–2130, RE Columbia

       Special Products AKOS–2130

(*Agent/contact*)

       Jule Styne   Betty Comden   Adolph Green

       c/o DG, Inc.   c/o DG, Inc.   c/o DG, Inc.

(*Libretto, Music, Orchestrations*) Tams–Witmark Music Library;

       same as (*Agent/contact*)

TAMBOURINES TO GLORY

(*Source*) *Tambourines to Glory* (novel) by Langston Hughes

(*Book*) Langston Hughes

(*Lyrics*) Langston Hughes

(*Music*) Jobe Huntley

(*Producer*) Joel Schenker, Hexter Productions, Inc.

       & Sydney S. Baron

Little Theatre   Broadway

November 2, 1963   24 performances

(*Stars*) Robert Guillaume, Louis Gossett, Micki Grant

Theatre World 63–64, p. 48

Best Plays 63–64, p. 312

New Yorker 39:95 N 9 '63

       Newsweek 62:72 N 18 '63

New York Times 1963, N 4, 47:1

NYTC 1963:207

(*Published libretto*) In *Five Plays by Langston Hughes*, Indiana
        Univ. Press, 1968

(*Published sheet music*) Chappell

(*Original cast recording*) NA

(*Agent/contact*)   Langston Hughes Estate   Theodore Presser Company
                           c/o Harold Ober Assoc.   Presser Place
                           40 E. 49th Street   Bryn Mawr, PA 19010
                           New York, N.Y.   10017
                           ATTN: Wendy Schmalz

(*Libretto*) NYPL RM1681, RM2948; LC Langston Hughes 14Aug56
        DU43139, Langston Hughes & Jobe Huntley 10Oct58 EU544061;
        same as (*Agent/contact*)

(*Music, Orchestrations*) Theodore Presser Company

TENDERLOIN

(*Source*) *Tenderloin* (novel) by Samuel Hopkins Adams

(*Book*) George Abbott & Jerome Weidman

(*Lyrics*) Sheldon Harnick

(*Music*) Jerry Bock

(*Producer*) Robert E. Griffith & Harold S. Prince

Forty–Sixth Street Theatre   Broadway

October 17, 1960   216 performances

(*Stars*) Maurice Evans, Ron Husman, Eileen Rodgers

Theatre World 60–61, p. 29

Best Plays 60–61, pp. 301–2

America 104:354+ D 3 '60

        Chr Cent 77:1382 N 23 '60

        Dance Mag il 34:33 D '60

        Nation 191:353 N 5 '60

        New Yorker 36:86 O 29 '60

        Newsweek 56:84 O 31 '60

        Sat R 43:39 N 5 '60

Theatre Arts 44:12 D '60

Time il 76:68 O 31 '60

New York Times 1960, O 18, 47:2

New York Times 1960, O 30, II, 1:1

NYTC 1960:205

(*Published libretto*) Random House, 1961

(*Published sheet music*) New York Times Music Corp./Sunbeam

(*Original cast recording*) OP Capitol WAO/SWAO–1492

(*Agent/contact*) Tams–Witmark Music Library

(*Libretto*) NYPL RM143, RM2065; same as (*Agent/contact*)

(*Music, Orchestrations*) Same as (*Agent/contact*)

TEXAS, L'IL DARLIN'

(*Source*) Original

(*Book*) John Whedon* & Sam Moore*

(*Lyrics*) Johnny Mercer

(*Music*) Robert Emmett Dolan

(*Producer*) Studio Productions, Inc. & Anthony Brady Farrell
        Productions

Mark Hellinger Theatre	Broadway
November 25, 1949	293 performances

(*Stars*) NA

Theatre World 49–50, pp. 41–2

Best Plays 49–50, pp. 361–62

Cath World 170:309 Ja '50

Commonweal 51:293 D 16 '49

New Yorker 25:70–1 D 3 '49

Newsweek il 34:84 D 5 '49

Theatre Arts il 34:9 F '50

Time il 54:66 D 5 '49

New York Times 1949, N 26, 10:5

NYTC 1949:214

(*Published libretto*) NA

(*Published sheet music*) Chappell & Co.

(*Original cast recording*) OP Decca DL–5188; RE Columbia Special
      Products X–14878 (w/*MEXICAN HAYRIDE*)
(*Agent/contact*)

John Whedon	Johnny Mercer Foundation	Robert Emmett
c/o DG, Inc.	32107 Lindero Canyon Rd.,	Dolan Estate
	Ste 222	c/o ASCAP
	Westlake Village, CA	
	91361	

(*Libretto*) NYPL NCOF+; LC John Ogden Whedon, Samuel Moore &
      Robert Emmett Dolan 24Oct49 DU21877; same as (*Agent/contact*)
(*Music*) LC Johnny Mercer & Robert Emmett Dolan 10Jan50 EU190766;
      same as (*Agent/contact*)
(*Orchestrations*) Same as (*Agent/contact*)

*At press time, neither Mr. Whedon nor Mr. Moore was interested
      in soliciting further productions of this property

THANK HEAVEN FOR THE HEATHEN
See *HEATHEN!*

13 DAUGHTERS
(*Source*) Original
(*Book*) Eaton Magoon, Jr.
(*Lyrics*) Eaton Magoon, Jr.
(*Music*) Eaton Magoon, Jr.
(*Producer*) Jack H. Silverman

| Fifty–Fourth Street Theatre | Broadway |
| March 2, 1961 | 28 performances |

(*Stars*) Don Ameche
Theatre World 60–61, p. 72
Best Plays 60–61, pp. 327–29
New Yorker 37:112 Mr 11 '61
New York Times 1961, Mr 3, 17:2
NYTC 1961:350

(*Published libretto*) NA

(*Published sheet music*) Ross Jungnickel, Inc./Hilland Range
        Songs, Inc.

(*Original cast recording*) OP Mahalo M–3003 (Original Hawaiian Cast)

(*Agent/contact*) Music Theatre International

(*Libretto*) NYPL RM1476, NCOF+; LC (Performing Arts Reading Room)
        ML50/.M213T5; same as (*Agent/contact*)

(*Music, Orchestrations*) Same as (*Agent/contact*)

THREE WISHES FOR JAMIE

(*Source*) *The Three Wishes for Jamie McRuin* (novel)
        by Charles O'Neal

(*Book*) Charles O'Neal & Abe Burrows

(*Lyrics*) Ralph Blane

(*Music*) Ralph Blane

(*Producer*) Albert Lewis & Arthur Lewis

Mark Hellinger Theatre   Broadway

March 21, 1952   91 performances

(*Stars*) John Raitt, Anne Jeffreys, Charlotte Rae

Theatre World 51–52, p. 112

Best Plays 51–52, pp. 315–16

Cath World 175:148 My '52

        Commonweal 56:14 Ap 11 '52

        Life il 32:119+ Ap 14 '52

        New Yorker 28:62 Mr 29 '52

        Newsweek il 39:84 Mr 31 '52

        Sat R 35:27 Ap 5 '52

        Theatre Arts 36:91 My '52

        Time 59:69 Mr 31 '52

New York Times 1952, Mr 22, 9:2

NYTC 1952:332

(*Published libretto*) NA

(*Published sheet music*) Chappell & Co., Inc.

(*Original cast recording*) OP Capitol S–317, RE Stet Records DS–15012

(*Agent/contact*) Samuel French, Inc.

(*Libretto, Music, Orchestrations*) Same as (*Agent/contact*)

TIMBUKTU!

(*Source*) *Kismet* (musical comedy) book by Charles Lederer & Luther
Davis, music and lyrics by Robert Wright & George Forrest, adapted
from *Kismet* (play) by Edward Knoblock

(*Book*) Luther Davis

(*Lyrics*) Robert Wright & George Forrest*

(*Music*) Robert Wright & George Forrest, based on themes by
Alexander Borodin*

(*Producer*) Luther Davis

Mark Hellinger Theatre   Broadway

March 1, 1978   221 performances

(*Stars*) Eartha Kitt, Melba Moore

Theatre World 77–78, p. 34

Best Plays 77–78, pp. 364–65

Encore il 7:26–7 Ap 3 '78

      NY 11:89–90 Mr 20 '78

      New Leader 61:28 Mr 27 '78

      Newsweek il 91:95 Mr 13 '78

      Sat R 5:26 Ap 29 '78

      Theatre Crafts il 12:13–15+ My '78

      Time il 111:75 Mr 13 '78

New York Times 1978, Mr 2, III, 15:1

      New York Times 1978, Mr 12, II, 3:1

NYTC 1978:365

(*Published libretto*) NA

(*Published sheet music*) Frank Music Corp./Bradley Pubs.

(*Original cast recording*) OP April–Blackwood SS–33782–01
      (Original Record Cast)

(*Agent/contact*) Music Theatre International

(*Libretto, Music, Orchestrations*) Same as (*Agent/contact*)

*Wright–Forrest score composed for **KISMET** augmented
      for **TIMBUKTU!** with new arrangements and several new songs

A TIME FOR SINGING

(*Source*) *How Green Was My Valley* (novel) by Richard Llewellyn
(*Book*) Gerald Freedman & John Morris
(*Lyrics*) Gerald Freedman & John Morris
(*Music*) John Morris
(*Producer*) Alexander H. Cohen

Broadway Theatre   Broadway
May 21, 1966   41 performances

(*Stars*) Shani Wallis, Tessie O'Shea
Theatre World 65–66, p. 78
Best Plays 65–66, pp. 410–12
America 114:881–2 Je 25 '66
       Commonweal 84:370 Je 17 '66
       Dance Mag 40:25 Jl '66
       New Yorker 42:79 My 28 '66
       Newsweek 67:89 Je 6 '66
       Sat R 49:34 Je 11 '66
New York Times 1966, My 23, 48:2
NYTC 1966:305
(*Published libretto*) NA
(*Published sheet music*) Chappell & Co.
(*Original cast recording*) OP Warner Bros. W/HS–1639

(*Agent/contact*)   Gerald Freedman   John Morris
               150 W. 87th Street   317 Millwood Road
               New York, N.Y. 10024   Chappaqua, N.Y. 10514

(*Libretto, Music, Orchestrations*) Same as (*Agent/contact*)

TOPLITZKY OF NOTRE DAME

(*Source*) Original
(*Book*) George Marion, Jr., additional dialogue and lyrics by
       Jack Barnett
(*Lyrics*) George Marion, Jr., additional dialogue and lyrics by
       Jack Barnett
(*Music*) Sammy Fain
(*Producer*) William Cahn

Century Theatre   Broadway
December 26, 1946   60 performances
(*Stars*) Warde Donovan
Theatre World 46–47, p. 63
Best Plays 46–47, p. 450
Cath World 164:455 F '47
       New Yorker 22:48+ Ja 11 '47
       Newsweek 29:64 Ja 6 '47
       Time il 49:56 Ja 6 '47
New York Times 1946, D 27, 13:4
NTYC 1946:201
(*Published libretto*) NA
(*Published sheet music*) Harms
(*Original cast recording*) NA
(*Agent/contact*)
     George Marion, Jr. Estate   Sammy Fain   Jack Barnett
     c/o AGAC   c/o DG, Inc.   c/o ASCAP
(*Libretto*) NYPL NCOF+; same as (*Agent/contact*)
(*Music, Orchestrations*) Same as (*Agent/contact*)

TOVARICH
(*Source*) *Tovarich* (play) by Jacques Deval, as adapted by
       Robert E. Sherwood
(*Book*) David Shaw
(*Lyrics*) Anne Croswell*
(*Music*) Lee Pockriss*
(*Producer*) Abel Farbman & Sylvia Harris, in association with
       Joseph Harris
Broadway Theatre   Broadway
March 18, 1963   264 performances
(*Stars*) Vivien Leigh, Jean Pierre Aumont
Theatre World 62–63, pp. 80–1
Best Plays 62–63, pp. 302–3

America 108:651 My 4 '63
        Commonweal 78:224 My 17 '63
        Nat R 14:535–7 Jl 2 '63
        Nation 196:334 Ap 20 '63
        New Yorker 39:108+ Mr 30 '63
        Newsweek 61:78 Ap 1 '63
        Sat R 46:40 Ap 6 '63
        Theatre Arts il 47:14–5+ My '63
        Time il 81:46 Mr 29 '63
New York Times 1963, Ja 23, 5:6
        New York Times 1963, Mr 20, 5:1
        New York Times 1963, Mr 21, 8:3
NYTC 1963:308
(*Published libretto*) NA
(*Published sheet music*) Piedmont Music Co./Edward B. Marks Music Corp.
(*Original cast recording*) OP Capitol TAO/STAO–1940, RE Capitol
        STAO–11653
(*Agent/contact*)   Anne Croswell
                    c/o DG, Inc.
(*Libretto*) NYPL RM7177; same as (*Agent/contact*)
(*Music, Orchestrations*) Same as (*Agent/contact*)

*Program credits one song, "You'll Make an Elegant Butler (I'll Make
        an Elegant Maid)," by Joan Javits & Philip Springer

A TREE GROWS IN BROOKLYN

(*Source*) *A Tree Grows in Brooklyn* (novel) by Betty Smith
(*Book*) Betty Smith & George Abbott
(*Lyrics*) Dorothy Fields
(*Music*) Arthur Schwartz
(*Producer*) George Abbott, in association with Robert Fryer
Alvin Theatre   Broadway
April 19, 1951   267 performances

(*Stars*) Shirley Booth

Theatre World 50–51, pp. 108–9

Best Plays 50–51, pp. 363–64

Cath World 173:229 Je '51

       Commonweal 54:88 My 4 '51

       Life 30:97–8+ My 7 '51

       Mus Am 71:34 Jl '51

       Nation 172:403 Ap 28 '51

       New Repub 124:20 My 14 '51

       New Yorker 27:56+ Ap 28 '51

       Newsweek il 37:53 Ap 30 '51

       Sat R Lit il 34:23–4 My 5 '51

       Time il 57:89 Ap 30 '51

New York Times 1951, Ap 20, 24:3

       New York Times 1951, Ap 29, II, 1:1

       New York Times 1951, My 20, II, 1:1

NYTC 1951:291

(*Published libretto*) Harper, 1951

(*Published sheet music*) Chappell

(*Original cast recording*) OP Columbia ML–4405,

       RE Columbia Special Products AML–4405

(*Agent/contact*)   Arthur Schwartz Estate

                      c/o Samuel French, Inc.

(*Libretto*) NYPL RM7836; Samuel French, Inc.; same as

       (*Agent/contact*)

(*Music, Orchestrations*) Samuel French, Inc.; same as

       (*Agent/contact*)

TRICKS

(*Source*) *The Pranks of Scapin* (*Les Fourberies de Scapin*)

       (play) by Molière

(*Book*) Jon Jory

(*Lyrics*) Lonnie Burstein

(*Music*) Jerry Blatt

(*Producer*) Herman Levin
Alvin Theatre   Broadway
January 8, 1973   8 performances
(*Stars*) Rene Auberjonois
Theatre World 72–73, p. 46
Best Plays 72–73, p. 347
New Yorker 48:59 Ja 20 '73
New York Times 1972, My 26, 14:2
        New York Times 1973, Ja 9, 29:1
NYTC 1973:391
(*Published libretto*) Samuel French, Inc., 1971
(*Published sheet music*) UniChappell
(*Original cast recording*) NA
(*Agent/contact*) Samuel French, Inc.
(*Libretto, Music, Orchestrations*) Same as (*Agent/contact*)

TWILIGHT ALLEY
See *BEGGAR'S HOLIDAY*

U.S.S. PINAFORE; OR, NOT TONIGHT, JOSEPHINE!
See *MEMPHIS BOUND*

THE UTTER GLORY OF MORRISSEY HALL
(*Source*) Original
(*Book*) Clark Gessner & Nagle Jackson
(*Lyrics*) Clark Gessner
(*Music*) Clark Gessner
(*Producer*) Arthur Whitelaw, Albert W. Selden, H. Ridgely
        Bullock & Marc Howard
Mark Hellinger Theatre   Broadway
May 13, 1979   1 performance
(*Stars*) Celeste Holm
Theatre World 78–79, p. 49

Best Plays 78–79, pp. 390–91
New Yorker 55:105 My 21 '79
New York Times 1979, My 14, III, 13:1
NYTC 1979:235
(*Published libretto*) Samuel French, Inc., 1982
(*Published sheet music*) NA
(*Original cast recording*) Original Cast Records OC–7918
(*Agent/contact*) Samuel French, Inc.
(*Libretto, Music, Orchestrations*) Same as (*Agent/contact*)

THE VAMP
(*Source*) Original
(*Book*) John Latouche & Sam Locke
(*Lyrics*) John Latouche
(*Music*) James Mundy
(*Producer*) Oscar Lerman, Martin Cohen & Alexander Carson
Winter Garden Theatre   Broadway
November 10, 1955   60 performances
(*Stars*) Carol Channing, Will Geer, Bibi Osterwald
Theatre World 55–56, p. 60
Best Plays 55–56, pp. 360–62
Cath World 182:310 Ja '56
          Commonweal 63:285 D 16 '55
          Look il 19:108+ N 29 '55
          New Yorker 31:121 N 19 '55
          Newsweek 46:68 N 21 '55
          Sat R 38:26 N 26 '55
          Theatre Arts il 40:20–1 Ja '56
          Time 66:110+ N 21 '55
New York Times 1955, N 11, 30:1
NYTC 1955:210
(*Published libretto*) NA
(*Published sheet music*) Robbins–Wise
(*Original cast recording*) NA

(*Agent/contact*)

Sam D. Locke	James Mundy	John Latouche
c/o Lucky Kroll Agency	c/o Lucy Kroll Agency	Estate
390 West End Avenue	390 West End Avenue	c/o ASCAP
New York, N.Y. 10024	New York, N.Y. 10024	

(*Libretto*) LC John Latouche & Sam Locke 5Nov54 DU38373;
       same as (*Agent/contact*)

(*Music, Orchestrations*) Same as (*Agent/contact*)

VIA GALACTICA

(*Source*) Original

(*Book*) Christopher Gore & Judith Ross

(*Lyrics*) Christopher Gore

(*Music*) Galt MacDermot

(*Producer*) George W. George, Barnard S. Strauss & Nat Shapiro

Uris Theatre   Broadway

November 28, 1972   7 performances

(*Stars*) Raul Julia, Virginia Vestoff, Keene Curtis

Theatre World 72–73, p. 36

Best Plays 72–73, pp. 343–4

America 127:570 D 30 '72

       New Yorker 48:109 D 9 '72

       Opera N il 37:24 Ja 20 '73

New York Times 1972, N 30, 33:1

       New York Times 1972, D 10, II, 5:1

NYTC 1972:174

(*Published libretto*) NA

(*Published sheet music*) NA

(*Original cast recording*) NA

(*Agent/contact*) Samuel French, Inc. (FOR FUTURE RELEASE)

(*Libretto*) LC Christopher Gore 29Jun70 DU77587;
       same as (*Agent/contact*)

(*Music, Orchestrations*) Same as (*Agent/contact*)

WALKING HAPPY

(*Source*) *Hobson's Choice* (play) by Harold Brighouse

(*Book*) Roger O. Hirson & Ketti Frings

(*Lyrics*) Sammy Cahn

(*Music*) James Van Heusen

(*Producer*) Cy Feuer & Ernest H. Martin, Lester Linsk

Lunt–Fontanne Theatre   Broadway

November 26, 1966   161 performances

(*Stars*) George Rose, Louise Troy

Theatre World 66–67, p. 33

Best Plays 66–67, pp. 374–75

America 116:160 Ja 28 '67

      Dance Mag 41:76–7 Ja '67

      Nation 204:29 Ja 2 '67

      Newsweek 68:100 D 12 '66

      Time il 88:60 D 9 '66

New York Times 1966, N 28, 47:1

      New York Times 1966, D 18, II, 3:1

NYTC 1966:225

(*Published libretto*) Samuel French, Inc., 1967

(*Published sheet music*) Shapiro, Bernstein & Co.

(*Original cast recording*) OP Capitol VAS/SVAS–2631

(*Agent/contact*) Samuel French, Inc.

(*Libretto*) NYPL RM2241, RM2242, NCOF+

(*Music, Orchestrations*) Same as (*Agent/contact*)

THE WALTZ OF THE STORK

(*Source*) Original

(*Book*) Melvin Van Peebles

(*Lyrics*) Melvin Van Peebles, with Ted Hayes & Mark Barkan

(*Music*) Melvin Van Peebles, with Ted Hayes & Mark Barkan

(*Producer*) Melvin Van Peebles

Century Theater   Broadway

January 5, 1982   160 performances

(*Stars*) NA

Theatre World 81–82, p. 21
Best Plays 81–82, pp. 327–28
New Yorker 57:85 Ja 11 '82
     People 17:57–8+ F 15 '82
New York Times 1982, Ja 6, III, 16:4
NYTC 1982:398
(*Published libretto*) NA
(*Published sheet music*) NA
(*Original cast recording*) NA
(*Agent/contact*)   Melvin Van Peebles   Mark Barkan
                    353 W. 56th Street   c/o DG, Inc.
                    New York, N.Y.   10019
(*Libretto, Music, Orchestrations*) Same as (*Agent/contact*)

WHAT'S UP

(*Source*) Original
(*Book*) Alan Jay Lerner* & Arthur Pierson
(*Lyrics*) Alan Jay Lerner* & Arthur Pierson
(*Music*) Frederick Loewe
(*Producer*) Mark Warnon
National Theatre   Broadway
November 11, 1943   63 performances
(*Stars*) William Tabbert
NO ENTRY AVAIL
Best Plays 43–44, pp. 426–27
Cath World 158:395 Ja '44
     Commonweal 39:144 N 26 '43
New York Times 1943, N 12, 24:6
     New York Times 1943, N 21, II, 1:1
NYTC 1943:229
(*Published libretto*) NA
(*Published sheet music*) Crawford Music Corp.
(*Original cast recording*) NA

(*Agent/contact*)   Alan Jay Lerner Estate   Frederick Loewe
                      c/o David Grossberg   c/o ASCAP
                      30 N. La Salle Street
                      New York, N.Y.   10027
(*Libretto, Music, Orchestrations*) Same as (*Agent/contact*)

*At press time, the Alan Jay Lerner Estate was not interested in
    soliciting further productions of this property

WHO TO LOVE
See *CRY FOR US ALL*

WHOOP-UP
(*Source*) *Stay Away, Joe* (novel) by Dan Cushman
(*Book*) Cy Feuer, Ernest H. Martin & Dan Cushman
(*Lyrics*) Norman Gimbel
(*Music*) Moose Charlap
(*Producer*) Cy Feuer & Ernest H. Martin
Sam S. Shubert Theatre   Broadway
December 22, 1958   56 performances
(*Stars*) Paul Ford, Sylvia Sims
Theatre World 58–59, p. 78
Best Plays 58–59, pp. 314–15
America 100:558–9 F 7 '59
         Cath World 188:506 Mr '59
         Dance Mag 33:18 F '59
         New Yorker 34:50+ Ja 3 '59
         Sat R 42:67 Ja 10 '59
         Theatre Arts il 43:9 Mr '59
New York Times 1958, D 23, 2:7
NYTC 1958:161
(*Published libretto*) NA
(*Published sheet music*) Saunders Publications, Inc.
(*Original cast recording*) OP MGM Records E/SE–3745

(*Agent/contact*)

Feuer & Martin Productions	Moose Charlap Estate	Norman Gimbel
1600 Broadway	c/o Sandra Charlap	c/o DG, Inc.
New York, N.Y. 10019	40 E. 62nd Street	
	New York, N.Y. 10021	

(*Libretto, Music, Orchestrations*) Same as (*Agent/contact*)

WILD AND WONDERFUL

(*Source*) Original work (title unavailable) by Bob Brotherton
   & Bob Miller
(*Book*) Phil Phillips
(*Lyrics*) Bob Goodman
(*Music*) Bob Goodman
(*Producer*) Rick Hobard & Raymonde Weil

Lyceum Theatre	Broadway
December 7, 1971	1 performance

(*Stars*) Ann Reinking, Pam Blair, Walter Willison
Theatre World 71–72, p. 26
Best Plays 71–72, pp. 326–27
NO CRIT AVAIL
New York Times 1971, D 8, 71:1
NYTC 1971:170
(*Published libretto*) NA
(*Published sheet music*) NA
(*Original cast recording*) NA
(*Agent/contact*)   Rick Hobard
                234 W. 44th Street
                New York, N.Y.   10036
(*Libretto, Music, Orchestrations*) Same as (*Agent/contact*)

WILDCAT

(*Source*) Original
(*Book*) N. Richard Nash

(*Lyrics*) Carolyn Leigh
(*Music*) Cy Coleman
(*Producer*) Michael Kidd & N. Richard Nash
Alvin Theatre   Broadway
December 16, 1960   172 performances
(*Stars*) Lucille Ball, Keith Andes
Theatre World 60–61, p. 55
Best Plays 60–61, pp. 313–14
America 104:546 Ja 21 '61
      Coronet il 49:16 Ap '61
      Nation 191:531 D 31 '60
      New Yorker 36:38 D 24 '60
      Newsweek 56:53 D 26 '60
      Sat R 43:28 D 31 '60
      Theatre Arts il 45:9–10 F '61
New York Times 1960, D 17, 20:2
NYTC 1960:134
(*Published libretto*) NA
(*Published sheet music*) Edwin H. Morris/Charles Hansen Distrib.
(*Original cast recording*) OP RCA LOC/LSO–1060
(*Agent/contact*) Tams–Witmark Music Library
(*Libretto*) NYPL RM7297; same as (*Agent/contact*)
(*Music, Orchestrations*) Same as (*Agent/contact*)

WORKING*
(*Source*) *Working* (collection) by Studs Terkel
(*Book*) Stephen Schwartz
(*Lyrics*) Craig Carnelia, Micki Grant, Mary Rodgers & Susan
      Birkenhead, Stephen Schwartz & James Taylor
(*Music*) Craig Carnelia, Micki Grant, Mary Rodgers & Susan
      Birkenhead, Stephen Schwartz & James Taylor
(*Producer*) Stephen R. Friedman, Irwin Meyer & Joseph Harris
Forty–Sixth Street Theatre   Broadway
May 14, 1978   25 performances

(*Stars*) Patti Lupone
Theatre World 77–78, p. 48
Best Plays 77–78, pp. 376–78
Commonweal 105:498 Ag 4 '78
      Harper 257:78–9 D '78
      Horizon il 21:28–33 Ap '78
      NY 11:77–8 My 29 '78
      Nation 226:676 Je 3 '78
      New Leader 61:24 Je 5 '78
      New Yorker 54:84 My 29 '78
      Sat R 5:24 Jl 8 '78
      Time 111:83 My 29 '78
New York Times 1978, My 15, III, 15:5
      New York Times 1978, My 28, II, 3:1
NYTC 1978:274
(*Published libretto*) NA
(*Published sheet music*) Country Road Music, Inc.
(*Original cast recording*) OP Columbia JS–35411, RE Columbia
      Special Products AJS–35411
(*Agent/contact*) Music Theatre International
(*Libretto, Music, Orchestrations*) Same as (*Agent/contact*)

*Subsequently produced on television for *Broadway on Showtime*,
      available at NYPL Billy Rose Collection, Lincoln Center, NCOX 368

THE YEARLING

(*Source*) *The Yearling* (novel) by Marjorie Kinnan Rawlings
(*Book*) Herbert Martin & Lore Noto
(*Lyrics*) Herbert Martin
(*Music*) Michael Leonard
(*Producer*) Lore Noto
Alvin Theatre   Broadway
December 10, 1965   3 performances

(*Stars*) David Wayne
Theatre World 65–66, p. 44
Best Plays 65–66, pp. 390–91
NO CRIT AVAIL
New York Times 1965, D 11, 25:1
NYTC 1965:221
(*Published libretto*) Dramatic Publishing Company, 1973
(*Published sheet music*) Mayfair Music Corp./Emanuel Music Corp.
(*Original cast recording*) OP Unnamed label CA–300 (Original
          Broadway Cast recorded live)
(*Agent/contact*) Dramatic Publishing Company
(*Libretto*) NYPL RM398, RM4489
(*Music, Orchestrations*) Same as (*Agent/contact*)

YELLOW DRUM
See *THE GRASS HARP*

YOUNG ABE LINCOLN
(*Source*) Original
(*Book*) Richard N. Bernstein & John Allen
(*Lyrics*) Joan Javits
(*Music*) Victor Ziskin
(*Producer*) Arthur Shimkin
Eugene O'Neill Theatre   Broadway
April 25, 1961*   27 performances
(*Stars*) NA
Theatre World 60–61, p. 87
NO ENTRY AVAIL
NO CRIT AVAIL
New York Times 1961, Ap 26, 36:1
NO CRIT AVAIL
(*Published libretto*) NA
(*Published sheet music*) Fairway Pub. Corp./Chappell
(*Original cast recording*) OP Golden 76, RE Wonderland WLP–76

(*Agent/contact*)
      Joan Javits Zeeman   John Allen   Victor Ziskin
      520 Hammocks Road   c/o DG, Inc.   c/o ASCAP
      Larchmont, N.Y.   10538
(*Libretto, Music, Orchestrations*) Same as (*Agent/contact*)

*Subsequently produced on tour by PART (Performing Arts Reptertory
      Theatre), N.Y.

YOURS IS MY HEART*
(*Source*) *The Yellow Jacket* (*Die Gelbe Jacke*) (operetta) by
      Franz Lehar, libretto by Victor Leon
(*Book*) Harry Graham, Ira Cobb & Karl Farkas*
(*Lyrics*) Harry Graham, Ira Cobb & Karl Farkas*
(*Music*) Franz Lehar, adapted by Felix Guenther
(*Producer*) Arthur Spitz
Shubert Theatre*   Broadway*
September 5, 1946*   36 performances
(*Stars*) Richard Tauber
Theatre World 46–47, p. 12
Best Plays 46–47, pp. 418–19
NO CRIT AVAIL
New York Times 1946, S 6, 16:5
NYTC 1946:351
(*Published libretto*) Glocken Verlad Ltd., 1954, as *THE LAND OF
      SMILES*
(*Published sheet music*) Chappell & Co., Inc. as *THE LAND OF SMILES*
(*Original cast recording*) NA
(*Agent/contact*)   The Shubert Organization
            234 W. 44th Street
            New York, N.Y.   10036

(*Libretto, Music, Orchestrations*) Same as (*Agent/contact*)

*Previously produced out of town at Shubert Theatre, Newark, 10/6/30,
    under title **PRINCE CHU CHANG**, adapted by Edgar Smith and
    Henry Clarke, with lyrics by Harry B. Smith; subsequently produced
    out of town at Shubert Theatre, Boston, 12/26/32, under title **THE
    LAND OF SMILES**, with book and lyrics by Ludwig Herzer and
    Fritz Lohner

THE ZULU AND THE ZAYDA
(*Source*) "Zulu and the Zayda" (short story) by Dan Jacobson
(*Book*) Howard Da Silva & Felix Leon
(*Lyrics*) Howard Da Silva & Felix Leon
(*Music*) Harold Rome
(*Producer*) Theodore Mann & Dore Schary
Cort Theatre   Broadway
November 10, 1965   179 performances
(*Stars*) Menasha Skulnik, Ossie Davis, Louis Gossett
Theatre World 65–66, p. 30
Best Plays 65–66, pp. 383–84
America 113:762 D 11 '65
        Commonweal 83:316 D 10 '65
        New Yorker 41:149 N 20 '65
        Newsweek il 66:97 N 22 '65
        Time il 86:97 N 19 '65
        Vogue 147:72 Ja 1 '66
New York Times 1965, N 11, 59:1
NYTC 1965:278
(*Published libretto*) Dramatists Play Service, Inc., 1966
(*Published sheet music*) Florence Music Co., Inc./
        Chappell & Co., Inc.
(*Original cast recording*) OP Columbia KOL–6480/KOS–2880
(*Agent/contact*) Dramatists Play Service, Inc.
(*Libretto*) NYPL RM2244, RM401, NCOF+
(*Music, Orchestrations*) Same as (*Agent/contact*)

THE SHOWS THAT CLOSED IN TRY–OUT OR PREVIEW

ALICE (See *BUT NEVER JAM TODAY*)*

(*Source*) *Alice in Wonderland* and *Through the Looking Glass*
  (novels) by Lewis Carroll

(*Book*) Vinnette Carroll

(*Lyrics*) Micki Grant

(*Music*) Micki Grant

(*Producer*) Mike Nichols & Lewis Allen, Urban Arts Corp. & Anita McShane

Forrest Theatre, Philadelphia   pre–Broadway

May 31, 1978   Out–of–Town

(*Stars*) Alice Ghostley, Paula Kelly

Theatre World 77–78, p. 161

Best Plays 78–79, pp. 394–95

NO CRIT AVAIL

New York Times 1978, Je 10, 11:1

  New York Times 1978, Je 10, II, 1:3

  New York Times 1978, D 23, 23:6

Broadway Bound, pp. 16–21

(*Published libretto*) NA

(*Published sheet music*) NA (Fiddleback Music Pub. Co., Inc.)

(*Original cast recording*) NA

(*Agent/contact*) Micki Grant   Vinnette Carroll
       c/o Migra Music Co., Inc. c/o DG, Inc.
       250 W. 94th Street, #6G
       New York, N.Y. 10025

(*Libretto*) NYPL NCOF+ 82–776 as *BUT NEVER JAM TODAY*; LC
  Vinnette Justine Carroll 9Jan75 DU92993 as *BLACK ALICE;*
  OR, BUT NEVER JAM TODAY; same as (*Agent/contact*)

(*Music, Orchestrations*)

Fiddleback Music Pub. Comp. Same as (*Agent/contact*)
 Inc./Tommy Valando
1270 Avenue of the Americas
New York, N.Y. 10020

*Previously titled *BLACK ALICE; OR, BUT NEVER JAM TODAY*;
 ALICE was rewritten with new score by Bob Larimer & Bert
 Keyes, and premiered off–Broadway 7/31/79 under the title *BUT
 NEVER JAM TODAY*

THE AMAZING ADELE

(*Source*) *Le Don d'Adèle* (play) by Pierre Barillet & Jean–Pierre Gredy
(*Book*) Anita Loos
(*Lyrics*) Albert Selden
(*Music*) Albert Selden
(*Producer*) Albert Selden, Morton Gottlieb & Henry David Epstein
Shubert Theatre, Philadelphia pre–Broadway
December 26, 1955 Out–of–Town
(*Stars*) Tammy Grimes
Theatre World 55–56, p. 170
NO ENTRY AVAIL
NO CRIT AVAIL
NO CRIT AVAIL
Broadway Bound, pp. 23–25
(*Published libretto*) NA
(*Published sheet music*) Edwin H. Morris & Co.
(*Original cast recording*) NA
(*Agent/contact*)

Albert Selden	Anita Loos Estate	Morton Gottlieb
609 Camino Rancheros	c/o Ray Pierre Corsini	165 W. 46th Street
Santa Fe, NM 87501	12 Beekman Place	New York, N.Y. 10036
	New York, N.Y. 10022	

(*Libretto*) NYPL NCOF+; same as (*Agent/contact*)
(*Music, Orchestrations*) Same as (*Agent/contact*)

*AT THE GRAND**

(*Source*) *Grand Hotel* (*Menschen im Hotel*) (novel and play) by
         Vicki Baum

(*Book*) Luther Davis

(*Lyrics*) Robert Wright & George Forrest

(*Music*) Robert Wright & George Forrest

(*Producer*) Edwin Lester, California Civic Light Opera Association

Philharmonic Auditorium, Los Angeles   pre–Broadway

July 7, 1958   Out–of–Town

(*Stars*) Paul Muni, Joan Diener

Theatre World 58–59, p. 185

NO ENTRY AVAIL

Newsweek il 52:82 Jl 21 '58

New York Times 1958, Ag 13, 24:3

Broadway Bound, pp. 37–40

(*Published libretto*) NA

(*Published sheet music*) NA (Frank Music Corp.)

(*Original cast recording*) NA

(*Agent/contact*)	Luther Davis	Robert Wright &
	c/o DG, Inc.	George Forrest
		c/o DG, Inc.

(*Libretto*) NYPL RM1577 as *GRAND HOTEL*;
         same as (*Agent/contact*)

(*Music, Orchestrations*) Same as (*Agent/contact*)

*Previously titled *GRAND HOTEL*

BACK COUNTRY

(*Source*) *The Playboy of the Western World* (play) by J.M. Synge

(*Book*) Jacques Levy

(*Lyrics*) Jacques Levy

(*Music*) Stanley Walden

(*Producer*) Eugene V. Wolsk & Harvey Granet

Wilbur Theatre, Boston   pre–Broadway

August 15, 1978   Out–of–Town

(*Stars*) Rex Everhart, Barbara Andres

Theatre World 78–79, p. 158

Best Plays 78–79, pp. 396–98

NO CRIT AVAIL

New York Times 1978, Je 10, II, 1:3

Broadway Bound, pp. 40–41

(*Published libretto*) NA

(*Published sheet music*) NA

(*Original cast recording*) NA

(*Agent/contact*)   Stanley Walden   Jacques Levy

                           Miller Hill Road, R.D. 7   478 W. Broadway

                           Hopewell Junction, N.Y.   New York, N.Y. 10012

                                        12537

(*Libretto, Music, Orchestrations*) Same as (*Agent/contact*)

THE BAKER'S WIFE

(*Source*) *The Baker's Wife* (*La Femme du Boulanger*) (screenplay)
         by Marcel Pagnol & Jean Giono

(*Book*) Joseph Stein

(*Lyrics*) Stephen Schwartz

(*Music*) Stephen Schwartz

(*Producer*) David Merrick

Dorothy Chandler Pavilion, Los Angeles   pre–Broadway

May 11, 1976   Out–of–Town

(*Stars*) Topol/Paul Sorvino*, Patti Lupone

Theatre World 76–77, p. 155

Best Plays 76–77, pp. 312–13

NO CRIT AVAIL

New York Times 1976, N 11, 54:4

Broadway Bound, pp. 42–22

(*Published libretto*) NA

(*Published sheet music*) NA (Heelstone Music)
(*Original cast recording*) Take Home Tunes THT–772
(*Agent/contact*)   Stephen Schwartz   Joseph Stein
                           c/o Paramuse Artists Assoc.   c/o DG, Inc.
                           1414 Avenue of the Americas
                           New York, N.Y.   10019
                           ATTN: Shirley Bernstein
(*Libretto*) NYPL RM8001; same as (*Agent/contact*)
(*Music, Orchestrations*) Same as (*Agent/contact*)

*Paul Sorvino replaced Topol in the leading role on
        pre–Broadway tour

BLACK ALICE; OR, BUT NEVER JAM TODAY
See *ALICE*

BONANZA BOUND!
(*Source*) Original
(*Book*) Betty Comden & Adolph Green
(*Lyrics*) Betty Comden & Adolph Green
(*Music*) Saul Chaplin
(*Producer*) Herman Levin, Paul Feigay & Oliver Smith
Shubert Theatre, Philadelphia   pre–Broadway
December 26, 1947   Out-of-Town
(*Stars*) Adolph Green, Gwen Verdon (chorus)
Theatre World 47–48, p. 145
NO ENTRY AVAIL
Theatre Arts il 32:19–23 F '48
NO CRIT AVAIL
Broadway Bound, pp. 65–67
(*Published libretto*) NA
(*Published sheet music*) Crawford Music Corp.
(*Original cast recording*) OP Unnamed label LP–508/JJA–19764 (Original
        Philadelphia Cast)

(*Agent/contact*)

Betty Comden	Adolph Green	Saul Chaplin
c/o DG, Inc.	c/o DG, Inc.	c/o ASCAP

(*Libretto, Music*) MCNY; same as (*Agent/contact*)
(*Orchestrations*) Same as (*Agent/contact*)

BRAIN
See *BRAINCHILD*

BRAINCHILD*
(*Source*) Original
(*Book*) Maxine Klein
(*Lyrics*) Hal David
(*Music*) Michel Legrand
(*Producer*) Adela Holzer

Forrest Theatre, Philadelphia	pre–Broadway
March 25, 1974	Out–of–Town

(*Stars*) Tovah Feldshuh
Theatre World 73–74, p. 153
Best Plays 73–74, pp. 371–72
NO CRIT AVAIL
New York Times 1974, Mr 17, 107:1
Broadway Bound, pp. 67–68
(*Published libretto*) NA
(*Published sheet music*) NA (Chappell & Co., Inc.)
(*Original cast recording*) OP Rescued From Oblivion RFO–104 (Original
        Demo Recording)
(*Agent/contact*)

Maxine Klein	Hal David	Michel Legrand
c/o Little Flags Theatre	c/o ASCAP	c/o DG, Inc.
22 Sunset Street		
Roxbury, MA 02120		

(*Libretto*) NYPL RM7768; LC Maxine Klein 10Sept73 DU87962 as
        BRAIN; same as (*Agent/contact*)

(*Music, Orchestrations*) Same as (*Agent/contact*)

*Previously titled *BRAIN*

*BREAKFAST AT TIFFANY'S**
(*Source*) *Breakfast at Tiffany's* (novel) by Truman Capote
(*Book*) Nunnally Johnson/Abe Burrows/Edward Albee**
(*Lyrics*) Bob Merrill***
(*Music*) Bob Merrill***
(*Producer*) David Merrick
Forrest Theatre, Philadelphia   pre–Broadway
October 10, 1966   Preview
(*Stars*) Mary Tyler Moore, Richard Chamberlain
Theatre World 66–67, p. 182
Best Plays 66–67, pp. 395–96
Newsweek 68:45 D 26 '66
New York Times 1966, D 15, 60:1
Broadway Bound, pp. 206–10 as *HOLLY GOLIGHTLY*
(*Published libretto*) NA
(*Published sheet music*) NA
(*Original cast recording*) OP SPM Records CO–4788 (Original
          Cast recorded live)
(*Agent/contact*)
          Bob Merrill   Edward Albee
          c/o UCLA Theatre Arts Dept.   c/o DG, Inc.
          Los Angeles, CA 90024
(*Libretto*) NYPL RM6623, RM6624, RM6625, RM6626, RM6627;
          same as (*Agent/contact*)
(*Music, Orchestrations*) Same as (*Agent/contact*)

*Previously presented under title *HOLLY GOLIGHTLY*
**Nunnally Johnson was replaced by Abe Burrows, who was then
          replaced by Edward Albee, as book writer
***At press time, Mr. Merrill was not interested in soliciting
          further productions of this property

*THE CAREFREE HEART**

(*Source*) *The Doctor In Spite of Himself* (*Le Medecin Malgré*) and
   The Imaginary Invalid (*Le Malade Imaginaire*) (plays) by Molière
(*Book*) Robert Wright & George Forrest
(*Lyrics*) Robert Wright & George Forrest
(*Music*) Robert Wright & George Forrest
(*Producer*) Lynn Loesser & Shamus Locke
Cass Theatre, Detroit   pre–Broadway
September 30, 1957   Out–of–Town
(*Stars*) Jack Carter, Virginia Martin
Theatre World 57–58, p. 184
NO ENTRY AVAIL
Theatre Arts il 41:78 N '57
New York Times 1959, O 14, 52:4 as *THE LOVE DOCTOR*
Broadway Bound, pp. 77–79
(*Published libretto*) NA
(*Published sheet music*) Frank Music Corp.
(*Original cast recording*) NA
(*Agent/contact*)   Robert Wright & George Forrest
          c/o DG, Inc.
(*Libretto, Music*) LC (Performing Arts Reading Room) ML50/.F728D6,
   LC Robert Craig Wright & George Forrest 14Jan55 DU38944 as
   THE DOCTOR IN SPITE OF HIMSELF; same as
   (*Agent/contact*)
(*Orchestrations*) Same as (*Agent/contact*)

*Previously titled *THE DOCTOR IN SPITE OF HIMSELF*;
   subsequently titled *SPEAK, LUCINDA!*;
   previously presented under title *THE LOVE DOCTOR*

CHU CHEM
(*Source*) Original
(*Book*) Ted Allan
(*Lyrics*) Jack Haines & Jack Wohl

(*Music*) Mitch Leigh
(*Producer*) Cheryl Crawford & Mitch Leigh
New Locust Theater, Philadelphia   pre–Broadway
November 15, 1966   Out–of–Town
(*Stars*) Menasha Skulnik, Molly Picon, Marcia Rodd
Theatre World 66–67, p. 183
Best Plays 66–67, p. 395
NO CRIT AVAIL
New York Times 1966, N 12, 23:2
        New York Times 1966, N 18, 38:2
        New York Times 1966, N 21, 59:1
Broadway Bound, pp. 87–88
(*Published libretto*) NA
(*Published sheet music*) NA (Andrew Scott, Inc.)
(*Original cast recording*) NA
(*Agent/contact*)

Mitch Leigh	Ted Allan	Jack Wohl
c/o Music Makers, Inc.	c/o DG, Inc.	c/o DG, Inc.
200 Central Park South		
New York, N.Y. 10019		

(*Libretto, Music, Orchestrations*) Same as (*Agent/contact*)

COLETTE (See *COLETTE*, off–Broadway Section)*
(*Source*) *Earthly Paradise* (collection) by Colette, edited by
        Robert Phelps
(*Book*) Tom Jones
(*Lyrics*) Tom Jones
(*Music*) Harvey Schmidt
(*Producer*) Harry Rigby, The Kennedy Center, The Denver Center &
        James M. Nederlander**

5th Avenue Theater, Seattle**   pre–Broadway**

February 9, 1982**   Out–of–Town**

(*Stars*) Diana Rigg

Theatre World 81–82, p. 114

> Theatre World 82–83, p. 122

Best Plays 81–82, pp. 343–44

> Best Plays 82–83, p. 429

NO CRIT AVAIL

New York Times 1981, Mr 9, II, 16:1

> New York Times 1981, Mr 20, 17:1
>
> New York Times 1983, Ap 11, III, 23:4

NO CRIT AVAIL

(*Published libretto*) NA

(*Published sheet music*) Portfolio Music, Inc./Chappell & Co., Inc.

> (Original off–Broadway production)

(*Original cast recording*) OP MIO International MCS–3001 (Original

> off–Broadway Cast)

(*Agent/contact*) Music Theatre International (FOR FUTURE RELEASE)

(*Libretto*) NYPL NCOF+; RM8055 (Original off–Broadway);

> same as (*Agent/contact*)

(*Music, Orchestrations*) Same as (*Agent/contact*)

COLETTE was first produced in an earlier version, book by Elinor

> Jones, also entitled *COLETTE*, which premiered off–Broadway
>
> 6/6/70

**COLETTE* was subsequently rewritten and produced off–off–Broadway

> under the title *COLETTE COLLAGE*, 3/31/83, by the York
>
> Players at the Church of the Heavenly Rest for 17 performances

COMEDY (See *SMILE, SMILE, SMILE*)*
(*Source*) "The Great Magician" (commedia dell'arte scenario) by
      Basillio Locatelli
(*Book*) Lawrence Carra
(*Lyrics*) Hugo Peretti, Luigi Creatore & George David Weiss
(*Music*) Hugo Peretti, Luigi Creatore & George David Weiss
(*Producer*) Edgar Lansbury, Stuart Duncan & Joseph Beruh
Colonial Theatre, Boston   pre–Broadway
November 6, 1972   Out–of–Town
(*Stars*) George S. Irving, Joseph Bova
Theatre World 72–73, p. 165
Best Plays 72–73, p. 361
NO CRIT AVAIL
NO CRIT AVAIL
Broadway bound, pp. 94–95
(*Published libretto*) NA
(*Published sheet music*) NA (Godspell Music Corp./Valando Music,
      Inc.); Music Maximus Ltd./ Screen Gems–Columbia as *SMILE,*
      SMILE, SMILE
(*Original cast recording*) NA
(*Agent/contact*)

George David Weiss	Luigi Creatore	Hugo Peretti	Edgar Lansbury
c/o DG, Inc.	c/o ASCAP	c/o AGAC	1650 Broadway
			New York, N.Y.
			10019

(*Libretto, Music, Orchestrations*) Same as (*Agent/contact*)

COMEDY was rewritten and premiered off–Broadway 4/04/73 under
    the title *SMILE, SMILE, SMILE*

COOL OFF!

(*Source*) *Faust* (play) by Johann Wolfgang von Goethe (suggested by)

(*Book*) Jerome Weidman

(*Lyrics*) Howard Blankman

(*Music*) Howard Blankman

(*Producer*) Barbara Griner

Forrest Theatre, Philadelphia   pre–Broadway

March 31, 1964   Out–of–Town

(*Stars*) Stanley Holloway, Hermione Baddeley

NO ENTRY AVAIL

Best Plays 63–64, pp. 380–81

NO CRIT AVAIL

NO CRIT AVAIL

Broadway Bound, pp. 98–99

(*Published libretto*) NA

(*Published sheet music*) Chappell & Co., Inc.

(*Original cast recording*) NA

(*Agent/contact*)

    Howard Blankman   Jerome Weidman

    c/o DG, Inc.   c/o DG, Inc.

(*Libretto, Music, Orchestrations*) Same as (*Agent/contact*)

DADDY GOODNESS

(*Source*) *Daddy Goodness* (play) by Richard Wright & Louis Sapin

(*Book*) Ron Miller & Shauneille Perry

(*Lyrics*) Ron Miller

(*Music*) Ken Hirsch

(*Producer*) Ashton Springer, in association with Marty Markinson,
    Joseph Harris & Donald Tick

Forrest Theater, Philadelphia   pre–Broadway
August 16, 1979   Out–of–Town
(*Stars*) Clifton Davis, Freyda Payne
Theatre World 79–80, p. 175
Best Plays 79–80, pp. 399–400
NO CRIT AVAIL
NO CRIT AVAIL
Broadway Bound, pp. 107–109
(*Published libretto*) NA
(*Published sheet music*) NA
(*Original cast recording*) NA
(*Agent/contact*)
                     Ron Miller   Ken Hirsch
                     c/o AGAC   c/o DG, Inc.
(*Libretto, Music, Orchestrations*) Same as (*Agent/contact*)

THE DOCTOR IN SPITE OF HIMSELF
See *THE CAREFREE HEART*

EX–LOVER
See *PLEASURE AND PALACES*

1491
(*Source*) Original
(*Book*) Meredith Willson, Richard Morris & Ira Barmak
(*Lyrics*) Meredith Willson
(*Music*) Meredith Willson
(*Producer*) Edwin Lester, California Civic Light Opera
Dorothy Chandler Pavilion, Los Angeles   pre–Broadway
September 2, 1969   Out–of–Town
(*Stars*) Chita Rivera, John Cullum, Jean Fenn
NO ENTRY AVAIL

NO ENTRY AVAIL
NO CRIT AVAIL
NO CRIT AVAIL
NO CRIT AVAIL
(*Published libretto*) NA
(*Published sheet music*) NA (Frank Music Corp.)
(*Original cast recording*) NA
(*Agent/contact*)   Meredith Willson Estate
                         c/o William Morris Agency
                         151 El Camino Drive
                         Beverly Hills, CA   90212
                         ATTN: Gayle Nachlis
(*Libretto*) NYPL NCOF+; same as (*Agent/contact*)
(*Music*) LC Frank Music Corp. & Rinimer Corp. 6Aug69 EU131151;
    same as (*Agent/contact*)
(*Orchestrations*) Same as (*Agent/contact*)

GLAD TO SEE YOU
(*Source*) Original
(*Book*) Fred Thompson & Eddie Davis
(*Lyrics*) Sammy Cahn
(*Music*) Jule Styne
(*Producer*) David Wolper
Shubert Theatre, Philadelphia   pre–Broadway
November 13, 1944   Out–of–Town
(*Stars*) Jane Withers, Eddie Foy, Jr., Gene Barry
Theatre World 1944–45, p. 104
NO ENTRY AVAIL
NO CRIT AVAIL
NO CRIT AVAIL
Broadway Bound, pp. 169–71
(*Published libretto*) NA
(*Published sheet music*) Chappell
(*Original cast recording*) NA

(*Agent/contact*)   Jule Styne   Sammy Cahn
                        c/o DG, Inc.   c/o Edward Traubner
                                          1849 Sawtelle Blvd.
                                          Los Angeles, CA   90025

(*Libretto, Music, Orchestrations*) Same as (*Agent/contact*)

GONE WITH THE WIND*

(*Source*) *Gone With the Wind* (novel) by Margaret Mitchell
(*Book*) Horton Foote
(*Lyrics*) Harold Rome
(*Music*) Harold Rome
(*Producer*) Harold Fielding
Dorothy Chandler Pavilion, Los Angeles   pre–Broadway
August 28, 1973   Out–of–Town
(*Stars*) Pernell Roberts, Lesley Ann Warren
Theatre World 73–74, p. 151
NO ENTRY AVAIL
NO CRIT AVAIL
New York Times 1972, Ap 27, 48:1
      New York Times 1972, My 21, II, 12:6
      New York Times 1973, Jl 26, 42:6
Broadway Bound, pp. 173–78
(*Published libretto*) NA
(*Published sheet music*) Chappell
(*Original cast recording*) OP Columbia(E) SCX–9252, RE AEI–1113
      (Original London Cast)
(*Agent/contact*)
      Harold Fielding, Ltd.   Harold Rome   Horton Foote
      13 Bruton Street   c/o DG, Inc.   c/o Lucy Kroll
      London WI, England   390 West End Avenue
                                            New York, N.Y. 10024

(*Libretto, Music, Orchestrations*) Same as (*Agent/contact*)

*Previously titled *SCARLETT*; book chronicling the making of
     SCARLETT entitled *The Scarlett Letters*, Random House, 1971

GRAND HOTEL
See *AT THE GRAND*

HALLOWEEN
(*Source*) *Saltpeter and Rhubarb* (play) by Sidney Michaels
(*Book*) Sidney Michaels
(*Lyrics*) Sidney Michaels
(*Music*) Mitch Leigh
(*Producer*) Albert Selden & Jerome Minskoff
Bucks County Playhouse, New Hope, PA   pre–Broadway
September 20, 1972   Out–of–Town
(*Stars*) David Wayne, Dick Shawn
NO ENTRY AVAIL
Best Plays 72–73, p. 360
NO CRIT AVAIL
NO CRIT AVAIL
Broadway Bound, pp. 181–82
(*Published libretto*) NA
(*Published sheet music*) NA (Andrew Scott, Inc.)
(*Original cast recording*) NA
(*Agent/contact*)

Mitch Leigh	Sidney Michaels	Albert Selden
c/o Music Makers, Inc.	c/o DG, Inc.	609 Camino Rancheros
200 Central Park South		Santa Fe, NM 87501
New York, N.Y. 10019		

(*Libretto, Music, Orchestrations*) Same as (*Agent/contact*)

HELEN OF TROY
See *LA BELLE*

HELLO, SUCKER!

(*Source*) Original

(*Book*) Larry B. Marks & Robert Ennis Turoff

(*Lyrics*) Wilson Stone

(*Music*) Wilson Stone

(*Producer*) Ben Segal & Bob Hall, for the Connecticut Performing
        Arts Foundation

Oakdale Musical Theatre, Wallingford, CT*   pre–Broadway

July 21, 1969*   Out–of–Town

(*Stars*) Martha Raye

NO ENTRY AVAIL

NO ENTRY AVAIL

NO CRIT AVAIL

NO CRIT AVAIL

NO CRIT AVAIL

(*Published libretto*) NA

(*Published sheet music*) NA

(*Original cast recording*) NA

(*Agent/contact*)   Wilson Stone   Larry B. Marks
                       c/o DG, Inc.   c/o DG, Inc.

(*Libretto*) NYPL NCOF+; LC Larry B. Marks & Robert Ennis Turoff
        18Jul69 DU74800; same as (*Agent/contact*)

(*Music, Orchestrations*) Same as (*Agent/contact*)

*Previously presented at Casa Manana Dinner Theatre, TX,
        05/17/69

HOLLY GOLIGHTLY
See *BREAKFAST AT TIFFANY'S*

HOME AGAIN
See *HOME AGAIN, HOME AGAIN*

*HOME AGAIN, HOME AGAIN**

(*Source*) Original

(*Book*) Russell Baker

(*Lyrics*) Barbara Fried

(*Music*) Cy Coleman

(*Producer*) Irwin Meyer, Stephen R. Friedman, Kenneth Laub &
        Warner Plays, Inc.

American Shakespeare Festival, Stratford, CT   pre–Broadway

March 10, 1979   Out–of–Town

(*Stars*) Dick Shawn, Lisa Kirk

Theatre World 78–79, p. 180

Best Plays 78–79, pp. 398–99

NO CRIT AVAIL

New York Times 1979, F 7, III, 13:2

        New York Times 1979, F 11, VI, p. 9

        New York Times 1979, Ap 14, 15:4

        New York Times 1979, Je 10, II, 1:3

Broadway Bound, pp. 211–12

(*Published libretto*) NA

(*Published sheet music*) NA (Notable Music, Inc.)

(*Original cast recording*) NA

(*Agent/contact*)

Cy Coleman	Russell Baker	Barbara Fried
c/o DG, Inc.	c/o *New York Times*	c/o DG, Inc.
	229 W. 43rd Street	
	New York, N.Y. 10036	

(*Libretto, Music, Orchestrations*) Same as (*Agent/contact*)

*Previously titled **HOME AGAIN**; subsequently revised and titled
        10 DAYS TO BROADWAY, then presented under the title
        13 DAYS TO BROADWAY

HOT SEPTEMBER

(*Source*) *Picnic* (play) by William Inge

(*Book*) Paul Osborn

(*Lyrics*) Rhoda Roberts

(*Music*) Kenneth Jacobson

(*Producer*) Leland Hayward & David Merrick

Shubert Theatre, Boston   pre–Broadway

September 14, 1965   Out–of–Town

(*Stars*) Eddie Bracken

Theatre World 65–66, p. 198

Best Plays 65–66, pp. 443–44

NO CRIT AVAIL

NO CRIT AVAIL

Broadway Bound, pp. 217–19

(*Published libretto*) NA

(*Published sheet music*) Valando Music Corp.

(*Original cast recording*) NA

(*Agent/contact*)

      Kenneth Jacobson   Rhoda Roberts   Paul Osborn

      47 W. 68th Street   c/o ASCAP   c/o DG, Inc.

      New York, N.Y.   10023

(*Libretto*) NYPL RM7774; same as (*Agent/contact*)

(*Music, Orchestrations*) Same as (*Agent/contact*)

HOW DO YOU DO, I LOVE YOU

(*Source*) Original

(*Book*) Michael Stewart

(*Lyrics*) Richard Maltby, Jr.*

(*Music*) David Shire*

(*Producer*) Lee Guber & Shelly Gross

Shady Grove Music Fair, Gaithersburg, MD   pre–Broadway
October 19, 1967   Out–of–Town
(*Stars*) Phyllis Newman, Carole Cook
NO ENTRY AVAIL
NO ENTRY AVAIL
NO CRIT AVAIL
NO CRIT AVAIL
NO CRIT AVAIL
(*Published libretto*) NA
(*Published sheet music*) Chappell
(*Original cast recording*) NA
(*Agent/contact*)

    Michael Stewart   Richard Maltby, Jr.   David Shire
    c/o Helen Harvey   c/o DG, Inc.   c/o DG, Inc.
    410 W. 24th Street
    New York, N.Y. 10011

    Guber/Gross, Inc.
    32 E. 57th Street
    New York, N.Y. 10011
(*Libretto*) NYPL RM4513; LC Michael Stewart 16Jan67 DU67737;
        same as (*Agent/contact*)
(*Music, Orchestrations*) Same as (*Agent/contact*)

*At press time, neither Mr. Maltby nor Mr. Shire was interested
        in soliciting further productions of this property

IN GAY NEW ORLEANS
(*Source*) Original
(*Book*) Forbes Randolph
(*Lyrics*) Forbes Randolph
(*Music*) Carl Fredrickson
(*Producer*) Forbes Randolph

Colonial Theatre, Boston   pre–Broadway
December 25, 1946   Out–of–Town
(*Stars*) NA
Theatre World 46–47, pp. 136–37
NO ENTRY AVAIL
NO CRIT AVAIL
NO CRIT AVAIL
Broadway Bound, pp. 228–29
(*Published libretto*) NA
(*Published sheet music*) NA
(*Original cast recording*) NA
(*Agent/contact*)   Carl Fredrickson
                         c/o ASCAP
(*Libretto, Music, Orchestrations*) Same as (*Agent/contact*)

JOLEY
(*Source*) Original
(*Book*) Herbert Hartig
(*Lyrics*) Herbert Hartig
(*Music*) Milton DeLugg
(*Producer*) Bob Funking & Bill Stutler, by special arrangement
        with Jeff Britton
Northstage Theatre, Glen Cove, N.Y.   pre–Broadway
March 2, 1979   Out–of–Town
(*Stars*) Larry Kert
Theatre World 78–79, p. 161
NO ENTRY AVAIL
NO CRIT AVAIL
New York Times 1979, F 23, IV, 2:5
        New York Times 1979, Mr 4, XXI, 7:1
        New York Times 1979, Je 24, XXI, 6:3
NO CRIT AVAIL
(*Published libretto*) NA
(*Published sheet music*) NA (Amy Dee Music)

(*Original cast recording*) NA

(*Agent/contact*)

Herbert Hartig	Milton DeLugg	Jeff Britton
c/o DG, Inc.	c/o DG, Inc.	1501 Broadway
		New York, N.Y. 10036

(*Libretto, Music, Orchestrations*) Same as (*Agent/contact*)

KICKS & CO.

(*Source*) Original

(*Book*) Oscar Brown, Jr. & Robert Nemiroff

(*Lyrics*) Oscar Brown, Jr.

(*Music*) Oscar Brown, Jr.

(*Producer*) Burt Charles D'Lugoff & Robert Nemiroff

Arie Crown Theatre, Chicago   pre–Broadway

October 11, 1961   Out–of–Town

(*Stars*) Burgess Meredith, Al Freeman, Jr.

Theatre World 61–62, p. 192

Best Plays 61–62, pp. 335–36

Ebony il 16:73–4+ Je '61

      Life il 50:102 Ap 7 '61

      Time 79:74 Mr 30 '62

NO CRIT AVAIL

Broadway Bound, pp. 241–42

(*Published libretto*) NA

(*Published sheet music*) Edwin B. Marks Music Corp.

(*Original cast recording*) NA

(*Agent/contact*)	Oscar Brown, Jr.	Robert Nemiroff
	855 Drexel Square,	c/o DG, Inc.
	First Floor	
	Chicago, IL 60615	

(*Libretto*) LC Oscar Brown, Jr. 1Sep61 DU53880;

      same as (*Agent/contact*)

(*Music, Orchestrations*) Same as (*Agent/contact*)

*LA BELLE**

(*Source*) *La Belle Hélène* (opera) by Jacques Offenbach
(*Book*) Brendan Gill, based on the translation by Bill Hoffman
(*Lyrics*) Marshall Barer
(*Music*) William Roy, based on the themes of Jacques Offenbach
(*Producer*) Gerard Oestreicher
Shubert Theatre, Philadelphia   pre–Broadway
August 13, 1962   Out–of–Town
(*Stars*) Joan Diener, Howard Da Silva, George Segal
Theatre World 62–63, p. 203
Best Plays 62–63, pp. 346–47
NO CRIT AVAIL
NO CRIT AVAIL
Broadway Bound, pp. 54–58
(*Published libretto*) NA
(*Published sheet music*) NA
(*Original cast recording*) NA
(*Agent/contact*)

Brendan Gill**	Marshall Barer	Gerard Oestreicher
c/o *New Yorker* Magazine	1718 Main Street	680 Madison Avenue
25 W. 43rd Street	Venice, CA 90291	New York, N.Y. 10022
New York, N.Y. 10036		

(*Libretto*) NYPL NCOF+; LC Bill Hoffman & Marshall Barer 26Oct60
        DU51936 as *HELEN OF TROY*; same as (*Agent/contact*)
(*Music, Orchestrations*) Chappell Music; same as (*Agent/contact*)

*Previously titled *HELEN OF TROY*

**At press time, Mr. Gill was not interested in soliciting
        further productions of this property

THE LAND OF SMILES
See *YOURS IS MY HEART*

THE LAST MINSTREL SHOW
(*Source*) Original
(*Book*) Joe Taylor Ford
(*Lyrics*) Traditional (Various lyricists)*
(*Music*) Traditional (Various composers)*
(*Producer*) Ken Marsolais, Martin Markinson & Donald Tick
Wilbur Theatre, Boston   pre–Broadway
March 20, 1978   Out–of–Town
(*Stars*) Della Reese, Gregory Hines
Theatre World 77–78, p. 162
Best Plays 77–78, pp. 382–84
NO CRIT AVAIL
NO CRIT AVAIL
Broadway Bound, pp. 257–59
(*Published libretto*) NA
(*Published sheet music*) NA (Cherry Lane Music Company)
(*Original cast recording*) NA
(*Agent/contact*)   Joe Taylor Ford
                         Butternut Farm
                         East Ryegate, VT 05042
(*Libretto*) NYPL RM341; same as (*Agent/contact*)
(*Music, Orchestrations*) Same as (*Agent/contact*)

*No listing given. *Theatre World* lists the following musical numbers:
        "Always Left Them Laughing," "At the Garbage Gentlemen's Ball,"
        "Can't You Hear Me Callin' Caroline," "Darktown Is Out Tonight,"
        "Dixie, Do Lord," "Down Where the Watermelon Grows," "Gee, I'm
        Glad I'm from Dixie," "Good News," "Happy Days in Dixieland," "A
        High Old Time in Dixie," "I Don't Mind Walkin' in the Rain," "I'll
        Lend You Anything," "Oh, Dem Golden Slippers," "Pickaninny's
        Paradise," "She's Getting More Like the White Folk Every Day,"
        "Shine, Shine, Shine," "Strut Miss Lizzie," "'T Ain't No Sin," "Turkey
        in the Straw," "Wait 'Til the Sun Shines, Nelly," "Waitin' for the
        Robert E. Lee," "What He'd Done for Me," "When the Bell in the
        Lighthouse Rings Ding–Dong"

THE LITTLE PRINCE AND THE AVIATOR

(*Source*) *The Little Prince* (novel) by Antoine de Saint–Exupery

(*Book*) Hugh Wheeler

(*Lyrics*) Don Black

(*Music*) John Barry

(*Producer*) A. Joseph Tandet

Alvin Theater   pre–Broadway

January 1, 1982   Preview

(*Stars*) Michael York, Ellen Greene

Theatre World 81–82, p. 47

Best Plays 81–82, pp. 341–42

NO CRIT AVAIL

New York Times 1981, Ja 21, III, 17:1

    New York Times 1981, N 20, III, 2:2

    New York Times 1982, illus, Ja 17, II, 8:1

    New York Times 1982, Ja 20, III, 21:1

NO CRIT AVAIL

(*Published libretto*) NA

(*Published sheet music*) NA

(*Original cast recording*) NA

(*Agent/contact*)

Hugh Wheeler	Don Black	John Barry
c/o DG, Inc.	c/o DG, Inc.	c/o Traubner & Flynn
		1849 Sawtelle Blvd.
		Los Angeles, CA 90025

(*Libretto, Music, Orchestrations*) Same as (*Agent/contact*)

LOCK UP YOUR DAUGHTERS!

(*Source*) *Rape Upon Rape* (play) by Henry Fielding

(*Book*) Bernard Miles

(*Lyrics*) Lionel Bart

(*Music*) Laurie Johnson

(*Producer*) Douglas Crawford & The Mermaid Theatre

Shubert Theatre, New Haven*   pre–Broadway*

April 27, 1960   Out-of-Town
(*Stars*) Nancy Dussault, George S. Irving
Theatre World 59-60, p. 197
NO ENTRY AVAIL
New Yorker 35:81 Ag 29 '59
NO CRIT AVAIL
Broadway Bound, pp. 272-75
(*Published libretto*) Samuel French, Inc., 1967
(*Published sheet music*) Peter Maurice Music Co., Ltd./Sam Fox
        Pub. Co.
(*Original cast recording*) OP Decca(E) LK-4320/SKL-4070, RE That's
        Entertainment(E) TER-1049 (Original London Cast)
(*Agent/contact*) Samuel French, Inc.
(*Libretto, Music, Orchestrations*) Same as (*Agent/contact*)

*Previously produced in London

LOLITA, MY LOVE
(*Source*) *Lolita* (novel) by Vladimir Nabokov
(*Book*) Alan Jay Lerner*
(*Lyrics*) Alan Jay Lerner*
(*Music*) John Barry
(*Producer*) Norman Twain & Stone Widney
Shubert Theatre, Philadelphia   pre-Broadway
February 16, 1971   Out-of-Town
(*Stars*) John Neville, Dorothy Loudon
Theatre World 70-71, p. 175
Best Plays 70-71, pp. 318-19
NO CRIT AVAIL
New York Times 1971, F 19, 26:1
        New York Times 1971, Mr 5, 24:4
        New York Times 1971, Mr 30, 23:1
Broadway Bound, pp. 275-77
(*Published libretto*) NA
(*Published sheet music*) Edwin H. Morris/Charles Hansen

(*Original cast recording*) Blue Pear Records BP–1009 (Original
      Cast recorded live)
(*Agent/contact*)   Alan Jay Lerner Estate   John Barry
                c/o David Grossberg   c/o Traubner & Flynn
                30 N. La Salle Street   1849 Sawtelle Blvd.
                New York, N.Y. 10027   Los Angeles, CA 90025
(*Libretto, Music, Orchestrations*) Same as (*Agent/contact*)

*At press time, the Alan Jay Lerner Estate was not interested in
      soliciting further productions of this property

THE LOVE DOCTOR
See *THE CAREFREE HEART*

LOVE IN THE SNOW
(*Source*) Original
(*Book*) Rowland Leigh
(*Lyrics*) Rowland Leigh
(*Music*) Ralph Benatzky
(*Producer*) Messrs. Shubert
Bushnell Memorial Theatre, Hartford   pre–Broadway
March 15, 1946   Out–of–Town
(*Stars*) NA
Theatre World 45–46, p. 131
NO ENTRY AVAIL
NO CRIT AVAIL
NO CRIT AVAIL
Broadway Bound, pp. 277–78
(*Published libretto*) NA
(*Published sheet music*) NA
(*Original cast recording*) NA

(*Agent/contact*)   Rowland Leigh Estate   The Shubert Organization
                          c/o ASCAP   234 W. 44th Street
                                                     New York, N.Y.   10036
(*Libretto*) LC Jacob J. Shubert 7June46 DU3493; same as
        (*Agent/contact*)
(*Music*) LC Jacob J. Shubert 7June46 EU25232–25247, 14June46
        EU25947–25950; same as (*Agent/contact*)
(*Orchestrations*) Same as (*Agent/contact*)

*LOVE MATCH**
(*Source*) Original
(*Book*) Christian Hamilton
(*Lyrics*) Richard Maltby, Jr.**
(*Music*) David Shire**
(*Producer*) Center Theater Group, by arrangement with Elliot
        Martin and Ivor David Balding Associates
Palace West Theater, Phoenix   pre–Broadway
November 3, 1968   Out–of–Town
(*Stars*) Hal Linden, Patricia Routledge
Theatre World 68–69, p. 197
Best Plays 68–69, pp. 417–18
NO CRIT AVAIL
New York Times 1968, D 25, 42:1
Broadway Bound, pp. 279–80
(*Published libretto*) NA
(*Published sheet music*) NA
(*Original cast recording*) NA
(*Agent/contact*)   Richard Maltby, Jr.   David Shire
                          c/o DG, Inc.   c/o DG, Inc.
(*Libretto*) NYPL NCOF+, RM7507; LC Christian Hamilton 27Mar67
        DU68367 as *THE LOVING COUPLE*; same as (*Agent/contact*)
(*Music, Orchestrations*) Same as (*Agent/contact*)

*Previously titled *THE LOVING COUPLE*
**At press time, neither Mr. Maltby nor Mr. Shire was interested
        in soliciting further productions of this property

THE LOVING COUPLE
See *LOVE MATCH*

MARIANNE
(*Source*) Original
(*Book*) Sylvia Regan & Kenneth White
(*Lyrics*) Beatrice & Lothar Metzl, with Robert B. Sour
(*Music*) Abraham Ellstein
(*Producer*) B.P. Schulberg & Marion Gering
Shubert Theatre, New Haven   pre–Broadway
December 30, 1943   Out–of–Town
(*Stars*) NA
NO ENTRY AVAIL
NO ENTRY AVAIL
NO CRIT AVAIL
NO CRIT AVAIL
Broadway Bound, pp. 295–96
(*Published libretto*) NA
(*Published sheet music*) NA
(*Original cast recording*) NA
(*Agent/contact*)   Sylvia Regan Ellstein
                         55 E. 9th Street
                         New York, N.Y.   10003
(*Libretto, Music, Orchestrations*) Same as (*Agent/contact*)

MATA HARI (See *BALLAD FOR A FIRING SQUAD*)*
(*Source*) Original
(*Book*) Jerome Coopersmith
(*Lyrics*) Martin Charnin
(*Music*) Edward Thomas
(*Producer*) David Merrick
National Theatre, Washington D.C.   pre–Broadway
November 18, 1967   Out–of–Town
(*Stars*) Pernell Roberts, Marisa Mell

Theatre World 67–68, p. 185

Best Plays 67–68, pp. 380–81

Look il 32:82–4 F 6 '68

New York Times 1967, N 9, 60:3

       New York Times 1967, D 1, 51:1

Broadway Bound, pp. 299–301

(*Published libretto*) NA

(*Published sheet music*) Mesquite Music Corp./Edwin H. Morris

(*Original cast recording*) NA

(*Agent/contact*)

Jerome Coopersmith	Edward Thomas	Martin Charnin
160 Hendrickson Avenue	c/o Somat Music	c/o DG, Inc.
Rockville Centre, N.Y.	157 W. 57th Street	
11570	New York, N.Y. 10019	

(*Libretto*) NYPL RM6434; NCOF+ as *BALLAD FOR A FIRING SQUAD*;
    LC Jerome Coopersmith, Edward Thomas & Martin Charnin
    2Jan69 DU73210 as *BALLAD FOR A FIRING SQUAD*;
    same as (*Agent/contact*)

(*Music, Orchestrations*) Same as (*Agent/contact*)

MATA HARI was rewritten and premiered off–Broadway 12/11/68
    under the title *BALLAD FOR A FIRING SQUAD*

MISS MOFFAT

(*Source*) *The Corn is Green* (play) by Emlyn Williams

(*Book*) Emlyn Williams & Joshua Logan

(*Lyrics*) Emlyn Williams

(*Music*) Albert Hague

(*Producer*) Eugene V. Wolsk, Joshua Logan & Slade Brown

Shubert Theatre, Philadelphia	pre–Broadway
October 7, 1974	Out–of–Town

(*Stars*) Bette Davis, Nell Carter

Theatre World 74–75, p. 160
Best Plays 74–75, pp. 350–51
NO CRIT AVAIL
New York Times 1974, Ag 11, III, 13:3
New York Times 1974, S 11, 37:1
New York Times 1974, O 22, 46:1
Broadway Bound, pp. 313–15
(*Published libretto*) NA
(*Published sheet music*) NA (Revelation Music Publishing Corp.)
(*Original cast recording*) NA
(*Agent/contact*)

Joshua Logan	Emlyn Williams	Albert Hague
c/o DG, Inc.	DG, Inc.	c/o DG, Inc.

(*Libretto, Music, Orchestrations*) Same as (*Agent/contact*)

A MONTH OF SUNDAYS
(*Source*) *Excursion* (play) by Victor Wolfson
(*Book*) Burt Shevelove
(*Lyrics*) Burt Shevelove & Ted Fetter
(*Music*) Albert Selden
(*Producer*) Carly Wharton
Shubert Theatre, Boston   pre–Broadway
December 25, 1951   Out–of–Town
(*Stars*) Nancy Walker, Gene Lockhart
Theatre World 51–52, p. 160
NO ENTRY AVAIL
NO CRIT AVAIL
NO CRIT AVAIL
Broadway Bound, pp. 319–21
(*Published libretto*) NA
(*Published sheet music*) Spitzer Songs, Inc.
(*Original cast recording*) NA

(*Agent/contact*)   Albert Selden   Burt Shevelove
                 609 Camino Rancheros   c/o Coleman & Rosenberg
                 Santa Fe, NM 87501   210 E. 58th Street
                                         New York, N.Y. 10022

(*Libretto, Music, Orchestrations*) Same as (*Agent/contact*)

A MOTHER'S KISSES

(*Source*) *A Mother's Kisses* (novel) by Bruce Jay Friedman
(*Book*) Bruce Jay Friedman*
(*Lyrics*) Richard Adler*
(*Music*) Richerd Adler*
(*Producer*) Lester Osterman, Richard Horner & Lawrence Kasha,
     in association with Frederic S. & Barbara Mates
Shubert Theatre, New Haven   pre–Broadway
September 23, 1968   Out–of–Town
(*Stars*) Bea Arthur
Theatre World 68–69, p. 179
Best Plays 68–69, pp. 416–17
NO CRIT AVAIL
New York Times 1968, S 10, 40:4
     New York Times 1968, O 15, 39:3
Broadway Bound, pp. 324–26
(*Published libretto*) NA
(*Published sheet music*) Cromwell Music, Inc.
(*Original cast recording*) NA
(*Agent/contact*)
     Richard Adler   Bruce Jay Friedman   Lester Osterman
     c/o DG, Inc.   c/o DG, Inc.   246 E. 54th Street
                                    New York, N.Y. 10022

(*Libretto*) NYPL RM4439, RM7129; same as (*Agent/contact*)

(*Music, Orchestrations*) Same as (*Agent/contact*)

*In all publicity, Bruce Jay Friedman is given sole authorship credit and
    Richard Adler sole lyricist/composer credit; however, the
    manuscript/promptscript filed with NYPL Billy Rose Collection gives
    Jerome Chodorov sole authorship credit, and Richard Adler & Bob
    Merrill lyricist/composer credit

NEFERTITI

(*Source*) *Brothers* (play) by Christopher Gore
(*Book*) Christopher Gore
(*Lyrics*) Christopher Gore
(*Music*) David Spangler
(*Producer*) Sherwin M. Goldman
Blackstone Theatre, Chicago   pre–Broadway
September 20, 1977   Out–of–Town
(*Stars*) Andrea Marcovicci
Theatre World 77–78, p. 163
Best Plays 77–78, pp. 379–80
NO CRIT AVAIL
New York Times 1977, S 20, 38:3
Broadway Bound, pp. 333–36
(*Published libretto*) NA
(*Published sheet music*) NA
(*Original cast recording*) Take Home Tunes THT–7810
(*Agent/contact*)

Christopher Gore	David Spangler	Sherwin M. Goldman Prods.
c/o DG, Inc.	c/o DG, Inc.	1501 Broadway
		New York, N.Y. 10036

(*Libretto*) LC Christopher Gore 16Sep77 DU105327; same as
        (*Agent/contact*)
(*Music*) LC David Spangler & Christopher Gore 3May78 PAu–19–567; same
        as (*Agent/contact*)
(*Orchestrations*) Same as (*Agent/contact*)

ONE NIGHT STAND
(*Source*) Original
(*Book*) Herb Gardner
(*Lyrics*) Herb Gardner
(*Music*) Jule Styne
(*Producer*) Joseph Kipness, Lester Osterman, Joan Culman,
          James M. Nederlander & Alfred Taubman
Nederlander Theater   pre-Broadway
October 20, 1980   Preview
(*Stars*) Jack Weston
Theatre World 80–81, p. 168
Best Plays 80–81, pp. 380–81
NO CRIT AVAIL
New York Times 1980, Ag 13, III, 15:1
          New York Times 1980, O 27, III, 16:4
Broadway Bound, pp. 5–6
(*Published libretto*) NA
(*Published sheet music*) (Chappell)
(*Original cast recording*) Original Cast Records OC–8134
(*Agent/contact*)

Jule Styne	Herb Gardner	Lester Osterman
c/o DG, Inc.	c/o DG, Inc.	246 E. 54th Street
		New York, N.Y. 10022

(*Libretto, Music, Orchestrations*) Same as (*Agent/contact*)

PEG*
(*Source*) *Peg O' My Heart* (play) by J. Hartley Manners,
          original libretto by Mike Sawyer
(*Book*) Robert Emmett
(*Lyrics*) Johnny Brandon
(*Music*) Johnny Brandon
(*Producer*) Lee Guber & Shelly Gross
Valley Forge Music Theatre, Devon, PA   pre-Broadway
July 10, 1967   Out-of-Town
(*Stars*) Eartha Kitt

NO ENTRY AVAIL
NO ENTRY AVAIL
NO CRIT AVAIL
NO CRIT AVAIL
NO CRIT AVAIL
(*Published libretto*) NA
(*Published sheet music*) NA
(*Original cast recording*) NA
(*Agent/contact*)

Johnny Brandon	Robert Emmett	Guber/Gross Inc.
c/o DG, Inc.	c/o DG, Inc.	32 E. 57th Street
		New York, N.Y. 10022

(*Libretto*) NYPL RM5834, RM5835, RM5836; LC Johnny Brandon & Robert
      E. Richardson 30Jan84 PAu–617–677 as *SING ME SUNSHINE*; same
      as (*Agent/contact*)
(*Music, Orchestrations*) Same as (*Agent/contact*)

*Subsequently revised and titled *SING ME SUNSHINE*, book by Johnny
      Brandon & Robert E. Richardson, lyrics and music by Johnny Brandon

THE PINK JUNGLE
(*Source*) Original
(*Book*) Leslie Stevens
(*Lyrics*) Vernon Duke
(*Music*) Vernon Duke
(*Producer*) Paul Gregory

Alcazar Theatre, San Francisco	pre–Broadway
October 14, 1959	Out-of-Town

(*Stars*) Agnes Moorehead, Leif Erickson, Ginger Rogers
Theatre World 59–60, p. 192
NO ENTRY AVAIL

NO CRIT AVAIL
NO CRIT AVAIL
Broadway Bound, pp. 368–70
(*Published libretto*) NA
(*Published sheet music*) NA (Vernon Duke Music Corp.)
(*Original cast recording*) NA
(*Agent/contact*)   Vernon Duke Estate   Leslie Stevens
                         c/o Kay McCracken Duke   c/o DG, Inc.
                         407 Vance Street
                         Pacific Palisades, CA 90272
(*Libretto*) NYPL RM2473; same as (*Agent/contact*)
(*Music, Orchestrations*) Same as (*Agent/contact*)

*PLEASURES AND PALACES**
(*Source*) *Once There Was a Russian* (play) by Sam Spewack
(*Book*) Sam Spewack & Frank Loesser**
(*Lyrics*) Frank Loesser**
(*Music*) Frank Loesser**
(*Producer*) Allen B. Whitehead, in association with Frank
        Productions, Inc.
Fisher Theatre, Detroit   pre–Broadway
March 11, 1965   Out–of–Town
(*Stars*) John McMartin, Phyllis Newman
Theatre World 64–65, p. 225
Best Plays 64–65, p. 371
NO CRIT AVAIL
New York Times 1965, Ap 9, 18:1
        New York Times 1965, My 2, II, 4:5
Broadway Bound, pp. 371–72
(*Published libretto*) NA
(*Published sheet music*) NA (Frank Music Corp.)
(*Original cast recording*) NA

(*Agent/contact*)   Frank Loesser Estate
                    c/o Music Theatre International
(*Libretto*) NYPL RM4599 as *EX–LOVER*; same as (*Agent/contact*)
(*Music, Orchestrations*) Same as (*Agent/contact*)

*Previously titled *EX–LOVER*

**At press time, the Frank Loesser Estate was not interested
   in soliciting further productions of this property

*PRETTYBELLE**
(*Source*) *Prettybelle* (novel) by Jean Arnold
(*Book*) Bob Merrill
(*Lyrics*) Bob Merrill
(*Music*) Jule Styne
(*Producer*) Alexander H. Cohen
Shubert Theatre, Boston   pre–Broadway
February 1, 1971   Out–of–Town
(*Stars*) Angela Lansbury
Theatre World 70–71, p. 174
Best Plays 70–71, pp. 316–18
NO CRIT AVAIL
New York Times 1971, Ja 2, 11:1
       New York Times 1971, Mr 3, 34:3
Broadway Bound, pp. 381–83
(*Published libretto*) NA
(*Published sheet music*) Valando Music Inc./Chappell & Co.
(*Original cast recording*) Original Cast Records OC–8238
(*Agent/contact*)   Jule Styne   Bob Merrill
                    c/o DG, Inc.   c/o UCLA Theatre Arts Dept.
                                        Los Angeles, CA 90024
(*Libretto*) NYPL RM7381 as *THE RAPE OF PRETTYBELLE*;
       same as (*Agent/contact*)

(Music, Orchestrations) Same as *(Agent/contact)*

*Previously titled *THE RAPE OF PRETTYBELLE*

PRINCE CHU CHANG
See *YOURS IS MY HEART*

THE PRINCE OF GRAND STREET
(Source) Original
(Book) Bob Merrill*
(Lyrics) Bob Merrill*
(Music) Bob Merrill*
(Producer) Robert Whitehead & Roger L. Stevens, The Shubert Organization
Forrest Theatre, Philadelphia   pre–Broadway
March 7, 1978   Out–of–Town
(Stars) Robert Preston
Theatre World 77–78, p. 163
Best Plays 77–78, pp. 381–82
NO CRIT AVAIL
New York Times 1978, Ja 11, III, 15:1
        New York Times 1978, Ap 11, 44:4
Broadway Bound, pp. 383–85
(Published libretto) NA
(Published sheet music) NA
(Original cast recording) NA
(Agent/contact)

Bob Merrill	Robert Whitehead
c/o UCLA Theatre Arts Dept.	1501 Broadway
Los Angeles, CA 90024	New York, N.Y. 10019

(Libretto, Music, Orchestrations) Same as *(Agent/contact)*

*At press time, Mr. Merrill was not interested in soliciting
        further productions of this property

RACHAEL LILY ROSENBLOOM
See *RACHAEL LILY ROSENBLOOM AND DON'T YOU EVER FORGET IT*

*RACHAEL LILY ROSENBLOOM AND DON'T YOU EVER FORGET IT**
(*Source*) Original
(*Book*) Paul Jabara & Tom Eyen
(*Lyrics*) Paul Jabara
(*Music*) Paul Jabara
(*Producer*) Robert Stigwood, Ahmet Ertegun, Gatchell & Neufeld
Broadhurst Theatre   pre–Broadway
November 26, 1973   Preview
(*Stars*) Andre De Shields, Ellen Greene, Anita Morris
Theatre World 73–74, p. 152
Best Plays 73–74, pp. 370–71
NO CRIT AVAIL
New York Times 1973, D 4, 52:10
Broadway Bound, p. 4
(*Published libretto*) NA
(*Published sheet music*) NA (Casserole Music Corporation)
(*Original cast recording*) NA
(*Agent/contact*)   Paul Jabara   Robert Stigwood Organization
                     c/o BMI   1775 Broadway
                                   New York, N.Y.   10019
(*Libretto*) LC Paul Jabara 1Jun71 DU80236;
      same as (*Agent/contact*)
(*Music, Orchestrations*) Same as (*Agent/contact*)

*Previously titled *RACHAEL LILY ROSENBLOOM*

THE RAPE OF PRETTYBELLE
See *PRETTYBELLE*

A REEL AMERICAN HERO*
(*Source*) Original
(*Book*) Judith GeBauer & Burt Vinocur
(*Lyrics*) Gerald Hillman & Stephanie Peters
(*Music*) Gordon Kent & Stephanie Peters
(*Producer*) Gerald Paul Hillman
Rialto Theater   pre–Broadway
March 25, 1981   Preview
(*Stars*) NA
Theatre World 80–81, p. 169
Best Plays 80–81, pp. 383
NO CRIT AVAIL
New York Times 1981, F 20, III, 2:3
        New York Times 1981, Mr 24, III, 20:3
Broadway Bound, pp. 6–7
(*Published libretto*) NA
(*Published sheet music*) NA
(*Original cast recording*) NA
(*Agent/contact*)   Chareeva Productions   Gerald Hillman
                        101 Fifth Avenue   601 West End Avenue
                        New York, N.Y. 10003   New York, N.Y. 10024
(*Libretto*) LC Basic International Investments 9Jun80 PAu–280–314 as
        THE WORLD OF BLACK AND WHITE; same as (*Agent/contact*)
(*Music, Orchestrations*) Same as (*Agent/contact*)

*Previously titled *THE WORLD OF BLACK AND WHITE*

REUBEN REUBEN
(*Source*) Original
(*Book*) Marc Blitzstein
(*Lyrics*) Marc Blitzstein

(*Music*) Marc Blitzstein
(*Producer*) Cheryl Crawford
Shubert Theatre, Boston   pre–Broadway
October 10, 1955   Out–of–Town
(*Stars*) Eddie Albert, Kaye Ballard, George Gaynes
Theatre World 55–56, p. 166
NO ENTRY AVAIL
NO CRIT AVAIL
NO CRIT AVAIL
Broadway Bound, pp. 400–402
(*Published libretto*) NA
(*Published sheet music*) Chappell & Co.
(*Original cast recording*) NA
(*Agent/contact*)   Marc Blitzstein Estate
                       c/o ASCAP
(*Libretto*) NYPL RM2920; same as (*Agent/contact*)
(*Music, Orchestrations*) Same as (*Agent/contact*)

ROYAL FLUSH

(*Source*) "The Green Bird" ("L'Augelinno Belverde") (commedia dell'arte
         scenario) by Carlo Gozzi, as translated and adapted by Nina Savo
(*Book*) Jay Thompson & Robert Schlitt
(*Lyrics*) Jay Thompson
(*Music*) Jay Thompson
(*Producer*) L. Slade Brown & Robert Linden
Shubert Theatre, New Haven   pre–Broadway
December 30, 1964   Out–of–Town
(*Stars*) Kaye Ballard, Jill O'Hara, Jane Connell
Theatre World 64–65, p. 223
Best Plays 64–65, p. 371
NO CRIT AVAIL
NO CRIT AVAIL
Broadway Bound, pp. 409–11

(*Published libretto*) NA
(*Published sheet music*) NA
(*Original cast recording*) NA
(*Agent/contact*)

Gilbert Parker	Jay Thompson
c/o William Morris Agency	403–B 75th Avenue N.
1350 Avenue of the Americas	Myrtle Beach, SC 29577
New York, N.Y. 10019	

(*Libretto*) NYPL RM7801; same as (*Agent/contact*)
(*Music, Orchestrations*) Same as (*Agent/contact*)

SAY HELLO TO HARVEY!

(*Source*) *Harvey* (play) by Mary Chase
(*Book*) Leslie Bricusse
(*Lyrics*) Leslie Bricusse
(*Music*) Leslie Bricusse
(*Producer*) Michael McAloney & Ed Mirvish, in association with
          Joyce Sloane

Royal Alexandra Theater, Toronto	pre–Broadway
September 14, 1981	Out–of–Town

(*Stars*) Donald O'Connor, Patricia Routledge
NO ENTRY AVAIL
Best Plays 81–82, p. 341
NO CRIT AVAIL
NO CRIT AVAIL
NO CRIT AVAIL
(*Published libretto*) NA
(*Published sheet music*) (Stage & Screen Music, Ltd.)
(*Original cast recording*) NA
(*Agent/contact*)   Leslie Bricusse
          c/o DG, Inc.
(*Libretto, Music, Orchestrations*) Same as (*Agent/contact*)

SCARLETT
See *GONE WITH THE WIND*

SHEBA
(*Source*) *Come Back Little Sheba* (play) by William Inge
(*Book*) Lee Goldsmith
(*Lyrics*) Lee Goldsmith
(*Music*) Clinton C. Ballard, Jr.
(*Producer*) Sidney Eden

1st Chicago Center, Chicago	pre–Broadway
July 24, 1974	Out–of–Town

(*Stars*) Kaye Ballard, George D. Wallace
NO ENTRY AVAIL
NO ENTRY AVAIL
NO CRIT AVAIL
NO CRIT AVAIL
NO CRIT AVAIL
(*Published libretto*) NA
(*Published sheet music*) NA
(*Original cast recording*) NA

(*Agent/contact*)	Lee Goldsmith	Clint Ballard, Jr.
	c/o DG, Inc.	c/o DG, Inc.

(*Libretto, Music, Orchestrations*) Same as (*Agent/contact*)

SHOOTIN' STAR
(*Source*) Original
(*Book*) Walter Hart, Louis Jacobs & Halsted Welles
(*Lyrics*) Bob Russell
(*Music*) Sol Kaplan
(*Producer*) Max Liebman & Joseph Kipness

Shubert Theatre, New Haven	pre–Broadway
April 4, 1946	Out–of–Town

(*Stars*) Howard Da Silva, Doretta Morrow

Theatre World 45–46, p. 132

NO ENTRY AVAIL

NO CRIT AVAIL

NO CRIT AVAIL

Broadway Bound, pp. 429–30

(*Published libretto*) NA

(*Published sheet music*) Famous Music Corp.

(*Original cast recording*) NA

(*Agent/contact*)   Sol Kaplan   Hannah Russell

                           c/o DG, Inc.   1324 Sunset Plaza Drive

                                                   Los Angeles, CA   90069

(*Libretto*) NYPL NCOF+; MCNY; LC Jay Lawrence, Lee Willis & Halsted
         Welles 31Mar46 DU2318; same as (*Agent/contact*)

(*Music, Orchestrations*) Same as (*Agent/contact*)

SING ME SUNSHINE

See *PEG*

SNOOPY!!!

(*Source*) "Peanuts" (comic strip) by Charles M. Schulz

(*Book*) Warren Lockhart, Arthur Whitelaw & Michael L. Grace*

(*Lyrics*) Hal Hackady

(*Music*) Larry Grossman

(*Producer*) Arthur Whitelaw, Michael L. Grace, Susan Bloom,
         Warren Lockhart & Charles M. Schulz Creative Associates

Little Fox Theatre, San Francisco   pre–Broadway*

December 9, 1975*   Out–of–Town

(*Stars*) Pamela Myers*

Theatre World 75–76, p. 172

         Theatre World 82–83, p. 87

Best Plays 82–83, pp. 400–1
NY 16:79 Ja 17 '83
New York Times 1982, N 19, III, 2:3
NO CRIT AVAIL
(*Published libretto*) NA
(*Published sheet music*) UniChappell
(*Original cast recording*) DRG Records 6103; Polydor(E)
          820 247–1 (Original London Cast)
(*Agent/contact*) Tams–Witmark Music Library
(*Libretto, Music, Orchestrations*) Same as (*Agent/contact*)

SNOOPY!!! subsequently revised and premiered off–Broadway 12/20/82,
          book by Charles M. Schulz Creative Associates, Warren Lockhart &
          Arthur Whitelaw, starring Lorna Luft

SPEAK, LUCINDA!
See *THE CAREFREE HEART*

A SONG FOR CYRANO
(*Source*) *Cyrano de Bergerac* (play) by Edmond Rostand
(*Book*) J. Vincent Smith (Jose Ferrer)
(*Lyrics*) Robert Wright & George Forrest
(*Music*) Robert Wright & George Forrest
(*Producer*) Pocono Playhouse

Pocono Playhouse, Mountainhome, PA*	pre–Broadway
September 4, 1972	Out–of–Town

(*Stars*) José Ferrer
NO ENTRY AVAIL
NO ENTRY AVAIL
NO CRIT AVAIL
NO CRIT AVAIL
NO CRIT AVAIL
(*Published libretto*) NA

(*Published sheet music*) NA
(*Original cast recording*) NA
(*Agent/contact*)   Robert Wright & George Forrest
                          c/o DG, Inc.
(*Libretto*) LC Jose V. Ferrer 8Nov77 DU105977;
        same as (*Agent/contact*)
(*Music, Orchestrations*) Same as (*Agent/contact*)

*Previously presented at Elitch Gardens Theatre, Denver, CO

SPOTLIGHT
(*Source*) Story (title unavailable) by Leonard Starr
(*Book*) Richard Seff
(*Lyrics*) Lyn Duddy
(*Music*) Jerry Bresler
(*Producer*) Sheldon R. Lubliner
National Theatre, Washington, D.C.   pre–Broadway
January 11, 1978   Out–of–Town
(*Stars*) Gene Barry
Theatre World 77–78, p. 164
Best Plays 77–78, pp. 380–81
NO CRIT AVAIL
New York Times 1978, Ja 11, III, 15:1
Broadway Bound, pp. 435–36
(*Published libretto*) NA
(*Published sheet music*) NA
(*Original cast recording*) NA
(*Agent/contact*)

        Richard Seff   Lyn Duddy   Jerry Bresler
        399 E. 72nd Street   c/o ASCAP   c/o ASCAP
        New York, N.Y.   10021
(*Libretto, Music, Orchestrations*) Same as (*Agent/contact*)

SPRING IN BRAZIL
(*Source*) Original
(*Book*) Philip Rapp
(*Lyrics*) Robert Wright & George Forrest
(*Music*) Robert Wright & George Forrest
(*Producer*) Monte Proser, in association with the Messrs. Shubert
Shubert Theatre, Boston   pre–Broadway
October 1, 1945   Out–of–Town
(*Stars*) Milton Berle, Rose Marie
Theatre World 45–46, p. 126
NO ENTRY AVAIL
NO CRIT AVAIL
NO CRIT AVAIL
Broadway Bound, pp. 436–38
(*Published libretto*) NA
(*Published sheet music*) NA
(*Original cast recording*) NA
(*Agent/contact*)

Robert Wright	George Forrest	The Shubert Organization
c/o DG, Inc.	c/o DG, Inc.	234 W. 44th Street
		New York, N.Y. 10036

(*Libretto, Music, Orchestrations*) Same as (*Agent/contact*)

STRIP FOR ACTION
(*Source*) *Strip for Action* (play) by Howard Lindsay & Russell
        Crouse
(*Book*) Paul Streger & Eli Basse
(*Lyrics*) Harold Adamson
(*Music*) Jimmy McHugh
(*Producer*) Howard Hoyt, Igor Cassini & William G. Costin
Shubert Theater, New Haven   pre–Broadway
March 17, 1956   Out–of–Town
(*Stars*) Hal Linden, Yvonne Adair
Theatre World 55–56, p. 171

NO ENTRY AVAIL
NO CRIT AVAIL
New York Times 1956, Ap 6, 13:6
Broadway Bound, pp. 451–53
(*Published libretto*) NA
(*Published sheet music*) Robbins Music Corp.
(*Original cast recording*) NA
(*Agent/contact*)

Paul Streger	Harold Adamson Estate	Jimmy McHugh Estate
c/o DG, Inc.	c/o AGAC	c/o Samuel French, Inc.

(*Libretto*) NYPL RM312; same as (*Agent/contact*)
(*Music, Orchestrations*) Same as (*Agent/contact*)

SWEET BYE AND BYE
(*Source*) Original
(*Book*) S.J. Perelman & Albert Hirschfeld
(*Lyrics*) Ogden Nash
(*Music*) Vernon Duke
(*Producer*) Nat Karson
Shubert Theatre, New Haven   pre–Broadway
October 10, 1946   Out–of–Town
(*Stars*) Dolores Gray
Theatre World 46–47, p. 136
NO ENTRY AVAIL
NO CRIT AVAIL
NO CRIT AVAIL
Broadway Bound, pp. 455–57
(*Published libretto*) NA
(*Published sheet music*) Harms
(*Original cast recording*) NA

(*Agent/contact*)

Vernon Duke Estate	Ogden Nash Estate	S.J. Perelman
c/o Kay McCracken Duke	c/o ASCAP	Estate
407 Vance Street		c/o Samuel French, Inc.
Pacific Palisades, CA 90272		

(*Libretto*) NYPL NCOF+; same as (*Agent/contact*)

(*Music, Orchestrations*) Same as (*Agent/contact*)

SWING*

(*Source*) Original

(*Book*) Conn Fleming

(*Lyrics*) Alfred Uhry

(*Music*) Robert Waldman

(*Producer*) Stuart Ostrow, in association with Edgar M.
  Bronfman

Playhouse, Wilmington, DE   pre–Broadway

February 25, 1980   Out-of-Town

(*Stars*) NA

Theatre World 79–80, p. 175

Best Plays 79–80, pp. 400–1

NO CRIT AVAIL

New York Times 1980, F 16, 19:2

Broadway Bound, pp. 459–61

(*Published libretto*) NA

(*Published sheet music*) NA

(*Original cast recording*) NA

(*Agent/contact*)

Conn Fleming	Alfred Uhry	Robert Waldman
c/o DG, Inc.	c/o DG, Inc.	c/o DG, Inc.

(*Libretto, Orchestrations*) Same as (*Agent/contact*)

(*Music*) LC Robert Waldman & Alfred Uhry 28Jan80 PAu–169–370,
16Apr80 PAu–214–178; same as (*Agent/contact*)

*Subsequently revised and presented off–Broadway under the title
DREAM TIME

10 DAYS TO BROADWAY
See *HOME AGAIN, HOME AGAIN*

THAT'S THE TICKET!
(*Source*) Original
(*Book*) Julius J. & Philip G. Epstein
(*Lyrics*) Harold Rome
(*Music*) Harold Rome
(*Producer*) Joseph Kipness, John Pransky & Al Beckman
Shubert Theatre, Philadelphia   pre–Broadway
September 24, 1948   Out–of–Town
(*Stars*) Leif Erickson, Kaye Ballard
Theatre World 48–49, p. 135
NO ENTRY AVAIL
NO CRIT AVAIL
NO CRIT AVAIL
Broadway Bound, pp. 464–66
(*Published libretto*) NA
(*Published sheet music*) Crawford Music Corp./Gemini Music
        Pub./Chappell
(*Original cast recording*) NA
(*Agent/contact*)   Julius J. Epstein   Harold Rome
                       c/o DG, Inc.   c/o DG, Inc.
(*Libretto*) NYPL RM8356, NCOF+; same as (*Agent/contact*)
(*Music, Orchestrations*) Same as (*Agent/contact*)

13 DAYS TO BROADWAY
See *HOME AGAIN, HOME AGAIN*

TREASURE ISLAND
(*Source*) *Treasure Island* (novel) by Robert Louis Stevenson
(*Book*) Tom Tippett
(*Lyrics*) John Clifton
(*Music*) John Clifton
(*Producer*) Adelaide Sutherland; Shepard, Clifton & Thompson, in
       association with Theatre Now, Inc.
DuPont Playhouse, Wilmington, DE   pre–Broadway
January 20, 1975   Out–of–Town
(*Stars*) NA
Theatre World 74–75, p. 172
NO ENTRY AVAIL
NO CRIT AVAIL
NO CRIT AVAIL
NO CRIT AVAIL
(*Published libretto*) NA
(*Published sheet music*) NA
(*Original cast recording*) NA
(*Agent/contact*)   Tom Tippett   John Clifton
                 c/o DG, Inc.   c/o DG, Inc.
(*Libretto, Music, Orchestrations*) Same as (*Agent/contact*)

TRUCKLOAD
(*Source*) Original
(*Book*) Hugh Wheeler
(*Lyrics*) Wes Harris
(*Music*) Louis St. Louis
(*Producer*) Adela Holzer, The Shubert Organization & Dick Clark
Lyceum Theatre   pre–Broadway
September 6, 1975   Preview

(*Stars*) Deborah Allen
Theatre World 75–76, p. 155
NO ENTRY AVAIL
NO CRIT AVAIL
NO CRIT AVAIL
Broadway Bound, p. 5
(*Published libretto*) NA
(*Published sheet music*) NA (Flamin' Mama Music)
(*Original cast recording*) NA
(*Agent/contact*)

Hugh Wheeler	Louis St. Louis	The Shubert Organization
c/o DG, Inc.	c/o DG, Inc.	234 W. 44th Street
		New York, N.Y. 10036

(*Libretto, Music, Orchestrations*) Same as (*Agent/contact*)

W.C.

(*Source*) *W.C., His Follies and Fortunes* (biography) by Robert
        Lewis Taylor
(*Book*) Milton Sperling & Sam Locke
(*Lyrics*) Al Carmines
(*Music*) Al Carmines
(*Producer*) Lee Guber & Shelly Gross, in association with David
        Black

Painters Mill Music Fair, Owings Mills, MD	pre–Broadway
June 15, 1971	Out–of–Town

(*Stars*) Mickey Rooney, Bernadette Peters, Virginia Martin
NO ENTRY AVAIL
NO ENTRY AVAIL
NO CRIT AVAIL
NO CRIT AVAIL
Broadway Bound, pp. 488–89

(*Published libretto*) NA
(*Published sheet music*) NA
(*Original cast recording*) NA
(*Agent/contact*)

Al Carmines	Sam D. Locke	Guber/Gross, Inc.
c/o DG, Inc.	c/o Lucy Kroll Agency	32 E. 57th Street
	390 West End Avenue	New York, N.Y. 10022
	New York, N.Y. 10024	

(*Libretto*) NYPL RM5689; same as (*Agent/contact*)
(*Music, Orchestrations*) Same as (*Agent/contact*)

WE TAKE THE TOWN

(*Source*) *Viva Villa!* (screenplay) by Ben Hecht
(*Book*) Felice Bauer & Matt Dubey
(*Lyrics*) Matt Dubey*
(*Music*) Harold Karr
(*Producer*) Stuart Ostrow

| Shubert Theatre, New Haven | pre—Broadway |
| February 19, 1962 | Out—of—Town |

(*Stars*) Robert Preston, Kathleen Widdoes, John Cullum
Theatre World 61–62, p. 195
Best Plays 61–62, pp. 337–38
Seventeen 21:86–7+ Je '62
NO CRIT AVAIL
Broadway Bound, pp. 494–96
(*Published libretto*) NA
(*Published sheet music*) Chappell & Co., Inc.
(*Original cast recording*) NA
(*Agent/contact*)

| Matt Dubey | Harold Karr |
| c/o DG, Inc. | c/o ASCAP |

(*Libretto, Music, Orchestrations*) Same as (*Agent/contact*)

*At press time, Mr. Dubey reported *WE TAKE THE TOWN*
        was being revised for Broadway production and therefore
        was presently unavailable for production

WHEN DO THE WORDS COME TRUE?

(*Source*) Original
(*Book*) John Meyer
(*Lyrics*) John Meyer
(*Music*) John Meyer
(*Producer*) Bucks County Theatre, in association with Madeline
        Lee Gilford & Gerard Oestreicher

Bucks County Playhouse, New Hope, PA	pre–Broadway
April 16, 1971	Out–of–Town

(*Stars*) Gloria De Haven
Theatre World 70–71, p. 190
NO ENTRY AVAIL
NO CRIT AVAIL
NO CRIT AVAIL
NO CRIT AVAIL
(*Published libretto*) NA
(*Published sheet music*) NA
(*Original cast recording*) NA

(*Agent/contact*)	John Meyer	Gerard Oestricher
	c/o ASCAP	680 Madison Avenue
		New York, N.Y. 10022

(*Libretto*) NYPL NCOF+ 73–1868; same as (*Agent/contact*)
(*Music, Orchestrations*) Same as (*Agent/contact*)

WINDY CITY
(*Source*) Original
(*Book*) Philip Yordan
(*Lyrics*) Paul Francis Webster
(*Music*) Walter Jurman
(*Producer*) Richard Kollmar

Shubert Theatre, New Haven	pre–Broadway
April 18, 1946	Out–of–Town

(*Stars*) NA
Theatre World 45–46, pp. 132–33
NO ENTRY AVAIL
NO CRIT AVAIL
NO CRIT AVAIL
Broadway Bound, pp. 504–506
(*Published libretto*) NA
(*Published sheet music*) Chappell
(*Original cast recording*) NA

(*Agent/contact*)	Paul Francis Webster	Walter Jurmann Estate
	c/o ASCAP	c/o ASCAP

(*Libretto*) NYPL NCOF+; same as (*Agent/contact*)
(*Music, Orchestrations*) Same as (*Agent/contact*)

THE WORLD OF BLACK AND WHITE
See *A REEL AMERICAN HERO*

ZENDA
(*Source*) *The Prisoner of Zenda* (novel) by Anthony Hope
(*Book*) Everett Freeman
(*Lyrics*) Leonard Adelson, Sid Kuller & Martin Charnin
(*Music*) Vernon Duke
(*Producer*) San Francisco Civic Light Opera Company, Edwin
        Lester, director

Curran Theatre, San Francisco	pre–Broadway

August 5, 1963   Out–of–Town
(*Stars*) Alfred Drake, Chita Rivera, Anne Rogers
Theatre World 63–64, p. 175
Best Plays 63–64, pp. 379–80
NO CRIT AVAIL
NO CRIT AVAIL
Broadway Bound, pp. 513–14
(*Published libretto*) NA
(*Published sheet music*) Morley Music Co./Edwin H. Morris
(*Original cast recording*) Blue Pear Records BP–1007 (Original Cast
        recorded live)
(*Agent/contact*)

Vernon Duke Estate	Leonard Adelson Estate	Sid Kuller
c/o Kay McCracken Duke	c/o Scott Adelson	c/o DG, Inc.
407 Vance Street	1617 Manning Street	
Pacific Palisades, CA	Los Angeles, CA 90024	Martin Charnin
90272		c/o DG, Inc.

(*Libretto*) NYPL RM1975; same as (*Agent/contact*)
(*Music, Orchestrations*) Same as (*Agent/contact*)

THE OFF–BROADWAY SHOWS AND A SELECTION
OF OFF–OFF–BROADWAY SHOWS

AESOP'S FABLES

(*Source*) *Aesop's Fables* (collection) by Aesopus
(*Book*) Jon Swan
(*Lyrics*) William Russo
(*Music*) William Russo
(*Producer*) William Russo

Mercer Arts Center   off–Broadway
August 17, 1972   58 performances

(*Stars*) NA
Theatre World 72–73, p. 95
Best Plays 72–73, pp. 369–70
NO CRIT AVAIL
New York Times 1972, Ag 18, 13:1
NO CRIT AVAIL
(*Published libretto*) NA
(*Published sheet music*) NA
(*Original cast recording*) NA

(*Agent/contact*)   William Russo   Jon Swan
                       621 W. Buckingham Place   c/o DG, Inc.
                       Chicago, IL   60657

(*Libretto, Music, Orchestrations*) Same as (*Agent/contact*)

AFTER STARDRIVE

(*Source*) Original
(*Book*) Kathleen Cramer & O–Lan Shepard
(*Lyrics*) Kathleen Cramer & O–Lan Shepard
(*Music*) Kathleen Cramer & O–Lan Shepard
(*Producer*) La Mama Experimental Theater Club

La Mama   off–off–Broadway
May 8, 1981   17 performances
(*Stars*) NA
NO ENTRY AVAIL
Best Plays 80–81, p. 430
New Yorker 57:115–6 My 25 '81
New York Times 1981, My 16, 15:3
NO CRIT AVAIL
(*Published libretto*) NA
(*Published sheet music*) NA
(*Original cast recording*) NA
(*Agent/contact*)   Kathleen Cramer   O–Lan Shepard
                        c/o Lois Berman   c/o Lois Berman
                        240 W. 44th Street   240 W. 44th Street
                        New York, N.Y.   10036   New York, N.Y.   10036
(*Libretto*) LC Kathleen Cramer & O–Lan Shepard 30Nov81
        PAu–354–900; same as (*Agent/contact*)
(*Music, Orchestrations*) Same as (*Agent/contact*)

ALICE AT THE PALACE
See *ALICE IN CONCERT*

*ALICE IN CONCERT**
(*Source*) *Alice in Wonderland* and *Through the Looking Glass*
        (novels) by Lewis Carroll
(*Book*) Elizabeth Swados
(*Lyrics*) Elizabeth Swados
(*Music*) Elizabeth Swados
(*Producer*) New York Shakespeare Festival

Public Theater   off–Broadway
December 29, 1980   32 performances
(*Stars*) Meryl Streep
Theatre World 80–81, p. 134
Best Plays 80–81, pp. 393, 395
NY il 14:38 Ja 19 '81
     New Yorker 56:90–1 Ja 19 '81
     Newsweek il 97:87 Ja 19 '81
     Time il 117:77 Ja 19 '81
New York Times 1981, Ja 8, III, 17:1
NYTC 1981:359
(*Published libretto*) Samuel French, Inc., 1986
(*Published sheet music*) NA
(*Original cast recording*) NA
(*Agent/contact*) Samuel French, Inc.
(*Libretto, Music, Orchestrations*) Same as (*Agent/contact*)

*Previously presented under the title **WONDERLAND IN CONCERT**;
    subsequently produced on television under the title ***ALICE AT THE***
    PALACE, available at NYPL Billy Rose Collection, Lincoln Center,
    NCOX 257

ALL IN LOVE
(*Source*) *The Rivals* (play) by Richard Brinsley Sheridan
(*Book*) Bruce Geller
(*Lyrics*) Bruce Geller
(*Music*) Jacques Urbont
(*Producer*) Jacques Urbont, J. Terry Brown & Stella Holt
Martinique Theatre   off–Broadway
November 10, 1961   141 performances
(*Stars*) Dom De Luise
Theatre World 61–62, p. 137
Best Plays 61–62, pp. 312–13

Commonweal 75:389 Ja 5 '62
> New Yorker 37:96+ N 18 '61

New York Times 1961, N 11, 15:2

NO CRIT AVAIL

(*Published libretto*) NA

(*Published sheet music*) Edwin B. Marks Music Corp.

(*Original cast recording*) OP Mercury OCM–2204/OCS–6204

(*Agent/contact*) Music Theatre International

(*Libretto*) NYPL RM6808; same as (*Agent/contact*)

(*Music, Orchestrations*) Same as (*Agent/contact*)

ALL KINDS OF GIANTS

(*Source*) Original

(*Book*) Tom Whedon

(*Lyrics*) Tom Whedon

(*Music*) Sam Pottle

(*Producer*) Noel Weiss

Cricket Theatre	off–Broadway
December 18, 1961	16 performances

(*Stars*) NA

Theatre World 61–62, p. 140

Best Plays 61–62, p. 316

New Yorker 37:58–9 Ja 6 '62

New York Times 1961, D 19, 40:1

NO CRIT AVAIL

(*Published libretto*) NA

(*Published sheet music*) Edwin H. Morris & Co.

(*Original cast recording*) NA

(*Agent/contact*)	Tom Whedon	Sam Pottle Estate
	c/o ASCAP	c/o ASCAP

(*Libretto, Music, Orchestrations*) Same as (*Agent/contact*)

AM I ASKING TOO MUCH
(*Source*) Original
(*Book*) Ken Rubenstein
(*Lyrics*) Ken Rubenstein
(*Music*) Ken Rubenstein
(*Producer*) The Rubenstein Theater Foundation
Katie Murphy Amphitheater, Fashion
      Institute of Technology   off-Broadway
April 3, 1979   11 performances
(*Stars*) Judith Jamison
Theatre World 78–79, p. 90
NO ENTRY AVAIL
Dance Mag 53:28 Jl '79
New York Times 1979, Ap 6, III, 15:2
NO CRIT AVAIL
(*Published libretto*) NA
(*Published sheet music*) NA
(*Original cast recording*) NA
(*Agent/contact*)   Ken Rubenstein
                 26 Gramercy Park South
                 New York, N.Y.   10003
(*Libretto, Music, Orchestrations*) Same as (*Agent/contact*)

AMERICAN MAN ON THE MOON
See *MAN ON THE MOON*

AMERICAN PRINCESS
(*Source*) Original
(*Book*) Leonard Orr, Jed Feuer, David Hurwitz
(*Lyrics*) Leonard Orr
(*Music*) Jed Feuer
(*Producer*) F & C Productions

Intar Theatre   off–off–Broadway
September 23, 1982   15 performances
(*Stars*) NA
Theatre World 82–83, p. 79
Best Plays 82–83, p. 431
NO CRIT AVAIL
New York Times 1982, O 12, III, 10:3
NO CRIT AVAIL
(*Published libretto*) NA
(*Published sheet music*) NA
(*Original cast recording*) NA
(*Agent/contact*)   Leonard Orr
                         c/o DG, Inc.
(*Libretto, Music, Orchestrations*) Same as (*Agent/contact*)

THE AMOROUS FLEA

(*Source*) *The School for Wives* (*L'Ecole Des Femmes*)
          (play) by Molière
(*Book*) Jerry Devine
(*Lyrics*) Bruce Montgomery
(*Music*) Bruce Montgomery
(*Producer*) Charles Hollerith, Jr. & Jerry Devine
East 78th Street Playhouse/York Theatre*   off–Broadway
February 17, 1964   93 performances
(*Stars*) NA
Theatre World 63–64, p. 219
Best Plays 63–64, p. 359
New Yorker 40:108–9 F 29 '64
New York Times 1964, F 18, 26:1
NO CRIT AVAIL
(*Published libretto*) Dramatists Play Service, Inc., 1964

(*Published sheet music*) Saunders Pubs., Inc./Frank Distrib. Corp.

(*Original cast recording*) NA

(*Agent/contact*) Dramatists Play Service, Inc.

(*Libretto*) NYPL NCOF+

(*Music, Orchestrations*) Same as (*Agent/contact*)

*Transferred to the York Theatre 3/20/64

APE OVER BROADWAY

(*Source*) Original

(*Book*) Mary McCartney & Bart Andrews*

(*Lyrics*) Bill Vitale

(*Music*) Stephen Ross**

(*Producer*) Allan Brown, Renee Semes Herz & Bill Vitale

Bert Wheeler Theatre   off–Broadway

March 12, 1975   11 performances

(*Stars*) NA

Theatre World 74–75, p. 83

NO ENTRY AVAIL

NO CRIT AVAIL

NO CRIT AVAIL

NO CRIT AVAIL

(*Published libretto*) NA

(*Published sheet music*) NA

(*Original cast recording*) NA

(*Agent/contact*)

       William Vitale   Bart Andrews

       c/o ASCAP   c/o ASCAP

(*Libretto*) NYPL RM6897, RM7384, NCOF+ 84–1040; LC Andrew Herz &
    William Vitale 1Feb71 DU79057; same as (*Agent/contact*)

(*Music, Orchestrations*) Same as (*Agent/contact*)

*In all publicity, Mary McCartney & Bart Andrews are given authorship
     credit; however, LC copyright DU79057 gives Andrew Herz sole
     authorship credit

**At press time, Mr. Ross was not interested in soliciting further
     productions of this property

APPLE PIE
(*Source*) Original
(*Book*) Myrna Lamb
(*Lyrics*) Myrna Lamb
(*Music*) Nicholas Meyers
(*Producer*) New York Shakespeare Festival
Public Theater   off–Broadway
February 12, 1976   72 performances
(*Stars*) Robert Guillaume
Theatre World 75–76, p. 137
Best Plays 75–76, p. 365
New Yorker 52:82 F 23 '76
New York Times 1976, F 13, 18:1
     New York Times 1976, F 22, II, 1:7
NO CRIT AVAIL
(*Published libretto*) NA
(*Published sheet music*) NA
(*Original cast recording*) NA
(*Agent/contact*)   Myrna Lamb   Nicholas Meyers
                      400 W. 43rd Street, #43T   315 E. 77th Street, #3F
                      New York, N.Y. 10036   New York, N.Y.   10021

(*Libretto*) LC Nicholas Meyers & Myrna Lamb 18Jun74 DU90788; same
      as (*Agent/contact*)
(*Music, Orchestrations*) Same as (*Agent/contact*)

ARABIAN NIGHTS

(*Source*) Original
(*Book*) George Marion, Jr.
(*Lyrics*) Carmen Lombardo & John Jacob Loeb
(*Music*) Carmen Lombardo & John Jacob Loeb
(*Producer*) Guy Lombardo

Jones Beach Theatre	off–Broadway
July 2, 1967*	63 performances

(*Stars*) NA
Theatre World 67–68, p. 101
NO ENTRY AVAIL
America 91:386 Jl 10 '54
    America 93:458–9 Ag 6 '55
    America 117:139 Ag 5 '67
    Cath World 179:391 Ag '54
    Dance Mag il 29:30–5 Ag '55
    Dance Mag 41:24–5 Ag '67
New York Times 1954, Je 25, 15:2
    New York Times 1955, Je 24, 16:1
    New York Times 1967, Jl 3, 12:1
NO CRIT AVAIL
(*Published libretto*) NA
(*Published sheet music*) Shapiro, Bernstein & Co.
(*Original cast recording*) OP Decca DL–9013

(*Agent/contact*)	Carmen Lombardo Estate	John Jacob Loeb Estate
	c/o Fred E. Ahlert	c/o Fred E. Ahlert
	8150 Beverly Blvd.	8150 Beverly Blvd.
	Los Angeles, CA 90048	Los Angeles, CA 90048

George Marion, Jr. Estate
c/o Georgette Marion
447 E. 14th Street
New York, NY   10009

(*Libretto*) NYPL RM678; LC Guy Lombardo Enterprises, Inc. 24Aug54
DU37748; same as (*Agent/contact*)

(*Music, Orchestrations*) Same as (*Agent/contact*)

ARABIAN NIGHTS previously played 1954 and 1955 summer seasons
at Jones Beach Theatre, opening 6/24/54 and 6/23/55 respectively;
however, no record of run appears in either *Best Plays* or *Theatre
World* yearbooks

AROUND THE WORLD IN 80 DAYS

(*Source*) *Around the World in 80 Days* (novel) by Jules Verne
(*Book*) Sig Herzig
(*Lyrics*) Harold Adamson
(*Music*) Victor Young/Sammy Fain*
(*Producer*) Guy Lombardo

Jones Beach Theatre   off–Broadway
June 22, 1963   73 performances

(*Stars*) Fritz Weaver, Robert Clary
NO ENTRY AVAIL
Best Plays 63–64, pp. 343–44
America 109:122 Ag 3 '63
New York Times 1963, Je 24, 22:1
New York Times 1964, Je 29, 33:2
NO CRIT AVAIL
(*Published libretto*) NA
(*Published sheet music*) Liza Music Corp./Fain Music Co./Adamson
Music Co.

(Original cast recording) OP Everest LPBR–4001/SDBR–1020 (Original
      Record Cast)
(Agent/contact) Tams–Witmark Music Library
(Libretto) NYPL RM4271, RM6688; same as *(Agent/contact)*
(Music, Orchestrations) Same as *(Agent/contact)*

*Victor Young's movie score augmented with new material by
      Sammy Fain

AS YOU LIKE IT
(Source) As You Like It (play) by William Shakespeare
(Book) Dran & Tani Seitz
(Lyrics) Dran & Tani Seitz
(Music) John Balamos
(Producer) ANTA Matinee Theater Series/Lucille Lortel
Theater de Lys   off–Broadway
October 27, 1964   1 performance
(Stars) Jon Cypher
NO ENTRY AVAIL
Best Plays 64–65, p. 361
NO CRIT AVAIL
NO CRIT AVAIL
NO CRIT AVAIL
(Published libretto) NA
(Published sheet music) NA
(Original cast recording) NA
(Agent/contact)   John Balamos
                       154 E. 97th Street
                       New York, N.Y.   10029
(Libretto, Music) LC Dran & Tani Seitz 14Mar57 DU44351;
      same as *(Agent/contact)*
(Orchestrations) Same as *(Agent/contact)*

THE ATHENIAN TOUCH

(*Source*) Original

(*Book*) Arthur Goodman & J. Albert Fracht

(*Lyrics*) David Eddy

(*Music*) Willard Straight

(*Producer*) David Brown, in association with Ronald Toyser

Jan Hus Playhouse   off–Broadway

January 14, 1964   1 performance

(*Stars*) Butterfly McQueen

Theatre World 63–64, p. 214

Best Plays 63–64, p. 356

NO CRIT AVAIL

New York Times 1964, Ja 15, 25:4

NO CRIT AVAIL

(*Published libretto*) NA

(*Published sheet music*) NA

(*Original cast recording*) OP Broadway East OC/OSC–101,
          RE Broadway East OCM–101

(*Agent/contact*)   David Eddy   Arthur Goodman
                         c/o DG, Inc.   c/o ASCAP

(*Libretto, Music, Orchestrations*) Same as (*Agent/contact*)

AUTUMN'S HERE*

(*Source*) "The Legend of Sleepy Hollow" (short story) by
          Washington Irving

(*Book*) Norman Dean

(*Lyrics*) Norman Dean

(*Music*) Norman Dean

(*Producer*) Bob Hadley

Bert Wheeler Theatre   off–Broadway

October 25, 1966   80 performances

(*Stars*) NA

Theatre World 66–67, p. 116

Best Plays 66–67, pp. 404–5

NO CRIT AVAIL

New York Times 1966, O 26, 40:1

NO CRIT AVAIL

(*Published libretto*) NA

(*Published sheet music*) NA

(*Original cast recording*) NA

(*Agent/contact*) NO CONT AVAIL

(*Libretto*) LC Norman H. Van Diest 11Aug64 DU60759;
   same as (*Agent/contact*)

(*Music, Orchestrations*) Same as (*Agent/contact*)

*Previously titled *SLEEPY HOLLOW*

BABES IN THE WOOD

(*Source*) *A Midsummer Night's Dream* (play) by William Shakespeare

(*Book*) Rick Besoyan

(*Lyrics*) Rick Besoyan

(*Music*) Rick Besoyan

(*Producer*) Sandy Farber & Aaron Schroeder

Orpheum Theatre   off–Broadway

December 28, 1964   45 performances

(*Stars*) Ruth Buzzi

Theatre World 64–65, p. 160

Best Plays 64–65, pp. 351–52

New Yorker 40:84 Ja 9 '65

New York Times 1964, D 29, 21:2

NO CRIT AVAIL

(*Published libretto*) Broadway Play Publishing, Inc., 1983

(*Published sheet music*) Sealark Ent. Inc./A. Schroeder Music
   Corp./Cimino Pubs. Inc.

(*Original cast recording*) NA (Studio Cast tape available from Broadway
        Play Publishing, Inc.)
(*Agent/contact*) Broadway Play Publishing, Inc.
(*Libretto*) NYPL RM2054
(*Music, Orchestrations*) Same as (*Agent/contact*)

BALLAD FOR A FIRING SQUAD (See *MATA HARI*)*
(*Source*) Original
(*Book*) Jerome Coopersmith
(*Lyrics*) Martin Charnin
(*Music*) Edward Thomas
(*Producer*) Edward Thomas, by special arrangement with Lucille
        Lortel Productions, Inc.
Theatre de Lys   off–Broadway
December 11, 1968   7 performances
(*Stars*) NA
Theatre World 68–69, p. 130
Best Plays 68–69, p. 439
New Yorker 44:65 D 21 '68
New York Times 1968, D 12, 64:2
NO CRIT AVAIL
(*Published libretto*) NA
(*Published sheet music*) Mesquite Music Corp./Edwin H. Morris as
        MATA HARI
(*Original cast recording*) NA
(*Agent/contact*)

Jerome Coopersmith	Edward Thomas	Martin Charnin
160 Hendrickson Avenue	c/o Somat Music	c/o DG, Inc.
Rockville Centre, N.Y.	157 W. 57th Street	
11570	New York, N.Y. 10019	

(*Libretto*) NYPL NCOF+; RM6434 as *MATA HARI*; LC Jerome
> Coopersmith, Edward Thomas & Martin Charnin 2Jan69 DU73210;
> same as (*Agent/contact*)

(*Music, Orchestrations*) Same as (*Agent/contact*)

*BALLAD FOR A FIRING SQUAD was first produced in an earlier
> version entitled *MATA HARI* which premiered in pre–Broadway
> try–out 11/18/67, but closed before scheduled New York opening

BALLAD FOR BIMSHIRE

(*Source*) Original

(*Book*) Irving Burgie & Loften Mitchell

(*Lyrics*) Irving Burgie

(*Music*) Irving Burgie

(*Producer*) Ossie Davis, Bernard Waltzer & Page Productions

Mayfair Theatre   off–Broadway

October 15, 1963   74 performances

(*Stars*) Robert Hooks, Ossie Davis

Theatre World 63–64, p. 199

Best Plays 63–64, pp. 348–49

America 109:643 N 16 '63

> New Yorker 39:113–4 O 26 '63

New York Times 1963, O 16, 54:1

NO CRIT AVAIL

(*Published libretto*) NA

(*Published sheet music*) Burlington Music Corp./Keys Popular Song
> Distrib., Inc.

(*Original cast recording*) OP London AM–48002/AMS–78002

(*Agent/contact*)   Irving Burgie   Loften Mitchell
>   c/o ASCAP   c/o Drama Dept.
>   State University of New York
>   Binghamton, N.Y.   13901

(*Libretto*) LC (Performing Arts Reading Room) ML50/.B9657B32;
      same as (*Agent/contact*)
(*Music, Orchestrations*) Same as (*Agent/contact*)

THE BALLAD OF JOHNNY POT

(*Source*) Original
(*Book*) Carolyn Richter
(*Lyrics*) Carolyn Richter
(*Music*) Clinton C. Ballard, Jr.
(*Producer*) Wyler Productions & Bob McDevitt
Theatre Four   off–Broadway
April 26, 1971   16 performances
(*Stars*) Betty Buckley, John Bennett Perry
Theatre World 70–71, p. 112
Best Plays 70–71, p. 349
NO CRIT AVAIL
New York Times 1971, Ap 27, 52:1
NO CRIT AVAIL
(*Published libretto*) NA
(*Published sheet music*) Edwin H. Morris
(*Original cast recording*) NA
(*Agent/contact*)   Clint Ballard, Jr.
                         c/o DG, Inc.
(*Libretto, Music, Orchestrations*) Same as (*Agent/contact*)

THE BANKER'S DAUGHTER

(*Source*) *The Streets of New York* (play) by Dion Boucicault
(*Book*) Edward Eliscu
(*Lyrics*) Edward Eliscu
(*Music*) Sol Kaplan
(*Producer*) Claire Nichtern & Paul Libin

Jan Hus Playhouse   off–Broadway
January 22, 1962   68 performances
(*Stars*) Phil Leeds
Theatre World 61–62, p. 148
Best Plays 61–62, p. 320
America 106:633 F 10 '62
        New Yorker 37:70+ F 3 '62
New York Times 1962, Ja 23, 37:1
NO CRIT AVAIL
(*Published libretto*) NA
(*Published sheet music*) Chappell & Co.
(*Original cast recording*) NA
(*Agent/contact*)   Edward Eliscu   Sol Kaplan
                         Brushy Hill Road   c/o DG, Inc.
                         Newtown, CT   06470
(*Libretto, Music, Orchestrations*) Same as (*Agent/contact*)

*THE BAR THAT NEVER CLOSES**
(*Source*) Original
(*Book*) Louisa Rose & Marco Vassi
(*Lyrics*) Louisa Rose, John Braswell & Tom Mandel
(*Music*) Tom Mandel
(*Producer*) Albert Poland & Bruce Mailman
Astor Place Theater   off–Broadway
December 3, 1972   33 performances
(*Stars*) NA
Theatre World 72–73, p. 106
Best Plays 72–73, p. 387
NO CRIT AVAIL
(*Published libretto*) NA
(*Published sheet music*) NA
(*Original cast recording*) NA

(*Agent/contact*)
    Tom Mandel   John Braswell
    2350 Broadway   c/o Sarah Lawrence
    New York, N.Y.10024   College
                           1 Meadway
    Albert Poland   Bronxville, N.Y. 10708
    226 W. 47th Street
    New York, N.Y.   10036
(*Libretto, Music, Orchestrations*) Same as (*Agent/contact*)

*Previously titled *EVERYTHING FOR ANYBODY*

BE KIND TO PEOPLE WEEK
(*Source*) Original
(*Book*) Jack Bussins & Ellsworth Olin (Naura Hayden)
(*Lyrics*) Jack Bussins & Ellsworth Olin (Naura Hayden)
(*Music*) Jack Bussins & Ellsworth Olin (Naura Hayden)
(*Producer*) J. Arthur Elliott
Belmont Theater   off–Broadway
March 23, 1975   100 performances
(*Stars*) Nell Carter
Theatre World 74–75, p. 84
Best Plays 74–75, p. 379
NO CRIT AVAIL
New York Times 1975, Mr 24, 40:3
NO CRIT AVAIL
(*Published libretto*) NA
(*Published sheet music*) NA
(*Original cast recording*) NA

(*Agent/contact*)   Naura Hayden
                          c/o BMI
(*Libretto*) LC Naura Hayden 1Feb72 DU82219;
            same as (*Agent/contact*)
(*Music, Orchestrations*) Same as (*Agent/contact*)

BEA'S PLACE

(*Source*) Original
(*Book*) Daniel O'Connor
(*Lyrics*) John Goodwin
(*Music*) John Goodwin
(*Producer*) Public Players, Inc.

Westbeth Theatre Center	off–Broadway
May 9, 1979	16 performances

(*Stars*) NA
Theatre World 78–79, p. 95
NO ENTRY AVAIL
NO CRIT AVAIL
NO CRIT AVAIL
NO CRIT AVAIL
(*Published libretto*) NA
(*Published sheet music*) NA
(*Original cast recording*) NA

(*Agent/contact*)	John Goodwin	Daniel O'Connor
	c/o DG, Inc.	c/o DG, Inc.

(*Libretto, Orchestrations*) Same as (*Agent/contact*)
(*Music*) LC Johnnie Ray Goodwin 6Aug79 PAu–137–646;
            same as (*Agent/contact*)

BEAUTIFUL DREAMER

(*Source*) Original
(*Book*) William Engvick
(*Lyrics*) Stephen Foster

(*Music*) Stephen Foster
(*Producer*) Joseph F. Moon, Catherine Connor, Wickland Company &
          Rob Holley

Madison Avenue Playhouse	off–Broadway
December 27, 1960	24 performances

(*Stars*) NA
Theatre World 60–61, p. 146
NO ENTRY AVAIL
NO CRIT AVAIL
New York Times 1960, D 28, 22:1
NO CRIT AVAIL
(*Published libretto*) NA
(*Published sheet music*) NA
(*Original cast recording*) NA

(*Agent/contact*)   William Engvick   Ernestine Perrie
                6 Camino Del Cielo   Box #306
                Orinda, CA 94563   Remsenberg, N.Y.   11960

(*Libretto, Music, Orchestrations*) Same as (*Agent/contact*)

BELLA
(*Source*) Original
(*Book*) Tom O'Malley & Lance Barklie
(*Lyrics*) Tom O'Malley
(*Music*) Jane Douglass
(*Producer*) Lance Barklie & Ned Hendrickson

Gramercy Arts Theatre	off–Broadway
November 16, 1961	6 performances

(*Stars*) NA
Theatre World 61–62, p. 131
Best Plays 61–62, p. 313
New Yorker 37:95–6 N 25 '61

New York Times 1961, N 17, 40:1
NO CRIT AVAIL
(*Published libretto*) NA
(*Published sheet music*) NA (Barton Music Corp.)
(*Original cast recording*) NA
(*Agent/contact*)   Jane Douglass White
                 c/o ASCAP
(*Libretto, Music, Orchestrations*) Same as (*Agent/contact*)

BILLY NONAME
(*Source*) Original
(*Book*) William Wellington Mackey
(*Lyrics*) Johnny Brandon
(*Music*) Johnny Brandon
(*Producer*) Robert E. Richardson & Joe Davis
Truck & Warehouse Theater   off–Broadway
March 2, 1970   48 performances
(*Stars*) NA
Theatre World 69–70, p. 123
Best Plays 69–70, pp. 359–60
Dance Mag 44:89–91 My '70
        New Yorker 46:122 Mr 14 '70
New York Times 1970, Mr 3, 37:1
NYTC 1970:285
(*Published libretto*) NA
(*Published sheet music*) NA (Big Seven Music Corp.)
(*Original cast recording*) OP Roulette SROC-11
(*Agent/contact*)   Johnny Brandon
                 c/o DG, Inc.
(*Libretto*) LC Johnny Brandon & William Wellington Mackey
        25Aug69 DU75198; same as (*Agent/contact*)
(*Music, Orchestrations*) Same as (*Agent/contact*)

*A BISTRO CAR ON THE CNR**

(*Source*) Original

(*Book*) D.R. Andersen

(*Lyrics*) Merv Campone & Richard Ouzounian

(*Music*) Patrick Rose

(*Producer*) Jeff Britton & Bob Bisaccia

Playhouse Theater   off–Broadway

March 23, 1978   82 performances

(*Stars*) Tom Wopat

Theatre World 77–78, p. 81

Best Plays 77–78, p. 421

New Yorker 54:112 Ap 3 '78

New York Times 1978, Mr 24, III, 3:1

NO CRIT AVAIL

(*Published libretto*) NA

(*Published sheet music*) NA (Delloraine Music as *JUBALAY*)

(*Original cast recording*) OP Unnamed label JP–9001 as *JUBALAY*

        (1974 Canadian Cast); OP Berandol BER–9069 (1979 Canadian Cast)

(*Agent/contact*)   D.R. Andersen   Jeff Britton

                c/o DG, Inc.   1501 Broadway

                                       New York, N.Y.   10036

(*Libretto, Music, Orchestrations*) Same as (*Agent/contact*)

*Originally presented under title *JUBALAY*

BLACK ALICE; OR, BUT NEVER JAM TODAY

See *BUT NEVER JAM TODAY*

BLOW, BUGLES, BLOW

See *BUGLES AT DAWN*

BROKEN TOYS!
(*Source*) Original
(*Book*) Keith Berger
(*Lyrics*) Keith Berger
(*Music*) Keith Berger
(*Producer*) Dani Ruska & Marina Spinola
Actors Playhouse   off–Broadway
July 16, 1982   29 performances
(*Stars*) NA
Theatre World 82–83, p. 75
Best Plays 82–83, p. 376
NO CRIT AVAIL
NO CRIT AVAIL
NO CRIT AVAIL
(*Published libretto*) NA
(*Published sheet music*) NA
(*Original cast recording*) NA
(*Agent/contact*) NO CONT AVAIL
(*Libretto, Music, Orchestrations*) Same as (*Agent/contact*)

BUGLES AT DAWN*
(*Source*) *The Red Badge of Courage* (novel) by Stephen Crane
(*Book*) David Vando
(*Lyrics*) David Vando
(*Music*) Mark Barkan
(*Producer*) Courage Productions
ATA/Chernuchin Theatre   off–off–Broadway
October 10, 1982   12 performances
(*Stars*) NA
Theatre World 82–83, p. 80
NO ENTRY AVAIL
NO CRIT AVAIL
New York Times 1982, O 11, III, 13:1
NO CRIT AVAIL

(*Published libretto*) NA
(*Published sheet music*) NA
(*Original cast recording*) NA
(*Agent/contact*)   David Vando   Mark Barkan
                           c/o DG, Inc.   c/o DG, Inc.
(*Libretto, Music*) LC David Vando & Mark Barkan 13Apr81
        PAu–286–838 as *BLOW, BUGLES, BLOW*, David Vando & Mark
        Barkan 21Sep82 PAu–439–823; same as (*Agent/contact*)
(*Orchestrations*) Same as (*Agent/contact*)

*Previously titled *BLOW, BUGLES, BLOW*

BUT NEVER JAM TODAY (See *ALICE*)*
(*Source*) *Alice in Wonderland* and *Through the Looking Glass*
        (novels) by Lewis Carroll
(*Book*) Vinnette Carroll & Bob Larimer
(*Lyrics*) Bob Larimer
(*Music*) Bert Keyes & Bob Larimer
(*Producer*) Arch Nadler, Anita McShane, Urban Arts Theater
Longacre Theatre   off–Broadway
July 31, 1979   8 performances
(*Stars*) NA
Theatre World 79–80, p. 14
Best Plays 79–80, pp. 357–59
NY 12:82–3 Ag 13 '79
New York Times 1979, Ag 1, III, 18:5
NYTC 1979:168
(*Published libretto*) NA
(*Published sheet music*) NA
(*Original cast recording*) NA

(*Agent/contact*)

Bob Larimer	Bert Keyes	Vinnette Carroll
c/o Nadler & Larimer	c/o DG, Inc.	c/o DG, Inc.

1350 Avenue of the Americas

New York, N.Y.   10019

(*Libretto*) NYPL NCOF+ 82–776; LC Vinnette Justine Carroll 9Jan75
DU92993 as *BLACK ALICE; OR, BUT NEVER JAM TODAY*;
same as (*Agent/contact*)

(*Music, Orchestrations*) Same as (*Agent/contact*)

*BUT NEVER JAM TODAY was first produced in an earlier version
entitled *ALICE* with score by Micki Grant, which premiered in
pre–Broadway try–out 6/31/78, but closed before scheduled New
York opening; previously titled *BLACK ALICE; OR, BUT NEVER
JAM TODAY*

BUY BONDS, BUSTER! (See *O SAY CAN YOU SEE!*)*

(*Source*) Original

(*Book*) Jack Holmes

(*Lyrics*) Bob (M.B.) Miller

(*Music*) Jack Holmes

(*Producer*) Wits' End

Theatre de Lys	off–Broadway
June 4, 1972	1 performance

(*Stars*) Virginia Martin

Theatre World 72–73, p. 87

Best Plays 72–73, p. 365

NO CRIT AVAIL

New York Times 1972, Je 5, 41:1

NO CRIT AVAIL

(*Published libretto*) NA

(*Published sheet music*) NA (Sunbeam Music Corp. as *O SAY CAN
YOU SEE!*)

(*Original cast recording*) Sunbeam XTV–87195/6 as *O SAY CAN
YOU SEE!*

(*Agent/contact*)　　　　　Jack Holmes

　　　　　　　　　　　　　65 W. 95th Street, #7B

　　　　　　　　　　　　　New York, N.Y.　10025

(*Libretto*) LC Robert D. Miller & William Conklin 14Sep61 DU53924

　　　　as *O SAY CAN YOU SEE!*; same as (*Agent/contact*)

(*Music, Orchestrations*) Same as (*Agent/contact*)

*BUY BONDS, BUSTER! was first produced in an earlier version entitled

　　　O SAY CAN YOU SEE! which premiered off–Broadway 10/08/62

BY HEX!

(*Source*) Original

(*Book*) John Rengier

(*Lyrics*) Howard Blankman/additional lyrics by Richard Gehman &

　　　　John Rengier

(*Music*) Howard Blankman

(*Producer*) Lester Hackett & George Ortman

Tempo Playhouse　　　　off–Broadway

June 18, 1956　　　　　40 performances

(*Stars*) NA

Theatre World 55–56, p. 148

NO ENTRY AVAIL

NO CRIT AVAIL

New York Times 1956, Je 19, 25:1

NO CRIT AVAIL

(*Published libretto*) Dramatists Play Service, Inc., 1956

(*Published sheet music*) Chappell & Co., Inc.

(*Original cast recording*) NA

(*Agent/contact*) Dramatists Play Service

(*Libretto, Music, Orchestrations*) Same as (*Agent/contact*)

CARTOONS FOR A LUNCH HOUR
(*Source*) Original
(*Book*) Loften Mitchell
(*Lyrics*) Loften Mitchell & Rudy Stevenson
(*Music*) Rudy Stevenson
(*Producer*) Seven Ages Performances Ltd.
Perry Street Theatre   off-off-Broadway
November 28, 1978   28 performances
(*Stars*) NA
Theatre World 78-79, p. 82
Best Plays 78-79, p. 458
NO CRIT AVAIL
NO CRIT AVAIL
NO CRIT AVAIL
(*Published libretto*) NA
(*Published sheet music*) NA
(*Original cast recording*) NA
(*Agent/contact*)   Loften Mitchell   Rudy Stevenson
                       c/o Drama Dept.   c/o ASCAP
                       State University of New York
                       Binghamton, N.Y.   13901
(*Libretto, Music, Orchestrations*) Same as (*Agent/contact*)

CASTAWAYS
(*Source*) *She Would Be a Soldier* (play) by Mordecai Noah
(*Book*) Anthony Stimac, D.R. Andersen & Ron Whyte
(*Lyrics*) Steve Brown
(*Music*) Don Pippin
(*Producer*) Jeff Britton
Promenade Theatre   off-Broadway
February 7, 1977   1 performance
(*Stars*) Kathleen Widdoes
Theatre World 76-77, p. 97
Best Plays 76-77, pp. 338

New Yorker 53:78 F 21 '77
New York Times 1977, F 8, 24:1
NO CRIT AVAIL
(*Published libretto*) NA
(*Published sheet music*) NA
(*Original cast recording*) NA
(*Agent/contact*)

Anthony Stimac	D.R. Andersen	Don Pippin	Ron Whyte
7 Stuyvesant Oval	c/o DG, Inc.	c/o DG, Inc.	c/o DG, Inc.
New York, N.Y. 10009			

(*Libretto*) LC Donald W. Pippin, Steve Brown & Anthony Stimac 14Nov75
        DU96795; same as (*Agent/contact*)
(*Music, Orchestrations*) Same as (*Agent/contact*)

CAUTION: A LOVE STORY

(*Source*) Original
(*Book*) Tom Eyen
(*Lyrics*) Tom Eyen
(*Music*) Bruce Kirle
(*Producer*) Theater of the Eye Repertory Company

La Mama	off–off–Broadway
April 2, 1969	10 performances

(*Stars*) Arthur Hill
NO ENTRY AVAIL
NO ENTRY AVAIL
Sat R 52:53–4 Ap 19 '69
New York Times 1969, Ap 4, 45:1
NO CRIT AVAIL
(*Published libretto*) NA
(*Published sheet music*) NA
(*Original cast recording*) NA

(*Agent/contact*)   Tom Eyen   Bruce Kirle
                     c/o I.C.M.   225 Central Park West, #914
                     40 W. 57th Street   New York, N.Y.   10024
                     New York, N.Y.   10019
                     ATTN: Bridget Aschenburg
(*Libretto, Music, Orchestrations*) Same as (*Agent/contact*)

CHANGES
(*Source*) Original
(*Book*) Dorothy Love
(*Lyrics*) Danny Apolinar
(*Music*) Addy Fieger
(*Producer*) Dorothy Love & John Britton
Theater de Lys   off–Broadway
February 19, 1980   7 performances
(*Stars*) Larry Kert, Kelly Bishop
Theatre World 79–80, p. 107
Best Plays 79–80, p. 446
NO CRIT AVAIL
New York Times 1980, F 20, III, 19:1
NO CRIT AVAIL
(*Published libretto*) NA
(*Published sheet music*) NA
(*Original cast recording*) NA
(*Agent/contact*)
                     Danny Apolinar   Addy Fieger
                     888 Eighth Avenue   115 Central Park West
                     New York, N.Y.   New York, N.Y.   10023
                         10019
(*Libretto, Music, Orchestrations*) Same as (*Agent/contact*)

*CHARLOTTE SWEET**

(*Source*) Original

(*Book*) Michael Colby

(*Lyrics*) Michael Colby

(*Music*) Gerald Joe Markoe

(*Producer*) Power Productions and Stan Raiff

Westside Arts/Cheryl Crawford Theater   off–Broadway

August 12, 1982   102 performances

(*Stars*) NA

Theatre World 82–83, p. 77

Best Plays 82–83, pp. 378–79

NY 15:82+ Ag 23 '82

      Time il 120:84 Ag 30 '82

New York Times 1982, My 3, III, 17:1

      New York Times 1982, Ag 6, II, 3:4

      New York Times 1982, S 17, III, 2:4

NYTC 1982:234

(*Published libretto*) Samuel French, Inc., 1983

(*Published sheet music*) Matthew Frankel/Hal Leonard

(*Original cast recording*) John Hammond Records W2X–38680

(*Agent/contact*) Samuel French, Inc.

(*Libretto*) LC Michael Colby & Gerald Jay Markoe 1Jul82

      PAu–416–102

(*Music*) LC Gerald Jay Markoe 3May82 PAu–397–660, Michael Colby &

      Gerald Jay Markoe 23May83 PA–204–784, 23May83 PA–204–785;

      same as (*Agent/contact*)

(*Orchestrations*) Same as (*Agent/contact*)

*Videotaped performance available at NYPL Billy Rose Collection,

      Lincoln Center, NCOV227

*CHASE A RAINBOW**
(*Source*) Original
(*Book*) Harry Stone
(*Lyrics*) Harry Stone
(*Music*) Harry Stone
(*Producer*) Joan Dunham & Segue Productions
Theater Four   off–Broadway
June 12, 1980   6 performances
(*Stars*) Virginia Sandifur
Theatre World 80–81, p. 76
Best Plays 80–81, p. 387
NO CRIT AVAIL
New York Times 1980, Je 14, 13:1
NO CRIT AVAIL
(*Published libretto*) NA
(*Published sheet music*) NA
(*Original cast recording*) NA
(*Agent/contact*)   Harry Stone
                         c/o Segue Productions
                         31 Shadyside Avenue
                         Upper Grandview, N.Y.   10960
(*Libretto*) LC Harry F. Stonum 15May80 PAu–199–763;
        same as (*Agent/contact*)
(*Music, Orchestrations*) Same as (*Agent/contact*)

*Previously presented under title *LISTEN, WORLD*

CHRISTY
(*Source*) *The Playboy of the Western World* (play) by J.M. Synge
(*Book*) Bernie Spiro
(*Lyrics*) Bernie Spiro
(*Music*) Lawrence J. Blank
(*Producer*) Joseph Lillis & Joan Spiro

Bert Wheeler Theatre   off–Broadway
October 14, 1975   40 performances
(*Stars*) NA
NO ENTRY AVAIL
Best Plays 75–76, p. 363
NO CRIT AVAIL
New York Times 1975, O 16, 44:6
NO CRIT AVAIL
(*Published libretto*) NA
(*Published sheet music*) NA (Myra Music Company)
(*Original cast recording*) Original Cast Records OC–7913
(*Agent/contact*)   Bernie Spiro
                       50 W. 97th Street, #8R
                       New York, N.Y.   10025
(*Libretto*) LC Bernard Spiro 80ct75 DU96295;
        same as (*Agent/contact*)
(*Music*) LC Myra Music Comp. 17Jan74 EU457370;
        same as (*Agent/contact*)
(*Orchestrations*) NA

THE COCKEYED TIGER
(*Source*) Original
(*Book*) Eric Blau
(*Lyrics*) Eric Blau/additional songs by Bert Kalmar & Harry Ruby,
        Betty Comden & Adolph Green
(*Music*) Nicholas Meyers/additional songs by Bert Kalmar & Harry
        Ruby, Betty Comden & Adolph Green
(*Producer*) James J. Wisner
Astor Place Theater   off–Broadway
January 13, 1977   5 performances
(*Stars*) Elly Stone

Theatre World 76–77, p. 96
Best Plays 76–77, p. 338
New Yorker 52:65 Ja 24 '77
New York Times 1977, Ja 14, III, 4:1
NO CRIT AVAIL
(*Published libretto*) NA
(*Published sheet music*) NA
(*Original cast recording*) NA
(*Agent/contact*)   Eric Blau   Nicholas Meyers
                         c/o DG, Inc.   315 E. 77th Street
                                                      New York, N.Y.   10021
(*Libretto, Music, Orchestrations*) Same as (*Agent/contact*)

COLETTE (See *COLETTE*, pre–Broadway Section)*
(*Source*) *Earthly Paradise* (collection) by Colette, edited by
        Robert Phelps
(*Book*) Elinor Jones
(*Lyrics*) Tom Jones
(*Music*) Harvey Schmidt
(*Producer*) Cheryl Crawford, in association with Mary W. John
Ellen Stewart Theater**   off–Broadway**
May 6, 1970**   101 performances **
(*Stars*) Zoe Caldwell, Barry Bostwick
Theatre World 69–70, p. 135
Best Plays 69–70, p. 367
Nation 210:636 My 25 '70
        New Repub 162:18 Je 13 '70
        New Yorker 46:105–6 My 16 '70
        Newsweek 75:121 My 18 '70
New York Times 1970, My 7, 60:1
        New York Times 1970, My 17, II, 1:1
        New York Times 1970, O 15, 58:1
NYTC 1970:228
(*Published libretto*) NA

(*Published sheet music*) Portfolio Music, Inc./Chappell & Co.
(*Original cast recording*) OP MIO International MCS–3001
(*Agent/contact*) Music Theatre International (FOR FUTURE RELEASE)
(*Libretto*) NYPL NCOF+, RM8055; same as (*Agent/contact*)
(*Music, Orchestrations*) Same as (*Agent/contact*)

COLETTE was rewritten with book by Tom Jones, and produced in
pre–Broadway try–out 2/09/82 but closed before scheduled New
York opening

**COLETTE* was subsequently rewritten and produced off–off–Broadway
under the title *COLETTE COLLAGE* 3/31/83 by the York Players
at the Church of the Heavenly Rest for 17 performances

COLETTE COLLAGE
See *COLETTE*

CONEY ISLAND COOKIE JAR
See *GOD BLESS CONEY*

THE CONTRAST
(*Source*) *The Contrast* (play) by Royall Tyler
(*Book*) Anthony Stimac
(*Lyrics*) Steve Brown
(*Music*) Don Pippin
(*Producer*) Peter Cookson

Eastside Playhouse   off–Broadway
November 27, 1972   24 performances
(*Stars*) NA
Theatre World 72–73, p. 105
Best Plays 72–73, pp. 385–86
Nation 215:637 D 18 '72
New York Times 1972, N 28, 51:1
        New York Times 1972, D 24, II, 7:1
NO CRIT AVAIL
(*Published libretto*) Samuel French, Inc., 1972
(*Published sheet music*) NA
(*Original cast recording*) NA
(*Agent/contact*) Samuel French, Inc.
(*Libretto, Music, Orchestrations*) Same as (*Agent/contact*)

THE COOLEST CAT IN TOWN
(*Source*) Original
(*Book*) William Gleason
(*Lyrics*) William Gleason
(*Music*) Diane Leslie
(*Producer*) A. Arthur Altman, Joseph H. Lillis, Jr.
        & Jean Altman
City Center Little Theatre   off–Broadway
June 22, 1978   37 performances
(*Stars*) NA
Theatre World 78–79, p. 69
Best Plays 78–79, p. 409
NO CRIT AVAIL
New York Times 1978, Je 30, III, 11:2
NO CRIT AVAIL
(*Published libretto*) Dramatic Publishing Company, 1977
(*Published sheet music*) NA
(*Original cast recording*) NA (Studio Cast tape available from
        Dramatic Publishing Company)

(*Agent/contact*) Dramatic Publishing Company

(*Libretto, Orchestrations*) Same as (*Agent/contact*)

(*Music*) LC Diane Leslie 30May78 PAu-51-963;
        same as (*Agent/contact*)

COTTON PATCH GOSPEL

(*Source*) *The Cotton Patch Version of Matthew and John*
        (scripture) by Clarence Jordan

(*Book*) Tom Key & Russell Treyz

(*Lyrics*) Harry Chapin

(*Music*) Harry Chapin

(*Producer*) Philip M. Getter

Lambs Theater   off–Broadway

October 21, 1981   193 performances

(*Stars*) NA

Theatre World 81–82, p. 54

Best Plays 81–82, pp. 369–70

Chr Century 99:515 Ap 28 '82

        Chr Today il 26:44 F 19 '82

New York Times 1981, O 22, III, 17:3

        New York Times 1981, N 22, XXI, 19:1

NO CRIT AVAIL

(*Published libretto*) Dramatic Publishing Company, 1982

(*Published sheet music*) NA

(*Original cast recording*) Chapin Productions CP–101 (Original
        Cast recorded live), available from Dramatic Publishing Company

(*Agent/contact*) Dramatic Publishing Company

(*Libretto, Music, Orchestrations*) Same as (*Agent/contact*)

COUNTED AS MINE
See *LADY OF MEXICO*

CRAZY NOW
(*Source*) Original
(*Book*) Richard Smithies & Maura Cavanagh
(*Lyrics*) Richard Smithies & Maura Cavanagh
(*Music*) Norman Sachs
(*Producer*) B.F. Productions
Eden Theater   off–Broadway
September 17, 1972   1 performance
(*Stars*) NA
Theatre World 72–73, p. 95
Best Plays 72–73, pp. 372
NO CRIT AVAIL
New York Times 1972, S 11, 45:3
NO CRIT AVAIL
(*Published libretto*) NA
(*Published sheet music*) NA
(*Original cast recording*) NA
(*Agent/contact*)   Maura Cavanagh/Richard Smithies   Norman Sachs
                     91 First Avenue   c/o DG, Inc.
                     New York, N.Y.   10003
(*Libretto*) LC Richard Smithies & Maura Cavanagh 8Sep72 DU84584;
        same as (*Agent/contact*)
(*Music, Orchestrations*) Same as (*Agent/contact*)

CROESUS AND THE WITCH
(*Source*) "Croesus" (folk tale) from *Aesop's Fables* by Aesopus
(*Book*) Vinnette Carroll
(*Lyrics*) Micki Grant
(*Music*) Micki Grant

(*Producer*) Urban Arts Corps/Vinette Carroll
Urban Arts Corps Center   off–off–Broadway
August 24, 1971   NA performances
(*Stars*) NA
NO ENTRY AVAIL
Best Plays 71–72, p. 386
New Yorker 47:54 S 4 '71
New York Times 1971, Ag 27, 18:1
NO CRIT AVAIL
(*Published libretto*) Broadway Play Publishing, Inc., 1984
        (w/*HANSEL & GRETL IN THE 1980'S*)
(*Published sheet music*) Broadway Play Publishing, Inc.
(*Original cast recording*) NA
(*Agent/contact*) Broadway Play Publishing, Inc.
(*Libretto*) LC Vinnette J. Carroll & Micki Grant 8Sep72 DU84623
(*Music, Orchestrations*) Same as (*Agent/contact*)

THE CRYSTAL HEART
(*Source*) Original
(*Book*) William Archibald
(*Lyrics*) William Archibald
(*Music*) Baldwin Bergersen
(*Producer*) Charles Kasher
East 74th Street Theatre   off–Broadway
February 15, 1960   9 performances
(*Stars*) Mildred Dunnock, Virginia Vestoff
Theatre World 59–60, p. 147
NO ENTRY AVAIL
New Yorker 36:104–6 F 27 '60
New York Times 1960, F 16, 31:2
NO CRIT AVAIL

(*Published libretto*) NA
(*Published sheet music*) Chappell
(*Original cast recording*) OP Unnamed label CK–1, RE Blue Pear
      Records BP–1001 (Original Cast recorded live)
(*Agent/contact*)   Baldwin Bergersen   William Archibald Estate
                   c/o DG, Inc.   c/o Samuel French, Inc.
(*Libretto*) NYPL RM328, NCOF+; same as (*Agent/contact*)
(*Music, Orchestrations*) Same as (*Agent/contact*)

A DAY IN THE LIFE OF JUST ABOUT EVERYONE

(*Source*) Original
(*Book*) Earl Wilson, Jr. & Michael Sawyer
(*Lyrics*) Earl Wilson, Jr.
(*Music*) Earl Wilson, Jr.
(*Producer*) Robert Shelley, in association with Lawrence Simon
      & Midge LaGuardia
Bijou Theater   off–Broadway
March 9, 1971   7 performances
(*Stars*) NA
Theatre World 70–71, p. 103
Best Plays 70–71, p. 346
New Yorker 47:96 Mr 20 '71
New York Times 1971, Mr 10, 31:1
NO CRIT AVAIL
(*Published libretto*) NA
(*Published sheet music*) NA (Damila Music, Inc.)
(*Original cast recording*) NA
(*Agent/contact*)   Earl Wilson, Jr.
                   c/o DG, Inc.
(*Libretto, Music*) LC Damila Music, Inc./Earl Wilson, Jr. 20May71
      EU250813; same as (*Agent/contact*)
(*Orchestrations*) Same as (*Agent/contact*)

DEAR OSCAR
(*Source*) Original
(*Book*) Caryl Gabrielle Young
(*Lyrics*) Caryl Gabrielle Young
(*Music*) Addy O. Fieger
(*Producer*) Mary W. John
Playhouse Theatre   off–Broadway
November 16, 1972   5 performances
(*Stars*) Russ Thacker
Theatre World 72–73, p. 102
Best Plays 72–73, pp. 341–43
NO CRIT AVAIL
New York Times 1972, N 17, 37:1
NYTC 1972:179
(*Published libretto*) NA
(*Published sheet music*) NA
(*Original cast recording*) NA
(*Agent/contact*)   Addy Fieger   Caryl Gabrielle Young
                       115 Central Park West   c/o DG, Inc.
                       New York, N.Y.   10023
(*Libretto*) LC Addy O. Fieger 14May71 DU80205; same as
      (*Agent/contact*)
(*Music, Orchestrations*) Same as (*Agent/contact*)

THE DEATH OF VON RICHTOFEN AS WITNESSED FROM EARTH
(*Source*) Orginal
(*Book*) Des McAnuff
(*Lyrics*) Des McAnuff
(*Music*) Des McAnuff

(*Producer*) New York Shakespeare Festival

Public/Newman Theater   off–Broadway

July 29, 1982   45 performances

(*Stars*) John Vickery, Bob Gunton, Mark Linn–Baker

Theatre World 82–83, p. 115

Best Plays 82–83, pp. 377–78

NY il 15:42 Ag 9 '82

   Newsweek il 100:68 Ag 9 '82

   Time il 120:74 Ag 9 '82

New York Times 1982, illus, My 2, II, 1:1

   New York Times 1982, My 7, III, 2:2

   New York Times 1982, Jl 25, II, 1:1

   New York Times 1982, Jl 30, III, 3:1

   New York Times 1982, Ag 10, III, 11:1

NYTC 1982:223

(*Published libretto*) NA

(*Published sheet music*) NA

(*Original cast recording*) NA

(*Agent/contact*) Des McAnuff   Joseph Papp

       c/o La Jolla Playhouse c/o Public Theatre

       P.O. Box #12039   425 Lafayette Street

       La Jolla, CA   92037 New York, N.Y.   10003

(*Libretto*) NYPL RM851; same as (*Agent/contact*)

(*Music, Orchestrations*) Same as (*Agent/contact*)

THE DECAMERON*

(*Source*) *The Decameron* (collection) by Giovanni Boccaccio

(*Book*) Yvonne Tarr

(*Lyrics*) Yvonne Tarr

(*Music*) Edward Earle

(*Producer*) Selma Tamber & William Tarr

East 74th Street Theatre   off–Broadway

April 12, 1961   39 performances

(*Stars*) NA

Theatre World 60–61, p. 175

NO ENTRY AVAIL

NO CRIT AVAIL

New York Times 1961, Ap 13, 32:1

NO CRIT AVAIL

(*Published libretto*) NA

(*Published sheet music*) Larry Shayne Music, Inc./G. Schirmer,
        Inc.

(*Original cast recording*) NA

(*Agent/contact*)   Edward Earle
                      91 Christopher Street
                      New York, N.Y.   10014

(*Libretto*) LC (Performing Arts Reading Room) ML50/.E15D4; LC Yvonne
        Young Tarr 29Mar61 DU52892 as *LOVE TALES FROM THE
        DECAMERON*; same as (*Agent/contact*)

(*Music, Orchestrations*) Same as (*Agent/contact*)

*Previously titled *LOVE TALES FROM THE DECAMERON*

DIAMOND STUDS (THE LIFE OF JESSE JAMES, A SALOON MUSICAL)

(*Source*) Original

(*Book*) Jim Wann

(*Lyrics*) Bland Simpson & Jim Wann

(*Music*) Bland Simpson & Jim Wann

(*Producer*) The Chelsea Theater Group of Brooklyn

Westside Theatre   off–Broadway

January 14, 1975   232 performances

(*Stars*) NA

Theatre World 74–75, p. 79

Best Plays 74–75, pp. 372–73

New Yorker 50:70 Ja 27 '75
    Newsweek il 85:69 Ja 27 '75
    Sat R il 2:39 Mr 22 '75
New York Times 1975, Ja 15, 50:1
    New York Times 1975, Mr 2, II, 5:1
NYTC 1975:345
(*Published libretto*) Samuel French, Inc., 1976
(*Published sheet music*) NA
(*Original cast recording*) NA
(*Agent/contact*) Samuel French, Inc.
(*Libretto, Music, Orchestrations*) Same as (*Agent/contact*)

THE DIFFICULT WOMAN

(*Source*) *A Difficult Widow* (*Una Viuda Dificil*) (play) by
    Conrado Nalé Roxlo, as translated by Ruth C. Gillespie
(*Book*) Malcolm Stuart Boyland & Maurice Alevy
(*Lyrics*) Morty Neff & George Mysels
(*Music*) Richard Freitas*
(*Producer*) Nikardi Productions & Donald C. Fetzko
Barbizon–Plaza Theatre   off–Broadway
April 25, 1962   3 performances
(*Stars*) NA
Theatre World 61–62, p. 158
Best Plays 61–62, pp. 329–30
NO CRIT AVAIL
New York Times 1962, Ap 26, 22:7
NO CRIT AVAIL
(*Published libretto*) NA
(*Published sheet music*) NA
(*Original cast recording*) NA
(*Agent/contact*)

| Richard Freitas | George Mysels | Morty Neff |
| c/o DG, Inc. | c/o AGAC | c/o ASCAP |

(*Libretto*) LC Maurice Alevy 15Jun62 DU55651;
        same as (*Agent/contact*)
(*Music, Orchestrations*) Same as (*Agent/contact*)

*At press time, Mr. Freitas was not interested in soliciting
        further productions of this property

DISPATCHES

(*Source*) *Dispatches* (collection) by Michael Herr
(*Book*) Elizabeth Swados
(*Lyrics*) Elizabeth Swados
(*Music*) Elizabeth Swados
(*Producer*) Joseph Papp
Public/Cabaret Theater   off–Broadway
April 18, 1979   63 performances
(*Stars*) NA
Theatre World 78–79, p. 135
Best Plays 78–79, pp. 425, 428
NY 12:85 My 7 '79
        New Yorker 55:95–6 Ap 30 '79
        Newsweek il 93:98 Ap 30 '79
New York Times 1979, Ap 19, III, 17:1
NYTC 1979:252
(*Published libretto*) NA
(*Published sheet music*) NA
(*Original cast recording*) NA
(*Agent/contact*)   Elizabeth Swados   Joseph Papp
                       c/o Advanced Management   c/o Public Theater
                         Services   425 Lafayette Street
                       280 Madison Avenue   New York, N.Y. 10003
                       New York, N.Y.   10016

(*Libretto*) NYPL NCOF+ 79–972; same as (*Agent/contact*)
(*Music, Orchestrations*) Same as (*Agent/contact*)

DOCTOR SELAVY'S MAGIC THEATER*

(*Source*) Original
(*Book*) Richard Foreman
(*Lyrics*) Tom Hendry
(*Music*) Stanley Silverman
(*Producer*) Lyn Austin & Oliver Smith/Lenox Arts Center
        Production
Mercer–O'Casey Theater   off–Broadway
November 23, 1972   144 performances
(*Stars*) NA
Theatre World 72–73, p. 103
Best Plays 72–73, pp. 384–85
HiFi 23:MA 27–8 Mr '73
        Nation 215:597 D 11 '72
        New Yorker 48:109 D 9 '72
        Newsweek 80:70 D 4 '72
New York Times 1972, N 24, 47:1
        New York Times 1972, D 3, II, 32:3
NO CRIT AVAIL
(*Published libretto*) NA
(*Published sheet music*) NA
(*Original cast recording*) OP United Artists LA–196–G
(*Agent/contact*) Rodgers & Hammerstein Theatre Library
(*Libretto, Music, Orchestrations*) Same as (*Agent/contact*)

*Videotaped performance of 1984 revival available at NYPL
        Billy Rose Collection, Lincoln Center, NCOV 302

DOUBLE FEATURE*
(*Source*) Original
(*Book*) Jeffrey Moss
(*Lyrics*) Jeffrey Moss
(*Music*) Jeffrey Moss
(*Producer*) Allen Grossman, Karl Allison, Nan Pearlman, in
         association with The Common at St. Peter's Church
St. Peter's Church**   off–Broadway**
October 8, 1981   7 performances
(*Stars*) Pamela Blair, Don Scardino
Theatre World 81–82, p. 53
Best Plays 81–82, p. 365
New Yorker 57:141 O 19 '81
New York Times 1981, O 9, III, 3:5
NO CRIT AVAIL
(*Published libretto*) NA
(*Published sheet music*) NA
(*Original cast recording*) NA
(*Agent/contact*)   Jeffrey Moss
                  c/o DG, Inc.
(*Libretto*) LC Jeffrey Moss 26Dec79 PAu–189–208;
        same as (*Agent/contact*)
(*Music, Orchestrations*) Same as (*Agent/contact*)

*Previously titled *PARTNERS*

**Previously produced at Long Wharf Theater, New Haven, CT

DOWNRIVER*
(*Source*) *The Adventures of Huckleberry Finn* (novel) by
        Mark Twain
(*Book*) Jeff Tambornino

(*Lyrics*) John Braden
(*Music*) John Braden
(*Producer*) St. Clement's Church
St. Clement's Church Theater   off–off–Broadway
December 19, 1975   NA
(*Stars*) NA
NO ENTRY AVAIL
Best Plays 75–76, p. 401
NO CRIT AVAIL
NO CRIT AVAIL
NO CRIT AVAIL
(*Published libretto*) NA
(*Published sheet music*) NA
(*Original cast recording*) Take Home Tunes THT–7811
(*Agent/contact*) Music Theatre International
(*Libretto*) LC Jeff Tambornino 28Feb72 DU82730 as *HUCKLEBERRY
        FINN*; same as (*Agent/contact*)
(*Music, Orchestrations*) Same as (*Agent/contact*)

*Previously titled *HUCKLEBERRY FINN*

DRAT!
(*Source*) Original
(*Book*) Fred Bluth
(*Lyrics*) Fred Bluth
(*Music*) Steven Metcalf
(*Producer*) Theatre 1972 (Richard Barr–Charles Woodward)
McAlpin Rooftop Theatre   off–Broadway
October 18, 1971   1 performance
(*Stars*) Bonnie Franklin, Jane Connell
Theatre World 71–72, p. 86
Best Plays 71–72, p. 357
NO CRIT AVAIL
New York Times 1971, O 19, 53:1

NO CRIT AVAIL
(*Published libretto*) NA
(*Published sheet music*) NA
(*Original cast recording*) NA
(*Agent/contact*)   Steven Metcalf   Richard Barr/Charles Woodward
                       c/o DG, Inc.   226 W. 47th Street
                                             New York, N.Y.   10036
(*Libretto*) NYPL RM258; same as (*Agent/contact*)
(*Music, Orchestrations*) Same as (*Agent/contact*)

DREAM TIME
See *SWING*

DREAMSTUFF
(*Source*) *The Tempest* (play) by William Shakespeare (freely adapted)
(*Book*) Howard Ashman, additional material by William Shakespeare
(*Lyrics*) Dennis Green
(*Music*) Marsha Malamet
(*Producer*) WPA Theatre
WPA Theatre   off–off–Broadway
April 2, 1976   17 performances
(*Stars*) NA
NO ENTRY AVAIL
Best Plays 75–76, pp. 405–6
NO CRIT AVAIL
New York Times 1976, illus, Apr 5, 45:1
NO CRIT AVAIL
(*Published libretto*) NA
(*Published sheet music*) NA

(*Original cast recording*) NA
(*Agent/contact*)   Howard Ashman   WPA Theatre
                         c/o DG, Inc.   138 Fifth Avenue
                                               New York, N.Y.   10003
(*Libretto*) LC Howard Ashman 27Feb76 DU98186;
        same as (*Agent/contact*)
(*Music, Orchestrations*) Same as (*Agent/contact*)

*A DRIFTER, THE GRIFTER & HEATHER MC BRIDE**
(*Source*) Original
(*Book*) John Gallagher
(*Lyrics*) John Gallagher
(*Music*) Bruce Petsche
(*Producer*) Popcorn Productions
47th Street Theatre   off–Broadway
June 20, 1982   9 performances
(*Stars*) NA
Theatre World 82–83, p. 74
Best Plays 82–83, p. 371
NO CRIT AVAIL
New York Times 1982, Je 27, 46:3
NO CRIT AVAIL
(*Published libretto*) NA
(*Published sheet music*) NA
(*Original cast recording*) NA
(*Agent/contact*)   John Gallagher
                         c/o DG, Inc.
(*Libretto*) LC John Gallagher & Bruce A. Petsche 9Jul80 PAu–214–276
        as *INTERNATIONAL BERNIE & COMPANY*; same as
        (*Agent/contact*)
(*Music, Orchestrations*) Same as (*Agent/contact*)

*Previously titled *INTERNATIONAL BERNIE & COMPANY*

THE DRUNKARD
(*Source*) *The Drunkard* (melodrama) by W.H. Smith
(*Book*) Bro Herrod
(*Lyrics*) Barry Manilow
(*Music*) Barry Manilow
(*Producer*) Bro Herrod & Peter Perry
13th Street Theatre   off–Broadway
April 13, 1970   48 performances
(*Stars*) NA
Theatre World 69–70, p. 131
Best Plays 69–70, p. 365
New Yorker 46:97 Ap 25 '70
New York Times 1970, Ap 14, 54:1
NO CRIT AVAIL
(*Published libretto*) NA
(*Published sheet music*) NA
(*Original cast recording*) NA
(*Agent/contact*) Music Theatre International
(*Libretto, Music, Orchestrations*) Same as (*Agent/contact*)

DYNAMITE TONITE
(*Source*) Original
(*Book*) Arnold Weinstein
(*Lyrics*) Arnold Weinstein
(*Music*) William Bolcom
(*Producer*) Actors Studio Inc.
York Playhouse   off–Broadway
March 15, 1964   1 performance
(*Stars*) Barbara Harris, Gene Wilder
Theatre World 63–64, p. 224
Best Plays 63–64, p. 361

Commonweal 86:126 Ap 14 '67

      Commonweal 86:152–4 Ap 21 '67

New York Times 1964, Mr 16, 36:2

      New York Times 1967, Mr 16, 52:2

NO CRIT AVAIL

(*Published libretto*) NA

(*Published sheet music*) NA (Trio Music Co., Inc.)

(*Original cast recording*) NA

(*Agent/contact*)	Arnold Weinstein	William Bolcom
	c/o I.C.M.	c/o I.C.M.
	40 W. 57th Street	40 W. 57th Street
	New York, N.Y. 10019	New York, N.Y. 10019
	Attn: Luis Sanjurjo	Attn: Luis Sanjurjo

(*Libretto, Music, Orchestrations*)

	Edward B. Marks Music;	same as (*Agent/contact*)
	c/o Belwin–Mills	
	1619 Broadway, top floor	
	New York, N.Y. 10036	

EDEN SKIDOO

See *UP EDEN*

THE EGG AND I

(*Source*) *The Egg and I* (novel) by Betty MacDonald

(*Book*) Hal Pockriss

(*Lyrics*) Wilfred Sales

(*Music*) Frank Brents

(*Producer*) William Gyimes

Jan Hus Playhouse   off–Broadway

September 10, 1958   21 performances

(*Stars*) Diana Sands, Isabel Sanford

NO ENTRY AVAIL

NO ENTRY AVAIL

New Yorker 34:78+ S 27 '58
New York Times 1958, S 11, 43:4
NO CRIT AVAIL
(*Published libretto*) NA
(*Published sheet music*) NA
(*Original cast recording*) NA
(*Agent/contact*) NO CONT AVAIL
(*Libretto, Music, Orchestrations*) Same as (*Agent/contact*)

EL BRAVO!
(*Source*) Original
(*Book*) Jose Fernandez & Thom Schiera
(*Lyrics*) John Clifton
(*Music*) John Clifton
(*Producer*) Kenneth Waissman, with Edward Mazvinsky & Sidney
        Shlenker

Entermedia Theater   off–Broadway
June 16, 1981   42 performances
(*Stars*) NA
Theatre World 81–82, p. 49
Best Plays 81–82, pp. 350–51
NO CRIT AVAIL
New York Times 1981, Je 17, III, 23:4
NO CRIT AVAIL
(*Published libretto*) NA
(*Published sheet music*) NA
(*Original cast recording*) NA

(*Agent/contact*)

John Clifton	Jose Fernandez	Thom Schiera	Kenneth Waissman
c/o DG, Inc.	c/o DG, Inc.	c/o DG, Inc.	1501 Broadway
			New York, N.Y.
			10036

(*Libretto, Music, Orchestrations*) Same as (*Agent/contact*)

ELIZABETH AND ESSEX

(*Source*) *Elizabeth the Queen* (play) by Maxwell Anderson
(*Book*) Michael Stewart* & Mark Bramble
(*Lyrics*) Richard Engquist
(*Music*) Doug Katsaros
(*Producer*) Encompass Theater/Roger Cunningham

South Street Theater	off–Broadway
February 24, 1980	24 performances

(*Stars*) Estelle Parsons
Theatre World 79–80, p. 105
Best Plays 79–80, p. 455
NY 13:67 Mr 24 '80
New York Times 1980, F 25, III, 15:1
NYTC 1980:331
(*Published libretto*) NA
(*Published sheet music*) NA
(*Original cast recording*) NA
(*Agent/contact*)

Michael Stewart	Mark Bramble	Doug Katsaros
c/o Helen Harvey	c/o Helen Harvey	c/o "It's the Score"
410 W. 24th Street	410 W. 24th Street	320 W. 46th Street,
New York, N.Y.	New York, N.Y.	4th Fl.
10011	10011	New York, N.Y. 10036

Richard Engquist

c/o DG, Inc.

(*Libretto, Music, Orchestrations*) Same as (*Agent/contact*)

*At press time, Mr. Stewart advised that *ELIZABETH AND ESSEX*
     was being revised for Broadway production and therefore was
     presently unavailable for production

ERNEST IN LOVE

(*Source*) *The Importance of Being Ernest* (play) by Oscar Wilde

(*Book*) Anne Croswell

(*Lyrics*) Anne Croswell

(*Music*) Lee Pockriss

(*Producer*) Noel Behn & Robert Kamlot

Gramercy Arts Theatre   off–Broadway

May 4, 1960   111 performances

(*Stars*) Leila Martin

Theatre World 59–60, p. 168

Best Plays 59–60, p. 359

New Yorker 36:117 My 21 '60

          Time il 75:70 Je 6 '60

New York Times 1960, My 5, 39:4

NO CRIT AVAIL

(*Published libretto*) NA

(*Published sheet music*) Edwin H. Morris & Co.

(*Original cast recording*) OP Columbia OL–5530/OS–2027

(*Agent/contact*) Music Theatre International

(*Libretto*) NYPL RM3228; same as (*Agent/contact*)

(*Music, Orchestrations*) Same as (*Agent/contact*)

AN EVENING WITH JOAN CRAWFORD
(*Source*) Original
(*Book*) Julian Neil
(*Lyrics*) Joseph Church, Richard Schill, Nick Branch, Kristine
        Zbornik, Julian Neil & Lee Sparks
(*Music*) Joseph Church, Richard Schill, Nick Branch, Kristine
        Zbornik, Julian Neil & Lee Sparks
(*Producer*) Joe Bianco, in association with Monroe Arnold
Orpheum Theater   off–Broadway
January 28, 1981   15 performances
(*Stars*) NA
Theatre World 80–81, p. 92
Best Plays 80–81, p. 417
NO CRIT AVAIL
New York Times 1981, Ja 30, III, 8:5
NO CRIT AVAIL
(*Published libretto*) NA
(*Published sheet music*) NA
(*Original cast recording*) NA
(*Agent/contact*)   Olim Associates, Inc.   Joseph Church
                      1540 Broadway   144 Willow Street
                      New York, N.Y. 10036   Brooklyn, N.Y. 11201
(*Libretto, Music, Orchestrations*) Same as (*Agent/contact*)

EVERYTHING FOR ANYBODY
See *THE BAR THAT NEVER CLOSES*

F. JASMINE ADDAMS
(*Source*) *The Member of the Wedding* (novel and play) by Carson
        McCullers*
(*Book*) Carson McCullers*, G. Wood & Theodore Mann
(*Lyrics*) G. Wood
(*Music*) G. Wood

(*Producer*) Circle–in–the–Square (Theodore Mann/Paul Libin)
        & David J. Seltzer
Circle–in–the–Square   off–Broadway
October 27, 1971   6 performances
(*Stars*) Neva Small
Theatre World 71–72, p. 88
Best Plays 71–72, p. 358
America 125:427 N 20 '71
        New Yorker 47:115–6 N 6 '71
New York Times 1971, O 28, 49:1
NO CRIT AVAIL
(*Published libretto*) NA
(*Published sheet music*) NA
(*Original cast recording*) NA
(*Agent/contact*)
    Carson McCullers Estate   G. Wood   Theodore Mann
    c/o Fitelson, Lasky & Aslan   c/o DG, Inc.   1633 Broadway
    551 Fifth Avenue   New York, N.Y.
    New York, N.Y. 10176   10019
(*Libretto*) NYPL NCOF+ 73–1771; same as (*Agent/contact*)
(*Music, Orchestrations*) Same as (*Agent/contact*)

*At press time, the Carson McCullers Estate was not interested in
    soliciting further productions of this property

FASHION
(*Source*) *Fashion; or, Life in New York* (play) by Anna Cora Mowatt
(*Book*) Anthony Stimac
(*Lyrics*) Steve Brown
(*Music*) Don Pippin
(*Producer*) R. Scott Lucas

McAlpin Rooftop Theatre   off–Broadway
February 17, 1974   62 performances
(*Stars*) NA
Theatre World 73–74, p. 82
Best Plays 73–74, p. 396
New Yorker 50:68–9 Mr 4 '74
        Time 103:104 Mr 11 '74
New York Times 1974, F 19, 25:1
NYTC 1974:294
(*Published libretto*) Samuel French, Inc., 1974
(*Published sheet music*) Edwin H. Morris/Wren Music
(*Original cast recording*) NA
(*Agent/contact*) Samuel French, Inc.
(*Libretto, Music, Orchestrations*) Same as (*Agent/contact*)

FESTIVAL
(*Source*) "Aucassin and Nicolette" (*chante-fable*) anonymous
(*Book*) Stephen Downs & Randall Martin
(*Lyrics*) Stephen Downs & Randall Martin
(*Music*) Stephen Downs & Bruce Vilanch
(*Producer*) Roger Berlind, Franklin R. Levy & Mike Wise
Downstairs at City Center   off–Broadway
May 16, 1979   5 performances
(*Stars*) Mike Rupert
Theatre World 78–79, p. 96
Best Plays 78–79, p. 442
NO CRIT AVAIL
New York Times 1979, My 18, III, 3:4
NO CRIT AVAIL
(*Published libretto*) Samuel French, Inc., 1983
(*Published sheet music*) NA
(*Original cast recording*) Original Cast Records OC–7916
(*Agent/contact*) Samuel French, Inc.
(*Libretto, Music, Orchestrations*) Same as (*Agent/contact*)

FIXED

(*Source*) Original

(*Book*) Robert Maurice Riley

(*Lyrics*) Gene Bone & Howard Fenton

(*Music*) Gene Bone & Howard Fenton, additional lyrics by Langston
        Hughes

(*Producer*) Theater of the Riverside Church/Anita L. Thomas

Theater of the Riverside Church   off–off–Broadway

December 20, 1977   28 performances

(*Stars*) NA

NO ENTRY AVAIL

Best Plays 77–78, p. 457

NO CRIT AVAIL

New York Times 1977, D 21, III, 15:1

NO CRIT AVAIL

(*Published libretto*) NA

(*Published sheet music*) NA (Bonfen Music Pub.)

(*Original cast recording*) NA

(*Agent/contact*)   Howard Fenton   Robert Maurice Riley
                       c/o DG, Inc.   c/o DG, Inc.

(*Libretto, Orchestrations*) Same as (*Agent/contact*)

(*Music*) LC Bonfen Music Pub. 24Jul78 PAu–42–855;
          same as (*Agent/contact*)

FLY BLACKBIRD

(*Source*) Original

(*Book*) C. Bernard Jackson & James Hatch

(*Lyrics*) C. Bernard Jackson & James Hatch

(*Music*) C. Bernard Jackson & James Hatch

(*Producer*) Helen Jacobson

Mayfair Theatre   off–Broadway

February 5, 1962   127 performances

(*Stars*) Robert Guillaume, Micki Grant

Theatre World 61–62, p. 152

Best Plays 61–62, p. 322

America 106:773–4 Mr 10 '62

       Nation 194:201 Mr 3 '62

       New Yorker 37:94–5 F 17 '62

       Theatre Arts il 46:61–3 My '62

New York Times 1962, F 6, 26:2

       New York Times 1962, Ap 29, II, 1:1

NO CRIT AVAIL

(*Published libretto*) In *Black Theater, U.S.A.*, The Free Press
       (MacMillan Pub., Inc.), 1974

(*Published sheet music*) Edward B. Marks Music Corp.

(*Original cast recording*) OP Mercury OCM–2206/OCS–6206

(*Agent/contact*)   C. Bernard Jackson   James Hatch

                 c/o DG, Inc.   c/o Hatch–Billops Archives

                                    491 Broadway, Fifth Floor

                                    New York, N.Y.   10012

(*Libretto*) NYPL NCOF+; LC (Performing Arts Reading Room)
       ML50/.H3456F62; LC Clarence B. Jackson & James V. Hatch 9Mar61
       DU52735; same as (*Agent/contact*)

(*Music, Orchestrations*) Same as (*Agent/contact*)

FORTUNA

(*Source*) *Fortuna con 'F' Maiuscula* (play) by Eduardo de Filippo
       & Armando Curcio

(*Book*) Arnold Weinstein

(*Lyrics*) Arnold Weinstein

(*Music*) Francis Thorne

(*Producer*) Sam Cohn & John Wulp

Maidman Playhouse   off–Broadway

January 3, 1962   5 performances

(*Stars*) Jane Connell, Pat Birch

Theatre World 61–62, p. 143

Best Plays 61–62, p. 317

New Yorker 37:67 Ja 13 '62

New York Times 1962, Ja 4, 26:1
NO CRIT AVAIL
(*Published libretto*) NA
(*Published sheet music*) Edwin H. Morris/Morley Music Co., Inc.
(*Original cast recording*) NA
(*Agent/contact*)   Arnold Weinstein
                       c/o I.C.M.
                       40 W. 57th Street
                       New York, N.Y.   10019
                       ATTN: Luis Sanjurjo
(*Libretto*) NYPL NCOF+; same as (*Agent/contact*)
(*Music, Orchestrations*) Same as (*Agent/contact*)

FOUR JEWS IN A ROOM BITCHING
See *MARCH OF THE FALSETTOS*

FOURTUNE
(*Source*) Original
(*Book*) Bill Russell
(*Lyrics*) Bill Russell
(*Music*) Ronald Melrose
(*Producer*) Jonathon Scharer
Actor's Playhouse   off–Broadway
April 27, 1980   241 performances
(*Stars*) NA
Theatre World 79–80, p. 118
Best Plays 79–80, p. 449
NY 13:42 Ag 4 '80
New York Times 1980, Ap 29, III, 8:5
NO CRIT AVAIL
(*Published libretto*) NA
(*Published sheet music*) NA
(*Original cast recording*) NA

(*Agent/contact*)	Bill Russell	Ronald Melrose
	c/o Susan Schulman	c/o Susan Schulman
	165 West End Avenue	165 West End Avenue
	New York, N.Y. 10023	New York, N.Y. 10023

(*Libretto*) LC Ronald Melrose & Bill Russell 19Jun78 PAu–27–606;
  same as (*Agent/contact*)

(*Music, Orchestrations*)
    Jonathon Scharer; same as (*Agent/contact*)
    11 Riverside Drive
    New York, N.Y. 10023

FRANCIS

(*Source*) Original

(*Book*) Joseph Leonardo

(*Lyrics*) Kenny Morris

(*Music*) Steve Jankowski

(*Producer*) The Praxis Group, in association with the National
  Franciscan Communications Conference

The Commons at St. Peters Church	off–Broadway
December 22, 1981	30 performances

(*Stars*) NA

Theatre World 81–82, p. 59

Best Plays 81–82, pp. 383–84

NO CRIT AVAIL

New York Times 1981, illus, D 27, 60:1

NO CRIT AVAIL

(*Published libretto*) NA

(*Published sheet music*) NA

(*Original cast recording*) NA

(*Agent/contact*) Joseph Leonardo
     c/o DG, Inc.

(*Libretto, Music, Orchestrations*) Same as (*Agent/contact*)

FRIMBO

(*Source*) *All Aboard with E.M. Frimbo* (novel) by Rogers E.M.
        Whitaker & Anthony Hiss
(*Book*) John L. Haber
(*Lyrics*) Jim Wann
(*Music*) Howard Harris
(*Producer*) Dodger Productions, John L. Haber & Louis Busch Hager
Grand Central Terminal Tracks 39 to 42   off–Broadway
November 9, 1980   1 performance
(*Stars*) Deborah May
Theatre World 80–81, p. 87
Best Plays 80–81, pp. 409–10
NO CRIT AVAIL
New York Times 1980, N 10, III, 20:4
NO CRIT AVAIL
(*Published libretto*) NA
(*Published sheet music*) NA
(*Original cast recording*) NA
(*Agent/contact*)   John L. Haber   Howard Harris
                c/o Howard Rosenstone   c/o Howard Rosenstone
                3 E. 48th Street, 4th Fl. 3 E. 48th Street, 4th Fl.
                New York, N.Y. 10017   New York, N.Y. 10017
(*Libretto, Music, Orchestrations*) Same as (*Agent/contact*)

FROM BROOKS WITH LOVE
(*Source*) Original
(*Book*) Wayne Sheridan
(*Lyrics*) Wayne Sheridan
(*Music*) George Koch, Russ Taylor
(*Producer*) Joseph L. Runner
Harold Clurman Theatre   off–off–Broadway
March 30, 1983   4 performances
(*Stars*) NA

Theatre World 82–83, p. 91
Best Plays 82–83, p. 431
NO CRIT AVAIL
New York Times 1983, Ap 9, I, 17:2
NO CRIT AVAIL
(*Published libretto*) NA
(*Published sheet music*) NA
(*Original cast recording*) NA
(*Agent/contact*) NO CONT AVAIL
(*Libretto, Music, Orchestrations*) Same as (*Agent/contact*)

THE FUTURE
(*Source*) Original
(*Book*) Al Carmines
(*Lyrics*) Al Carmines
(*Music*) Al Carmines
(*Producer*) Judson Poets' Theater
Judson Memorial Church   off–off–Broadway
March 22, 1974   16 performances
(*Stars*) NA
NO ENTRY AVAIL
Best Plays 73–74, p. 408
New Yorker 50:106 Ap 15 '74
New York Times 1974, Mr 27, 34:2
NO CRIT AVAIL
(*Published libretto*) NA
(*Published sheet music*) NA
(*Original cast recording*) NA
(*Agent/contact*)   Al Carmines
                         c/o DG, Inc.
(*Libretto, Music, Orchestrations*) Same as (*Agent/contact*)

THE GATES OF PARADISE

(*Source*) Original
(*Book*) Ed Kuczewski
(*Lyrics*) Bill Vitale
(*Music*) Bill Vitale
(*Producer*) The Fantasy Factory
Neill Gallery   off–Broadway
November 25, 1977   12 performances
(*Stars*) NA
Theatre World 77–78, p. 72
NO ENTRY AVAIL
NO CRIT AVAIL
NO CRIT AVAIL
NO CRIT AVAIL
(*Published libretto*) NA
(*Published sheet music*) NA
(*Original cast recording*) NA
(*Agent/contact*)   William Vitale
                         c/o ASCAP
(*Libretto*) LC Ed Kuczewski & Bill Vitale 24Jan77 DU102065; same
            as (*Agent/contact*)
(*Music, Orchestrations*) Same as (*Agent/contact*)

GENTLEMEN, BE SEATED!

(*Source*) Original
(*Book*) Jerome Moross & Edward Eager
(*Lyrics*) Edward Eager
(*Music*) Jerome Moross
(*Producer*) New York City Center of Music and Drama
New York City Center   off–Broadway
October 10, 1963   3 performances
(*Stars*) Dick Shawn, Alice Ghostley
NO ENTRY AVAIL
Best Plays 63–64, p. 348

NO CRIT AVAIL
NO CRIT AVAIL
NO CRIT AVAIL
(*Published libretto*) NA
(*Published sheet music*) Chappell
(*Original cast recording*) NA
(*Agent/contact*)   Jerome Moross Estate   Edward Eager Estate
                         c/o Susan Tarjan   c/o AGAC
                         6951 S.W. 134th Street
                         Miami, FL   33156
(*Libretto*) LC (Performing Arts Reading Room) ML50/.M873G52; same
        as (*Agent/contact*)
(*Music, Orchestrations*) Same as (*Agent/contact*)

GET THEE TO CANTERBURY
(*Source*) *The Canterbury Tales* (collection) by Geoffrey Chaucer
(*Book*) Jan Steen & David Secter
(*Lyrics*) David Secter
(*Music*) Paul Hoffert
(*Producer*) David Secter
Sheridan Square Playhouse   off–Broadway
January 25, 1969   20 performances
(*Stars*) NA
Theatre World 68–69, p. 136
Best Plays 68–69, pp. 444–45
NO CRIT AVAIL
New York Times 1969, Ja 26, 74:1
NO CRIT AVAIL
(*Published libretto*) NA
(*Published sheet music*) NA
(*Original cast recording*) NA

(*Agent/contact*)   David Secter   Paul Hoffert
                       231 Second Avenue   73 Brookview Drive
                       New York, N.Y.   10003   Toronto, Canada M6A 2K5
(*Libretto, Music, Orchestrations*) Same as (*Agent/contact*)

GIFT OF THE MAGI
(*Source*) "Gift of the Magi" (short story) by O. Henry
(*Book*) Ronnie Britton
(*Lyrics*) Ronnie Britton
(*Music*) Ronnie Britton
(*Producer*) Wayne Clark & Joseph Tiraco, Larry J. Pontillo
Players Theatre   off–Broadway
December 1, 1975   48 performances
(*Stars*) NA
Theatre World 75–76, p. 76
Best Plays 75–76, pp. 376–77
NO CRIT AVAIL
New York Times 1975, D 2, 47:1
NYTC 1975:95
(*Published libretto*) NA
(*Published sheet music*) NA
(*Original cast recording*) NA
(*Agent/contact*)   Ronnie Britton
                       c/o DG, Inc.
(*Libretto*) NYPL NCOF+ 77–1954; LC Ronnie Britton 5Aug74 DU91180;
        same as (*Agent/contact*)
(*Music, Orchestrations*) Same as (*Agent/contact*)

THE GLORIOUS AGE
(*Source*) Original
(*Book*) Cy Young & Mark Gordon
(*Lyrics*) Cy Young
(*Music*) Cy Young

(*Producer*) Jane Manning & Carol McGroder, in association with
        Wendell Minnick
Theater Four   off–Broadway
May 11, 1975   14 performances
(*Stars*) Don Scardino
Theatre World 74–75, p. 89
Best Plays 74–75, p. 382
NO CRIT AVAIL
New York Times 1975, My 12, 39:1
NO CRIT AVAIL
(*Published libretto*) NA
(*Published sheet music*) NA
(*Original cast recording*) NA
(*Agent/contact*)   Cy Young
                       4151 Arch Drive, #109
                       Studio City, CA 91604
(*Libretto, Orchestrations*) Same as (*Agent/contact*)
(*Music*) LC Cy Young 17Apr75 EU588405; same as (*Agent/contact*)

*GOD BLESS CONEY**
(*Source*) Original
(*Book*) John Glines*
(*Lyrics*) John Glines*
(*Music*) John Glines*
(*Producer*) Paul B. Reynolds
Orpheum Theater   off–Broadway
May 3, 1972   3 performances
(*Stars*) NA
Theatre World 71–72, p. 109
Best Plays 71–72, pp. 377
NO CRIT AVAIL
New York Times 1972, My 4, 55:2
NO CRIT AVAIL
(*Published libretto*) NA
(*Published sheet music*) NA

(Original cast recording) NA
(Agent/contact)   John Glines
                       28 Willow Street
                       Brooklyn, N.Y.   11201
(Libretto) LC John Glines 20Dec71 DU82519 as *CONEY ISLAND*
        COOKIE JAR, John Glines 27Dec77 DU106701 as *GULP!*;
        same as *(Agent/contact)*
(Music, Orchestrations) Same as *(Agent/contact)*

*Previously titled *CONEY ISLAND COOKIE JAR*;
        subsequently rewritten and presented under the title *GULP!*, book
        by J.B. Hamilton & Stephen Greco, lyrics by J.B. Hamilton & Robin
        Jones, music by Scott Kingman

GOD BLESS YOU, MR. ROSEWATER
(Source) *God Bless You, Mr. Rosewater* (novel) by Kurt Vonnegut, Jr.
(Book) Howard Ashman
(Lyrics) Howard Ashman & Dennis Green
(Music) Alan Menken
(Producer) Edith Vonnegut & Warner Theatre Productions
Entermedia Theatre   off–Broadway
October 14, 1979   49 performances
(Stars) Janie Sell
Theatre World 79–70, p. 93
Best Plays 79–80, pp. 427–28
NY 12:87 N 5 '79
        New Yorker 55:82 O 29 '79
        Newsweek il 94:114 O 29 '79
        People il 12:36–9 O 15 '79
New York Times 1979, My 21, III, 14:4
        New York Times 1979, O 15, III, 16:1
        New York Times 1979, N 4, II, 3:2
NYTC 1979:104

(*Published libretto*) Samuel French, Inc., 1980, as
    KURT VONNEGUT'S GOD BLESS YOU, MR. ROSEWATER
(*Published sheet music*) NA (Warner Bros. Music Corp./
    Warner–Tamerlane Pub. Comp.)
(*Original cast recording*) NA
(*Agent/contact*) Samuel French, Inc.
(*Libretto, Music, Orchestrations*) Same as (*Agent/contact*)

GOGO LOVES YOU

(*Source*) *L'Ecole Des Cocottes* (play) by Paul Armont
(*Book*) Anita Loos
(*Lyrics*) Gladys Shelley
(*Music*) Claude Leveiliee
(*Producer*) Fredana Productions

Theatre de Lys	off–Broadway
October 9, 1964	2 performances

(*Stars*) NA
Theatre World 64–65, p. 151
Best Plays 64–65, pp. 343–44
NO CRIT AVAIL
New York Times 1964, O 10, 19:2
NO CRIT AVAIL
(*Published libretto*) NA
(*Published sheet music*) NA (Vadfer Music, Inc.)
(*Original cast recording*) NA

(*Agent/contact*)	Gladys Shelley	Anita Loos Estate
	875 Fifth Avenue	c/o Ray Pierre Corsini
	New York, N.Y. 10021	12 Beekman Place
		New York, N.Y. 10022

(*Libretto, Music, Orchestrations*) Same as (*Agent/contact*)

THE GOLDEN SCREW

(*Source*) Original

(*Book*) Tom Sankey

(*Lyrics*) Tom Sankey

(*Music*) Tom Sankey

(*Producer*) Pandora Productions, in association with Delancey Productions

Provincetown Playhouse   off–Broadway

January 30, 1967   40 performances

(*Stars*) NA

Theatre World 66–67, p. 128

Best Plays 66–67, p. 411

New Yorker 42:116+ F 11 '67

New York Times 1967, Ja 31, 52:1

      New York Times 1967, Mr 26, II, 1:2

NO CRIT AVAIL

(*Published libretto*) In *The New Underground Theatre*, Bantam, 1968

(*Published sheet music*) NA

(*Original cast recording*) OP Atco 33–208

(*Agent/contact*)   Tom Sankey

            c/o Bantam Books, Inc.

            666 Fifth Avenue

            New York, N.Y.   10019

(*Libretto, Music, Orchestrations*) Same as (*Agent/contact*)

GREAT BIG RIVER

See *LIVIN' THE LIFE*

THE GREAT MACDADDY

(*Source*) *The Palm Wine Drinkard* (novel) by Amos Tutuola

      (suggested by)

(*Book*) Paul Carter–Harrison

(*Lyrics*) Paul Carter–Harrison

(*Music*) Coleridge–Taylor Perkinson

(*Producer*) The Negro Ensemble Company

St. Marks Playhouse   off–Broadway

February 12, 1974   72 performances
(*Stars*) Al Freeman, Jr., Cleavon Little, Robert Hooks
Theatre World 73–74, p. 117
Best Plays 73–74, pp. 394–95
New Yorker 50:84 F 25 '74
       Time 103:69 F 25 '74
New York Times 1974, F 13, 51:6
      New York Times 1974, F 24, II, 1:1
      New York Times 1974, Mr 3, II, 3:1
NYTC 1974:364
(*Published libretto*) In *Kuntu Drama: Plays of the African
      Continuum*, Grove, 1974
(*Published sheet music*) NA
(*Original cast recording*) NA
(*Agent/contact*)   Paul Carter–Harrison   Coleridge–Taylor Perkinson
               151 Chauncly   c/o ASCAP
               Brooklyn, N.Y.   11233

               Negro Ensemble Company
               165 W. 46th Street
               New York, N.Y.   10036
(*Libretto, Music, Orchestrations*) Same as (*Agent/contact*)

GREAT SCOT!

(*Source*) Original
(*Book*) Mark Conradt & Gregory Dawson
(*Lyrics*) Nancy Leeds
(*Music*) Don McAfee
(*Producer*) Scotia Productions, in association with Edward H.
      Davis
Theatre Four   off–Broadway
November 10, 1965   38 performances
(*Stars*) NA
Theatre World 65–66, p. 131

Best Plays 65–66, pp. 424–25
NO CRIT AVAIL
New York Times 1965, N 12, 56:3
NO CRIT AVAIL
(*Published libretto*) Dramatists Play Service, 1969
(*Published sheet music*) Valando Music Corp.
(*Original cast recording*) NA
(*Agent/contact*) Dramatists Play Service, Inc.
(*Libretto, Music, Orchestrations*) Same as (*Agent/contact*)

GREEN POND
(*Source*) Original
(*Book*) Robert Montgomery
(*Lyrics*) Robert Montgomery
(*Music*) Mel Marvin
(*Producer*) Chelsea Theater Center
Academy of Music, Brooklyn/Westside Theater*   off–Broadway
November 22, 1977   32 performances
(*Stars*) Christine Ebersole
Theatre World 77–78, p. 105
Best Plays 77–78, pp. 410–11
NO CRIT AVAIL
New York Times 1977, D 15, III, 19:1
NO CRIT AVAIL
(*Published libretto*) NA
(*Published sheet music*) Macmillan Perf. Arts Music/G. Schirmer
(*Original cast recording*) NA
(*Agent/contact*)   Robert Montgomery   Mel Marvin
                       c/o ASCAP   c/o DG, Inc.
(*Libretto, Music, Orchestrations*) Same as (*Agent/contact*)

*Transferred to Westside Theater 12/7/77

GULP!

See *GOD BLESS CONEY*

THE HAGGADAH, A PASSOVER CANTATA

(Source) *Moses, Portrait of a Leader* (novel) by Elie Wiesel,
        portions of the *Haggadah* (scripture), and the *Old Testament*
        (scripture)

(Book) Elizabeth Swados

(Lyrics) Elizabeth Swados

(Music) Elizabeth Swados

(Producer) New York Shakespeare Festival

Public Theater   off–Broadway

March 31, 1980   64 performances

(Stars) NA

Theatre World 79–80, p. 149

        Theatre World 80–81, p. 135

Best Plays 79–80, pp. 415, 417–18

        Best Plays 80–81, pp. 393, 396

NY 13:79 Ap 21 '80

        Sat R il 7:56 My '80

New York Times 1980, Ap 2, III, 22:4

NO CRIT AVAIL

(Published libretto) Samuel French, Inc., 1982

(Published sheet music) NA

(Original cast recording) NA

(Agent/contact) Samuel French, Inc.

(Libretto, Orchestrations) Same as *(Agent/contact)*

(Music) LC Elizabeth Swados 9Jul82 PA–143–618;
        same as *(Agent/contact)*

HALF–PAST WEDNESDAY*

(Source) "Rumpelstiltskin" (folk tale) from *Grimm's Fairy Tales* by
        Jakob & Wilhelm Grimm

(*Book*) Anna Marie Barlow
(*Lyrics*) Robert Colby & Nita Jonas
(*Music*) Robert Colby
(*Producer*) Hal Raywin & Jerome Rudolph
Orpheum Theatre   off–Broadway
April 6, 1962   6 performances
(*Stars*) Dom De Luise
Theatre World 61–62, p. 161
Best Plays 61–62, pp. 327–28
NO CRIT AVAIL
New York Times 1962, Ap 7, 16:2
NO CRIT AVAIL
(*Published libretto*) NA
(*Published sheet music*) Sharkey Music, Inc./Sam Fox Pubs. Co.
(*Original cast recording*) OP Columbia CL–1917/CS–8717, RE Harmony
        HL–9560/HS–14560 as *RUMPELSTILTSKIN*
(*Agent/contact*)
        Robert Colby   Anna Marie Barlow   Nita Jonas
        37 W. 57th Street   c/o DG, Inc.   c/o ASCAP
        New York, N.Y.   10019
(*Libretto*) NYPL NCOF+; LC (Performing Arts Reading Room)
        ML50/.C682H3; LC Anna Marie Barlow, Robert Colby & Nita Jonas
        1May62 DU55371; same as (*Agent/contact*)
(*Music, Orchestrations*) Same as (*Agent/contact*)

*Subsequently titled *RUMPELSTILTSKIN*

THE HAPPY HYPOCRITE
(*Source*) "The Happy Hypocrite, A Fairy Tale For Tired Men" (short
        story) by Max Beerbohm
(*Book*) Edward Eager
(*Lyrics*) Edward Eager
(*Music*) James Bredt (Bernard Pagenstecher)
(*Producer*) Arete Spero

Bouwerie Lane Theater   off–Broadway
September 5, 1968   17 performances
(*Stars*) NA
Theatre World 68–69, p. 117
Best Plays 68–69, p. 427
New Yorker 44:129–30 S 14 '68
New York Times 1968, S 6, 38:1
NO CRIT AVAIL
(*Published libretto*) NA
(*Published sheet music*) Chappell & Co., Inc.
(*Original cast recording*) NA
(*Agent/contact*)   Bernard Pagenstecher   Edward Eager Estate
                         8000 Baymeadows Cir. E., #59   c/o AGAC
                         Jacksonville, FL   32216
(*Libretto*) LC Edward Eager & Bernard Pagenstecher 12Jan61 DU52460,
        22Nov66 DU67287; same as (*Agent/contact*)
(*Music, Orchestrations*) Same as (*Agent/contact*)

HARD JOB BEING GOD

(*Source*) *Old Testament* (scripture)
(*Book*) Tom Martel
(*Lyrics*) Tom Martel
(*Music*) Tom Martel
(*Producer*) Bob Yde & Andy Wiswell
Edison Theatre   off–Broadway
May 15, 1972   6 performances
(*Stars*) NA
Theatre World 71–72, p. 110
Best Plays 71–72, pp. 345–46
New Yorker 48:82+ My 27 '72
New York Times 1972, My 16, 49:1
NO CRIT AVAIL
(*Published libretto*) NA
(*Published sheet music*) Screen Gems–Columbia Pubs.
(*Original cast recording*) OP GWP Records ST–2036

(*Agent/contact*)   Tom Martel
                        1489 South Riverview Drive
                        Gardnerville, NV   89410
(*Libretto, Music, Orchestrations*) Same as (*Agent/contact*)

HARLEQUINADE
See *HEAD OVER HEELS*

HAVE I GOT ONE FOR YOU
(*Source*) Original
(*Book*) Jerry Blatt & Lonnie Burstein
(*Lyrics*) Jerry Blatt & Lonnie Burstein
(*Music*) Jerry Blatt
(*Producer*) Harlan P. Kleiman
Theatre Four   off–Broadway
January 7, 1968   1 performance
(*Stars*) Gloria De Haven
Theatre World 67–68, p. 122
Best Plays 67–68, p. 398
NO CRIT AVAIL
New York Times 1968, Ja 8, 32:1
NO CRIT AVAIL
(*Published libretto*) NA
(*Published sheet music*) NA (Pamco Music, Inc.)
(*Original cast recording*) OP Unnamed label LP–272 (Original Cast
        recorded live)
(*Agent/contact*)   Jerry Blatt
                        36 Morton Street
                        New York, N.Y.   10014
(*Libretto*) NYPL RM3492; same as (*Agent/contact*)
(*Music, Orchestrations*) Same as (*Agent/contact*)

*HEAD OVER HEELS**

(*Source*) *The Wonder Hat* (play) by Kenneth Sawyer Goodman & Ben
        Hecht
(*Book*) William S. Kilbourne, Jr. & Albert T. Viola
(*Lyrics*) William S. Kilbourne, Jr.
(*Music*) Albert T. Viola
(*Producer*) Aristotle Productions
Harold Clurman Theater   off–Broadway
December 15, 1981   22 performances
(*Stars*) NA
Theatre World 81–82, p. 59
Best Plays 81–82, pp. 383
NO CRIT AVAIL
New York Times 1981, illus, D 19, 17:5
NO CRIT AVAIL
(*Published libretto*) Samuel French, Inc., 1983
(*Published sheet music*) NA
(*Original cast recording*) NA
(*Agent/contact*) Samuel French, Inc.
(*Libretto*) LC Albert T. Viola & William S. Kilbourne, Jr.
        27Aug80 PAu–239–289 as *HARLEQUINADE*
(*Music*) LC Albert T. Viola & William S. Kilbourne, Jr.
        17Nov82 PA–155–629 as *HARLEQUINADE*; same as
        (*Agent/contact*)
(*Orchestrations*) Same as (*Agent/contact*)

*Previously titled *HARLEQUINADE*

THE HEEBIE JEEBIES
(*Source*) Original
(*Book*) Mark Hampton & Stuart Ross
(*Lyrics*) Various lyricists*
(*Music*) Various composers*
(*Producer*) Spencer Tandy, Joseph Butt & Peter Alsop

Westside Arts/Downstairs**   off–Broadway
June 18, 1981   37 performances
(*Stars*) NA
Theatre World 81–82, p. 49
Best Plays 81–82, p. 351
NO CRIT AVAIL
New York Times 1981, illus, Je 19, III, 4:5
NO CRIT AVAIL
(*Published libretto*) NA
(*Published sheet music*) NA
(*Original cast recording*) NA
(*Agent/contact*) NO CONT AVAIL
(*Libretto*) LC Mark Hampton & Stuart Ross 22Feb79 PAu–85–990;
        same as (*Agent/contact*)
(*Music, Orchestrations*) Same as (*Agent/contact*)

*No listing given. *New York Times* states, "Contemporary pop tunes
        the Boswell Sisters sang between 1930 and 1936"

**Previously produced at the Berkshire Theater Festival

HELEN
(*Source*) Original
(*Book*) Lucia Victor
(*Lyrics*) Johnny Brandon
(*Music*) Johnny Brandon
(*Producer*) AMAS Repertory Theater   off–Broadway
February 22, 1979   12 performances
(*Stars*) NA
Theatre World 78–79, p. 99
Best Plays 78–79, p. 446
NO CRIT AVAIL
NO CRIT AVAIL

NO CRIT AVAIL
(*Published libretto*) NA
(*Published sheet music*) NA
(*Original cast recording*) NA
(*Agent/contact*)   Johnny Brandon
                        c/o DG, Inc.
(*Libretto*) LC Johnny Brandon & Lucia Victor 3Mar78 PAu–4–957;
        same as (*Agent/contact*)
(*Music, Orchestrations*) Same as (*Agent/contact*)

HI, PAISANO!
(*Source*) Original
(*Book*) Ernest Chambers
(*Lyrics*) June Carroll
(*Music*) Robert Holton
(*Producer*) Aaron Gardner
York Playhouse   off–Broadway
September 30, 1961   3 performances
(*Stars*) NA
Theatre World 61–62, p. 130
Best Plays 61–62, p. 308
New Yorker 37:131–2 O 7 '61
New York Times 1961, O 2, 36:2
NO CRIT AVAIL
(*Published libretto*) NA
(*Published sheet music*) NA
(*Original cast recording*) NA
(*Agent/contact*)

Robert W. Holton	Vassili Lambrinos	June Carroll
210 Riverside Drive	Olympic Towers	132 N. Mansfield Avenue
New York, N.Y. 10025	641 Fifth Avenue	Los Angeles, CA 90036
	New York, N.Y. 10022	

    Ernest Chambers
    c/o ASCAP
(*Libretto, Music, Orchestrations*) Same as (*Agent/contact*)

HIJINKS!

(*Source*) *Captain Jinks of the Horse Marines* (play) by Clyde
        Fitch
(*Book*) Robert Kalfin, Steve Brown & John McKinney
(*Lyrics*) Various lyricists*
(*Music*) Various composers**
(*Producer*) Chelsea Theater Center, The Fisher Theater Foundation
        & Roger L. Stevens
Chelsea Theater Center/Cheryl Crawford Theater   off–Broadway
December 17, 1980   39 performances
(*Stars*) NA
Theatre World 80–81, p. 91
Best Plays 80–81, pp. 414–15
New Yorker 56:62 Ja 5 '81
New York Times 1980, D 19, III, 6:1
NO CRIT AVAIL
(*Published libretto*) Samuel French, Inc., 1982
(*Published sheet music*) NA
(*Original cast recording*) NA
(*Agent/contact*) Samuel French, Inc.
(*Libretto, Orchestrations*) Same as (*Agent/contact*)
(*Music*) LC John McKinney 3Oct81 PA–120–130;
        same as (*Agent/contact*)

*G. Clifton Bingham, Steve Brown, Alfred Bunn, Robert Burns, J.E.
        Carpenter, Robert Cooms, George Cooper, Barney Fagan, Stephen
        Foster, Mrs. Mary E. Hewitt, Joseph E. Howard, Francis Scott Key,
        George Leybourne, William Lingard, Harry Miller, John Howard
        Payne, Billy Reeves, Eben E. Rexford, Andrew B. Sterling, J.J.
        Walker, Septimus Winner, Henry Clay Work

**M.W. Balfe, Ernest R. Ball, Frank Campbell, Robert Cooms, H.P. Danks,
        Barney Fagan, Stephen Foster, S. Glover, Joseph E. Howard, Alfred
        Lee, William Lingard, J.L. Molloy, John Howard Payne, Charles E.
        Pratt, J.P. Skelly, Giuseppe Verdi, Friedrich von Flotow, Harry von
        Tilzer, W.V. Wallace, Septimus Winner, Henry Clay Work

HOBO
(*Source*) Original
(*Book*) John Dooley
(*Lyrics*) John Dooley
(*Music*) John Dooley
(*Producer*) George E. Burns
Gate Theatre   off–Broadway
April 10, 1961   32 performances
(*Stars*) Ron Holgate
Theatre World 60–61, p. 174
NO ENTRY AVAIL
New Yorker 37:118–19 Ap 22 '61
New York Times 1961, Ap 11, 41:2
NO CRIT AVAIL
(*Published libretto*) NA
(*Published sheet music*) NA
(*Original cast recording*) NA
(*Agent/contact*)   John Dooley
                         c/o DG, Inc.
(*Libretto, Music, Orchestrations*) NA

HOORAY! IT'S A GLORIOUS DAY . . . AND ALL THAT
(*Source*) Original
(*Book*) Maurice Teitelbaum & Charles Grodin
(*Lyrics*) Ethel Bieber & Maurice Teitelbaum
(*Music*) Arthur Gordon
(*Producer*) Jeff Britton
Theatre Four   off–Broadway
March 9, 1966   15 performances
(*Stars*) Ron Holgate
Theatre World 65–66, p. 157
Best Plays 65–66, p. 432
New Yorker 42:163–4 Mr 19 '66
New York Times 1966, Mr 10, 28:1

NO CRIT AVAIL

(*Published libretto*) NA

(*Published sheet music*) NA

(*Original cast recording*) NA

(*Agent/contact*)

Arthur Gordon	Ethel Bieber	Jeff Britton
75 Knightbridge Road	c/o ASCAP	1501 Broadway
Great Neck, N.Y. 11021		New York, N.Y. 10036

(*Libretto, Music, Orchestrations*) Same as (*Agent/contact*)

HORATIO

See *SMILING THE BOY FELL DEAD*

HORSEMAN, PASS BY

(*Source*) Poetry (titles unavailable) by William Butler Yeats

(*Book*) Rocco Bufano & John Duffy

(*Lyrics*) Rocco Bufano & John Duffy

(*Music*) John Duffy

(*Producer*) John A. McQuiggan

Fortune Theater   off–Broadway

January 15, 1969   37 performances

(*Stars*) Barbara Barrie, Laurence Luckinbill, Will Geer

Theatre World 68–69, p. 135

Best Plays 68–69, pp. 443–44

New Yorker 44:77–8 Ja 25 '69

New York Times 1969, Ja 16, 46:4

NO CRIT AVAIL

(*Published libretto*) NA

(*Published sheet music*) NA

(*Original cast recording*) NA

(*Agent/contact*)   John Duffy

120 W. 70th Street

New York, N.Y. 10023

(*Libretto, Music, Orchestrations*) Same as (*Agent/contact*)

HOT GROG
(*Source*) Original
(*Book*) Jim Wann
(*Lyrics*) Bland Simpson & Jim Wann
(*Music*) Bland Simpson & Jim Wann
(*Producer*) The Phoenix Theater

| Marymount Manhattan Theater | off–Broadway |
| October 6, 1977 | 22 performances |

(*Stars*) Mimi Kennedy
Theatre World 77–78, p. 132
Best Plays 77–78, pp. 404–6
NO CRIT AVAIL
New York Times 1977, O 18, 32:1
NO CRIT AVAIL
(*Published libretto*) Samuel French, Inc., 1980
(*Published sheet music*) NA
(*Original cast recording*) NA
(*Agent/contact*) Samuel French, Inc.
(*Libretto*) LC James C. Wann 28Dec78 PAu–120–495
(*Music, Orchestrations*) Same as (*Agent/contact*)

HOTEL PASSIONATO*
(*Source*) Hotel Paradiso (*L'Hôtel du Libre Echange*) (play) by
      Georges Feydeau & Maurice Desvallières
(*Book*) Jerome J. Schwartz
(*Lyrics*) Joan Javits
(*Music*) Philip Springer
(*Producer*) Slade Brown

| East Seventy–Fourth Street Theatre | off–Broadway |
| October 22, 1965 | 11 performances |

(*Stars*) Marian Mercer, Jo Anne Worley, Linda Lavin, Paul Sand
Theatre World 65–66, p. 130
Best Plays 65–66, p. 423
New Yorker 41:116 N 6 '65

New York Times 1965, O 23, 16:1

NO CRIT AVAIL

(*Published libretto*) NA

(*Published sheet music*) NA

(*Original cast recording*) NA

(*Agent/contact*)   Joan Javits Zeeman   Philip Springer

                         520 Hommocks Road   c/o ASCAP

                         Larchmont, N.Y.   10538

(*Libretto*) NYPL RM610, RM4519, NCOF+; LC Jerome J. Schwartz

        13Jan65 DU62000; same as (*Agent/contact*)

(*Music, Orchestrations*) Same as (*Agent/contact*)

*Previously titled *WHAT A NIGHT!*

THE HOUSE OF LEATHER

(*Source*) Original

(*Book*) Frederick Gaines

(*Lyrics*) Dale F. Menten & Frederick Gaines

(*Music*) Dale F. Menten

(*Producer*) William H. Semans & Richard K. Shapiro, in

        association with Marshall Naify

Ellen Stewart Theatre   off–Broadway

March 18, 1970   1 performance

(*Stars*) Barry Bostwick, Jonelle Allen

Theatre World 69–70, p. 124

Best Plays 69–70, p. 361

New Yorker 46:86+ Mr 28 '70

New York Times 1969, My 18, II, 3:1

        New York Times 1970, Mr 19, 56:1

NO CRIT AVAIL

(*Published libretto*) NA

(*Published sheet music*) NA

(*Original cast recording*) OP Fontana SRF–67591

(*Agent/contact*)	Frederick Gaines	Dale F. Menten
	c/o Ellen Neuwald	6630 Minnewashta Parkway
	905 West End Avenue	Excelsior, MN 55331
	New York, N.Y. 10025	

(*Libretto, Music, Orchestrations*) Same as (*Agent/contact*)

THE HOUSEWIVES' CANTATA

(*Source*) Original
(*Book*) William Holtzman
(*Lyrics*) June Siegel
(*Music*) Mira J. Spektor
(*Producer*) Cheryl Crawford & Eryk Spektor

Theater Four	off–Broadway
February 18, 1980	24 performances

(*Stars*) NA
Theatre World 79–80, p. 107
Best Plays 79–80, pp. 445–46
NO CRIT AVAIL
New York Times 1980, F 19, III, 5:1
NO CRIT AVAIL
(*Published libretto*) NA
(*Published sheet music*) NA
(*Original cast recording*) Original Cast Records OC–8133
(*Agent/contact*)

Mira J. Spektor	June Siegel	William Holtzman
262 Central Park West	c/o DG, Inc.	c/o DG, Inc.
New York, N.Y. 10024		

(*Libretto, Music, Orchestrations*) Same as (*Agent/contact*)

HOW TO GET RID OF IT

(*Source*) *Amédée* (play) by Eugène Ionesco
(*Book*) Eric Blau

(*Lyrics*) Eric Blau
(*Music*) Mort Shuman
(*Producer*) 3W Productions, Inc.
Astor Place Theatre   off–Broadway
November 17, 1974   10 performances
(*Stars*) NA
Theatre World 74–75, p. 74
Best Plays 74–75, p. 369
NO CRIT AVAIL
New York Times 1974, N 18, 51:1
NO CRIT AVAIL
(*Published libretto*) NA
(*Published sheet music*) NA
(*Original cast recording*) NA
(*Agent/contact*)   Eric Blau
                         c/o DG, Inc.
(*Libretto, Music, Orchestrations*) Same as (*Agent/contact*)

HOW'S THE HOUSE?
See *MUSICAL CHAIRS*

HUCKLEBERRY FINN
See *DOWNRIVER*

*I CAN'T KEEP RUNNING IN PLACE**
(*Source*) Original
(*Book*) Barbara Schottenfeld
(*Lyrics*) Barbara Schottenfeld
(*Music*) Barbara Schottenfeld
(*Producer*) Ray Gaspard, in association with Chris Silva, Stephen
        Dailey & Will Dailey

Westside Arts Theatre**   off-Broadway**
May 14, 1981   187 performances
(*Stars*) Helen Gallagher, Marcia Rodd
Theatre World 80–81, p. 102
Best Plays 80–81, p. 422
NY 14:97–8 My 25 '81
New York Times 1981, My 15, III, 4:5
NO CRIT AVAIL
(*Published libretto*) Samuel French, Inc., 1981
(*Published sheet music*) NA
(*Original cast recording*) Painted Smiles PS–1346
(*Agent/contact*) Samuel French, Inc.
(*Libretto*) LC Barbara Schottenfeld 1May82 PA–141–136
(*Music, Orchestrations*) Same as (*Agent/contact*)

*Previously titled *A WOMAN SUSPENDED*

**Previously produced off-off-Broadway at La Mama

I DREAMT I DWELT IN BLOOMINGDALE'S
(*Source*) Original
(*Book*) Jack Ramer
(*Lyrics*) Jack Ramer & Ernest McCarty
(*Music*) Ernest McCarty
(*Producer*) Sam Levine
Provincetown Playhouse   off-Broadway
February 12, 1970   6 performances
(*Stars*) NA
Theatre World 69–70, p. 120
Best Plays 69–70, p. 358
New Yorker 46:67 F 21 '70
New York Times 1970, F 13, 26:1
NO CRIT AVAIL
(*Published libretto*) NA

(*Published sheet music*) NA

(*Original cast recording*) NA

(*Agent/contact*) NO CONT AVAIL

(*Libretto*) NYPL RM4407; LC Jack Ramer & Ernest McCarty 27Oct69
      DU75701; same as (*Agent/contact*)

(*Music, Orchestrations*) Same as (*Agent/contact*)

I KNOCK AT THE DOOR

(*Source*) *I Knock at the Door, Swift Glances Back at Things that
      Made Me* (autobiography) by Sean O'Casey

(*Book*) Paul Shyre

(*Lyrics*) Paul Dick

(*Music*) Paul Dick

(*Producer*) Marc Hammerman

| Billy Munk Theatre | off–Broadway |
| April 12, 1976 | 4 performances |

(*Stars*) NA

Theatre World 75–76, p. 86

NO ENTRY AVAIL

NO CRIT AVAIL

NO CRIT AVAIL

NO CRIT AVAIL

(*Published libretto*) NA

(*Published sheet music*) NA

(*Original cast recording*) NA

(*Agent/contact*)   Paul Shyre   Paul Dick

                        c/o Ellen Neuwald   7261 Shore Road

                        905 West End Avenue   Brooklyn, N.Y.   11209

                        New York, N.Y.   10025

(*Libretto, Music, Orchestrations*) Same as (*Agent/contact*)

I TAKE THESE WOMEN
(*Source*) Original
(*Book*) J.J. Coyle
(*Lyrics*) Sandi Merle
(*Music*) Robert Kole
(*Producer*) King Stuart Productions
Nat Horne Theatre   off–Broadway
March 11, 1982   20 performances
(*Stars*) NA
Theatre World 81–82, p. 64
NO ENTRY AVAIL
NO CRIT AVAIL
NO CRIT AVAIL
NO CRIT AVAIL
(*Published libretto*) NA
(*Published sheet music*) NA
(*Original cast recording*) NA
(*Agent/contact*)   J.J. Coyle
                       c/o DG, Inc.
(*Libretto, Music, Orchestrations*) Same as (*Agent/contact*)

I WANT YOU!
(*Source*) Original
(*Book*) Stefan Kanfer & Jess J. Korman
(*Lyrics*) Stefan Kanfer, Jess J. Korman & Joseph Crayham
(*Music*) Stefan Kanfer, Jess J. Korman & Joseph Crayham
(*Producer*) Theodore J. Flicker, Sam W. Gelfman & Joseph Crayham,
             in association with David W. Carter
Maidman Playhouse   off–Broadway
September 14, 1961   4 performances
(*Stars*) NA
Theatre World 61–62, p. 128
Best Plays 61–62, pp. 305
NO CRIT AVAIL

New York Times 1961, S 15, 29:1
NO CRIT AVAIL
(*Published libretto*) NA
(*Published sheet music*) Morley Music Co., Inc./Edwin H. Morris &
          Co., Inc.
(*Original cast recording*) NA
(*Agent/contact*)   Stefan Kanfer
                         c/o Time, Inc.
                         Time & Life Bldg.
                         Rockefeller Center
                         New York, N.Y.   10020
(*Libretto, Music, Orchestrations*) Same as (*Agent/contact*)

INTERNATIONAL BERNIE & COMPANY
See *A DRIFTER, THE GRIFTER & HEATHER MC BRIDE*

IPHIGENIA
See *THE WEDDING OF IPHIGENIA AND IPHIGENIA IN CONCERT*

IT'S WILDE!
(*Source*) Original
(*Book*) Burton Wolfe
(*Lyrics*) Burton Wolfe
(*Music*) Randy Klein
(*Producer*) Stages Theatrical Productions Ltd.
Theater East   off–Broadway
May 21, 1980   7 performances
(*Stars*) NA
Theatre World 79–80, p. 120
Best Plays 79–80, p. 451
NO CRIT AVAIL
New York Times 1980, My 23, III, 7:1

NO CRIT AVAIL
(*Published libretto*) NA
(*Published sheet music*) NA
(*Original cast recording*) NA
(*Agent/contact*)   Burton Wolfe   Randy Klein
                           156 Olive Way   498 West End Avenue
                           Boca Raton, FL 33432   New York, N.Y.   10024
(*Libretto, Music, Orchestrations*) Same as (*Agent/contact*)

JAZZBO
See *JAZZBO BROWN*

*JAZZBO BROWN**
(*Source*) *The Jazz Singer* (play) by Samson Raphaelson
(*Book*) Stephen H. Lemberg
(*Lyrics*) Stephen H. Lemberg
(*Music*) Stephen H. Lemberg
(*Producer*) Barbara Gittler, in association with Morris Jaffe
City Light Theatre   off–Broadway
June 24, 1980   44 performances
(*Stars*) Andre De Shields
Theatre World 80–81, p. 77
NO ENTRY AVAIL
NO CRIT AVAIL
NO CRIT AVAIL
NO CRIT AVAIL
(*Published libretto*) NA
(*Published sheet music*) NA
(*Original cast recording*) NA
(*Agent/contact*)   Stephen Lemberg
                           c/o ASCAP

(*Libretto*) LC Stephen H. Lemberg 17Apr80 PAu–190–914 as
        JAZZBO; same as (*Agent/contact*)
(*Music, Orchestrations*) Same as (*Agent/contact*)

*Previously titled *JAZZBO*

JIMMY & BILLY

(*Source*) Original
(*Book*) David I. Levine
(*Lyrics*) David I. Levine
(*Music*) David I. Levine & Pat Curtis
(*Producer*) David I. Levine
Westside/Upstairs   off–Broadway
December 10, 1978   1 performance
(*Stars*) NA
NO ENTRY AVAIL
Best Plays 78–79, p. 432
NO CRIT AVAIL
NO CRIT AVAIL
NO CRIT AVAIL
(*Published libretto*) NA
(*Published sheet music*) NA
(*Original cast recording*) NA
(*Agent/contact*)   David I. Levine
                c/o DG, Inc.
(*Libretto, Music, Orchestrations*) Same as (*Agent/contact*)

JO

(*Source*) *Little Women* (novel) by Louisa May Alcott
(*Book*) Don Parks & William Dyer
(*Lyrics*) Don Parks & William Dyer
(*Music*) William Dyer
(*Producer*) Virginia Crandall

Orpheum Theatre   off–Broadway
February 12, 1964   63 performances
(*Stars*) Karin Wolfe, Susan Browning
Theatre World 63–63, p. 217
Best Plays 63–64, p. 358
America 110:322 Mr 7 '64
        New Yorker 40:92+ F 22 '64
New York Times 1964, F 13, 25:1
NO CRIT AVAIL
(*Published libretto*) Dramatists Play Service, Inc., 1964
(*Published sheet music*) Sunbeam Music Corp./Valando Music
(*Original cast recording*) NA
(*Agent/contact*) Dramatists Play Service, Inc.
(*Libretto, Music, Orchestrations*) Same as (*Agent/contact*)

JOAN

(*Source*) Original
(*Book*) Al Carmines
(*Lyrics*) Al Carmines
(*Music*) Al Carmines
(*Producer*) Theodore Mann, Paul Libin & Seymour Hacker
Circle in the Square   off–Broadway
June 19, 1972   64 performances
(*Stars*) NA
Theatre World 72–73, p. 89
Best Plays 72–73, p. 366
America 127:292–3 O 14 '72
        New Yorker 47:101 D 11 '71
        Sat R 55:72 Jl 8 '72
        Time il 100:72 Jl 10 '72
New York Times 1972, Je 20, 33:1
        New York Times 1972, Je 25, II, 1:1
NYTC 1972:235
(*Published libretto*) NA

(*Published sheet music*) NA

(*Original cast recording*) OP Judson JU–1001

(*Agent/contact*)   Al Carmines   Theodore Mann/Paul Libin
                           c/o DG, Inc.   1633 Broadway
                                                    New York, N.Y.   10019

(*Libretto, Music, Orchestrations*) Same as (*Agent/contact*)

JUBALAY

See *A BISTRO CAR ON THE CNR*

JUDGEMENT DAY

See *KA–BOOM!*

KABOOM!

(*Source*) Original

(*Book*) Ira Wallach*

(*Lyrics*) Ira Wallach*

(*Music*) Doris Schwerin

(*Producer*) Joseph Rhodes

Bottom Line Theatre   off–Broadway

May 1, 1974   1 performances

(*Stars*) NA

Theatre World 73–74, p. 88

Best Plays 72–73, p. 401

NO CRIT AVAIL

New York Times 1974, My 2, 64:3

NO CRIT AVAIL

(*Published libretto*) NA

(*Published sheet music*) NA

(*Original cast recording*) NA

(*Agent/contact*)   Ira Wallach   Doris Schwerin

345 W. 58th Street   c/o DG, Inc.

New York, N.Y.   10019

(*Libretto*) LC Ira Wallach & Doris H. Schwerin 6Jun74 EU496748;
    same as (*Agent/contact*)

(*Music, Orchestrations*) Same as (*Agent/contact*)

*At press time, Mr. Wallach was not interested in soliciting
    further productions of this property

*KA–BOOM!**

(*Source*) Original

(*Book*) Bruce Kluger

(*Lyrics*) Bruce Kluger

(*Music*) Joe Ercole

(*Producer*) Jim Payne, in association with Sherie Seff & Bruce Kluger

Carter Theater   off–Broadway

November 20, 1980   71 performances

(*Stars*) NA

Theatre World 80–81, p. 87

Best Plays 80–81, pp. 410–11

NO CRIT AVAIL

New York Times 1980, N 21, III, 21:1

NO CRIT AVAIL

(*Published libretto*) NA

(*Published sheet music*) NA

(*Original cast recording*) CYM Records CYM–8130

(*Agent/contact*)   Bruce Kluger

One Slade Avenue, #106

Baltimore, MD 21208

(*Libretto, Music*) LC Joseph C. Ercole 19Oct79 PAu–154–462;
    Bruce Lawrence Kluger 13Nov79 PAu–157–537 as *JUDGMENT DAY*;
    same as (*Agent/contact*)

(*Orchestrations*) Same as (*Agent/contact*)

*Previously titled *JUDGEMENT DAY*

KING OF THE WHOLE DAMN WORLD!

(*Source*) *Comic Strip* (play) by George Panetta
(*Book*) George Panetta
(*Lyrics*) Robert Larimer
(*Music*) Robert Larimer
(*Producer*) Norman Forman
Jan Hus Playhouse   off–Broadway
April 14, 1962   43 performances
(*Stars*) NA
Theatre World 61–62, p. 163
Best Plays 61–62, pp. 328–29
New Yorker 38:97 Ap 28 '62
        Sat R 45:29 My 5 '62
New York Times 1962, Ap 16, 32:2
NO CRIT AVAIL
(*Published libretto*) NA
(*Published sheet music*) Saunders Pubs., Inc./Frank Dist. Corp.
(*Original cast recording*) OP Unnamed label, unnumbered
(*Agent/contact*)   Robert Larimer
                       c/o DG, Inc.
(*Libretto, Music, Orchestrations*) Same as (*Agent/contact*)

KISS NOW

(*Source*) Original
(*Book*) Maxine Klein
(*Lyrics*) Maxine Klein
(*Music*) William S. Fischer
(*Producer*) John Ramsey, William Formaad & Milan Stitt

Martinique Theater   off–Broadway
April 20, 1971   4 performances
(*Stars*) NA
Theatre World 70–71, p. 109
Best Plays 70–71, p. 348
NO CRIT AVAIL
New York Times 1971, Ap 21, 40:4
NO CRIT AVAIL
(*Published libretto*) NA
(*Published sheet music*) NA
(*Original cast recording*) NA
(*Agent/contact*)   Maxine Klein   William S. Fischer
                       c/o Little Flags Theatre   c/o ASCAP
                       22 Sunset Street
                       Roxbury, MA 02120
(*Libretto, Music, Orchestrations*) Same as (*Agent/contact*)

KITTIWAKE ISLAND
(*Source*) Original
(*Book*) Arnold Sundgaard
(*Lyrics*) Arnold Sundgaard
(*Music*) Alec Wilder
(*Producer*) Joseph Beruh & Lawrence Carra
Martinique Theatre   off–Broadway
October 12, 1960   7 performances
(*Stars*) Lainie Kazan
Theatre World 60–61, p. 130
Best Plays 60–61, p. 350–51
New Yorker 36:93 O 22 '60
New York Times 1960, O 13, 43:1
NO CRIT AVAIL
(*Published libretto*) G. Schirmer, 1955
(*Published sheet music*) G. Schirmer

(*Original cast recording*) OP Adelphi AD–2015/6, RE Blue Pear
    Records BP–1003 (Original Cast recorded live)
(*Agent/contact*)   G. Schirmer, Inc.   Arnold Sundgaard
                         866 Third Avenue   c/o DG, Inc.
                         New York, N.Y.   10022
(*Libretto, Music, Orchestrations*) Same as (*Agent/contact*)

LADY AUDLEY'S SECRET

(*Source*) *Lady Audley's Secret* (novel) by Mary Elizabeth Braddon
(*Book*) Douglas Seale
(*Lyrics*) John Kuntz
(*Music*) George Goehring
(*Producer*) Hal Stoddard & Arnold H. Levy
Eastside Playhouse   off–Broadway
October 3, 1972   7 performances
(*Stars*) Russell Nype
Theatre World 72–73, p. 97
Best Plays 72–73, p. 377
Sat R 54:33 Ag 7 '71
New York Times 1972, O 4, 40:1
NO CRIT AVAIL
(*Published libretto*) NA
(*Published sheet music*) NA
(*Original cast recording*) NA
(*Agent/contact*) Music Theatre International
(*Libretto, Music, Orchestrations*) Same as (*Agent/contact*)

LADY DAY: A MUSICAL TRAGEDY

(*Source*) Original
(*Book*) Aishah Rahman
(*Lyrics*) Aishah Rahman
(*Music*) Archie Shepp, Stanley Cowell & Cal Massey
(*Producer*) Chelsea Theater Center of Brooklyn

Academy of Music, Brooklyn   off-Broadway
October 17, 1972   24 performances
(*Stars*) NA
Theatre World 72–73, p. 132
Best Plays 72–73, pp. 378–79
New Yorker 48:105–6+ N 4 '72
     Newsweek il 80:133–4 N 6 '72
New York Times 1972, O 26, 39:1
     New York Times 1972, N 5, II, 5:1
NYTC 1972:165
(*Published libretto*) NA
(*Published sheet music*) NA
(*Original cast recording*) NA
(*Agent/contact*)   Aishah Rahman   Archie Shepp
     c/o Hatch–Billops Archive   Box #801
     491 Broadway, Fifth Floor   Amherst, MA   01002
     New York, N.Y.   10012
(*Libretto*) LC Aishah Rahman 27Sep71 DU81405;
     same as (*Agent/contact*)
(*Music, Orchestrations*) Same as (*Agent/contact*)

*LADY OF MEXICO**
(*Source*) Original
(*Book*) Sister Mary Francis
(*Lyrics*) Sister Mary Francis
(*Music*) Joseph Roff
(*Producer*) The Blackfriars' Guild
The Blackfriars' Theatre   off-Broadway
October 16, 1962   56 performances
(*Stars*) NA
Theatre World 62–63, p. 140
NO ENTRY AVAIL
America 107:1106 N 17 '62
New York Times 1962, O 20, 13:2
NO CRIT AVAIL

(*Published libretto*) Gregorian Institute of America, 1961, Poor
    Clare Monastery, 1983, as *COUNTED AS MINE*
(*Published sheet music*) Gregorian Institute of America,
    Poor Clare Monastery as *COUNTED AS MINE*
(*Original cast recording*) NA
(*Agent/contact*)   Poor Clare Monastery
        809 E. 19th Street
        Roswell, NM 88201
        Attn: Mother M. Francis, P.C.C.
(*Libretto, Music, Orchestrations*) Same as (*Agent/contact*)

*Originally titled *COUNTED AS MINE*

LEAVE IT TO BEAVER IS DEAD

(*Source*) Original
(*Book*) Des McAnuff
(*Lyrics*) Des McAnuff
(*Music*) Larry David & Des McAnuff
(*Producer*) Joseph Papp
Public/Other Stage   off–Broadway
March 29, 1979   15 performances
(*Stars*) Mandy Patinkin
Theatre World 78–79, p. 134
Best Plays 78–79, p. 457
NO CRIT AVAIL
New York Times 1979, Ap 4, III, 20:5
NO CRIT AVAIL
(*Published libretto*) NA
(*Published sheet music*) NA
(*Original cast recording*) NA
(*Agent/contact*)   Des McAnuff   Joseph Papp
        c/o La Jolla Playhouse   c/o Public Theatre
        P.O. Box #12039   425 Lafayette Street
        La Jolla, CA 92037   New York, N.Y. 10003
(*Libretto, Music, Orchestrations*) Same as (*Agent/contact*)

THE LEGEND OF PARADISE ISLAND
See *PARADISE ISLAND*

THE LEGEND OF PETER GRANT
See *MEET PETER GRANT*

LES PARAPLUIES DE CHERBOURG
See *THE UMBRELLAS OF CHERBOURG*

LIFE IS NOT A DORIS DAY MOVIE
(*Source*) Original
(*Book*) Boyd Graham
(*Lyrics*) Boyd Graham
(*Music*) Stephen Graziano
(*Producer*) Reid–Dolph, Inc.
Top of the Gate   off–Broadway
June 25, 1982   37 performances
(*Stars*) Mary Testa, Neva Small
Theatre World 82–83, p. 73
Best Plays 82–83, pp. 373–74
NO CRIT AVAIL
New York Times 1982, Je 27, 46:4
(*Published libretto*) NA
(*Published sheet music*) NA
(*Original cast recording*) NA
(*Agent/contact*) NO CONT AVAIL
(*Libretto, Music, Orchestrations*) Same as (*Agent/contact*)

THE LIFE OF A MAN
(*Source*) Original
(*Book*) Al Carmines

(*Lyrics*) Al Carmines
(*Music*) Al Carmines
(*Producer*) Judson Poets' Theater
Judson Poets' Theater   off–off–Broadway
September 29, 1972   16 performances
(*Stars*) NA
NO ENTRY AVAIL
Best Plays 72–73, p. 400
Craft Horiz 32:10+ D '72
        New Yorker 48:125 O 14 '72
        Sat R 55:85 O 21 '72
New York Times 1972, O 4, 40:1
NO CRIT AVAIL
(*Published libretto*) NA
(*Published sheet music*) NA
(*Original cast recording*) NA
(*Agent/contact*)   Al Carmines
                       c/o DG, Inc.
(*Libretto, Music, Orchestrations*) Same as (*Agent/contact*)

LISTEN, WORLD
See **CHASE A RAINBOW**

LIVIN' THE LIFE*
(*Source*) *Life on the Mississippi* (collection), *The Adventures*
        of Huckleberry Finn (novel) and *The Adventures of Tom Sawyer*
        (novel) by Mark Twain
(*Book*) Dale Wasserman & Bruce Geller*
(*Lyrics*) Bruce Geller
(*Music*) Jack Urbont
(*Producer*) T. Edward Hambleton & Norris Houghton

Phoenix Theatre   off–Broadway
April 27, 1957   25 performances
(*Stars*) Edward Villella, Alice Ghostley
Theatre World 56–57, p. 166
Best Plays 56–57, pp. 371–72
America 97:270 My 25 '57
   Nation 184:427 My 11 '57
   New Yorker 33:142 My 4 '57
   Theatre Arts il 41:18 Jl '57
New York Times 1957, Ap 29, 20:1
NYTC 1957:281
(*Published libretto*) NA
(*Published sheet music*) G. Schirmer
(*Original cast recording*) NA
(*Agent/contact*)

Michael Colby	Jack Urbont	Dale Wasserman
c/o Algonquin Hotel	330 W. 72nd Street	c/o DG, Inc.
59 W. 44th Street	New York, N.Y. 10023	
New York, N.Y. 10036		

Bruce Geller Estate
707 North Arden Drive
Beverly Hills, CA 90210
(*Libretto*) NYPL NCOF+; same as (*Agent/contact*)
(*Music, Orchestrations*)
    Schirmer Music; same as (*Agent/contact*)
    40 W. 62nd Street
    New York, N.Y. 10023

*Subsequently presented under the title *GREAT BIG RIVER*, book and
  lyrics adapted by Michael Colby

A LOOK AT THE FIFTIES
(*Source*) Original
(*Book*) Al Carmines

(*Lyrics*) Al Carmines
(*Music*) Al Carmines
(*Producer*) Judson Poets' Theater
Judson Memorial Church   off–off–Broadway
April 14, 1972   12 performances
(*Stars*) NA
NO ENTRY AVAIL
NO ENTRY AVAIL
New Yorker 48:105 Ap 29 '72
New York Times 1972, Ap 20, 53:1
NO CRIT AVAIL
(*Published libretto*) NA
(*Published sheet music*) NA
(*Original cast recording*) NA
(*Agent/contact*)   Al Carmines
                       c/o DG, Inc.
(*Libretto, Music, Orchestrations*) Same as (*Agent/contact*)

LOOK WHERE I'M AT!

(*Source*) *Rain in the Doorway* (novel) by Thorne Smith
(*Book*) James Leasor & Gib Dennigan
(*Lyrics*) Frank H. Stanton* & Murray Semos
(*Music*) Jordan Ramin
(*Producer*) Jean Merie–Lee
Theatre Four   off–Broadway
March 5, 1971   5 performances
(*Stars*) Ron Husmann
Theatre World 70–71, p. 102
Best Plays 70–71, p. 346
NO CRIT AVAIL
New York Times 1971, Mr 6, 20:1
NO CRIT AVAIL
(*Published libretto*) NA
(*Published sheet music*) NA
(*Original cast recording*) NA

(*Agent/contact*)   Frank Stanton Enterprises   Jordan Ramin
                         2315 Foxhaven Drive   45 W. 69th Street
                         Franklin, TN 37064   New York, N.Y.   10023

                         Thorne Smith Estate
                         c/o Harold Matson Co., Inc.
                         276 Fifth Avenue
                         New York, N.Y.   10016
(*Libretto, Music, Orchestrations*) Same as (*Agent/contact*)

*At press time, Mr. Stanton was not interested in soliciting
        further productions of this property

LOTTA, OR THE BEST THING EVOLUTION'S EVER COME UP WITH
(*Source*) Original
(*Book*) Robert Montgomery
(*Lyrics*) Robert Montgomery
(*Music*) Robert Montgomery
(*Producer*) New York Shakespeare Festival
Public Theater/Anspacher   off–Broadway
November 21, 1973   54 performances
(*Stars*) Irene Cara, Jill Eikenberry
Theatre World 73–74, p. 126
Best Plays 73–74, p. 384
America 129:485 D 22 '73
        New Yorker 49:147 D 3 '73
        Newsweek 91 82:73 D 3 '73
New York Times 1973, N 23, 42:1
        New York Times 1973, D 2, II, 3:1
NYTC 1973:168
(*Published libretto*) NA
(*Published sheet music*) NA
(*Original cast recording*) NA

(*Agent/contact*)   Robert Montgomery   Joseph Papp
                       c/o Ellen Neuwald   c/o Public Theatre
                       905 West End Avenue   425 Lafayette Street
                       New York, N.Y. 10025   New York, N.Y. 10003
(*Libretto*) LC Robert Montgomery 7Mar74 DU89714;
        same as (*Agent/contact*)
(*Music, Orchestrations*) Same as (*Agent/contact*)

LOUIS

(*Source*) Original
(*Book*) Don Evans
(*Lyrics*) Don Evans
(*Music*) Michael Renzi
(*Producer*) Henry Street Settlement's New Federal Theatre
Henry Street Playhouse   off–off–Broadway
September 18, 1981   12 performances
(*Stars*) Ken Page, Debbie Allen, Tiger Haynes
Theatre World 81–82, p. 80
Best Plays 81–82, p. 401
NO CRIT AVAIL
NO CRIT AVAIL
NO CRIT AVAIL
(*Published libretto*) NA
(*Published sheet music*) NA
(*Original cast recording*) NA
(*Agent/contact*)   Don Evans   Michael Renzi
                       32 Oak Lane   c/o DG, Inc.
                       Trenton, NJ   08618
(*Libretto, Music, Orchestrations*) Same as (*Agent/contact*)

*LOVE AND LET LOVE**
(*Source*) *Twelfth Night* (play) by William Shakespeare
(*Book*) John Lollos
(*Lyrics*) John Lollos & Don Christopher
(*Music*) Stanley Jay Gelber
(*Producer*) L. & L.L. Company
Sheridan Square Playhouse   off–Broadway
January 3, 1968   14 performances
(*Stars*) Marcia Rodd, Virginia Vestoff
Theatre World 67–68, p. 122
Best Plays 67–68, pp. 397–98
New Yorker 43:58–9 Ja 13 '68
New York Times 1968, Ja 4, 30:1
NO CRIT AVAIL
(*Published libretto*) NA
(*Published sheet music*) Sam Fox Pub. Comp.
(*Original cast recording*) OP Sam Fox X4RS–0371 as *TWELFTH*
        NIGHT
(*Agent/contact*)
        Don Christopher   John Lollos   Stanley Jay Gelber
        c/o Caterpillar Music c/o DG, Inc.   c/o DG, Inc.
        8 Yale Street
        Nutley, NJ   07110
(*Libretto, Music, Orchestrations*) Same as (*Agent/contact*)

*Subsequently titled *TWELFTH NIGHT*

LOVE ME, LOVE MY CHILDREN
(*Source*) Original
(*Book*) Robert Swerdlow
(*Lyrics*) Robert Swerdlow
(*Music*) Robert Swerdlow
(*Producer*) Joel Schenker & Edward F. Kook

Mercer–O'Casey Theater   off–Broadway
November 3, 1971   187 performances
(*Stars*) NA
Theatre World 71–72, p. 89
Best Plays 71–72, pp. 359–60
New Yorker 47:66+ N 13 '71
New York Times 1971, N 4, 53:1
NYTC 1971:166
(*Published libretto*) NA
(*Published sheet music*) NA (Chappell)
(*Original cast recording*) NA
(*Agent/contact*)   Joel W. Schenker
                         234 W. 44th Street
                         New York, N.Y.   10036
(*Libretto, Music, Orchestrations*) Same as (*Agent/contact*)

LOVE TALES FROM THE DECAMERON
See **THE DECAMERON**

LULLABYE AND GOODNIGHT
(*Source*) Original
(*Book*) Elizabeth Swados
(*Lyrics*) Elizabeth Swados
(*Music*) Elizabeth Swados
(*Producer*) N.Y. Shakespeare Festival Public Theater
Public/Newman Theater   off–Broadway
February 9, 1982   30 performances
(*Stars*) NA
Theatre World 81–82, p. 97
Best Plays 81–82, pp. 335, 357–58
NY 15:52–4 F 22 '82
        New Yorker 58:54 F 22 '82

New York Times 1982, illus, F 10, III, 24:1
NO CRIT AVAIL
(*Published libretto*) NA
(*Published sheet music*) NA
(*Original cast recording*) NA
(*Agent/contact*)   Elizabeth Swados   Joseph Papp
                           c/o Advanced Management c/o Public Theatre
                             Services   425 Lafayette Street
                           280 Madison Avenue   New York, N.Y.   10003
                           New York, N.Y. 10016
(*Libretto, Music, Orchestrations*) Same as (*Agent/contact*)

LYLE

(*Source*) Children's books (titles unavailable) by Bernard Waber
(*Book*) Chuck Harner*
(*Lyrics*) Toby Garson
(*Music*) Janet Gari
(*Producer*) Marilyn Cantor Baker
McAlphin Rooftop Theatre   off–Broadway
March 20, 1970   3 performances
(*Stars*) NA
Theatre World 69–70, p. 125
Best Plays 69–70, p. 361
NO CRIT AVAIL
New York Times 1970, Mr 21, 16:2
NO CRIT AVAIL
(*Published libretto*) NA
(*Published sheet music*) NA
(*Original cast recording*) NA
(*Agent/contact*)
     Janet Gari   Toby Garson   Bernard Waber
     205 W. 54th Street   c/o ASCAP   3653 Bertha Drive
     New York, N.Y. 10019   Baldwin Harbor, N.Y. 11510

(*Libretto*) LC Janet Gari, Toby Garson & Sidney Miller 2Apr70
        DU76782; same as (*Agent/contact*)
(*Music, Orchestrations*) Same as (*Agent/contact*)

*In all publicity, Chuck Harner is given sole authorship credit; however,
        LC copyright DU76782 gives Sidney Miller & Toby Garson authorship
        credit

MACKEY
See *MACKEY OF APPALACHIA*

*MACKEY OF APPALACHIA**
(*Source*) Original
(*Book*) Walter Cool
(*Lyrics*) Walter Cool
(*Music*) Walter Cool
(*Producer*) The Blackfriars' Guild
The Blackfriars' Theatre   off–Broadway
October 6, 1965   54 performances
(*Stars*) NA
Theatre World 65–66, p. 123
Best Plays 65–66, p. 437
America 113:384–5 O 2 '65
NO CRIT AVAIL
NO CRIT AVAIL
(*Published libretto*) NA
(*Published sheet music*) NA
(*Original cast recording*) NA
(*Agent/contact*) NO CONT AVAIL
(*Libretto*) LC Walter D. Cool 26Jun64 DU60548;
        same as (*Agent/contact*)
(*Music, Orchestrations*) Same as (*Agent/contact*)

*Previously titled *MACKEY*

MADAME APHRODITE
(*Source*) Original
(*Book*) Tad Mosel
(*Lyrics*) Jerry Herman*
(*Music*) Jerry Herman*
(*Producer*) Howard Baker, Cynthia Baer & Robert Chambers
Orpheum Theatre   off–Broadway
December 29, 1961   13 performances
(*Stars*) Nancy Andrews, Steve Elmore
Theatre World 61–62, p. 139
Best Plays 61–62, p. 317
New Yorker 37:66 Ja 13 '62
New York Times 1961, D 30, 13:1
NO CRIT AVAIL
(*Published libretto*) NA
(*Published sheet music*) Vogue Music Corp.
(*Original cast recording*) NA
(*Agent/contact*)   Jerry Herman
                       c/o DG, Inc.
(*Libretto, Music, Orchestrations*) Same as (*Agent/contact*)

*At press time, Mr. Herman was not interested in soliciting
     further productions of this property

MAHALIA
(*Source*) *Just Mahalia Baby* (biography) by Laurraine Goreau
(*Book*) Don Evans
(*Lyrics*) Don Evans
(*Music*) John Lewis
(*Producer*) Carousel Group, Inc. & Lucy Productions Corp.
Henry Street Playhouse   off–Broadway
May 31, 1978   14 performances
(*Stars*) NA
Theatre World 77–78, p. 90

NO ENTRY AVAIL
Down Beat 45:12 O 5 '78
          Encore il 7:35 Je 19 '78
New York Times 1978, Je 6, III, 3:3
NO CRIT AVAIL
(*Published libretto*) NA
(*Published sheet music*) NA (MJQ Music)
(*Original cast recording*) NA
(*Agent/contact*)   Don Evans   J. Lloyd Grant
                        32 Oak Lane   505 Eighth Avenue
                        Trenton, NJ 08618   New York, N.Y.   10001
(*Libretto, Orchestrations*) Same as (*Agent/contact*)
(*Music*) LC MJQ Music Inc. 12Apr78 PAu–16–087; same as (*Agent/contact*)

THE MALADE WHO WAS IMAGINARY
See *'TOINETTE*

MAN BETTER MAN
(*Source*) Original
(*Book*) Errol Hill
(*Lyrics*) Errol Hill
(*Music*) Coleridge–Taylor Perkinson
(*Producer*) The Negro Ensemble Company
St. Marks Playhouse   off–Broadway
July 2, 1969   23 performances
(*Stars*) Esther Rolle
Theatre World 69–70, p. 140
Best Plays 69–70, pp. 336–37
New Yorker 45:58 Jl 12 '69
New York Times 1969, Jl 3, 22:1
          New York Times 1969, Jl 13, II, 1:1
          New York Times 1969, Jl 13, II, 3:6
NO CRIT AVAIL

(*Published libretto*) In *Three Plays From the Yale School of
       Drama*, Dutton, 1964
(*Published sheet music*) NA
(*Original cast recording*) NA
(*Agent/contact*)   Errol Hill   Coleridge–Taylor Perkinson
                      3 Haskins Road   c/o ASCAP
                      Hanover, NH   03755
(*Libretto*) LC Errol Gaston Hill 15Feb60 DU50459, 26Sep61 DU53995;
       same as (*Agent/contact*)
(*Music, Orchestrations*) Same as (*Agent/contact*)

MAN ON THE MOON*
(*Source*) Original
(*Book*) John Phillips
(*Lyrics*) John Phillips
(*Music*) John Phillips
(*Producer*) Andy Warhol, in association with Richard Turley
The Little Theatre   off–Broadway
January 29, 1975   5 performances
(*Stars*) Monique Van Vooren
Theatre World 74–75, p. 81
Best Plays 74–75, p. 339
New Yorker 50:74 F 10 '75
New York Times 1975, Ja 30, 28:1
NO CRIT AVAIL
(*Published libretto*) NA
(*Published sheet music*) NA (Intergalactic Music, Inc.)
(*Original cast recording*) NA
(*Agent/contact*)   Andy Warhol Estate
                      c/o Leo Castelli Gallery
                      420 W. Broadway
                      New York, N.Y.   10012
(*Libretto, Music, Orchestrations*) Same as (*Agent/contact*)

*Previously titled *AMERICAN MAN ON THE MOON*

MAN WITH A LOAD OF MISCHIEF
(*Source*) *The Man with a Load of Mischief* (play) by Ashley Dukes
(*Book*) Ben Tarver
(*Lyrics*) John Clifton & Ben Tarver
(*Music*) John Clifton
(*Producer*) Donald H. Goldman
Jan Hus Playhouse/Provincetown Playhouse*   off–Broadway
November 6, 1966   240 performances
(*Stars*) Reid Shelton
Theatre World 66–67, p. 119
Best Plays 66–67, pp. 406–7
New Yorker 42:178+ N 19 '66
New York Times 1966, N 7, 65:1
NO CRIT AVAIL
(*Published libretto*) NA
(*Published sheet music*) Scope Music/Vincent Youmans Co., Inc.
(*Original cast recording*) OP Kapp KRL–4508/KRS–5508
(*Agent/contact*) Samuel French, Inc.
(*Libretto, Music, Orchestrations*) Same as (*Agent/contact*)

*Transferred to the Provincetown Playhouse 5/14/67

*MARCH OF THE FALSETTOS**
(*Source*) Original
(*Book*) William Finn
(*Lyrics*) William Finn
(*Music*) William Finn
(*Producer*) Playwrights Horizons
Playwrights Horizons/Westside Arts**   off–Broadway
April 9, 1981   298 performances
(*Stars*) Michael Rupert
Theatre World 80–81, p. 142
Best Plays 80–81, p. 423
NY 14:59–60 Ap 27 '81

NY il 14:31–3 Je 8 '81

New Yorker 57:144–5 My 18 '81

Time 118:72 Ag 3 '81

New York Times 1981, ill, Ap 10, III, 3:1

New York Times 1981, Ap 26, II, 3:1

NO CRIT AVAIL

(*Published libretto*) Samuel French, Inc., 1981

(*Published sheet music*) NA

(*Original cast recording*) DRG Records SBL–12581

(*Agent/contact*) Samuel French, Inc.

(*Libretto, Orchestrations*) Same as (*Agent/contact*)

(*Music*) LC William Finn 22Sep82 PA–150–596;

   same as (*Agent/contact*)

*Previously presented under title *FOUR JEWS IN A ROOM BITCHING*

**Moved to Westside Arts/Cheryl Crawford Theatre on 11/9/81

MARDI GRAS!

(*Source*) Original

(*Book*) Sig Herzig

(*Lyrics*) Carmen Lombardo & John Jacob Loeb

(*Music*) Carmen Lombardo & John Jacob Loeb

(*Producer*) Guy Lombardo

Jones Beach Theater   off–Broadway

June 26, 1965   68 performances

(*Stars*) Juanita Hall, Ruth Kobart, Phil Leeds

NO ENTRY AVAIL

Best Plays 65–66, pp. 417–18

America 113:190 Ag 21 '65

America 115:140 Ag 6 '66

Sat R 49:48 Jl 30 '66

New York Times 1965, Je 28, 33:2

New York Times 1966, Ja 16, VII, 2:1

NO CRIT AVAIL
(*Published libretto*) NA
(*Published sheet music*) Lombardo Music, Inc.
(*Original cast recording*) NA
(*Agent/contact*)   Carmen Lombardo Estate   Sig Herzig
                           c/o Fred E. Ahlert, Jr.   11924 Montana Avenue
                           8150 Beverly Blvd.   Brentwood, CA   90049
                           Los Angeles, CA   90048

                           John Jacob Loeb Estate
                           c/o Fred E. Ahlert, Jr.
                           8150 Beverly Blvd.
                           Los Angeles, CA   90048
(*Libretto*) LC Siegfried M. Herzig 24Mar65 DU62532;
        same as (*Agent/contact*)
(*Music, Orchestrations*) Same as (*Agent/contact*)

THE MATINEE KIDS
(*Source*) Original
(*Book*) Garry Bormet & Gary Gardner
(*Lyrics*) Garry Bormet & Gary Gardner
(*Music*) Brian Lasser
(*Producer*) Fisher Theatre Foundation
BTA Theatre   off–Broadway
March 10, 1981   15 performances
(*Stars*) NA
Theatre World 80–81, p. 94
NO ENTRY AVAIL
NO CRIT AVAIL
NO CRIT AVAIL
NO CRIT AVAIL
(*Published libretto*) NA
(*Published sheet music*) NA
(*Original cast recording*) NA

(*Agent/contact*)   Garry Bormet   Gary Gardner
                        58 Bank Street   c/o UCLA Theater Arts Dept.
                        New York, N.Y. 10014 Los Angeles, CA   90024
(*Libretto, Music, Orchestrations*) Same as (*Agent/contact*)

A MATTER OF OPINION
(*Source*) Original
(*Book*) Mary Elizabeth Hauer
(*Lyrics*) Mary Elizabeth Hauer
(*Music*) Harold Danko & John Jacobson
(*Producer*) Miracle Expressions, Inc.
Players Theater   off–Broadway
September 30, 1980   8 performances
(*Stars*) NA
Theatre World 80–81, p. 83
Best Plays 80–81, p. 392
NO CRIT AVAIL
New York Times 1980, O 2, III, 18:5
NO CRIT AVAIL
(*Published libretto*) NA
(*Published sheet music*) NA
(*Original cast recording*) NA
(*Agent/contact*)   Mary E. Hauer   Harold Danko
                        1372–79th Street   344 W. 72nd Street
                        Brooklyn, N.Y. 11228 New York, N.Y.   10023
(*Libretto*) LC Mary Elizabeth Hauer 16Mar79 PAu–91–640;
            same as (*Agent/contact*)
(*Music, Orchestrations*) Same as (*Agent/contact*)

A MATTER OF TIME
(*Source*) Original
(*Book*) Hap Schlein & Russell Leib
(*Lyrics*) Philip F. Margo

(*Music*) Philip F. Margo
(*Producer*) Jeff Britton
Playhouse Theater   off–Broadway
April 27, 1975   1 performance
(*Stars*) NA
Theatre World 74–75, p. 87
Best Plays 74–75, p. 381
NO CRIT AVAIL
New York Times 1975, Ap 28, 37:1
NO CRIT AVAIL
(*Published libretto*) NA
(*Published sheet music*) NA
(*Original cast recording*) NA
(*Agent/contact*)   Jeff Britton   Philip Margo
                         1501 Broadway   1438 N. Gower Street
                         New York, N.Y.   10036 Los Angeles, CA 90028
(*Libretto*) LC Hap Schlein & Russell Leib 8Nov73 DU88673;
        same as (*Agent/contact*)
(*Music, Orchestrations*) Same as (*Agent/contact*)

MEET PETER GRANT*
(*Source*) *Peer Gynt* (play) by Henrik Ibsen
(*Book*) Elliot Arluck
(*Lyrics*) Elliot Arluck
(*Music*) Ted Harris
(*Producer*) Lee Bergman
Folksbiene Theatre   off–Broadway
May 8, 1961   33 performances
(*Stars*) David Hartman
NO ENTRY AVAIL
NO ENTRY AVAIL
New Yorker 37:120 My 20 '61
New York Times 1961, My 11, 41:4
NO CRIT AVAIL
(*Published libretto*) NA

(*Published sheet music*) NA (Shapiro, Bernstein & Co.)

(*Original cast recording*) NA

(*Agent/contact*)   Ted Harris   Elliot Arluck

                         1237 Avenue Z   c/o ASCAP

                         Brooklyn, N.Y.   11235

(*Libretto*) LC Theodore Harris & Elliot Arluck 24Mar59 DU48686 as

        THE LEGEND OF PETER GRANT; same as (*Agent/contact*)

(*Music, Orchestrations*) Same as (*Agent/contact*)

*Previously titled *THE LEGEND OF PETER GRANT*

MISS EMILY ADAM

(*Source*) "Rosemary and the Planet" (short story) by Winthrop Palmer

(*Book*) James Lipton

(*Lyrics*) James Lipton

(*Music*) Sol Berkowitz

(*Producer*) Paul E. Davis & Stanley G. Weiss, in association

        with Winthrop Palmer

Theatre Marquee   off—Broadway

March 29, 1960   21 performances

(*Stars*) NA

Theatre World 59–60, p. 159

NO ENTRY AVAIL

NO CRIT AVAIL

New York Times 1960, Mr 30, 43:1

NO CRIT AVAIL

(*Published libretto*) NA

(*Published sheet music*) Chappell

(*Original cast recording*) NA

(*Agent/contact*)   James Lipton   Sol Berkowitz

                         c/o DG, Inc.   46–36 Hamford Street

                                                   Douglaston, N.Y.   11362

(*Libretto, Music, Orchestrations*) Same as (*Agent/contact*)

MISS TRUTH

(*Source*) Original

(*Book*) Glory Van Scott

(*Lyrics*) Glory Van Scott

(*Music*) Glory Van Scott

(*Producer*) Apollo Theatre

Apollo Theatre   off–Broadway

June 5, 1979   16 performances

(*Stars*) NA

Theatre World 79–80, p. 82

NO ENTRY AVAIL

NO CRIT AVAIL

NO CRIT AVAIL

New York Times 1979, Jl 23, III, 17:1

(*Published libretto*) NA

(*Published sheet music*) NA

(*Original cast recording*) NA

(*Agent/contact*)   Dr. Glory Van Scott

                       c/o Hayes Registry

                       701 Seventh Avenue

                       New York, N.Y.   10036

(*Libretto, Music, Orchestrations*) Same as (*Agent/contact*)

MOD DONNA

(*Source*) Original

(*Book*) Myrna Lamb

(*Lyrics*) Myrna Lamb

(*Music*) Susan Hulsman Bingham

(*Producer*) New York Shakespeare Festival

Public Theater   off–Broadway

May 3, 1970   56 performances

(*Stars*) April Shawhan

Theatre World 69–70, p. 150

Best Plays 69–70, pp. 345–46

Harp Baz 103:6+ Jl '70

New Yorker 46:107 My 16 '70

Newsweek il 75:121 My 18 '70

Time il 95:62 My 25 '70

New York Times 1970, My 4, 48:1

New York Times 1970, My 10, II, 1:1

NO CRIT AVAIL

(*Published libretto*) In *The Mod Donna and Scyklon Z: Plays of Women's Liberation*, Pathfinder Press, Inc., 1971

(*Published sheet music*) NA

(*Original cast recording*) NA

(*Agent/contact*)   Myrna Lamb

400 W. 43rd Street

New York, N.Y.   10036

(*Libretto*) NYPL NCOF+; LC Myrna Lamb & Susan Hulsman Bingham 16Feb70 DU76414, 14Jul70 DU77674; same as (*Agent/contact*)

(*Music, Orchestrations*) Same as (*Agent/contact*)

MONTH OF SUNDAYS

(*Source*) *The Great Git-Away* (play) by Romeo Muller

(*Book*) Romeo Muller

(*Lyrics*) Jules Bass

(*Music*) Maury Laws

(*Producer*) Arthur Rankin, Jr. & Jules Bass

Theatre de Lys   off–Broadway

September 16, 1968   8 performances

(*Stars*) John Bennett Perry

Theatre World 68–69, p. 118

Best Plays 68–69, p. 428

New Yorker 44:89 S 28 '68

New York Times 1968, S 17, 50:1

NO CRIT AVAIL

(*Published libretto*) NA

(*Published sheet music*) NA

(*Original cast recording*) NA

(*Agent/contact*)	Jules Bass	Romeo Muller	Maury Laws
	c/o ASCAP	c/o DG, Inc.	c/o ASCAP

(*Libretto, Music, Orchestrations*) Same as (*Agent/contact*)

MORE THAN YOU DESERVE

(*Source*) Original

(*Book*) Michael Weller

(*Lyrics*) Michael Weller & Jim Steinman

(*Music*) Jim Steinman

(*Producer*) New York Shakespeare Festival Public Theater/Joseph Papp

Public Theater   off–Broadway

November 21, 1973   63 performances

(*Stars*) Fred Gwynne, Meat Loaf, Mary Beth Hurt

Theatre World 73–74, p. 126

Best Plays 73–74, pp. 384–85

New Yorker 49:58+ Ja 14 '74

New York Times 1974, Ja 4, 17:4

     New York Times 1974, Ja 13, II, 3:5

NO CRIT AVAIL

(*Published libretto*) NA

(*Published sheet music*) NA (Casserole Music Corp.)

(*Original cast recording*) NA

(*Agent/contact*)	Joseph Papp	Michael Weller
	c/o Public Theatre	c/o DG, Inc.
	425 Lafayette Street	
	New York, N.Y. 10003	

(*Libretto, Music, Orchestrations*) Same as (*Agent/contact*)

MORNING SUN

(*Source*) Story (title unavailable) by Mary Deasy

(*Book*) Fred Ebb*

(*Lyrics*) Fred Ebb*

(*Music*) Paul Klein

(*Producer*) T. Edward Hambleton & Martin Tahse
Phoenix Theatre   off–Broadway
October 6, 1963   9 performances
(*Stars*) Bert Convy, Patricia Neway
Theatre World 63–64, p. 198
Best Plays 63–64, p. 347
Theatre Arts 48:11+ Ja '64
New York Times 1963, O 7, 36:2
NO CRIT AVAIL
(*Published libretto*) NA
(*Published sheet music*) NA (Sunbeam Music Corp.)
(*Original cast recording*) NA
(*Agent/contact*)   Fred Ebb   Paul Klein
                      c/o DG, Inc.   24 Meter Fens
                                        New Rochelle, N.Y.   10804
(*Libretto, Music, Orchestrations*) Same as (*Agent/contact*)

*At press time, Mr. Ebb was not interested in soliciting further
     productions of this property

MOVIE BUFF

(*Source*) Original
(*Book*) Hiram Taylor
(*Lyrics*) Hiram Taylor & John Raniello
(*Music*) John Raniello
(*Producer*) Free Space Ltd.
Actors Playhouse   off–Broadway
March 14, 1977   22 performances
(*Stars*) NA
Theatre World 76–77, p. 100
Best Plays 76–77, pp. 339–40
NO CRIT AVAIL
New York Times 1977, Mr 15, 42:1
NO CRIT AVAIL
(*Published libretto*) NA

(Published sheet music) NA
(Original cast recording) NA
(Agent/contact)   John Raniello   Hiram Taylor
                121 Madison Avenue   40 First Avenue
                New York, N.Y. 10016   New York, N.Y. 10009
(Libretto, Music, Orchestrations) Same as *(Agent/contact)*

MUSICAL CHAIRS*
(Source) Original
(Book) Barry Berg, Ken Donnelly & Tom Savage
(Lyrics) Tom Savage
(Music) Tom Savage
(Producer) Lesley Savage & Bert Stratford
Rialto Theatre   off–Broadway
May 11, 1980   14 performances
(Stars) Ron Holgate
Theatre World 79–80, p. 67
Best Plays 79–80, pp. 397–98
NO CRIT AVAIL
New York Times 1980, My 15, III, 19:1
NYTC 1980:238
(Published libretto) Samuel French, Inc., 1982
(Published sheet music) NA
(Original cast recording) Original Cast Records OC–8024
(Agent/contact) Samuel French, Inc.
(Libretto) LC Tom Savage & Scott Newborn 1May79 PAu–102–352
      as *HOW'S THE HOUSE?*
(Music) LC Tom Savage 10Nov81 PA–140–039;
      same as *(Agent/contact)*
(Orchestrations) Same as *(Agent/contact)*

*Previously presented off–off–Broadway under the title *HOW'S THE HOUSE?*, book by Barry Berg, Scott Newborn & Tom Savage, music and lyrics by Tom Savage

MY WIFE AND I
(*Source*) Original
(*Book*) Bill Mahoney
(*Lyrics*) Bill Mahoney
(*Music*) Bill Mahoney
(*Producer*) Katydid Productions
Theatre Four   off–Broadway
October 10, 1966   8 performances
(*Stars*) NA
Theatre World 66–67, p. 112
Best Plays 66–67, p. 402
NO CRIT AVAIL
New York Times 1966, O 11, 53:2
NO CRIT AVAIL
(*Published libretto*) NA
(*Published sheet music*) NA
(*Original cast recording*) NA
(*Agent/contact*) NO CONT AVAIL
(*Libretto*) LC William F. Mahoney 19Aug65 DU63720;
       same as (*Agent/contact*)
(*Music, Orchestrations*) Same as (*Agent/contact*)

NEVERTHELESS THEY LAUGH
(*Source*) *He Who Gets Slapped* (play) by Leonid Andreyev
(*Book*) LaRue Watts
(*Lyrics*) LaRue Watts
(*Music*) Richard Lescsak
(*Producer*) Lambs Club
Lambs Club Theatre   off–Broadway
March 24, 1971   5 performances
(*Stars*) Bernadette Peters, David Holliday
Theatre World 70–71, p. 105
NO ENTRY AVAIL
NO CRIT AVAIL
NO CRIT AVAIL

NO CRIT AVAIL
(*Published libretto*) NA
(*Published sheet music*) NA
(*Original cast recording*) NA
(*Agent/contact*)   LaRue Watts
                       c/o DG, Inc.
(*Libretto*) LC LaRue Watts & Richard Lescsak 20Jul67 DU69316,
       29Jul71 DU80741; same as (*Agent/contact*)
(*Music, Orchestrations*) Same as (*Agent/contact*)

NEW YORK CITY STREET SHOW
(*Source*) Original
(*Book*) Peter Copani
(*Lyrics*) Peter Copani
(*Music*) Peter Copani
(*Producer*) Peter Copani & Victor Papa
Actors Playhouse   off–Broadway
April 28, 1977   20 performances
(*Stars*) NA
Theatre World 76–77, p. 104
Best Plays 76–77, pp. 341–42
New Yorker 53:59+ My 9 '77
NO CRIT AVAIL
NO CRIT AVAIL
(*Published libretto*) NA
(*Published sheet music*) NA
(*Original cast recording*) NA
(*Agent/contact*)   Peter Copani
                       59 Carmine Street
                       New York, N.Y. 10014
(*Libretto*) LC Peter Copani 6Sep78 PAu–59–942;
       same as (*Agent/contact*)
(*Music, Orchestrations*) Same as (*Agent/contact*)

NORTHCHESTER
See *THE RAINBOW RAPE TRICK*

NOT TONIGHT, BENVENUTO
(*Source*) Original
(*Book*) Virgil Engeran
(*Lyrics*) Virgil Engeran
(*Music*) Virgil Engeran
(*Producer*) Jim Payne & Virgil Engeran
Carter Theater   off–Broadway
June 5, 1979   1 performance
(*Stars*) NA
Theatre World 79–80, p. 82
Best Plays 79–80, p. 411
NO CRIT AVAIL
NO CRIT AVAIL
NO CRIT AVAIL
(*Published libretto*) NA
(*Published sheet music*) NA
(*Original cast recording*) NA
(*Agent/contact*)   Virgil Enterprises
                       325 W. 45th Street, Ste #800
                       New York, N.Y.   10036
(*Libretto, Music, Orchestrations*) Same as (*Agent/contact*)

NOW IS THE TIME FOR ALL GOOD MEN*
(*Source*) Original
(*Book*) Gretchen Cryer
(*Lyrics*) Gretchen Cryer
(*Music*) Nancy Ford
(*Producer*) David Cryer & Albert Poland
Theatre de Lys**   off–Broadway
September 26, 1967   112 performances
(*Stars*) David Cryer

Theatre World 67–68, p. 106

Best Plays 67–68, pp. 386–87

America 117:421–2 O 14 '67

     New Yorker 43:133–4 O 7 '67

New York Times 1967, S 27, 42:1

     New York Times 1967, O 27, 49:1

NO CRIT AVAIL

(*Published libretto*) Samuel French, Inc., 1967

(*Published sheet music*) NA (Kiki Music Corp.)

(*Original cast recording*) OP Columbia OL–6730/OS–3130

(*Agent/contact*) Samuel French, Inc.

(*Libretto*) NYPL NCOF+, RM8179; LC (Performing Arts Reading Room)
     ML50/.F714N72

(*Music*) LC (Performing Arts Reading Room) ML50/.F714N72;
     same as (*Agent/contact*)

(*Orchestrations*) Same as (*Agent/contact*)

*Previously titled ***WHAT'S IN THE WIND?***

**Videotaped performance of 1971 Equity Library production available
     at NYPL Billy Rose Collection, Lincoln Center, NCOV 8

O MARRY ME!

(*Source*) *She Stoops to Conquer* (play) by Oliver Goldsmith

(*Book*) Lola Pergament

(*Lyrics*) Lola Pergament

(*Music*) Robert Kessler

(*Producer*) Lily Turner

Gate Theatre   off–Broadway

October 27, 1961   21 performances

(*Stars*) Elly Stone

Theatre World 61–62, p. 130

Best Plays 61–62, pp. 310–11

New Yorker 37:130–2 N 4 '61

New York Times 1961, O 28, 13:1

NO CRIT AVAIL

(*Published libretto*) Chappell & Co., Ltd. (London), 1965

(*Published sheet music*) Chappell & Co., Ltd.

(*Original cast recording*) NA

(*Agent/contact*) Music Theatre International

(*Libretto, Music, Orchestrations*) Same as (*Agent/contact*)

O SAY CAN YOU SEE! (See *BUY BONDS, BUSTER!*)*

(*Source*) Original

(*Book*) Bill Conklin & Bob Miller

(*Lyrics*) Bill Conklin & Bob Miller

(*Music*) Jack Holmes**

(*Producer*) Greenville Company

Provincetown Playhouse   off–Broadway

October 8, 1962   24 performances

(*Stars*) Marcia Rodd

Theatre World 62–63, p. 139

Best Plays 62–63, p. 315

New Yorker 38:86+ O 20 '62

New York Times 1962, O 9, 45:1

NO CRIT AVAIL

(*Published libretto*) NA

(*Published sheet music*) NA (Sunbeam Music Corp.)

(*Original cast recording*) Sunbeam XTV–87195/6

(*Agent/contact*)   Jack Holmes   Bob Miller

                         65 W. 95th Street   c/o ASCAP

                         New York, N.Y. 10025

(*Libretto*) LC Robert D. Miller & William Conklin 14Sep61 DU53924;

      same as (*Agent/contact*)

(*Music, Orchestrations*) Same as (*Agent/contact*)

**O SAY CAN YOU SEE!* was rewritten and played off–Broadway

      6/04/72 under the title *BUY BONDS, BUSTER!*

**Mr. Holmes advises that only the latest version of *O SAY*

      CAN YOU SEE! is available for production

ODODO (TRUTH)
(*Source*) Original
(*Book*) Joseph A. Walker
(*Lyrics*) Joseph A. Walker
(*Music*) Dorothy A. Dinroe
(*Producer*) Negro Ensemble Company
St. Marks Playhouse   off–Broadway
November 24, 1970   48 performances
(*Stars*) Roxie Roker, Garrett Morris
Theatre World 70–71, p. 138
Best Plays 70–71, p. 337
New Yorker 46:162 D 5 '70
New York Times 1970, N 25, 26:1
          New York Times 1970, D 6, II, 5:1
NYTC 1970:124
(*Published libretto*) NA
(*Published sheet music*) NA
(*Original cast recording*) NA
(*Agent/contact*) Samuel French, Inc.
(*Libretto, Music, Orchestrations*) Same as (*Agent/contact*)

OF MICE AND MEN
(*Source*) *Of Mice and Men* (novel and play) by John Steinbeck
(*Book*) Ira J. Bilowit & Wilson Lehr
(*Lyrics*) Ira J. Bilowit
(*Music*) Alfred Brooks
(*Producer*) Ira J. Bilowit & Unicorn Productions
Provincetown Playhouse   off–Broadway
December 4, 1958   37 performances
(*Stars*) Art Lund, Jo Sullivan
Theatre World 58–59, p. 150
NO ENTRY AVAIL
New Yorker 34:109–11 D 13 '58
New York Times 1958, D 5, 38:1
NO CRIT AVAIL

(*Published libretto*) NA
(*Published sheet music*) NA
(*Original cast recording*) NA
(*Agent/contact*)   Ira J. Bilowit
                         c/o DG, Inc.
(*Libretto*) LC (Performing Arts Reading Room) ML50/B87403; LC Ira
        J. Bilowit 17Nov58 DU47996; same as (*Agent/contact*)
(*Music, Orchestrations*) Same as (*Agent/contact*)

OH, JOHNNY

(*Source*) Original
(*Book*) Paul Streitz
(*Lyrics*) Paul Streitz & Gary Cherpakov
(*Music*) Gary Cherpakov
(*Producer*) Paul Streitz, in association with Stephen Harcusz
Players Theater   off–Broadway
January 10, 1982   1 performance
(*Stars*) NA
Theatre World 81–82, p. 60
Best Plays 81–82, pp. 384–85
NO CRIT AVAIL
New York Times 1982, Ja 13, III, 18:6
NO CRIT AVAIL
(*Published libretto*) NA
(*Published sheet music*) NA
(*Original cast recording*) NA
(*Agent/contact*)   Gary Cherpakov
                         c/o ASCAP
(*Libretto, Music*) LC Gary Cherpakov & Paul Streitz 7Jan80
        PAu–164–260; same as (*Agent/contact*)
(*Orchestrations*) Same as (*Agent/contact*)

ON THE GOD–DAMN LOCK–IN!
See *ON THE LOCK–IN*

*ON THE LOCK–IN**
(*Source*) Original
(*Book*) David Langston Smyrl
(*Lyrics*) David Langston Smyrl
(*Music*) David Langston Smyrl
(*Producer*) New York Shakespeare Festival
Public/LuEsther Hall   off–Broadway
April 14, 1977   62 performances
(*Stars*) NA
Theatre World 76–77, p. 142
Best Plays 76–77, p. 337
New Yorker 53:59 My 9 '77
New York Times 1977, Ap 28, III, 23:1
NYTC 1977:225
(*Published libretto*) NA
(*Published sheet music*) NA
(*Original cast recording*) NA
(*Agent/contact*)   David Langston Smyrl   Joseph Papp
                        c/o DG, Inc.   c/o Public Theatre
                                                    425 Lafayette Street
                                                    New York, N.Y.   10003
(*Libretto*) LC David Langston Smyrl 14Jun75 DU95281 as *ON THE
        GOD–DAMN LOCK–IN!*; same as (*Agent/contact*)
(*Music, Orchestrations*) Same as (*Agent/contact*)

*Previously titled *ON THE GOD–DAMN LOCK–IN!*

*PARADISE ISLAND**
(*Source*) Original
(*Book*) Carmen Lombardo & John Jacob Loeb
(*Lyrics*) Carmen Lombardo & John Jacob Loeb
(*Music*) Carmen Lombardo & John Jacob Loeb
(*Producer*) Guy Lombardo
Jones Beach Theatre   off–Broadway

June 22, 1961   75 performances
(*Stars*) Arthur Treacher
NO ENTRY AVAIL
Best Plays 61–62, pp. 303–4
America 105:532 Jl 15 '61
New York Times 1961, Je 24, 11:1
    New York Times 1961, Je 28, 22:1
NO CRIT AVAIL
(*Published libretto*) NA
(*Published sheet music*) Marine Music Corp./Keys Hansen, Inc.
(*Original cast recording*) NA
(*Agent/contact*)   Carmen Lombardo Estate   John Jacob Loeb Estate
        c/o Fred E. Ahlert, Jr.   c/o Fred E. Ahlert, Jr.
        8150 Beverly Blvd.   8150 Beverly Blvd.
        Los Angeles, CA   90048   Los Angeles, CA   90048
(*Libretto*) LC (Performing Arts Reading Room) ML50/.L8422P4 as
    THE LEGEND OF PARADISE ISLAND;
    same as (*Agent/contact*)
(*Music, Orchestrations*) Same as (*Agent/contact*)

*Previously titled *THE LEGEND OF PARADISE ISLAND*

PARTNERS
See *DOUBLE FEATURE*

PEACE
(*Source*) *Peace* (play) by Aristophanes (freely adapted)
(*Book*) Tim Reynolds
(*Lyrics*) Tim Reynolds
(*Music*) Al Carmines
(*Producer*) Albert Poland & Franklin DeBoer
Astor Place Theater   off–Broadway
January 27, 1969   192 performances
(*Stars*) NA

Theatre World 68–69, p. 136

Best Plays 68–69, p. 445

Dance Mag 43:23+ Ap '69
  New Yorker 44:98–100 F 8 '69

New York Times 1969, Ja 28, 49:1
  New York Times 1969, F 16, II, 1:1
  New York Times 1970, S 2, 30:2

NYTC 1969:276

(*Published libretto*) NA

(*Published sheet music*) Caaz Music Comp./Chappell & Co., Inc.

(*Original cast recording*) OP Metromedia MP–33001

(*Agent/contact*) Samuel French, Inc.

(*Libretto, Music, Orchestrations*) Same as (*Agent/contact*)

THE PENNY FRIEND

(*Source*) *A Kiss for Cinderella* (play) by Sir James M. Barrie

(*Book*) William Roy

(*Lyrics*) William Roy

(*Music*) William Roy

(*Producer*) Thomas Hammond

Stage 73   off–Broadway

December 26, 1966   32 performances

(*Stars*) Bernadette Peters

Theatre World 66–67, p. 124

Best Plays 66–67, pp. 408–9

NO CRIT AVAIL

New York Times 1966, D 27, 46:1

NO CRIT AVAIL

(*Published libretto*) NA

(*Published sheet music*) NA

(*Original cast recording*) NA

(*Agent/contact*)   William Roy
                      c/o ASCAP

(*Libretto*) NYPL NCOF+; same as (*Agent/contact*)

(*Music, Orchestrations*) Same as (*Agent/contact*)

PHILEMON*

(*Source*) Original
(*Book*) Tom Jones
(*Lyrics*) Tom Jones
(*Music*) Harvey Schmidt
(*Producer*) Portfolio Productions
Portfolio Studio   off-Broadway
April 8, 1975   48 performances
(*Stars*) NA
Theatre World 74-75, p. 138
Best Plays 74-75, pp. 380-81
NO CRIT AVAIL
New York Times 1975, Ja 7, 28:1
          New York Times 1975, My 4, II, 5:1
NYTC 1975:255
(*Published libretto*) NA
(*Published sheet music*) NA
(*Original cast recording*) OP Gallery OC-1
(*Agent/contact*) Music Theatre International
(*Libretto, Music, Orchestrations*) Same as (*Agent/contact*)

*Subsequently produced on television for *Hollywood Television Theatre*
          (WNET), available at NYPL Billy Rose Collection, Lincoln Center,
          NCOX 117, NCOV 44

PIANO BAR

(*Source*) Original
(*Book*) Doris Willens & Rob Fremont
(*Lyrics*) Doris Willens
(*Music*) Rob Fremont
(*Producer*) Lantern Productions
Westside Theater   off-Broadway
June 8, 1978   125 performances
(*Stars*) Steve Elmore, Kelly Bishop

Theatre World 78–79, p. 67

Best Plays 78–79, pp. 408–9

NY il 11:62 Jl 17 '78

      New Yorker 54:54+ Je 19 '78

New York Times 1978, Je 9, III, 3:5

      New York Times 1978, Je 18, II, 3:1

      New York Times 1978, Jl 20, III, 15:1

NYTC 1978:181

(*Published libretto*) Samuel French, Inc., 1978

(*Published sheet music*) NA

(*Original cast recording*) Original Cast Records OC–7812

(*Agent/contact*) Samuel French, Inc.

(*Libretto*) LC Rob Fremont & Doris Willens 28May76 DU99154,
      11May78 PAu–18–461

(*Music, Orchestrations*) Same as (*Agent/contact*)

PIMPERNEL!

(*Source*) *The Scarlet Pimpernel* (novel) by Baroness Emmuska Orczy

(*Book*) William Kaye

(*Lyrics*) William Kaye

(*Music*) Mimi Stone

(*Producer*) Gerald Krone & Dorothy Olim

Gramercy Arts Theatre   off–Broadway

January 6, 1964   3 performances

(*Stars*) Leila Martin

Theatre World 63–64, p. 211

Best Plays 63–64, pp. 354–55

NO CRIT AVAIL

New York Times 1964, Ja 7, 26:6

NO CRIT AVAIL

(*Published libretto*) NA

(*Published sheet music*) NA

(*Original cast recording*) NA

(*Agent/contact*)   Mimi Stone   William Kaye
                     c/o Flora Roberts   c/o ASCAP
                     157 W. 57th Street
                     New York, N.Y. 10019
(*Libretto, Music, Orchestrations*) Same as (*Agent/contact*)

POP

(*Source*) *King Lear* (play) by William Shakespeare (freely adapted)
(*Book*) Larry Schiff & Chuck Knull
(*Lyrics*) Larry Schiff & Chuck Knull
(*Music*) Donna Cribari
(*Producer*) Brad Gromelski, in association with William Murphy III
Players Theater   off–Broadway
April 3, 1974   1 performances
(*Stars*) NA
Theatre World 73–74, p. 85
Best Plays 72–73, p. 398
NO CRIT AVAIL
New York Times 1974, Ap 4, 54:1
NO CRIT AVAIL
(*Published libretto*) NA
(*Published sheet music*) NA
(*Original cast recording*) NA
(*Agent/contact*)   Brad Gromelski   Donna Cribari
                     45 Hillside Avenue   14 Tower Hill Drive
                     Hastings–on–Hudson, N.Y. Port Chester, N.Y.
                              10706   10573

                     Larry Schiff   Chuck Knull
                     c/o DG, Inc.   c/o DG, Inc.
(*Libretto*) LC Lawrence L. Schiff & Charles H. Knull 22Apr74
         DU90179, 17Apr72 DU83129, 20Nov72 DP8224;
         same as (*Agent/contact*)
(*Music, Orchestrations*) Same as (*Agent/contact*)

THE PRINCE AND THE PAUPER

(*Source*) *The Prince and the Pauper* (novel) by Mark Twain

(*Book*) Verna Tomasson

(*Lyrics*) Verna Tomasson

(*Music*) George Fischoff

(*Producer*) Joseph Beinhorn

Judson Hall   off–Broadway

October 12, 1963   158 performances

(*Stars*) NA

NO ENTRY AVAIL

Best Plays 63–64, p. 348

NO CRIT AVAIL

NO CRIT AVAIL

NO CRIT AVAIL

(*Published libretto*) NA

(*Published sheet music*) Felsted Music Corp./Keys Pop Song Distrib.

(*Original cast recording*) OP London AM–28001/AMS–98001; OP Pickwick
       SPC–3204 (Original Television Cast)

(*Agent/contact*)   George Fischoff Music Co.   Verna Tomasson Safran

                  61–45 98th Street, #4E   230 Park Place

                  Rego Park, N.Y. 11374   Brooklyn, N.Y. 11238

                  Felsted Music Corp.

                  539 W. 25th Street

                  New York, N.Y. 10001

                  Attn: Carolyn Kalitt

(*Libretto*) LC (Performing Arts Reading Room) ML50/.F545P72;
     same as (*Agent/contact*)

(*Music, Orchestrations*) Same as (*Agent/contact*)

THE PRODIGAL SISTER

(*Source*) Original

(*Book*) J.E. Franklin

(*Lyrics*) J.E. Franklin & Micki Grant

(*Music*) Micki Grant
(*Producer*) Woodie King, Jr.
Theatre de Lys   off–Broadway
November 25, 1974   42 performances
(*Stars*) NA
Theatre World 74–75, p. 75
Best Plays 74–75, pp. 369–70
New Yorker 50:69–70 D 9 '74
New York Times 1974, Jl 6, 42:1
        New York Times 1974, N 26, 30:1
NYTC 1974:124
(*Published libretto*) Samuel French, Inc., 1974
(*Published sheet music*) NA (Fiddleback Music Pub. Co., Inc.)
(*Original cast recording*) NA
(*Agent/contact*) Samuel French, Inc.
(*Libretto, Music, Orchestrations*) Same as (*Agent/contact*)

PROMENADE
(*Source*) Original
(*Book*) Maria Irene Fornes
(*Lyrics*) Maria Irene Fornes
(*Music*) Al Carmines
(*Producer*) Edgar Lansbury & Joseph Beruh
Promenade Theatre   off–Broadway
June 4, 1969   259 performances
(*Stars*) Madeline Kahn, Alice Playten
Theatre World 69–70, p. 86
Best Plays 69–70, pp. 333–34
Life 67:8 Ag 1 '69
        Nation 208:837 Je 30 '69
        New Yorker 45:63 Jl 5 '69
        Newsweek il 73:107 Je 16 '69
New York Times 1969, Je 5, 56:1
        New York Times 1969, Je 15, II, 1:1
NYTC 1969:213

(Published libretto) In *The New Underground Theatre*, Bantam,
        1968; in *Promenade & Other Plays*, Winter House, 1971;
        in *Great Rock Musicals*, Stein and Day, 1979
(Published sheet music) Caaz Music Co.
(Original cast recording) OP RCA LSO–1161
(Agent/contact) Samuel French, Inc.
(Libretto) NYPL RM695, RM4574, NCOF+ 73–1865; same as *(Agent/contact)*
(Music, Orchestrations) Same as *(Agent/contact)*

RAINBOW
(Source) Original
(Book) James & Ted Rado
(Lyrics) James Rado
(Music) James Rado
(Producer) James & Ted Rado
Orpheum Theatre   off–Broadway
December 18, 1972   48 performances
(Stars) Meat Loaf
Theatre World 72–73, p. 107
Best Plays 72–73, pp. 359–60
New Yorker 48:47 D 30 '72
New York Times 1972, D 19, 50:3
NO CRIT AVAIL
(Published libretto) NA
(Published sheet music) NA (Chappell & Co.)
(Original cast recording) NA
(Agent/contact)   James Rado
                         c/o DG, Inc.
(Libretto, Music, Orchestrations) Same as *(Agent/contact)*

THE RAINBOW RAPE TRICK*
(Source) Original
(Book) Greg Reardon

(*Lyrics*) Greg Reardon & Ann K. Lipson

(*Music*) Ann K. Lipson

(*Producer*) Hyperion Productions

Bert Wheeler Theatre   off–Broadway

April 13, 1975   4 performances

(*Stars*) NA

Theatre World 74–75, p. 85

NO ENTRY AVAIL

NO CRIT AVAIL

NO CRIT AVAIL

NO CRIT AVAIL

(*Published libretto*) NA

(*Published sheet music*) NA

(*Original cast recording*) NA

(*Agent/contact*)   Greg Reardon
                      335 W. 84th Street
                      New York, N.Y.   10024

(*Libretto*) LC Ann K. Lipson & Gregory Reardon 15Jan73 DU85794
        as **NORTHCHESTER**; same as (*Agent/contact*)

(*Music, Orchestrations*) Same as (*Agent/contact*)

*Previously titled **NORTHCHESTER**

*REALLY ROSIE**

(*Source*) "The Sign on Rosie's Door" (short story) and *The
        Nutshell Library* (collection) by Maurice Sendak

(*Book*) Maurice Sendak

(*Lyrics*) Maurice Sendak

(*Music*) Carole King

(*Producer*) John H. P. Davis & Sheldon Riss, in association with
        Alexander S. Bowers & The Chelsea Theater Center

Chelsea Theater Center Upstairs Theater/
        American Place Theatre**   off–Broadway

October 14, 1980   274 performances

(*Stars*) NA

Theatre World 80–81, p. 84

Best Plays 80–81, p. 400

NY 13:49–50 O 27 '80

New York Times 1980, O 15, III, 21:5

NO CRIT AVAIL

(*Published libretto*) *Maurice Sendak's Really Rosie: Starring the*
        Nutshell Kids, Harper & Row, 1975; Samuel French, Inc., 1986

(*Published sheet music*) Colgems Music Corp.

(*Original cast recording*) Caedmon TRS–368; Ode SP–77027 (Original
        Television Cast)

(*Agent/contact*) Samuel French, Inc.

(*Libretto, Music, Orchestrations*) Same as (*Agent/contact*)

*Book chronicling the making of *REALLY ROSIE* entitled
        The Making of a Musical, Crown, 1982; videotaped performance of
        Musical Theatre Lab production at the Kennedy Center available at
        NYPL Billy Rose Collection, Lincoln Center, NCOV 155

**Transferred to the American Place Theater 11/26/80

THE RED WHITE AND BLACK

(*Source*) Original

(*Book*) Eric Bentley

(*Lyrics*) Eric Bentley

(*Music*) Brad Burg

(*Producer*) Donald Goldman

Players Theater   off–Broadway

March 30, 1971   1 performance

(*Stars*) Marilyn Sokol

Theatre World 70–71, p. 106

Best Plays 70–71, p. 347

NO CRIT AVAIL

New York Times 1971, Mr 6, 20:1

        New York Times 1971, Mr 31, 37:1

NO CRIT AVAIL
(*Published libretto*) NA
(*Published sheet music*) NA
(*Original cast recording*) NA
(*Agent/contact*)   Eric Bentley
                       194 Riverside Drive
                       New York, N.Y.   10025
(*Libretto, Orchestrations*) Same as (*Agent/contact*)
(*Music*) LC Bradley M. Burg 15May72 EU331933;
        same as (*Agent/contact*)

REUNION

(*Source*) Original
(*Book*) Melvin H. Freedman & Robert Kornfeld
(*Lyrics*) Melvin H. Freedman & Robert Kornfeld
(*Music*) Ron Roullier/additional songs by Carly Simon
        & Lucy Simon
(*Producer*) Sally E. Parry
The Cubiculo   off–off–Broadway
May 12, 1978   12 performances
(*Stars*) NA
Theatre World 77–78, p. 89
Best Plays 77–78, p. 463
NO CRIT AVAIL
NO CRIT AVAIL
NO CRIT AVAIL
(*Published libretto*) NA
(*Published sheet music*) NA
(*Original cast recording*) NA
(*Agent/contact*)

Melvin H. Freedman	Robert Kornfeld	Ron Roullier
5 White Street	c/o DG, Inc.	c/o DG, Inc.
New York, N.Y. 10013		

(*Libretto*) LC Robert J. Kornfeld & Melvin H. Freedman 7Apr76
        DU98438; same as (*Agent/contact*)
(*Music, Orchestrations*) Same as (*Agent/contact*)

RHINESTONE
(*Source*) Original
(*Book*) Bill Gunn
(*Lyrics*) Bill Gunn
(*Music*) Sam Waymon
(*Producer*) Richard Allen Center (Hazel J. Bryant, producer)
Richard Allen Center   off–off–Broadway
November 16, 1982   20 performances
(*Stars*) NA
Theatre World 82–83, p. 84
NO ENTRY AVAIL
NO CRIT AVAIL
New York Times 1982, N 23, III, 11:5
NO CRIT AVAIL
(*Published libretto*) NA
(*Published sheet music*) NA (Annubis Music)
(*Original cast recording*) NA
(*Agent/contact*) NO CONT AVAIL
(*Libretto, Orchestrations*) Same as (*Agent/contact*)
(*Music*) LC Annubis Music 26Dec78 PAu–84–113;
        same as (*Agent/contact*)

RIDE THE WINDS
(*Source*) Original
(*Book*) John Driver
(*Lyrics*) John Driver
(*Music*) John Driver
(*Producer*) Berta Walker & Bill Tchakirides
Bijou Theatre   off–Broadway
May 16, 1974   3 performances

(*Stars*) NA

Theatre World 73–74, p. 91

Best Plays 72–73, pp. 367–68

New York Times 1974, My 17, 32:5

NO CRIT AVAIL

(*Published libretto*) NA

(*Published sheet music*) Screen Gems–Columbia Pubs.

(*Original cast recording*) NA

(*Agent/contact*)   John Driver

                          c/o Helen Merrill Agency

                          337 W. 22nd Street

                          New York, N.Y.   10011

                          Attn: William Craver

(*Libretto, Music, Orchestrations*) Same as (*Agent/contact*)

RONDELAY*

(*Source*) *La Ronde* (play) by Arthur Schnitzler

(*Book*) Jerry Douglas

(*Lyrics*) Jerry Douglas

(*Music*) Hal Jordan

(*Producer*) Rick Hobard

Hudson West Theatre   off–Broadway

November 5, 1969   11 performances

(*Stars*) Carole Demas

Theatre World 69–70, p. 108

Best Plays 69–70, p. 345

NO CRIT AVAIL

New York Times 1969, N 6, 55:1

NO CRIT AVAIL

(*Published libretto*) NA

(*Published sheet music*) NA

(*Original cast recording*) NA

(*Agent/contact*)   Jerry Douglas   Rick Hobard

                      890 West End Avenue   234 W. 44th Street

                      New York, N.Y.   10025   New York, N.Y.   10036

(*Libretto*) NYPL RM4476; LC Jerry Douglas & Hal Jordan 21Mar66
       DU65386 as *ROUNDELAY*; same as (*Agent/contact*)
(*Music, Orchestrations*) Same as (*Agent/contact*)

*Previously titled *ROUNDELAY*

ROSA

(*Source*) *Rosa* (play) by Brenda Forbes
(*Book*) William Archibald
(*Lyrics*) William Archibald
(*Music*) Baldwin Bergersen
(*Producer*) Wendell Minnick

St. Clement's Theatre	off–off–Broadway
May 10, 1978	12 performances

(*Stars*) NA
Theatre World 77–78, p. 87
Best Plays 77–78, p. 466
NO CRIT AVAIL
NO CRIT AVAIL
NO CRIT AVAIL
(*Published libretto*) NA
(*Published sheet music*) NA
(*Original cast recording*) NA

(*Agent/contact*)	William Archibald Estate	Baldwin Bergersen
	c/o Samuel French, Inc.	c/o DG, Inc.

(*Libretto*) LC Baldwin Bergersen 22Dec75 DU97453;
       same as (*Agent/contact*)
(*Music, Orchestrations*) Same as (*Agent/contact*)

ROUNDELAY
See *RONDELAY*

RUMPELSTILTSKIN
See *HALF–PAST WEDNESDAY*

SAINTS
(*Source*) Original
(*Book*) Merle Kessler
(*Lyrics*) Merle Kessler
(*Music*) William Penn
(*Producer*) Musical Theatre Lab
Good Shepherd–Faith Church   off–Broadway
June 30, 1976   10 performances
(*Stars*) Marti Rolph
Theatre World 76–77, p. 89
NO ENTRY AVAIL
NO CRIT AVAIL
NO CRIT AVAIL
NO CRIT AVAIL
(*Published libretto*) NA
(*Published sheet music*) NA
(*Original cast recording*) NA
(*Agent/contact*)   William Penn
                       11800 Three Oaks Trail
                       Austin, TX   78759
(*Libretto*) LC William Penn & Merle Kessler 2Jan76 DU97265;
        same as (*Agent/contact*)
(*Music, Orchestrations*) Same as (*Agent/contact*)

SALAD DAYS
(*Source*) Original
(*Book*) Julian Slade & Dorothy Reynolds
(*Lyrics*) Julian Slade & Dorothy Reynolds
(*Music*) Julian Slade
(*Producer*) Nicholas Benton, Stanley Flink, William Freedman
        & Barry Morse

Barbizon–Plaza Theatre*   off–Broadway*
November 10, 1958   80 performances
(*Stars*) NA
Theatre World 58–59, p. 143
NO ENTRY AVAIL
Cath World 188:418 F '59
       Dance Mag il 38:18 F '59
       New Yorker 34:103–4 N 22 '58
       Sat R 41:24 N 29 '58
       Theatre Arts il 43:65 Ja '59
New York Times 1955, N 13, II, 3:1
       New York Times 1958, N 11, 24:1
NO CRIT AVAIL
(*Published libretto*) Samuel French, Ltd. (London), 1961
(*Published sheet music*) Francis Day & Hunter, Ltd. (London)
(*Original cast recording*) OP Quality(E) V–1570, Oriole(E) MG–20004,
       RE Embassy(E) EMB–31046, London(E) 5474 (Original London Cast);
       That's Entertainment(E) TER–1018 (London Revival Cast)
(*Agent/contact*) Tams–Witmark Music Library
(*Libretto, Music, Orchestrations*) Same as (*Agent/contact*)

*Previously and subsequently produced in London

SALVATION
(*Source*) Original
(*Book*) Peter Link & C.C. Courtney
(*Lyrics*) Peter Link & C.C. Courtney
(*Music*) Peter Link & C.C. Courtney
(*Producer*) David Black
Jan Hus Playhouse   off–Broadway
September 24, 1969   239 performances
(*Stars*) Barry Bostwick, Bette Midler (replacements)
Theatre World 69–70, p. 98
Best Plays 69–70, pp. 340–41

Chr Cent 86:1646–7 D 24 '69
> Commonweal 91:534–5 F 13 '70
> Dance Mag 43:84 N '69
> New Yorker 45:114 O 4 '69
> Newsweek il 74:133 O 6 '69
> Sat R 52:26 O 11 '69

New York Times 1969, Mr 13, 53:1
> New York Times 1969, S 25, 55:1
> New York Times 1969, O 5, II, 1:1
> New York Times 1970, F 15, II, 1:1

NYTC 1969:198
(*Published libretto*) NA
(*Published sheet music*) Chappell & Co., Inc.
(*Original cast recording*) OP Capitol SO–337
(*Agent/contact*) Music Theatre International
(*Libretto*) NYPL NCOF+; same as (*Agent/contact*)
(*Music, Orchestrations*) Same as (*Agent/contact*)

SAMBO

(*Source*) Original
(*Book*) Ron Steward
(*Lyrics*) Ron Steward
(*Music*) Ron Steward & Neal Tate
(*Producer*) New York Shakespeare Festival
Public Theater   off–Broadway
December 21, 1969   25 performances
(*Stars*) NA
Theatre World 69–70, p. 150
Best Plays 69–70, pp. 345–46
New Yorker 45:43 Ja 3 '70
New York Times 1969, D 22, 42:1
> New York Times 1970, Ja 11, II, 1:1
> New York Times 1970, Ja 11, II, 3:7
> New York Times 1970, Ja 23, 24:1

NYTC 1969:130

(*Published libretto*) NA

(*Published sheet music*) NA

(*Original cast recording*) NA

(*Agent/contact*)   Ron Steward   Joseph Papp

                  c/o ASCAP   c/o Public Theatre

                                    425 Lafayette Street

                                    New York, N.Y.   10003

(*Libretto, Music, Orchestrations*) Same as (*Agent/contact*)

SANDHOG

(*Source*) "St. Columba and the River" (short story) by Theodore Dreiser

(*Book*) Earl Robinson & Waldo Salt

(*Lyrics*) Earl Robinson & Waldo Salt

(*Music*) Earl Robinson & Waldo Salt

(*Producer*) T. Edward Hambleton, Norris Houghton, Rachel

        Productions, Howard DaSilva & Arnold Perl

Phoenix Theater   off–Broadway

November 23, 1954   48 performances

(*Stars*) Jack Cassidy

Theatre World 54–55, p. 134

Best Plays 54–55, pp. 376–77

America 92:326 D 18 '54

       Cath World 180:308–9 Ja '55

       Nation 179:518 D 11 '54

       New Yorker 30:86+ D 4 '54

       Newsweek 44:84 D 6 '54

       Sat R 38:62 Ja 1 '55

       Theatre Arts il 39:76, 91 F '55

New York Times 1954, N 24, 17:1

NYTC 1954:239

(*Published libretto*) Chappell, 1956

(*Published sheet music*) Chappell & Co., Inc.

(*Original cast recording*) OP Vanguard VRS-9001

(*Agent/contact*)	Earl Robinson	Waldo Salt
	3929 Calle Cita	c/o Fred S. Jamner
	Santa Barbara, CA 93110	760 N. La Cienega Blvd.
		Los Angeles, CA 90069

(*Libretto*) NYPL RM681, NCOF+; same as (*Agent/contact*)

(*Music, Orchestrations*) Same as (*Agent/contact*)

THE SAP OF LIFE

(*Source*) Original
(*Book*) Richard Maltby, Jr.
(*Lyrics*) Richard Maltby, Jr.
(*Music*) David Shire
(*Producer*) Quartet Productions
One Sheridan Square   off–Broadway
October 2, 1961   49 performances
(*Stars*) Jerry Dodge, Kenneth Nelson
Theatre World 61–62, p. 129
Best Plays 61–62, p. 308
New Yorker 37:166 O 14 '61
New York Times 1961, O 3, 44:1
NO CRIT AVAIL
(*Published libretto*) NA
(*Published sheet music*) NA
(*Original cast recording*) Blue Pear Records BP–1002

(*Agent/contact*)	Richard Maltby, Jr.	David Shire
	c/o DG, Inc.	c/o DG, Inc.

(*Libretto, Music, Orchestrations*) Same as (*Agent/contact*)

SAY WHEN!

(*Source*) Original
(*Book*) Keith Winter

(*Lyrics*) Keith Winter
(*Music*) Arnold Goland
(*Producer*) Walter Rosen Scholz
Plaza 9 Theater   off–Broadway
December 4, 1972   7 performances
(*Stars*) NA
NO ENTRY AVAIL
Best Plays 72–73, p. 388
NO CRIT AVAIL
New York Times 1972, D 5, 61:1
NO CRIT AVAIL
(*Published libretto*) NA
(*Published sheet music*) NA (Greenland Music, Inc.)
(*Original cast recording*) NA
(*Agent/contact*)   Arnold Goland
                          c/o ASCAP
(*Libretto*) LC Keith Winter & Arnold Goland 16Oct72 DU84962;
              same as (*Agent/contact*)
(*Music, Orchestrations*) Same as (*Agent/contact*)

SCARLET RIBBONS
See *SHE SHALL HAVE MUSIC*

THE SECRET LIFE OF WALTER MITTY
(*Source*) "The Secret Life of Walter Mitty" (short story) by James Thurber
(*Book*) Joe Manchester & Mervyn Nelson
(*Lyrics*) Earl Schuman
(*Music*) Leon Carr
(*Producer*) Joe Manchester & J.M. Fried
Players Theatre   off–Broadway
October 26, 1964   96 performances
(*Stars*) Cathryn Damon, Eugene Roche

Theatre World 64–65, p. 153

Best Plays 64–65, pp. 345–46

NO CRIT AVAIL

New York Times 1964, O 27, 44:5

NO CRIT AVAIL

(*Published libretto*) Samuel French, Inc., 1968

(*Published sheet music*) April Music, Inc./Cimino Pubs., Inc.

(*Original cast recording*) OP Columbia OL–6320/OS–2720, RE Columbia
    Special Products AOS–2720

(*Agent/contact*) Samuel French, Inc.

(*Libretto*) NYPL RM5635, NCOF+; LC (Performing Arts Reading Room)
    ML50/.C3113S42

(*Music, Orchestrations*) Same as (*Agent/contact*)

SENSATIONS

(*Source*) *Romeo & Juliet* (play) by William Shakespeare (freely
    adapted)

(*Book*) Paul Zakrzewski

(*Lyrics*) Paul Zakrzewski

(*Music*) Wally Harper

(*Producer*) John Bowab & Charles Celian

Theatre Four   off–Broadway

October 25, 1970   16 performances

(*Stars*) John Savage

Theatre World 70–71, p. 79

Best Plays 70–71, p. 335

New Yorker 46:135 N 7 '70

New York Times 1970, O 26, 48:2

NO CRIT AVAIL

(*Published libretto*) NA

(*Published sheet music*) Notable Music Co., Inc.

(*Original cast recording*) NA

(*Agent/contact*)   Wally Harper   Paul Zakrzewski
                      124 W. 79th Street   c/o ASCAP
                      New York, N.Y.   10024

(*Libretto, Music, Orchestrations*) Same as (*Agent/contact*)

SGT. PEPPER'S LONELY HEART'S CLUB BAND ON THE ROAD

(*Source*) "Sgt. Pepper's Lonely Hearts Club Band" (record album)
        featuring The Beatles

(*Book*) Robin Wagner

(*Lyrics*) John Lennon & Paul McCartney

(*Music*) John Lennon & Paul McCartney

(*Producer*) Robert Stigwood, Brian Avnet & Scarab Productions

Beacon Theatre   off–Broadway
November 17, 1974   66 performances

(*Stars*) Ted Neeley

Theatre World 74–75, p. 74

Best Plays 74–75, pp. 329–30

Time il 104:75 D 2 '74

New York Times 1974, N 18, 46:6

NO CRIT AVAIL

(*Published libretto*) NA

(*Published sheet music*) Maclean Music, Inc./Warner Bros. Pubs.,
        Inc.

(*Original cast recording*) NA

(*Agent/contact*)   Tom O'Horgan   Robert Stigwood
                      840 Broadway   Organization
                      New York, N.Y.   10003   1775 Broadway
                                                      New York, N.Y.   10019

(*Libretto, Music, Orchestrations*) Same as (*Agent/contact*)

SEXTET

(*Source*) Original

(*Book*) Harvey Perr & Lee Goldsmith

(*Lyrics*) Lee Goldsmith
(*Music*) Lawrence Hurwit
(*Producer*) Balemar Productions & Lawrence E. Sokol
Bijou Theatre   off–Broadway
March 3, 1974   9 performances
(*Stars*) Jerry Lanning, Dixie Carter
Theatre World 73–74, p. 83
Best Plays 73–74, p. 361
NO CRIT AVAIL
New York Times 1974, Mr 4, 36:1
NO CRIT AVAIL
(*Published libretto*) NA
(*Published sheet music*) NA
(*Original cast recording*) NA
(*Agent/contact*)   Lawrence S. Hurwit   Lee Goldsmith
                         13715 Biscayne Blvd.   c/o DG, Inc.
                         North Miami, FL 33181
(*Libretto, Music, Orchestrations*) Same as (*Agent/contact*)

SHE SHALL HAVE MUSIC*
(*Source*) *The Country Wife* (play) by William Wycherley
(*Book*) Stuart Bishop
(*Lyrics*) Dede Meyer
(*Music*) Dede Meyer
(*Producer*) Stuart Bishop, Dede Meyer & Edwin West
Theatre Marquee   off–Broadway
January 22, 1959   54 performances
(*Stars*) NA
Theatre World 58–59, p. 151
NO ENTRY AVAIL
NO CRIT AVAIL
New York Times 1959, Ja 23, 18:4
NO CRIT AVAIL

(*Published libretto*) NA

(*Published sheet music*) Chappell & Co., Inc.

(*Original cast recording*) OP Unnamed label FR–6205 (Original 1963
     Granville, OH Cast)

(*Agent/contact*)   Dede Meyer
                      c/o ASCAP

(*Libretto*) LC Stuart S. Bishop & Dede C. Meyer 13May57 DU44705,
     3Feb59 DU48355; same as (*Agent/contact*)

(*Music*) LC Deed Meyer 20Feb59 EP127753, 30Apr63 EU769815;
     same as (*Agent/contact*)

(*Orchestrations*) Same as (*Agent/contact*)

*Previously titled *SCARLET RIBBONS*

THE SHOEMAKER AND THE PEDDLER

(*Source*) Original

(*Book*) Armand Aulicino

(*Lyrics*) Armand Aulicino

(*Music*) Frank Fields

(*Producer*) Jullis Productions

East Seventy–Fourth Street Theatre   off–Broadway

October 14, 1960   43 performances

(*Stars*) NA

Theatre World 60–61, p. 133

Best Plays 60–61, pp. 352–53

New Yorker 36:92 O 22 '60

New York Times 1960, O 15, 27:4

NO CRIT AVAIL

(*Published libretto*) NA

(*Published sheet music*) NA (Sunbeam Music Corp.)

(*Original cast recording*) NA

(*Agent/contact*)   Frank Fields   Armand Aulicino
                      c/o ASCAP   255 Elderwood Avenue
                                            Pelham, N.Y.   10803

(*Libretto*) NYPL NCOF+; same as (*Agent/contact*)
(*Music, Orchestrations*) Same as (*Agent/contact*)

SHOEMAKER'S HOLIDAY
(*Source*) *The Shoemaker's Holiday* (play) by Thomas Dekker
(*Book*) Ted Berger
(*Lyrics*) Ted Berger
(*Music*) Mel Marvin
(*Producer*) Ken Costigan, in association with Robert Wissier
Orpheum Theatre			off–Broadway
March 2, 1967			6 performances
(*Stars*) Jerry Dodge
Theatre World 66–67, p. 135
Best Plays 66–67, p. 415
New Yorker 36:92 O 22 '60
	New Yorker 43:127–8+ Mr 11 '67
New York Times 1967, Mr 3, 25:1
	New York Times 1967, Je 3, 19:1
NO CRIT AVAIL
(*Published libretto*) NA
(*Published sheet music*) NA
(*Original cast recording*) NA
(*Agent/contact*)	Mel Marvin
			c/o DG, Inc.
(*Libretto*) LC (Performing Arts Reading Room) ML50/.M3897S5; LC Mel
	Marvin & Ted Berger 23Feb65 DU62377, 23Feb67 DU67901;
	same as (*Agent/contact*)
(*Music, Orchestrations*) Same as (*Agent/contact*)

SHOW ME WHERE THE GOOD TIMES ARE
(*Source*) *The Imaginary Invalid* (*Le Malade Imaginaire*)
	(play) by Molière

(*Book*) Lee Thuna
(*Lyrics*) Rhoda Roberts
(*Music*) Kenneth Jacobson
(*Producer*) Lorin E. Price & Barbara Lee Horn
Edison Theatre   off–Broadway
March 5, 1970   29 performances
(*Stars*) Cathryn Damon, John Bennett Perry
Theatre World 69–70, p. 123
Best Plays 69–70, p. 360
America 122:398 Ap 11 '70
          New Yorker 46:122 Mr 14 '70
New York Times 1970, Mr 6, 32:1
NO CRIT AVAIL
(*Published libretto*) Samuel French, Inc., 1970
(*Published sheet music*) Valando Music, Inc.
(*Original cast recording*) NA
(*Agent/contact*) Samuel French, Inc.
(*Libretto*) NYPL NCOF+
(*Music, Orchestrations*) Same as (*Agent/contact*)

SING MUSE!
(*Source*) Original
(*Book*) Erich Segal
(*Lyrics*) Erich Segal
(*Music*) Joseph Raposo
(*Producer*) Robert D. Feldstein
Van Dam Theatre   off–Broadway
December 6, 1961   39 performances
(*Stars*) Karen Morrow
Theatre World 61–62, p. 142
Best Plays 61–62, p. 315
New Yorker 37:68 Ja 20 '62

New York Times 1961, D 7, 52:1

NO CRIT AVAIL

(*Published libretto*) NA

(*Published sheet music*) Edwin H. Morris & Co., Inc.

(*Original cast recording*) OP Unnamed label CH–1093, RE Blue Pear
    Records BP–1004

(*Agent/contact*)	Erich Segal	Joe Raposo
	c/o Lazarow & Co.	881 Seventh Avenue
	119 W. 57th Street,	New York, N.Y. 10019
	Ste #1106	
	New York, N.Y. 10019	

(*Libretto*) LC Erich W. Segal 10May61 DU53194, 4Jan62 DU54524;
    same as (*Agent/contact*)

(*Music, Orchestrations*) Same as (*Agent/contact*)

SKYLINE

(*Source*) Original

(*Book*) Sonny Casella

(*Lyrics*) Sonny Casella

(*Music*) Sonny Casella

(*Producer*) Flair Theatrical Productions

American Theatre of Actors   off–off–Broadway

January 6, 1983   19 performances

(*Stars*) NA

Theatre World 82–83, p. 88

NO ENTRY AVAIL

NO CRIT AVAIL

NO CRIT AVAIL

NO CRIT AVAIL

(*Published libretto*) NA

(*Published sheet music*) NA (Springfield Music)

(*Original cast recording*) NA

(*Agent/contact*) NO CONT AVAIL

(*Libretto*) LC Springfield Music 17Mar82 PAu–383–463;

       same as (*Agent/contact*)

(*Music, Orchestrations*) Same as (*Agent/contact*)

SLEEPY HOLLOW

See *AUTUMN'S HERE*

SMILE, SMILE, SMILE (See *COMEDY*)*

(*Source*) "The Great Magician" (commedia dell'arte scenario) by

       Basillio Locatelli

(*Book*) Hugo Peretti, Luigi Creatore & George David Weiss**

(*Lyrics*) Hugo Peretti, Luigi Creatore & George David Weiss

(*Music*) Hugo Peretti, Luigi Creatore & George David Weiss

(*Producer*) Stuart Duncan

Eastside Playhouse   off–Broadway

April 4, 1973   7 performances

(*Stars*) NA

Theatre World 72–73, p. 117

Best Plays 72–73, p. 394

NO CRIT AVAIL

New York Times 1973, Ap 5, 51:1

NO CRIT AVAIL

(*Published libretto*) NA

(*Published sheet music*) Music Maximus Ltd./Screen Gems–Columbia

(*Original cast recording*) NA

(*Agent/contact*)

    Hugo Peretti   Luigi Creatore   George David Weiss

    c/o AGAC   c/o ASCAP   c/o DG, Inc.

(*Libretto, Music, Orchestrations*) Same as (*Agent/contact*)

SMILE, SMILE, SMILE was first produced in an earlier version
         entitled *COMEDY* which premiered in pre–Broadway try–out
         11/06/72, but closed before scheduled New York opening

**In all publicity, Hugo Peretti, Luigi Creatore & George David Weiss
         are given authorship credit; however, the Stuart Duncan manuscript
         gives Robert Russell sole authorship credit

SMILING THE BOY FELL DEAD*

(*Source*) Original
(*Book*) Ira Wallach
(*Lyrics*) Sheldon Harnick
(*Music*) David Baker
(*Producer*) Theodore Mann & George Kogel
Cherry Lane Theatre   off–Broadway
April 19, 1961   22 performances
(*Stars*) NA
Theatre World 60–61, p. 176
Best Plays 60–61, pp. 360–61
New Yorker 37:94 Ap 29 '61
         Theatre Arts 45:32 Je '61
New York Times 1961, Ap 20, 28:1
NO CRIT AVAIL
(*Published libretto*) NA
(*Published sheet music*) Sunbeam Music Corp./Valando
(*Original cast recording*) OP Sunbeam LB–549, RE Sunbeam LB549
(*Agent/contact*)

Ira Wallach	David Baker	Sheldon Harnick
345 W. 58th Street	c/o Flora Roberts	c/o David Cogan
New York, N.Y.	157 W. 57th Street	350 Fifth Avenue
10019	New York, N.Y.	New York, N.Y.
	10019	10003

(*Libretto, Music, Orchestrations*) Same as (*Agent/contact*)

*Previously presented under title *HORATIO*

SMITH

(*Source*) Original

(*Book*) Dean Fuller, Tony Hendra & Matt Dubey

(*Lyrics*) Matt Dubey & Dean Fuller

(*Music*) Matt Dubey & Dean Fuller

(*Producer*) Jordan Hott, Robert Anglund, Jack Millstein, Iris
        Kopelan & Alexander Bedrosian

Eden Theatre   off–Broadway

May 19, 1973   17 performances

(*Stars*) NA

Theatre World 72–73, p. 122

Best Plays 72–73, pp. 359–60

New Yorker 49:54 My 26 '73

New York Times 1973, My 21, 43:1

NYTC 1973:265

(*Published libretto*) Samuel French, Inc., 1972

(*Published sheet music*) NA

(*Original cast recording*) NA

(*Agent/contact*) Samuel French, Inc.

(*Libretto*) NYPL RM5046

(*Music, Orchestrations*) Same as (*Agent/contact*)

SOAP

(*Source*) Original

(*Book*) David Man

(*Lyrics*) David Man

(*Music*) Aaron Egigian

(*Producer*) Donald Arsenault

Lion Theatre   off–off–Broadway

September 11, 1982   16 performances
(*Stars*) NA
Theatre World 82–83, p. 78
Best Plays 82–83, p. 431
NO CRIT AVAIL
New York Times 1982, S 14, III, 10:5
NO CRIT AVAIL
(*Published libretto*) NA
(*Published sheet music*) NA
(*Original cast recording*) NA
(*Agent/contact*) NO CONT AVAIL
(*Libretto, Music, Orchestrations*) Same as (*Agent/contact*)

SOON

(*Source*) Original
(*Book*) Martin Duberman
(*Lyrics*) Scott Fagan
(*Music*) Joseph Martinez Kookoolis & Scott Fagan
(*Producer*) Bruce W. Stark & Sagittarius Productions, Inc.
Ritz Theater   off–Broadway
January 12, 1971   3 performances
(*Stars*) Barry Bostwick, Richard Gere, Peter Allen, Nell Carter
Theatre World 70–71, p. 89
Best Plays 70–71, p. 303
New Yorker 46:66 Ja 23 '71
New York Times 1971, Ja 13, 29:2
NYTC 1971:393
(*Published libretto*) NA
(*Published sheet music*) NA (Valando Music, Inc.)
(*Original cast recording*) NA
(*Agent/contact*)   Scott Fagan
                      c/o ASCAP
(*Libretto, Music, Orchestrations*) Same as (*Agent/contact*)

SPEED GETS THE POPPIES

(*Source*) Original

(*Book*) Lila Levant

(*Lyrics*) Lorenzo Fuller & Lila Levant

(*Music*) Lorenzo Fuller

(*Producer*) Daffodil Productions

Mercer–Brecht Theater   off–Broadway

July 25, 1972   7 performances

(*Stars*) NA

Theatre World 72–73, p. 94

Best Plays 72–73, p. 369

NO CRIT AVAIL

New York Times 1972, Jl 26, 21:3

NO CRIT AVAIL

(*Published libretto*) NA

(*Published sheet music*) NA

(*Original cast recording*) NA

(*Agent/contact*)   Lila Levant   Lorenzo Fuller

                         c/o DG, Inc.   c/o ASCAP

(*Libretto*) LC Lila Levant & Lorenzo Miller 17Nov71 DU81786,
        25Sep72 DU84798; same as (*Agent/contact*)

(*Music, Orchestrations*) Same as (*Agent/contact*)

STAG MOVIE

(*Source*) Original

(*Book*) David Newburge

(*Lyrics*) David Newburge

(*Music*) Jacques Urbont

(*Producer*) Robert L. Steele

Gate Theatre   off–Broadway

January 3, 1971   89 performances

(*Stars*) Adrienne Barbeau

Theatre World 70–71, p. 88

Best Plays 70–71, p. 340

NO CRIT AVAIL
New York Times 1971, Ja 4, 39:1
NO CRIT AVAIL
(*Published libretto*) NA
(*Published sheet music*) NA
(*Original cast recording*) NA
(*Agent/contact*)   David Newburge   Jack Urbont
                           55 Morton Street   330 W. 72nd Street
                           New York, N.Y.   10014   New York, N.Y.   10023
(*Libretto*) NYPL RM6907; same as (*Agent/contact*)
(*Music, Orchestrations*) Same as (*Agent/contact*)

STREET JESUS
(*Source*) Original
(*Book*) Peter Copani
(*Lyrics*) Peter Copani
(*Music*) Chris Staudt
(*Producer*) The Peoples Performing Company
Provincetown Playhouse   off–off–Broadway
November 16, 1974   52 performances
(*Stars*) NA
Theatre World 74–75, p. 73
Best Plays 74–75, p. 397
NO CRIT AVAIL
NO CRIT AVAIL
NO CRIT AVAIL
(*Published libretto*) NA
(*Published sheet music*) NA
(*Original cast recording*) NA
(*Agent/contact*)   Peter Copani
                           59 Carmine Street
                           New York, N.Y.   10014
(*Libretto*) LC Peter Copani & Chris Staudt 26Jul74 DU91194;
          same as (*Agent/contact*)
(*Music, Orchestrations*) Same as (*Agent/contact*)

THE STREETS OF GOLD
(*Source*) Original
(*Book*) Marvin Gordon
(*Lyrics*) Marvin Gordon
(*Music*) Ted Simons
(*Producer*) Ballet Concepto & The Workmen's Circle
Manhattan Center Ballroom Theatre   off–Broadway
November 25, 1977   12 performances
(*Stars*) NA
Theatre World 77–78, p. 72
NO ENTRY AVAIL
NO CRIT AVAIL
NO CRIT AVAIL
NO CRIT AVAIL
(*Published libretto*) NA
(*Published sheet music*) NA
(*Original cast recording*) NA
(*Agent/contact*)   Marvin Gordon   Ted Simons
                         387 Bleecker Street   110 Riverside Drive
                         New York, N.Y. 10014   New York, N.Y. 10024
(*Libretto, Music, Orchestrations*) Same as (*Agent/contact*)

SUNSET
See *PLATINUM*

THE SURVIVAL OF ST. JOAN
(*Source*) Original
(*Book*) James Lineberger
(*Lyrics*) James Lineberger
(*Music*) Hank & Gary Ruffin
(*Producer*) Haila Stoddard & Neal DuBrock
Anderson Theatre   off–Broadway
February 28, 1971   17 performances

(*Stars*) F. Murray Abraham, Lenny Baker
Theatre World 70–71, p. 100
Best Plays 70–71, pp. 345–46
NO CRIT AVAIL
New York Times 1971, Mr 1, 25:1
NO CRIT AVAIL
(*Published libretto*) NA
(*Published sheet music*) NA (Transmedia, Inc.)
(*Original cast recording*) OP Paramount PAS–9000
(*Agent/contact*) NO CONT AVAIL
(*Libretto*) NYPL RM7635; LC Transmedia, Inc. 20Oct69 DU5662; same
        as (*Agent/contact*)
(*Music, Orchestrations*) Same as (*Agent/contact*)

SWEET FEET
(*Source*) Original
(*Book*) Dan Graham
(*Lyrics*) Don Brockett
(*Music*) Don Brockett
(*Producer*) Proscenium Productions, Inc.
The New Theatre   off–Broadway
May 25, 1972   6 performances
(*Stars*) NA
Theatre World 71–72, p. 112
Best Plays 71–72, p. 379
NO CRIT AVAIL
New York Times 1972, My 26, 17:1
NO CRIT AVAIL
(*Published libretto*) NA
(*Published sheet music*) NA
(*Original cast recording*) NA
(*Agent/contact*)   Don Brockett Productions   Dan Graham
                       5600 Darlington Road   c/o DG, Inc.
                       Pittsburgh, PA   15217

(*Libretto*) LC R. Donald Brockett & Daniel E. Graham 1May72
        DU83417; same as (*Agent/contact*)
(*Music, Orchestrations*) Same as (*Agent/contact*)

SWEET MIANI

(*Source*) Original
(*Book*) Stuart Bishop
(*Lyrics*) Ed Tyler
(*Music*) Ed Tyler
(*Producer*) Edmund Brophy, in association with Donald Currie
Players Theatre   off–Broadway
September 25, 1962   22 performances
(*Stars*) NA
Theatre World 62–63, p. 137
Best Plays 62–63, pp. 314–15
New Yorker 38:183–4 O 13 '62
New York Times 1962, S 26, 33:2
NO CRIT AVAIL
(*Published libretto*) NA
(*Published sheet music*) NA
(*Original cast recording*) NA
(*Agent/contact*)   Edmund Tyler
                        c/o DG, Inc.
(*Libretto*) LC Ed Tyler & Stuart Bishop 19Sep62 DU56774;
        same as (*Agent/contact*)
(*Music, Orchestrations*) Same as (*Agent/contact*)

T.N.T.

(*Source*) Original
(*Book*) Richard Morrock
(*Lyrics*) Richard Morrock
(*Music*) Richard Morrock

(*Producer*) The Dynamite Limited Partnership
Players Theatre   off–Broadway
April 22, 1982   6 performances
(*Stars*) NA
Theatre World 81–82, p. 68
Best Plays 81–82, p. 390
NO CRIT AVAIL
NO CRIT AVAIL
NO CRIT AVAIL
(*Published libretto*) NA
(*Published sheet music*) NA
(*Original cast recording*) NA
(*Agent/contact*) NO CONT AVAIL
(*Libretto*) LC Richard Morrock 9Jul80 PAu–018;
      same as (*Agent/contact*)
(*Music, Orchestrations*) Same as (*Agent/contact*)

TANIA

(*Source*) Original
(*Book*) Mario Fratti
(*Lyrics*) Paul Dick
(*Music*) Paul Dick
(*Producer*) New York Theatre Ensemble/Lucille Talayco
New York Theatre Ensemble   off–off–Broadway
November 5, 1975   48 performances
(*Stars*) NA
Theatre World 75–76, p. 73
Best Plays 75–76, p. 397
NO CRIT AVAIL
NO CRIT AVAIL
NO CRIT AVAIL
(*Published libretto*) NA
(*Published sheet music*) NA
(*Original cast recording*) NA

(*Agent/contact*)   Mario Fratti
                      145 W. 55th Street
                      New York, N.Y.   10019
(*Libretto, Music, Orchestrations*) Same as (*Agent/contact*)

TATTERDEMALION
See *KING OF SCHNORRERS*

THE TATTOOED COUNTESS
(*Source*) *The Tattooed Countess* (novel) by Carl Van Vechten
(*Book*) Coleman Dowell*
(*Lyrics*) Coleman Dowell*
(*Music*) Coleman Dowell*
(*Producer*) Dick Randall, in association with Robert D. Feldstein
Barbizon–Plaza Theatre   off–Broadway
April 3, 1961   4 performances
(*Stars*) NA
Theatre World 60–61, p. 172
NO ENTRY AVAIL
NO CRIT AVAIL
New York Times 1961, My 4, 40:2
NO CRIT AVAIL
(*Published libretto*) NA
(*Published sheet music*) NA (Kiki Music Corp.)
(*Original cast recording*) NA
(*Agent/contact*) NO CONT AVAIL
(*Libretto*) LC John R. McKinney 2Apr57 DU444487;
          same as (*Agent/contact*)
(*Music, Orchestrations*) Same as (*Agent/contact*)

*In all publicity, Coleman Dowell is given sole authorship credit; however,
      LC copyright DU444487 gives John R. McKinney sole authorship
      credit

TELECAST
(*Source*) Original
(*Book*) Barry Harman
(*Lyrics*) Barry Harman
(*Music*) Martin Silvestri
(*Producer*) Harve Bronsten
St. Bart's Playhouse   off–Broadway
February 15, 1979   13 performances
(*Stars*) NA
Theatre World 78–79, p. 86
Best Plays 78–79, pp. 436–7
NO CRIT AVAIL
NO CRIT AVAIL
NO CRIT AVAIL
(*Published libretto*) NA
(*Published sheet music*) NA
(*Original cast recording*) NA
(*Agent/contact*)   Barry Harman   Martin Silvestri
                        35 W. 92nd Street   c/o DG, Inc.
                        New York, N.Y.   10025
(*Libretto, Music, Orchestrations*) Same as (*Agent/contact*)

TEN NIGHTS IN A BARROOM
(*Source*) *Ten Nights in a Barroom* (play) by W.W. Pratt
(*Book*) John Savoca & Marcia Taradash
(*Lyrics*) Martin Sherman
(*Music*) Stanley Silverman*
(*Producer*) The Greenwich Mews Players, Inc.
Greenwich Mews Theatre   off–Broadway
October 1, 1962   32 performances
(*Stars*) NA
Theatre World 62–63, p. 137
NO ENTRY AVAIL

NO CRIT AVAIL
NO CRIT AVAIL
NO CRIT AVAIL
(*Published libretto*) NA
(*Published sheet music*) NA
(*Original cast recording*) NA
(*Agent/contact*)   Martin Sherman   Stanley Silverman
                      c/o DG, Inc.   11 Riverside Drive
                                              New York, N.Y.   10023
(*Libretto*) LC John M. Savoca & Marcia Taradash 30Jul62 DU55904;
        same as (*Agent/contact*)
(*Music, Orchestrations*) Same as (*Agent/contact*)

*At press time, Mr. Silverman was not interested in soliciting
        further productions of this property

THAT 5 A.M. JAZZ
(*Source*) Original
(*Book*) Will Holt
(*Lyrics*) Will Holt
(*Music*) Will Holt
(*Producer*) Muriel Morse & Jan Stanwyck
Astor Place Playhouse   off-Broadway
October 19, 1964   94 performances
(*Stars*) James Coco
Theatre World 64–65, p. 152
Best Plays 64–65, pp. 344–45
New Yorker 40:129 O 31 '64
New York Times 1964, O 20, 42:2
NO CRIT AVAIL
(*Published libretto*) NA
(*Published sheet music*) NA
(*Original cast recording*) OP Unnamed label, unnumbered

(*Agent/contact*)   Will Holt
                         c/o Fifi Oscard Agency
                         19 W. 44th Street
                         New York, N.Y. 10036
                         Attn: Charles Hunt
(*Libretto*) LC Will Holt 25Jan63 DU56947, 17Sep64 DU61214;
        same as (*Agent/contact*)
(*Music, Orchestrations*) Same as (*Agent/contact*)

THAT HAT!

(*Source*) An Italian Straw Hat (*Un Chapeau de Paille d'Italie*)
        (play) by Eugène Labiche & Marc–Michel
(*Book*) Cy Young
(*Lyrics*) Cy Young
(*Music*) Cy Young
(*Producer*) Bonard Productions, in association with Katherine
        & Justin Sturm
Theatre Four   off–Broadway
September 23, 1964   1 performance
(*Stars*) Pierre Olaf
Theatre World 64–65, p. 149
Best Plays 64–65, p. 342
NO CRIT AVAIL
New York Times 1964, S 24, 45:1
NO CRIT AVAIL
(*Published libretto*) NA
(*Published sheet music*) NA (Thursday Music Corp.)
(*Original cast recording*) NA
(*Agent/contact*)   Cy Young
                         4151 Arch Drive, #109
                         Studio City, CA   91604
(*Libretto, Orchestrations*) Same as (*Agent/contact*)
(*Music*) LC Thursday Music Corp. 28Aug64 EU841503;
        same as (*Agent/contact*)

THAT'S WHAT'S HAPPENING, BABY
See *WHO'S WHO, BABY?*

THOUGHTS
(*Source*) Original
(*Book*) Lamar Alford
(*Lyrics*) Lamar Alford, Megan Terry & Jose Tapla
(*Music*) Lamar Alford
(*Producer*) Arthur Whitelaw, Seth Harrison, Dallas Alinder, in association
      with Peter Kean, by special arrangement with Lucille Lortel
Theatre de Lys   off–Broadway
March 19, 1973   24 performances
(*Stars*) NA
NO ENTRY AVAIL
Best Plays 72–73, p. 393
New Yorker 49:77 Mr 31 '73
New York Times 1973, F 5, 25:1
     New York Times 1973, Mr 20, 29:1
     New York Times 1973, Ap 1, II, 1:1
NO CRIT AVAIL
(*Published libretto*) NA
(*Published sheet music*) NA
(*Original cast recording*) NA
(*Agent/contact*)   Lamar Alford   Arthur Whitelaw
               216 E. 14th Street   132 E. 38th Street
               New York, N.Y. 10003   New York, N.Y. 10016
(*Libretto, Music, Orchestrations*) Same as (*Agent/contact*)

THE TIGER RAG
(*Source*) Original
(*Book*) Seyril Schochen
(*Lyrics*) Seyril Schochen

(*Music*) Kenneth Gaburo
(*Producer*) Tira Productions & Lorin Ellington Price
Cherry Lane Theatre   off–Broadway
February 16, 1961   14 performances
(*Stars*) Nancy Andrews
Theatre World 60–61, p. 166
NO ENTRY AVAIL
NO CRIT AVAIL
New York Times 1961, F 17, 20:2
        New York Times 1961, Mr 5, II, 1:1
NO CRIT AVAIL
(*Published libretto*) NA
(*Published sheet music*) NA
(*Original cast recording*) NA
(*Agent/contact*)   Seyril Schochen   Kenneth Gaburo
                        301 Hawthorn Avenue   c/o ASCAP
                        Boulder, CO   80302
(*Libretto*) NYPL RM8202; same as (*Agent/contact*)
(*Music, Orchestrations*) Same as (*Agent/contact*)

'TOINETTE*
(*Source*) *The Imaginary Invalid* (*Le Malade Imaginaire*)
        (play) by Molière
(*Book*) J.I. Rodale
(*Lyrics*) Dede Meyer
(*Music*) Dede Meyer
(*Producer*) Bickerstaff Productions
Theatre Marquee   off–Broadway
November 20, 1961   31 performances
(*Stars*) NA
Theatre World 61–62, p. 138
Best Plays 61–62, p. 313
New Yorker 37:121 D 2 '61
New York Times 1961, N 21, 46:1
NO CRIT AVAIL

(*Published libretto*) Rodale Press, 1969, as *THE MALADE WHO WAS*
        IMAGINARY, (one–act version)
(*Published sheet music*) NA
(*Original cast recording*) NA
(*Agent/contact*)   Dede Meyer   J.I. Rodale Estate
                        c/o ASCAP   c/o Rodale Press, Inc.
                                               33 East Minor Street
                                               Emmaus, PA   18049
(*Libretto*) NYPL NCOF+; LC J.I. Rodale 5May69 DP7035 as
        THE MALADE WHO WAS IMAGINARY; same as (*Agent/contact*)
(*Music, Orchestrations*) Same as (*Agent/contact*)

*Subsequently titled *THE MALADE WHO WAS IMAGINARY*

TOULOUSE
(*Source*) Original
(*Book*) Ronnie Britton
(*Lyrics*) Ronnie Britton
(*Music*) Ronnie Britton
(*Producer*) Wayne Clark, Ronnie Britton & Robert Speller
Ukranian Hall   off–Broadway
September 14, 1981   12 performances
(*Stars*) NA
Theatre World 81–82, p. 52
NO ENTRY AVAIL
NO CRIT AVAIL
NO CRIT AVAIL
NO CRIT AVAIL
(*Published libretto*) NA
(*Published sheet music*) NA
(*Original cast recording*) NA
(*Agent/contact*)   Ronnie Britton
                        c/o DG, Inc.

(*Libretto*) LC Ronnie Britton 13Mar78 SRu–362;
        same as (*Agent/contact*)
(*Music, Orchestrations*) Same as (*Agent/contact*)

TRIXIE TRUE, TEEN DETECTIVE

(*Source*) Original
(*Book*) Kelly Hamilton
(*Lyrics*) Kelly Hamilton
(*Music*) Kelly Hamilton
(*Producer*) Doug Cole, Joe Novak, Spencer Tandy & Joseph Butt
Theatre de Lys   off–Broadway
December 4, 1980   86 performances
(*Stars*) Marilyn Sokol
Theatre World 80–81, p. 90
Best Plays 80–81, p. 412
NO CRIT AVAIL
New York Times 1980, D 5, III, 3:1
        New York Times 1980, D 14, II, 3:1
NO CRIT AVAIL
(*Published libretto*) Samuel French, Inc., 1981
(*Published sheet music*) NA
(*Original cast recording*) NA
(*Agent/contact*) Samuel French, Inc.
(*Libretto*) LC Kelly Hamilton 5Dec79 PAu–157–784
(*Music*) LC Kelly Hamilton 4May81 PA–100–617;
        same as (*Agent/contact*)
(*Orchestrations*) Same as (*Agent/contact*)

TRUMPETS OF THE LORD

(*Source*) *God's Trombones* (collection) by James Weldon Johnson
(*Book*) Vinnette Carroll
(*Lyrics*) Vinnette Carroll
(*Music*) Vinnette Carroll

(*Producer*) Theodore Mann & Will B. Sandler

Astor Place Playhouse/One Sheridan Square*   off–Broadway

December 21, 1963   160 performances

(*Stars*) Cicely Tyson, Al Freeman, Jr.

Theatre World 63–64, p. 209

Best Plays 63–64, p. 354

New Yorker 39:60–1 Ja 4 '64

New York Times 1963, D 23, 22:3

   New York Times 1967, Je 1, 51:3

   New York Times 1969, Ap 30, 37:1

NO CRIT AVAIL

(*Published libretto*) NA

(*Published sheet music*) NA

(*Original cast recording*) NA

(*Agent/contact*) Vinnette Carroll   Theodore Mann

        c/o DG, Inc.   1633 Broadway

                 New York, N.Y. 10019

(*Libretto*) LC Vinnette Carroll 11Dec63 DU59078;

   same as (*Agent/contact*)

(*Music, Orchestrations*) Same as (*Agent/contact*)

*Transferred to One Sheridan Square 1/22/64

TWANGER

(*Source*) Original

(*Book*) Ronnie Britton

(*Lyrics*) Ronnie Britton

(*Music*) Ronnie Britton

(*Producer*) Wayne Clark

Van Dam Theatre   off–Broadway

November 15, 1972   23 performances

(*Stars*) NA

Theatre World 72–73, p. 102

NO ENTRY AVAIL

NO CRIT AVAIL

NO CRIT AVAIL
NO CRIT AVAIL
(*Published libretto*) NA
(*Published sheet music*) NA
(*Original cast recording*) NA
(*Agent/contact*)   Ronnie Britton
                         c/o DG, Inc.
(*Libretto*) NYPL NCOF+ 77–1953; LC Ronnie Britton 19May70 DU77192,
       17Dec70 DU220220; same as (*Agent/contact*)
(*Music*) LC Ronnie Britton 19Mar71 EU241621;
       same as (*Agent/contact*)
(*Orchestrations*) Same as (*Agent/contact*)

TWELFTH NIGHT
See *LOVE AND LET LOVE*

TWO IF BY SEA
(*Source*) Original
(*Book*) Priscilla B. Dewey & Charles Werner Moore
(*Lyrics*) Priscilla B. Dewey
(*Music*) Tony Hutchins
(*Producer*) The Tea Party Company
Circle–in–the–Square   off–Broadway
February 6, 1972   1 performance
(*Stars*) NA
Theatre World 71–72, p. 96
Best Plays 71–72, p. 372
NO CRIT AVAIL
(*Published libretto*) NA
(*Published sheet music*) NA
(*Original cast recording*) NA
(*Agent/contact*)   Priscilla B. Dewey   Tony Hutchins
                     307 Orchard Street   768 Chestnut Street
                     Millis, MA   02054   Needham, MA   02192

(*Libretto*) NYPL NCOF+; LC Priscilla B. Dewey 28Mar68
    DU71157, 5Feb76 DP9900; same as (*Agent/contact*)
(*Music, Orchestrations*) Same as (*Agent/contact*)

THE UMBRELLAS OF CHERBOURG*

(*Source*) *The Umbrellas of Cherbourg* (*Les Parapluies de Cherbourg*)
    (screenplay) by Jacques Demy, musical score by Michel Legrand
(*Book*) Jacques Demy, English translation by Sheldon Harnick
    & Charles Burr
(*Lyrics*) Jacques Demy, English translation by Sheldon Harnick
    & Charles Burr
(*Music*) Michel Legrand
(*Producer*) New York Shakespeare Festival/Joseph Papp
Public/Martinson Hall   off–Broadway
February 1, 1979   36 performances
(*Stars*) Laurence Guittard
Theatre World 78–79, p. 132
Best Plays 78–79, pp. 426–27
NY 12:70+ F 19 '79
    Nation 228:221–2 F 24 '79
    New Yorker 54:45 F 12 '79
    Newsweek il 93:62 F 12 '79
New York Times 1979, Ja 21, II, 1:3
    New York Times 1979, F 2, III, 3:4
    New York Times 1979, F 11, II, 3:1
NYTC 1979:325
(*Published libretto*) NA
(*Published sheet music*) Vogue Music
(*Original cast recording*) OP Accord(F) ACV–130011 (Original 1979
    French Cast) as *LES PARAPLUIES DE CHERBOURG*
(*Agent/contact*)   Nat Shapiro
                     157 W. 57th Street
                     New York, N.Y.   10019

(*Libretto*) NYPL NCOF+ 81–700; LC Sheldon Harnick 22Dec78
        PAu–72–079; same as (*Agent/contact*)
(*Music, Orchestrations*) Same as (*Agent/contact*)

*Previously presented under title *LES PARAPLUIES DE
        CHERBOURG*; videotaped performance available at NYPL Billy Rose
        Collection, Lincoln Center, NCOV 101

UP EDEN*

(*Source*) *Cosi Fan Tutte* (opera) by Wolfgang Amadeus Mozart,
        libretto by Lorenzo Da Ponte (freely adapted)
(*Book*) Robert Rosenblum & Howard Schuman
(*Lyrics*) Robert Rosenblum & Howard Schuman
(*Music*) Robert Rosenblum
(*Producer*) Jack Farren, in association with Evan William Mandel
Jan Hus Playhouse   off–Broadway
November 27, 1968   7 performances
(*Stars*) Blythe Danner, Bob Balaban
Theatre World 68–69, p. 128
Best Plays 68–69, p. 436
New Yorker 44:142 D 7 '68
New York Times 1968, N 27, 42:1
NO CRIT AVAIL
(*Published libretto*) NA
(*Published sheet music*) NA (Noma Music, Inc. as *EDEN SKIDOO*)
(*Original cast recording*) NA
(*Agent/contact*)   Robert Rosenblum
                         158 Waverly Place
                         New York, N.Y.   10014
(*Libretto*) NYPL RM3339, RM7482; RM 7481 as *EDEN SKIDOO*;
        LC (Performing Arts Reading Room) ML50/.R7964E32 as *EDEN
        SKIDOO*; LC Robert Jay Rosenblum & Howard Schuman 13Jul67
        DU69221 as *EDEN SKIDOO*; same as (*Agent/contact*)

(*Music*) LC (Performing Arts Reading Room) ML50/.R7964E32 as
      EDEN SKIDOO; same as (*Agent/contact*)
(*Orchestrations*) Same as (*Agent/contact*)

*Previously titled *EDEN SKIDOO*

UTOPIA!
(*Source*) Original
(*Book*) William Klenosky
(*Lyrics*) William Klenosky
(*Music*) William Klenosky
(*Producer*) Billy K Productions
Folksbiene Playhouse   off–Broadway
May 6, 1963   11 performances
(*Stars*) NA
Theatre World 62–63, p. 177
NO ENTRY AVAIL
NO CRIT AVAIL
New York Times 1963, My 7, 47:4
NO CRIT AVAIL
(*Published libretto*) NA
(*Published sheet music*) NA
(*Original cast recording*) NA
(*Agent/contact*) NO CONT AVAIL
(*Libretto, Music, Orchestrations*) Same as (*Agent/contact*)

VALMOUTH
(*Source*) *Valmouth* (novel) by Ronald Firbank
(*Book*) Sandy Wilson
(*Lyrics*) Sandy Wilson
(*Music*) Sandy Wilson
(*Producer*) Gene Andrewski

York Playhouse*   off–Broadway*
October 6, 1960   14 performances
(*Stars*) Elly Stone, Eugene Roche
Theatre World 60–61, p. 129
Best Plays 60–61, pp. 349–50
New Yorker 34:168–9 N 1 '58
        New Yorker 36:75–6 O 15 '60
New York Times 1960, O 7, 29:1
NO CRIT AVAIL
(*Published libretto*) Samuel French, Ltd. (London), 1985
(*Published sheet music*) NA
(*Original cast recording*) OP Pye(E) NPL/NSPL–18029, RE Pye(E)
        NSPL–83004, AEI–1123 (Original London Cast); That's
        Entertainment(E) TER–1019 (London Revival Cast)
(*Agent/contact*) Samuel French, Ltd. (London)
(*Libretto, Music, Orchestrations*) Same as (*Agent/contact*)

*Previously and subsequently produced in London

VONETTA SWEETWATER CARRIES ON . . .
(*Source*) Original
(*Book*) Johnny Brandon
(*Lyrics*) Johnny Brandon
(*Music*) Johnny Brandon
(*Producer*) Theatre Off Park
Theatre Off Park   off–off–Broadway
February 3, 1982   16 performances
(*Stars*) NA
Theatre World 81–82, p. 104
Best Plays 81–82, p. 408
NO CRIT AVAIL
NO CRIT AVAIL
NO CRIT AVAIL
(*Published libretto*) NA
(*Published sheet music*) NA

(*Original cast recording*) NA
(*Agent/contact*)   Johnny Brandon
                        c/o DG, Inc.
(*Libretto*) LC Johnny Brandon 16Nov81 PAu–356–298;
            same as (*Agent/contact*)
(*Music, Orchestrations*) Same as (*Agent/contact*)

WANTED
(*Source*) Original
(*Book*) David Epstein
(*Lyrics*) Al Carmines
(*Music*) Al Carmines
(*Producer*) Arthur D. Zinberg
Cherry Lane Theatre   off–Broadway
January 19, 1972   79 performances
(*Stars*) NA
Theatre World 71–72, p. 96
Best Plays 71–72, p. 372
New Yorker 47:74 Ja 29 '72
        Newsweek il 79:83 Ja 31 '72
New York Times 1972, Ja 20, 52:1
        New York Times 1972, Ja 30, II, 9:1
NYTC 1972:339
(*Published libretto*) NA
(*Published sheet music*) NA
(*Original cast recording*) NA
(*Agent/contact*)   David Epstein   Al Carmines
                        c/o Howard Rosenstone   c/o DG, Inc.
                        3 E. 48th Street
                        New York, N.Y.   10017
(*Libretto*) NYPL NCOF+ 73–1870a, NCOF+ 73–1870b;
            same as (*Agent/contact*)
(*Music, Orchestrations*) Same as (*Agent/contact*)

THE WEDDING OF IPHIGENIA AND IPHIGENIA IN CONCERT*
(*Source*) *Iphigenia in Aulis* and *Iphigenia in Tauris* (plays)
        by Euripides
(*Book*) Doug Dyer, Peter Link & Gretchen Cryer
(*Lyrics*) Doug Dyer, Peter Link & Gretchen Cryer
(*Music*) Peter Link
(*Producer*) New York Shakespeare Festival
Public/Martinson Hall   off–Broadway
December 16, 1971   139 performances
(*Stars*) Nell Carter, Andrea Marcovicci
Theatre World 71–72, p. 119
NO ENTRY AVAIL
Nation 214:28–9 Ja 3 '72
        New Yorker 47:57 D 25 '71
New York Times 1971, D 17, 28:2
NO CRIT AVAIL
(*Published libretto*) NA
(*Published sheet music*) NA
(*Original cast recording*) NA
(*Agent/contact*)   Peter Link   Joseph Papp
                        c/o On–Broadway Productions   c/o Public Theatre
                        400 W. 43rd Street, #38D   425 Lafayette Street
                        New York, N.Y. 10036   New York, N.Y. 10003
(*Libretto, Music, Orchestrations*) Same as (*Agent/contact*)

*Previously titled *IPHIGENIA*

WE'RE CIVILIZED?
(*Source*) Original
(*Book*) Alfred Aiken
(*Lyrics*) Alfred Aiken
(*Music*) Ray Haney
(*Producer*) Rendell Productions

Jan Hus Playhouse   off–Broadway
November 8, 1962   22 performances
(*Stars*) Karen Black
Theatre World 62–63, p. 145
Best Plays 62–63, p. 318
New Yorker 38:148 N 17 '62
New York Times 1962, N 9, 30:1
NO CRIT AVAIL
(*Published libretto*) NA
(*Published sheet music*) NA (Norwood Music, Inc.)
(*Original cast recording*) NA
(*Agent/contact*) NO CONT AVAIL
(*Libretto*) LC (Performing Arts Reading Room) ML50/.Z99W1998,
    ML50/.H2437W4; same as (*Agent/contact*)
(*Music, Orchestrations*) Same as (*Agent/contact*)

WHAT A KILLING!

(*Source*) Story (title unavailable) by Jack Waldron
(*Book*) Fred Hebert
(*Lyrics*) George Harwell & Joan Anania
(*Music*) George Harwell
(*Producer*) Jack Collins
Folksbiene Theatre   off–Broadway
March 27, 1961   1 performance
(*Stars*) Paul Hartman
Theatre World 60–61, p. 170
NO ENTRY AVAIL
NO CRIT AVAIL
New York Times 1961, Mr 28, 41:1
NO CRIT AVAIL
(*Published libretto*) NA
(*Published sheet music*) NA
(*Original cast recording*) NA
(*Agent/contact*) NO CONT AVAIL

(*Libretto*) LC Fred Hebert 31Oct60 DU51945;
        same as (*Agent/contact*)
(*Music, Orchestrations*) Same as (*Agent/contact*)

WHAT A NIGHT!
See *HOTEL PASSIONATO*

WHAT'S IN THE WIND?
See *NOW IS THE TIME FOR ALL GOOD MEN*

WHISPERS ON THE WIND
(*Source*) Original
(*Book*) John B. Kuntz
(*Lyrics*) John B. Kuntz
(*Music*) Lor Crane
(*Producer*) Bruce W. Paltrow, Mitchell Fink & Lucille Lortel
        Productions, Inc.
Theatre de Lys   off–Broadway
June 3, 1970   9 performances
(*Stars*) David Cryer, Nancy Dussault
Theatre World 70–71, p. 63
Best Plays 70–71, p. 332
New Yorker 46:90+ Je 13 '70
New York Times 1970, Je 4, 50:1
NO CRIT AVAIL
(*Published libretto*) Samuel French, Inc., 1971
(*Published sheet music*) NA (Valando Music, Inc.)
(*Original cast recording*) OP Friends of Lincoln Center SS–492
(*Agent/contact*) Samuel French, Inc.
(*Libretto*) LC John Kuntz & Lor Crane 16Sep68 DU72410
(*Music, Orchestrations*) Same as (*Agent/contact*)

WHO'S WHO, BABY?*
(*Source*) *Who's Who?* (play) by Guy Bolton & P.G. Wodehouse
(*Book*) Gerold Frank
(*Lyrics*) Johnny Brandon**
(*Music*) Johnny Brandon**
(*Producer*) Edmund J. Ferdinand & Charlotte Schiff
Players Theater   off–Broadway
January 29, 1968   16 performances
(*Stars*) NA
Theatre World 67–68, p. 126
Best Plays 67–68, pp. 400–1
New Yorker 43:90–1 F 10 '68
New York Times 1968, Ja 30, 36:1
NO CRIT AVAIL
(*Published libretto*) NA
(*Published sheet music*) Wemar Music Corp.
(*Original cast recording*) NA
(*Agent/contact*)   Johnny Brandon
                        c/o DG, Inc.
(*Libretto, Music, Orchestrations*) Same as (*Agent/contact*)

*Previously titled *THAT'S WHAT'S HAPPENING, BABY*

**At press time, Mr. Brandon was not interested in soliciting
        further productions of this property

WILL THE MAIL TRAIN RUN TONIGHT?
(*Source*) *Love Rides the Rails* (play) by Hugh Nevill (Morland
        Cady)
(*Book*) Malcolm L. LaPrade
(*Lyrics*) Malcolm L. LaPrade
(*Music*) Alyn Heim
(*Producer*) Jon Baisch

New Bowery Theatre   off–Broadway
January 9, 1964   8 performances
(*Stars*) NA
Theatre World 63–64, p. 213
Best Plays 63–64, p. 355
NO CRIT AVAIL
New York Times 1964, Ja 10, 18:1
NO CRIT AVAIL
(*Published libretto*) NA
(*Published sheet music*) NA
(*Original cast recording*) NA
(*Agent/contact*)   Malcolm LaPrade   Alyn Heim, Sr.
                      130 W. 16th Street   12 Old Quarry Road
                      New York, N.Y. 10011 Cedar Grove, NJ 07009
(*Libretto*) NYPL NCOF+ 79–758; LC (Performing Arts Reading Room)
        ML50/.H46SW52; LC Alyn J. Heim & Malcolm LaPrade 9Aug62
        DU55999; same as (*Agent/contact*)
(*Music, Orchestrations*) Same as (*Agent/contact*)

WINGS
(*Source*) *The Birds* (play) by Aristophanes
(*Book*) Robert McLaughlin & Peter Ryan
(*Lyrics*) Robert McLaughlin & Peter Ryan
(*Music*) Robert McLaughlin & Peter Ryan
(*Producer*) Stephen Wells, R.E. Lee, Jr. & Charles Walton
Eastside Playhouse   off–Broadway
March 16, 1975   9 performances
(*Stars*) NA
Theatre World 74–75, p. 83
Best Plays 74–75, p. 378
NO CRIT AVAIL
New York Times 1975, Mr 17, 34:3
NO CRIT AVAIL
(*Published libretto*) NA

(*Published sheet music*) NA (Dramatis Music Corp.)

(*Original cast recording*) NA

(*Agent/contact*) Theatre Maximus

(*Libretto, Orchestrations*) Same as (*Agent/contact*)

(*Music*) LC Robert McLaughlin & Peter Ryan 31Mar75 EU567894; same
as (*Agent/contact*)

A WOMAN SUSPENDED
See *I CAN'T KEEP RUNNING IN PLACE*

WONDERLAND IN CONCERT
See *ALICE IN CONCERT*

*YOU NEVER KNOW (revival)**
(*Source*) *By Candlelight* (play) by Siegfried Geyer

(*Book*) Rowland Leigh & George Abbott, adapted from the original
libretto by Robert Katscher, Siegfried Geyer & Karl Farkas**

(*Lyrics*) Cole Porter, additional lyrics by Robert Katscher**

(*Music*) Cole Porter & Robert Katscher**

(*Producer*) Stanley H. Handman

Eastside Playhouse   off–Broadway

March 12, 1973   8 performances

(*Stars*) NA

Theatre World 72–73, p. 113

Best Plays 72–73, pp. 392–93

NO CRIT AVAIL

New York Times 1973, Mr 13, 31:1

NO CRIT AVAIL

(*Published libretto*) NA

(*Published sheet music*) Chappell & Co., Inc. (Original Broadway
production)

(*Original cast recording*) NA

(*Agent/contact*) Samuel French, Inc.

(*Libretto*) NYPL RM8078; LC (Performing Arts Reading Room)
	ML50/.P8Y7 (Original Broadway libretto); same as (*Agent/contact*)

(*Music, Orchestrations*) Same as (*Agent/contact*)

*This revival included as it was substantially different from its
	original New York production

**The original 1938 Broadway production was rewritten by a host of
	different authors; the credits indicate that Siegfried Geyer's original
	play was turned into a musical play by Robert Katscher, Siegfried
	Geyer & Karl Farkas; this adaptation was then rewritten by Rowland
	Leigh & George Abbott. The 1973 revival was adapted from the
	original by Rowland Leigh; Cole Porter is given sole credit for the
	score

THE SHOWS THAT RAN LONGER THAN 300 PERFORMANCES

BUT ARE CURRENTLY UNAVAILABLE FOR PRODUCTION

AIN'T SUPPOSED TO DIE A NATURAL DEATH
(*Source*) Original
(*Book*) Melvin Van Peebles
(*Lyrics*) Melvin Van Peebles
(*Music*) Melvin Van Peebles
(*Producer*) Eugene V. Wolsk, Charles Blackwell, Emanuel Azenberg
       & Robert Malina

Ethel Barrymore Theatre/Ambassador Theatre*	Broadway
October 20, 1971	325 performances

(*Stars*) Garrett Morris
Theatre World 71–72, p. 15
Best Plays 71–72, pp. 316–17
Nation 213:476–7 N 8 '71
      New Yorker 47:101–2 O 30 '71
      Newsweek il 78:85–6 N 1 '71
      Sat R 54:10+ N 13 '71
      Time il 98:95 N 1 '71
New York Times 1971, O 21, 55:1
      New York Times 1971, N 7, II, 1:6
NYTC 1971:229
(*Published libretto*) Bantam, 1973 (novelized version)
(*Published sheet music*) NA
(*Original cast recording*) OP A&M Records SP–3510
(*Agent/contact*)

Melvin Van Peebles	Eugene V. Wolsk	Emanuel Azenburg
353 W. 56th Street	165 W. 46th Street	165 W. 46th Street
New York, N.Y. 10019	New York, N.Y. 10036	New York, N.Y. 10036

(*Libretto, Music, Orchestrations*) Same as (*Agent/contact*)

*Transferred to Ambassador Theatre 11/17/71

AS THE GIRLS GO
(*Source*) Original
(*Book*) William Roos
(*Lyrics*) Harold Adamson
(*Music*) Jimmy McHugh
(*Producer*) Michael Todd

Winter Garden Theatre	Broadway
November 13, 1948	420 performances

(*Stars*) Bobby Clark
Theatre World 48–49, pp. 45–7
Best Plays 48–49, pp. 394–95
Cath World 168:324 Ja '49
      Commonweal 49:231 D 10 '48
      Life il 25:89–90+ N 29 '48
      New Repub 119:37 D 6 '48
      New Yorker 24:58 N 20 '48
      Newsweek 32:80 N 22 '48
      Theatre Arts 33:18 Ja '49
      Time 52:85 N 22 '48
New York Times 1948, N 15, 21:2
NYTC 1948:159
(*Published libretto*) NA
(*Published sheet music*) Sam Fox Pubs. Co.
(*Original cast recording*) NA

(*Agent/contact*)	Jimmy McHugh Music	William E. Roos
	9301 Wilshire Blvd.,	Box #1112
	Ste #400	Edgartown, MA 02539
	Beverly Hills, CA 90210	

(*Libretto, Music, Orchestrations*) Same as (*Agent/contact*)

BOY MEETS BOY

(*Source*) Original

(*Book*) Bill Solly & Donald Ward

(*Lyrics*) Bill Solly

(*Music*) Bill Solly

(*Producer*) Edith O'Hara, in conjunction with Lee Barton &
        Christopher Larkin

Actors Playhouse   off–Broadway

September 17, 1975   463 performances

(*Stars*) NA

Theatre World 75–76, p. 70

Best Plays 75–76, pp. 361

NO CRIT AVAIL

New York Times 1975, S 18, 49:3

NO CRIT AVAIL

(*Published libretto*) In *Gay Plays: The First Collection*, Avon, 1979

(*Published sheet music*) Oublietta

(*Original cast recording*) OP JO Records & Publishing JO–13,
        RE AEI–1102; OP Private Editions FRC/PES–1 (Original Revival Cast)

(*Agent/contact*)   Bill Solly

                     c/o Helen Merrill

                     337 W. 22nd Street

                     New York, N.Y.   10011

(*Libretto*) LC Bill Solly 6Mar75 DU93574; same as (*Agent/contact*)

(*Music, Orchestrations*) Same as (*Agent/contact*)

COCO

(*Source*) Original

(*Book*) Alan Jay Lerner

(*Lyrics*) Alan Jay Lerner

(*Music*) André Previn
(*Producer*) Frederick Brisson

Mark Hellinger Theatre	Broadway
December 18, 1969	332 performances

(*Stars*) Katharine Hepburn
Theatre World 69–70, p. 26
Best Plays 69–70, pp. 309–10
America 122:54–5 Ja 17 '70
      Commonweal 91:558–9 F 20 '70
      Dance Mag il 44:72–8 F '70
      Dance Mag 44:84–5 Mr '70
      Life il 68:12 Ja 30 '70
      Nat R 22:370–1 Ap 7 '70
      Nation 210:61 Ja 19 '70
      New Yorker 45:38 D 27 '69
      Newsweek il 74:75–9 N 10 '69
      Newsweek il 74:58 D 29 '69
      Sat R 53:88 Ja 10 '70
      Time il 94:86–7 N 7 '69
      Time il 94:35 D 26 '69
New York Times 1969, D 19, 66:1
      New York Times 1969, D 28, II, 1:1
      New York Times 1970, Ag 7, 28:1
NYTC 1969:151
(*Published libretto*) NA
(*Published sheet music*) Chappell & Co.
(*Original cast recording*) OP Paramount PMS–1002
(*Agent/contact*)

Alan Jay Lerner Estate	André Previn	Frederick Brisson
c/o David Grossberg	c/o DG, Inc.	Productions
30 N. La Salle Street		c/o Dwight D. Frye
New York, N.Y. 10027		35 W. 90th Street
		New York, N.Y. 10024

(*Libretto*) NYPL RM6745, NCOF+; same as (*Agent/contact*)
(*Music, Orchestrations*) Same as (*Agent/contact*)

THE MAGIC SHOW
(*Source*) Original
(*Book*) Bob Randall
(*Lyrics*) Stephen Schwartz
(*Music*) Stephen Schwartz
(*Producer*) Edgar Lansbury, Joseph Beruh & Ivan Reitman

Cort Theatre	Broadway
May 28, 1974	1,859 performances

(*Stars*) Doug Henning, David Ogden Stiers
Theatre World 73–74, p. 56
Best Plays 73–74, p. 368
Comentary 58:75–6 N '74
        New Yorker 50:64 Je 10 '74
        Newsweek il 83:84 Je 10 '74
        Sr Schol il 106:33–4 Mr 27 '75
        Time il 103:106 Je 10 '74
New York Times 1974, My 29, 49:1
        New York Times 1974, Je 9, II, 1:5
        New York Times 1974, Jl 10, 44:1
NYTC 1974:254
(*Published libretto*) NA
(*Published sheet music*) Belwin Mills Pubs. Corp./Grey Dog Music
(*Original cast recording*) OP Bell 9003, RE Arista 9003
(*Agent/contact*)

Stephen Schwartz	Bob Randall	Lansbury/Beruh
c/o Paramuse Artists	c/o DG, Inc.	Productions, Inc.
Associates		1650 Broadway
1414 Avenue of the Americas		New York, N.Y. 10019
New York, N.Y. 10019		

(*Libretto*) LC Bob Randall 3Jul74 DU90759;
        same as (*Agent/contact*)
(*Music, Orchestrations*) Same as (*Agent/contact*)

TOUCH

(*Source*) Original

(*Book*) Kenn Long & Amy Saltz

(*Lyrics*) Kenn Long

(*Music*) Kenn Long & Jim Crozier

(*Producer*) Edith O'Hara & Albert Poland, in association with
        Robert S. Weinstein & The Two Arts Playhouse, Inc.

Village Arena Theatre/Martinique Theatre*   off–Broadway

November 8, 1970   422 performances

(*Stars*) NA

Theatre World 70–71, p. 82

Best Plays 70–71, p. 336

Nation 211:542 N 23 '70

        New Yorker 46:132 D 12 '70

New York Times 1970, N 9, 52:1

NO CRIT AVAIL

(*Published libretto*) NA

(*Published sheet music*) NA

(*Original cast recording*) OP Ampex A–50102

(*Agent/contact*)   Albert Poland
        226 W. 47th Street
        New York, N.Y.   10036

(*Libretto*) LC Kenn Long 27Nov70 DU78769; same as (*Agent/contact*)

(*Music*) LC Kenneth Long & James A. Crozier 13Jan71 EU224672;
        same as (*Agent/contact*)

(*Orchestrations*) Same as (*Agent/contact*)

*Transferred to Martinique Theatre 6/1/71

YOUR ARMS TOO SHORT TO BOX WITH GOD

(*Source*) *The Gospel According to St. Matthew* (scripture)

(*Book*) Vinnette Carroll

(*Lyrics*) Alex Bradford, Micki Grant

(*Music*) Alex Bradford, Micki Grant

(*Producer*) Frankie Hewitt, the Shubert Organization, in
    association with Theater Now, Inc.

Lyceum Theater   Broadway

December 22, 1976   429 performances

(*Stars*) Delores Hall, Patti LaBelle (touring company)

Theatre World 76–77, p. 47
    Theatre World 80–81, p. 8
    Theatre World 82–83, p. 14

Best Plays 76–77, p. 299
    Best Plays 80–81, p. 339
    Best Plays 82–83, p. 338

America 136:60 Ja 22 '77
    Chr Today il 20:16–17 Ja 30 '79
    Dance Mag 51:39–40 My '77
    Ebony il 35:122+ O '80
    Nation 224:61 Ja 15 '77
    New Yorker 52:60 Ja 3 '77
    Newsweek 89:66 Ja 10 '77
    Time il 109:55 Ja 24 '77

New York Times 1976, D 23, 20:1
    New York Times 1976, D 31, III, 3:6
    New York Times 1980, illus, Je 3, III, 7:1
    New York Times 1982, illus, S 10, III, 3:4
    New York Times 1982, O 22, III, 2:3

NYTC 1976:52
    NYTC 1980:223
    NYTC 1982:212

(*Published libretto*) NA

(*Published sheet music*) Blue Pearl Music Corp.

(*Original cast recording*) OP ABC Records AB–1004, RE MCA
    Records 37126

(*Agent/contact*)

Vinnette Carroll	Micki Grant	Alex Bradford
c/o DG, Inc.	c/o Fiddleback Music Pub. Co.	Estate
	1270 Avenue of the Americas,	c/o ASCAP
	Ste #2110	
	New York, N.Y. 10020	

(*Libretto*) LC Vinnette J. Carroll & Alex Bradford 20Nov75 DU96843;
      same as (*Agent/contact*)

(*Music, Orchestrations*) Same as (*Agent/contact*)

OPENING DATES

WHAT'S UP	November 11, 1943
MARIANNE	December 30, 1943 (OT)
JACKPOT	January 13, 1944
ALLAH BE PRAISED!	April 20, 1944
DREAM WITH MUSIC	May 18, 1944
GLAD TO SEE YOU	November 13, 1944 (OT)
SADIE THOMPSON	November 16, 1944
RHAPSODY	November 22, 1944
A LADY SAYS YES	January 10, 1945
THE FIREBRAND OF FLORENCE	March 22, 1945
MEMPHIS BOUND	May 24, 1945
HOLLYWOOD PINAFORE	May 31, 1945
MARINKA	July 18, 1945
MR. STRAUSS GOES TO BOSTON	September 6, 1945
CARIB SONG	September 27, 1945
SPRING IN BRAZIL	October 1, 1945 (OT)
POLONAISE	October 6, 1945
THE GIRL FROM NANTUCKET	November 8, 1945
ARE YOU WITH IT?	November 10, 1945
THE DAY BEFORE SPRING	November 22, 1945
BILLION DOLLAR BABY	December 21, 1945
NELLIE BLY	January 21, 1946
LUTE SONG	February 6, 1946
THE DUCHESS MISBEHAVES	February 13, 1946
LOVE IN THE SNOW	March 15, 1946 (OT)
ST. LOUIS WOMAN	March 30, 1946
SHOOTIN' STAR	April 4, 1946 (OT)

WINDY CITY	April 18, 1946 (OT)
AROUND THE WORLD	May 31, 1946
YOURS IS MY HEART	September 5, 1946
SWEET BYE AND BYE	October 10, 1946 (OT)
PARK AVENUE	November 4, 1946
IF THE SHOE FITS	December 5, 1946
IN GAY NEW ORLEANS	December 25, 1946 (OT)
TOPLITZKY OF NOTRE DAME	December 26, 1946
BEGGAR'S HOLIDAY	December 26, 1946
STREET SCENE	January 9, 1947
BAREFOOT BOY WITH CHEEK	April 3, 1947
LOUISIANA LADY	June 2, 1947
MUSIC IN MY HEART	October 2, 1947
BONANZA BOUND!	December 26, 1947 (OT)
LOOK, MA, I'M DANCIN'	January 29, 1948
HOLD IT!	May 5, 1948
SLEEPY HOLLOW	June 3, 1948
HEAVEN ON EARTH	September 16, 1948
MAGDALENA	September 20, 1948
THAT'S THE TICKET!	September 24, 1948 (OT)
LOVE LIFE	October 7, 1948
MY ROMANCE	October 19, 1948
AS THE GIRLS GO	November 13, 1948
LOST IN THE STARS	October 30, 1949
REGINA	October 31, 1949
TEXAS, L'IL DARLIN'	November 25, 1949
HAPPY AS LARRY	January 6, 1950
ARMS AND THE GIRL	February 2, 1950
GREAT TO BE ALIVE!	March 23, 1950
THE LIAR	May 18, 1950
THE BARRIER	November 2, 1950
OUT OF THIS WORLD	December 21, 1950
JOTHAM VALLEY	February 6, 1951
MAKE A WISH	April 18, 1951

A TREE GROWS IN BROOKLYN	April 19, 1951
FLAHOOLEY	May 14, 1951
COURTIN' TIME	June 13, 1951
SEVENTEEN	June 21, 1951
PAINT YOUR WAGON	November 12, 1951
A MONTH OF SUNDAYS	December 25, 1951 (OT)
THREE WISHES FOR JAMIE	March 21, 1952
BUTTRIO SQUARE	October 14, 1952
MY DARLIN' AIDA	October 27, 1952
HAZEL FLAGG	February 11, 1953
MAGGIE	February 18, 1953
CARNIVAL IN FLANDERS	September 8, 1953
THE GIRL IN PINK TIGHTS	March 5, 1954
BY THE BEAUTIFUL SEA	April 8, 1954
THE GOLDEN APPLE	April 20, 1954
ARABIAN NIGHTS	June 24, 1954
SANDHOG	November 23, 1954
MRS. PATTERSON	December 1, 1954
HIT THE TRAIL	December 2, 1954
HOUSE OF FLOWERS	December 30, 1954
ANKLES AWEIGH	April 18, 1955
SEVENTH HEAVEN	May 26, 1955
REUBEN REUBEN	October 10, 1955 (OT)
THE VAMP	November 10, 1955
PIPE DREAM	November 30, 1955
THE AMAZING ADELE	December 26, 1955 (OT)
STRIP FOR ACTION	March 17, 1956 (OT)
BY HEX!	June 18, 1956
SHANGRI–LA	June 31, 1956
CANDIDE	December 1, 1956
SHINBONE ALLEY	April 13, 1957
LIVIN' THE LIFE	April 27, 1957
SIMPLY HEAVENLY	August 20, 1957
THE CAREFREE HEART	September 30, 1957 (OT)

COPPER AND BRASS	October 17, 1957
RUMPLE	November 6, 1957
THE BODY BEAUTIFUL	January 23, 1958
OH CAPTAIN!	February 4, 1958
PORTOFINO	February 21, 1958
AT THE GRAND	July 7, 1958 (OT)
THE EGG AND I	September 10, 1958
GOLDILOCKS	October 11, 1958
SALAD DAYS	November 10, 1958
OF MICE AND MEN	December 4, 1958
WHOOP–UP	December 22, 1958
SHE SHALL HAVE MUSIC	January 22, 1959
JUNO	March 9, 1959
FIRST IMPRESSIONS	March 19, 1959
THE NERVOUS SET	May 12, 1959
HAPPY TOWN	October 7, 1959
THE PINK JUNGLE	October 14, 1959 (OT)
SARATOGA	December 7, 1959
BEG, BORROW, OR STEAL	February 10, 1960
THE CRYSTAL HEART	February 15, 1960
GREENWILLOW	March 8, 1960
MISS EMILY ADAM	March 29, 1960
LOCK UP YOUR DAUGHTERS!	April 27, 1960 (OT)
CHRISTINE	April 28, 1960
ERNEST IN LOVE	May 4, 1960
VALMOUTH	October 6, 1960
KITTIWAKE ISLAND	October 12, 1960
THE SHOEMAKER AND THE PEDDLER	October 14, 1960
TENDERLOIN	October 17, 1960
WILDCAT	December 16, 1960
BEAUTIFUL DREAMER	December 27, 1960
THE CONQUERING HERO	January 16, 1961
THE TIGER RAG	February 16, 1961
13 DAUGHTERS	March 2, 1961

WHAT A KILLING	March 27, 1961
THE HAPPIEST GIRL IN THE WORLD	April 3, 1961
THE TATTOOED COUNTESS	April 3, 1961
HOBO	April 10, 1961
THE DECAMERON	April 12, 1961
SMILING THE BOY FELL DEAD	April 19, 1961
YOUNG ABE LINCOLN	April 25, 1961
MEET PETER GRANT	May 8, 1961
DONNYBROOK!	May 18, 1961
PARADISE ISLAND	June 22, 1961
I WANT YOU	September 14, 1961
HI, PAISANO!	September 30, 1961
THE SAP OF LIFE	October 2, 1961
SAIL AWAY	October 3, 1961
KICKS & CO.	October 11, 1961 (OT)
LET IT RIDE!	October 12, 1961
KWAMINA	October 23, 1961
O MARRY ME!	October 27, 1961
KEAN	November 2, 1961
ALL IN LOVE	November 10, 1961
BELLA	November 16, 1961
THE GAY LIFE	November 18, 1961
'TOINETTE	November 20, 1961
SING MUSE!	December 6, 1961
ALL KINDS OF GIANTS	December 18, 1961
SUBWAYS ARE FOR SLEEPING	December 27, 1961
MADAME APHRODITE	December 29, 1961
FORTUNA	January 3, 1962
THE BANKER'S DAUGHTER	January 22, 1962
A FAMILY AFFAIR	January 27, 1962
FLY BLACKBIRD	February 5, 1962
WE TAKE THE TOWN	February 19, 1962 (OT)
ALL AMERICAN	March 19, 1962
I CAN GET IT FOR YOU WHOLESALE	March 22, 1962

HALF–PAST WEDNESDAY	April 6, 1962
KING OF THE WHOLE DAMN WORLD!	April 14, 1962
THE DIFFICULT WOMAN	April 25, 1962
BRAVO GIOVANNI	May 19, 1962
LA BELLE	August 13, 1962 (OT)
SWEET MIANI	September 25, 1962
TEN NIGHTS IN A BARROOM	October 1, 1962
O SAY CAN YOU SEE!	October 8, 1962
LADY OF MEXICO	October 16, 1962
MR. PRESIDENT	October 20, 1962
WE'RE CIVILIZED?	November 8, 1962
NOWHERE TO GO BUT UP	November 10, 1962
LITTLE ME	November 17, 1962
TOVARICH	March 18, 1963
SOPHIE	April 15, 1963
HOT SPOT	April 19, 1963
UTOPIA!	May 6, 1963
THE BEAST IN ME	May 16, 1963
AROUND THE WORLD IN 80 DAYS	June 22, 1963
ZENDA	August 5, 1963 (OT)
THE STUDENT GYPSY, OR THE PRINCE OF LIEDERKRANZ	September 30, 1963
MORNING SUN	October 6, 1963
GENTLEMEN, BE SEATED!	October 10, 1963
THE PRINCE AND THE PAUPER	October 12, 1963
BALLAD FOR BIMSHIRE	October 15, 1963
JENNIE	October 17, 1963
TAMBOURINES TO GLORY	November 2, 1963
THE GIRL WHO CAME TO SUPPER	December 8, 1963
TRUMPETS OF THE LORD	December 21, 1963
PIMPERNEL!	January 6, 1964
WILL THE MAIL TRAIN RUN TONIGHT?	January 9, 1964
THE ATHENIAN TOUCH	January 14, 1964
JO	February 12, 1964

FOXY	February 16, 1964
THE AMOROUS FLEA	February 17, 1964
DYNAMITE TONITE	March 15, 1964
COOL OFF!	March 31, 1964 (OT)
ANYONE CAN WHISTLE	April 4, 1964
CAFE CROWN	April 17, 1964
FADE OUT – FADE IN	May 26, 1964
THAT HAT!	September 23, 1964
GOGO LOVES YOU	October 9, 1964
THAT 5 A.M. JAZZ	October 19, 1964
THE SECRET LIFE OF WALTER MITTY	October 26, 1964
BEN FRANKLIN IN PARIS	October 27, 1964
AS YOU LIKE IT	October 27, 1964
SOMETHING MORE!	November 10, 1964
BAJOUR	November 23, 1964
I HAD A BALL	December 15, 1964
BABES IN THE WOOD	December 28, 1964
ROYAL FLUSH	December 30, 1964 (OT)
KELLY	February 6, 1965
PLEASURES AND PALACES	March 11, 1965 (OT)
DO I HEAR A WALTZ?	March 18, 1965
FLORA, THE RED MENACE	May 11, 1965
THE ROAR OF THE GREASEPAINT – THE SMELL OF THE CROWD	May 16, 1965
MARDI GRAS!	June 26, 1965
HOT SEPTEMBER	September 14, 1965 (OT)
PICKWICK	October 4, 1965
MACKEY OF APPALACHIA	October 6, 1965
DRAT! THE CAT!	October 10, 1965
ON A CLEAR DAY YOU CAN SEE FOREVER	October 17, 1965
HOTEL PASSIONATO	October 22, 1965
THE ZULU AND THE ZAYDA	November 10, 1965
GREAT SCOT!	November 10, 1965
SKYSCRAPER	November 13, 1965

ANYA	November 29, 1965
THE YEARLING	December 10, 1965
LA GROSSE VALISE	December 14, 1965
HOORAY! IT'S A GLORIOUS DAY . . . AND ALL THAT	March 9, 1966
POUSSE–CAFE	March 18, 1966
IT'S A BIRD . . . IT'S A PLANE . . . IT'S SUPERMAN	March 29, 1966
A TIME FOR SINGING	May 21, 1966
BREAKFAST AT TIFFANY'S	October 10, 1966 (PRE)
MY WIFE AND I	October 10, 1966
AUTUMN'S HERE	October 25, 1966
MAN WITH A LOAD OF MISCHIEF	November 6, 1966
CHU CHEM	November 15, 1966 (OT)
WALKING HAPPY	November 26, 1966
A JOYFUL NOISE	December 15, 1966
THE PENNY FRIEND	December 26, 1966
THE GOLDEN SCREW	January 30, 1967
SHOEMAKER'S HOLIDAY	March 2, 1967
SHERRY!	March 28, 1967
HALLELUJAH, BABY!	April 26, 1967
PEG	July 10, 1967 (OT)
NOW IS THE TIME FOR ALL GOOD MEN	September 26, 1967
HOW DO YOU DO, I LOVE YOU	October 19, 1967 (OT)
HENRY, SWEET HENRY	October 23, 1967
MATA HARI	November 18, 1967 (OT)
HOW NOW, DOW JONES	December 7, 1967
LOVE AND LET LOVE	January 3, 1968
HAVE I GOT ONE FOR YOU	January 7, 1968
THE HAPPY TIME	January 18, 1968
DARLING OF THE DAY	January 27, 1968
WHO'S WHO, BABY?	January 29, 1968
HERE'S WHERE I BELONG	March 3, 1968
THE EDUCATION OF H*Y*M*A*N K*A*P*L*A*N	April 4, 1968

I'M SOLOMON	April 23, 1968
THE HAPPY HYPOCRITE	September 5, 1968
MONTH OF SUNDAYS	September 16, 1968
A MOTHER'S KISSES	September 23, 1968 (OT)
HER FIRST ROMAN	October 20, 1968
MAGGIE FLYNN	October 23, 1968
LOVE MATCH	November 3, 1968 (OT)
UP EDEN	November 27, 1968
BALLAD FOR A FIRING SQUAD	December 11, 1968
THE FIG LEAVES ARE FALLING	January 2, 1969
HORSEMAN, PASS BY	January 15, 1969
CELEBRATION	January 22, 1969
GET THEE TO CANTERBURY	January 25, 1969
RED, WHITE, AND MADDOX	January 26, 1969
PEACE	January 27, 1969
CANTERBURY TALES	February 3, 1969
DEAR WORLD	February 6, 1969
COME SUMMER	March 18, 1969
BILLY	March 22, 1969
CAUTION: A LOVE STORY	April 2, 1969
PROMENADE	June 4, 1969
MAN BETTER MAN	July 2, 1969
HELLO, SUCKER!	July 21, 1969 (OT)
1491	September 2, 1969 (OT)
SALVATION	September 24, 1969
JIMMY	October 23, 1969
RONDELAY	November 5, 1969
BUCK WHITE	December 2, 1969
LA STRADA	December 14, 1969
COCO	December 18, 1969
SAMBO	December 21, 1969
I DREAMT I DWELT IN BLOOMINGDALE'S	February 12, 1970
GANTRY	February 14, 1970
GEORGY	February 26, 1970

BILLY NONAME	March 2, 1970
SHOW ME WHERE THE GOOD TIMES ARE	March 5, 1970
THE HOUSE OF LEATHER	March 18, 1970
LYLE	March 20, 1970
BLOOD RED ROSES	March 22, 1970
MINNIE'S BOYS	March 26, 1970
LOOK TO THE LILIES	March 29, 1970
CRY FOR US ALL	April 8, 1970
THE DRUNKARD	April 13, 1970
PARK	April 22, 1970
MOD DONNA	May 3, 1970
COLETTE	May 6, 1970
WHISPERS ON THE WIND	June 3, 1970
SENSATIONS	October 25, 1970
TOUCH	November 8, 1970
ODODO (TRUTH)	November 24, 1970
LOVELY LADIES, KIND GENTLEMEN	December 28, 1970
STAG MOVIE	January 3, 1971
SOON	January 12, 1971
ARI	January 15, 1971
PRETTYBELLE	February 1, 1971 (OT)
LOLITA, MY LOVE	February 16, 1971 (OT)
THE SURVIVAL OF ST. JOAN	February 28, 1971
LOOK WHERE I'M AT!	March 5, 1971
A DAY IN THE LIFE OF JUST ABOUT EVERYONE	March 9, 1971
NEVERTHELESS THEY LAUGH	March 24, 1971
THE RED WHITE AND BLACK	March 30, 1971
70, GIRLS, 70	April 15, 1971
WHEN DO THE WORDS COME TRUE?	April 16, 1971 (OT)
KISS NOW	April 20, 1971
FRANK MERRIWELL, OR HONOR CHALLENGED	April 24, 1971
THE BALLAD OF JOHNNY POT	April 26, 1971
EARL OF RUSTON	May 5, 1971

W.C.	June 15, 1971 (OT)
CROESUS AND THE WITCH	August 24, 1971
DRAT!	October 18, 1971
AIN'T SUPPOSED TO DIE A NATURAL DEATH	October 20, 1971
F. JASMINE ADDAMS	October 27, 1971
THE GRASS HARP	November 2, 1971
LOVE ME, LOVE MY CHILDREN	November 3, 1971
WILD AND WONDERFUL	December 7, 1971
THE WEDDING OF IPHIGENIA AND IPHIGENIA IN CONCERT	December 16, 1971
INNER CITY	December 19, 1971
ANNE OF GREEN GABLES	December 21, 1971
WANTED	January 19, 1972
TWO IF BY SEA	February 6, 1972
THE SELLING OF THE PRESIDENT	March 22, 1972
A LOOK AT THE FIFTIES	April 14, 1972
DIFFERENT TIMES	May 1, 1972
GOD BLESS CONEY	May 3, 1972
HARD JOB BEING GOD	May 15, 1972
DON'T PLAY US CHEAP!	May 16, 1972
HEATHEN!	May 21, 1972
SWEET FEET	May 25, 1972
BUY BONDS, BUSTER!	June 4, 1972
JOAN	June 19, 1972
SPEED GETS THE POPPIES	July 25, 1972
AESOP'S FABLES	August 17, 1972
A SONG FOR CYRANO	September 4, 1972 (OT)
CRAZY NOW	September 17, 1972
HALLOWEEN	September 20, 1972 (OT)
THE LIFE OF A MAN	September 29, 1972
LADY AUDLEY'S SECRET	October 3, 1972
DUDE	October 9, 1972
HURRY, HARRY	October 12, 1972
LADY DAY: A MUSICAL TRAGEDY	October 17, 1972

COMEDY	November 6, 1972 (OT)
LYSISTRATA	November 13, 1972
TWANGER	November 15, 1972
DEAR OSCAR	November 16, 1972
AMBASSADOR	November 19, 1972
DOCTOR SELAVY'S MAGIC THEATER	November 23, 1972
THE CONTRAST	November 27, 1972
VIA GALACTICA	November 28, 1972
THE BAR THAT NEVER CLOSES	December 3, 1972
SAY WHEN	December 4, 1972
RAINBOW	December 18, 1972
TRICKS	January 8, 1973
SHELTER	February 6, 1973
YOU NEVER KNOW (revival)	March 12, 1973
SEESAW	March 18, 1973
THOUGHTS	March 19, 1973
SMILE, SMILE, SMILE	April 4, 1973
CYRANO	May 13, 1973
SMITH	May 19, 1973
GONE WITH THE WIND	August 28, 1973 (OT)
MOLLY	November 1, 1973
GIGI	November 13, 1973
LOTTA, OR THE BEST THING EVOLUTION'S EVER COME UP WITH	November 21, 1973
MORE THAN YOU DESERVE	November 21, 1973
RACHAEL LILY ROSENBLOOM AND DON'T YOU EVER FORGET IT	November 26, 1973 (PRE)
THE GREAT MACDADDY	February 12, 1974
RAINBOW JONES	February 13, 1974
FASHION	February 17, 1974
SEXTET	March 3, 1974
THE FUTURE	March 22, 1974
BRAINCHILD	March 25, 1974 (OT)
POP	April 3, 1974
KABOOM!	May 1, 1974

RIDE THE WINDS	May 16, 1974
THE MAGIC SHOW	May 28, 1974
SHEBA	July 24, 1974 (OT)
MACK AND MABEL	October 6, 1974
MISS MOFFAT	October 7, 1974 (OT)
STREET JESUS	November 16, 1974
HOW TO GET RID OF IT	November 17, 1974
SGT. PEPPER'S LONELY HEART'S CLUB BAND ON THE ROAD	November 17, 1974
THE PRODIGAL SISTER	November 25, 1974
GOOD NEWS (revival)	December 23, 1974
DIAMOND STUDS (THE LIFE OF JESSE JAMES, A SALOON MUSICAL)	January 14, 1975
TREASURE ISLAND	January 20, 1975 (OT)
MAN ON THE MOON	January 29, 1975
GOODTIME CHARLEY	March 3, 1975
THE LIEUTENANT	March 9, 1975
THE ROCKY HORROR SHOW	March 10, 1975
APE OVER BROADWAY	March 12, 1975
WINGS	March 16, 1975
DOCTOR JAZZ	March 19, 1975
BE KIND TO PEOPLE WEEK	March 23, 1975
PHILEMON	April 8, 1975
THE RAINBOW RAPE TRICK	April 13, 1975
A MATTER OF TIME	April 27, 1975
THE GLORIOUS AGE	May 11, 1975
TRUCKLOAD	September 6, 1975 (PRE)
BOY MEETS BOY	September 17, 1975
CHRISTY	October 14, 1975
TANIA	November 5, 1975
BOCCACCIO	November 24, 1975
GIFT OF THE MAGI	December 1, 1975
SNOOPY!!!	December 9, 1975 (OT)
DOWNRIVER	December 19, 1975
HOME, SWEET HOMER	January 4, 1976

PACIFIC OVERTURES	January 11, 1976
APPLE PIE	February 12, 1976
ROCKABYE HAMLET	February 17, 1976
DREAMSTUFF	April 4, 1976
I KNOCK AT THE DOOR	April 12, 1976
REX	April 25, 1976
SO LONG, 174TH STREET	April 27, 1976
1600 PENNSYLVANIA AVENUE	May 4, 1976
THE BAKER'S WIFE	May 11, 1976 (OT)
SOMETHING'S AFOOT	May 27, 1976
SAINTS	June 30, 1976
THE ROBBER BRIDEGROOM	October 9, 1976
MUSIC IS	December 20, 1976
YOUR ARMS TOO SHORT TO BOX WITH GOD	December 22, 1976
THE COCKEYED TIGER	January 13, 1977
CASTAWAYS	February 7, 1977
MOVIE BUFF	March 14, 1977
ON THE LOCK-IN	April 14, 1977
NEW YORK CITY STREET SHOW	April 28, 1977
HAPPY END	May 7, 1977
NEFERTITI	September 20, 1977 (OT)
HOT GROG	October 6, 1977
THE ACT	October 29, 1977
GREEN POND	November 22, 1977
THE GATES OF PARADISE	November 25, 1977
THE STREETS OF GOLD	November 25, 1977
FIXED	December 20, 1977
SPOTLIGHT	January 11, 1978 (OT)
TIMBUKTU!	March 1, 1978
THE PRINCE OF GRAND STREET	March 7, 1978 (OT)
THE LAST MINSTREL SHOW	March 20, 1978 (OT)
A BISTRO CAR ON THE CNR	March 23, 1978
A HISTORY OF THE AMERICAN FILM	March 30, 1978
ANGEL	May 10, 1978

ROSA	May 10, 1978
REUNION	May 12, 1978
RUNAWAYS	May 13, 1978
WORKING	May 14, 1978
ALICE	May 31, 1978 (OT)
MAHALIA	May 31, 1978
PIANO BAR	June 8, 1978
THE COOLEST CAT IN TOWN	June 22, 1978
BACK COUNTRY	August 15, 1978 (OT)
KING OF HEARTS	October 22, 1978
PLATINUM	November 12, 1978
CARTOONS FOR A LUNCH HOUR	November 28, 1978
JIMMY & BILLY	December 10, 1978
BALLROOM	December 14, 1978
A BROADWAY MUSICAL	December 21, 1978
THE GRAND TOUR	January 11, 1979
SARAVA	January 11, 1979
THE UMBRELLAS OF CHERBOURG	February 1, 1979
TELECAST	February 15, 1979
HELEN	February 22, 1979
JOLEY	March 2, 1979 (OT)
HOME AGAIN, HOME AGAIN	March 10, 1979 (OT)
LEAVE IT TO BEAVER IS DEAD	March 29, 1979
AM I ASKING TOO MUCH	April 3, 1979
CARMELINA	April 8, 1979
MY OLD FRIENDS	April 12, 1979
DISPATCHES	April 18, 1979
BEA'S PLACE	May 9, 1979
THE UTTER GLORY OF MORRISSEY HALL	May 13, 1979
FESTIVAL	May 16, 1979
I REMEMBER MAMA	May 31, 1979
MISS TRUTH	June 5, 1979
NOT TONIGHT, BENVENUTO	June 5, 1979
THE MADWOMAN OF CENTRAL PARK WEST	June 13, 1979

GOT TU GO DISCO	June 25, 1979
BUT NEVER JAM TODAY	July 31, 1979
DADDY GOODNESS	August 16, 1979 (OT)
THE 1940'S RADIO HOUR	October 7, 1979
GOD BLESS YOU, MR. ROSEWATER	October 14, 1979
STRIDER: THE STORY OF A HORSE	November 14, 1979
KING OF SCHNORRERS	November 28, 1979
COMIN' UPTOWN	December 20, 1979
THE HOUSEWIVES' CANTATA	February 18, 1980
CHANGES	February 19, 1980
ELIZABETH AND ESSEX	February 24, 1980
SWING	February 25, 1980 (OT)
REGGAE	March 27, 1980
THE HAGGADEH, A PASSOVER CANTATA	March 31, 1980
HAPPY NEW YEAR	April 27, 1980
FOURTUNE	April 27, 1980
MUSICAL CHAIRS	May 11, 1980
IT'S WILDE!	May 21, 1980
BILLY BISHOP GOES TO WAR	May 29, 1980
IT'S SO NICE TO BE CIVILIZED	June 3, 1980
CHASE A RAINBOW	June 12, 1980
FEARLESS FRANK	June 15, 1980
JAZZBO BROWN	June 24, 1980
CHARLIE AND ALGERNON	September 14, 1980
A MATTER OF OPINION	September 30, 1980
REALLY ROSIE	October 14, 1980
ONE NIGHT STAND	October 20, 1980 (PRE)
FRIMBO	November 9, 1980
KA-BOOM!	November 20, 1980
TRIXIE TRUE, TEEN DETECTIVE	December 4, 1980
ONWARD, VICTORIA!	December 14, 1980
HIJINKS!	December 17, 1980
ALICE IN CONCERT	December 29, 1980
AN EVENING WITH JOAN CRAWFORD	January 28, 1981

BRING BACK BIRDIE	March 5, 1981
THE MATINEE KIDS	March 10, 1981
A REEL AMERICAN HERO	March 25, 1981 (PRE)
MARCH OF THE FALSETTOS	April 9, 1981
COPPERFIELD	April 13, 1981
AFTER STARDRIVE	May 8, 1981
I CAN'T KEEP RUNNING IN PLACE	May 14, 1981
EL BRAVO!	June 16, 1981
THE HEEBIE JEEBIES	June 18, 1981
SAY HELLO TO HARVEY!	September 14, 1981 (OT)
TOULOUSE	September 14, 1981
LOUIS	September 18, 1981
DOUBLE FEATURE	October 8, 1981
MARLOWE	October 12, 1981
COTTON PATCH GOSPEL	October 21, 1981
OH, BROTHER!	November 10, 1981
MERRILY WE ROLL ALONG	November 16, 1981
THE FIRST	November 17, 1981
HEAD OVER HEELS	December 15, 1981
FRANCIS	December 22, 1981
THE LITTLE PRINCE AND THE AVIATOR	January 1, 1982 (PRE)
WALTZ OF THE STORK	January 5, 1982
OH, JOHNNY	January 10, 1982
VONETTA SWEETWATER CARRIES ON . . .	February 3, 1982
COLETTE	February 9, 1982 (OT)
LULLABYE AND GOODNIGHT	February 9, 1982
I TAKE THESE WOMEN	March 11, 1982
LITTLE JOHNNY JONES (revival)	March 21, 1982
T.N.T.	April 22, 1982
IS THERE LIFE AFTER HIGH SCHOOL?	May 7, 1982
DO BLACK PATENT LEATHER SHOES REALLY REFLECT UP?	May 27, 1982
A DRIFTER, THE GRIFTER & HEATHER MC BRIDE	June 20, 1982

CLEAVAGE	June 23, 1982
LIFE IS NOT A DORIS DAY MOVIE	June 25, 1982
PLAY ME A COUNTRY SONG	June 27, 1982
SEVEN BRIDES FOR SEVEN BROTHERS	July 8, 1982
BROKEN TOYS!	July 19, 1982
THE DEATH OF VON RICHTOFEN AS WITNESSED FROM EARTH	July 29, 1982
CHARLOTTE SWEET	August 12, 1982
SOAP	September 11, 1982
A DOLL'S LIFE	September 23, 1982
AMERICAN PRINCESS	September 23, 1982
BUGLES AT DAWN	October 10, 1982
RHINESTONE	November 16, 1982
SKYLINE	January 6, 1983
MERLIN	February 13, 1983
FROM BROOKS WITH LOVE	March 30, 1983
DANCE A LITTLE CLOSER	May 11, 1983

SHOW TITLES

SOURCES

Breath of Spring (play)	256
Brothers (play)	325
Buona Sera, Mrs. Campbell (screenplay)	92
Buried Alive (novel)	106
Buttrio Square (play)	86
By Candlelight (play)	538
Bye Bye Birdie (musical comedy)	83
Caesar and Cleopatra (play)	154
Cafe Crown (play)	87
Candide (novel)	10, 88
The Canterbury Tales (collection)	90, 413
Captain Jinks of the Horse Marines (play)	428
The Captain's Paradise (screenplay)	222
Carnival in Flanders (screenplay)	93
A Christmas Carol (novel)	99
"Cinderella" (folk tale)	139, 166
Come Back Little Sheba (play)	335
The Comedy of Errors (play)	221
Comic Strip (play)	444
The Contrast (play)	382
The Corn is Green (play)	5, 322
Cosi Fan Tutte (opera)	529
The Cotton Patch Version of Matthew and John (scripture)	384
The Country Wife (play)	503
Creoles (novel)	193
The Crime of Giovanni Venturi (novel)	82
"Croesus" (folk tale)	385
Cry the Beloved Country (novel)	192
Cyrano de Bergerac (play)	104, 337
Daddy Goodness (play)	304
David Copperfield (novel)	101
The Decameron (collection)	81, 389
Der Blaue Engel (screenplay)	234
Die Gelbe Jacke (operetta)	291

SOURCE AUTHORS, LIBRETTISTS, COMPOSERS AND LYRICISTS

Work, Henry Clay	428
Wright, Richard	304
Wright, Robert	64, 177, 178, 199, 200, 276, 295, 300, 337, 338, 339
Wycherley, William	503
Yeats, William Butler	28, 430
Yellen, Sherman	239
Young, Caryl Gabrielle	388
Young, Cy	414, 415, 521
Young, Victor	255, 256, 358, 359
Yordan, Philip	347
Zakrzewski, Paul	501, 502
Zangwill, Israel	180
Zavin, Benjamin Bernard	119
Zbornik, Kristine	403
Zeeman, Joan Javits see Javits, Joan	
Zimmer, Bernard	93
Ziskin, Victor	290, 291
Zodrow, John	139, 140
Zuckmayer, Karl	234